POLITICIANS AND THE SLUMP

The Labour Government of

1929–1931

POLITICIANS AND THE SLUMP

The Labour Government of 1929-1931

ROBERT SKIDELSKY
RESEARCH FELLOW OF NUFFIELD COLLEGE, OXFORD

MACMILLAN
LONDON · MELBOURNE · TORONTO
1967

Published by
MACMILLAN & CO LTD
Little Essex Street London WC2
and also at Bombay Calcutta and Madras
Macmillan South Africa (Publishers) Pty Ltd Johannesburg
The Macmillan Company of Australia Pty Ltd Melbourne
The Macmillan Company of Canada Ltd Toronto

Printed in Great Britain by
ROBERT MACLEHOSE AND CO. LTD
The University Press, Glasgow

TO
MY MOTHER AND FATHER

CONTENTS

LIST OF ILLUSTRATIONS

PREFACE

I OWE an enormous debt of gratitude to Mr. Philip Williams of Nuffield College, Oxford, who read each successive draft with the sharpest eye for loose arguments, and without whose constant and helpful encouragement and criticism this book would never have been completed; also to Mr. Kenneth Tite of Magdalen College, Oxford, to whom I am indebted not only for numerous comments of substance, but also for critical observations on my punctuation. It is also a pleasure to thank my stepfather, Mr. Alexander Baylin, and my friends, Mr. Vijay Joshi, of Merton College, Oxford, and Mr. Vernon Bogdanor, of Brasenose College, for their many helpful comments on the portions of the manuscript which they read, and Mrs. Kay Watts, who typed the many stages of the 'final' draft with enormous efficiency and unfailing good humour.

Finally, it is a pleasure to acknowledge the help of those politicians, economists and civil servants, active in the period covered by my book, who talked to me or answered my enquiries in writing, especially: Mr. J. R. Bellerby, Lord Boothby, the late Lord Chuter-Ede, Dr. R. Forgan, Lord Henderson, the late Mrs. 'Molly' Hamilton, Sir Roy Harrod, Mr. W. A. Lee, Sir Oswald Mosley, the Hon. Sir Harold Nicolson, Mr. J. R. A. Oldfield, Mrs. Ishbel Peterkin, Mr. Morgan Philips Price, Lord Sorensen, the late Rt. Hon. E. J. Strachey, the Rt. Hon. G. R. Strauss, Mr. Wilfred Wellcock, and Sir Horace Wilson.

My acknowledgments are due to the following for permission to use and quote from various collections of papers:

General Council of the T.U.C. (General Council Papers)
Keynes Memorial Committee (Keynes Papers)
Lothian Trustees (Lothian Papers)
The Rt. Hon. Malcolm MacDonald (MacDonald Papers)
Sir Oswald Mosley (Mosley Papers)

Nuffield College (Hubert Henderson and Morrison Papers)
Passfield Trust (Passfield Papers)
Raymond Postgate (Lansbury Papers)
The Rt. Hon. G. R. Strauss (Diary)

In addition I am very grateful to the Librarians of the Library of Political and Economic Science, L.S.E., and the Marshall Library, Cambridge; to the Curator of Historical Records, Scottish Record Office; to the Secretary of the Research and Economic Department of the T.U.C.; and to Mr. David Marquand, M.P., for their courtesy and help to me while I was consulting the papers in their custody.

As I write, the promised relaxation of the fifty-year rule, designed to give access to the Cabinet and departmental papers of this period, remains merely a promise, so that I have not been able to look through the mass of papers jealously guarded by the Public Records Office. Nevertheless, I have been extremely fortunate in having had access to a wide range of relevant official and private papers without which large sections of this book could not have been written. This type of source material has been invaluable to expose processes of policy-making within government which would otherwise have remained obscure and to give a solid backing of evidence to what would otherwise have remained speculation or assertion. It has not produced any startling 'revelations', nor brought to light any 'secrets': on the whole journalists were remarkably good in sensing what was going on and the reasons for it. From this I assume that the effect of the release of these papers will largely be to give students better ammunition with which to defend their own, and blast rival, theories; and debate will continue undiminished — as it should.

INTRODUCTION

INTEREST in the Labour Government of 1929 to 1931 has centred almost exclusively on the events leading to the formation of the National Government on 24 August 1931. The political happenings of the previous two years have been obscured by the light that has played on the crisis itself. They are covered in scarcely more than a dozen pages or so in the standard general histories, and the complexity of issues and choices has never received a study comparable to that on the drama of the fight for the pound.

One unfortunate consequence of this is that it reinforces the tendency to view inter-war politics in terms of a struggle between socialism and capitalism, between the Labour Party and the Rest. This was undoubtedly an important cleavage, especially of sentiment, and as such should not be under-estimated. However, the real cleavage of opinion occurred not across this divide, but another: between the economic radicals and the economic conservatives. This cut right across party lines. There were economic radicals to be found in all parties, though it was the Liberal Party that came to stake its life on economic radicalism in the election of 1929. It is with this second cleavage, to which the political divide of 1931 is only tangentially and rather fortuitously related, that this book is primarily concerned. The real story of the domestic politics of the inter-war period is the defeat of the economic radicals by the economic conservatives.

The issue on which this debate centred was unemployment. Unemployment of 10 per cent of the labour force was endemic in the England of the nineteen-twenties. It is often argued that before Keynes's *General Theory* (1936) governments were bound to pursue conservative, orthodox, economic policies. Yet most economists and many businessmen rejected the 'treasury view', and dissent from orthodoxy increased progressively as traditional policies failed to restore prosperity. By 1929 there existed a substantial body of economic and political support for a radical unemployment policy embracing an expansionist monetary policy and a big programme of government investment.

It is sometimes argued that it was the lack of a parliamentary majority that prevented the Labour Government of 1929 to 1931 from following a radical unemployment policy. Yet the Labour Party never had such a policy, and in the election campaign of 1929 it attacked the Liberals' detailed programme of public investment under the cover of a vague and woolly 'socialism'. In office it followed the orthodox policies of its Conservative predecessors with only minor modifications. Yet in these two years the Liberals, who held the balance of power, were consistent advocates of a bolder approach. Thus 1929 was the major missed opportunity of the inter-war period, the one occasion when the electorate voted unambiguously against 'safety first' and in favour of economic innovation.

Why did the Labour Party fail to utilise this dissent for the ends of a radical unemployment policy? I have sought the answer in terms of the party's commitment to a Utopian socialism which incapacitated it from effectively working the parliamentary system and prevented it from coming to terms with economic reality. It suffered in those days from a split personality: on the one hand it was committed to constitutionalism; on the other it lacked a social democratic or gradualist programme without which tenure of power was bound to be rather barren of achievement. It thought in terms of a total solution to the problem of poverty, when what it was offered was the limited opportunity to cure unemployment. It was a parliamentary party with a Utopian ethic. It was not fit for the kind of power it was called upon to exercise.

For what was at issue between 1929 and 1931, with unemployment rising to nearly three million, was not Socialism versus Capitalism. It was interventionist Capitalism versus *laissez-faire* Capitalism. The Labour Party's commitment to a nebulous Socialism made it regard the work of the 'economic radicals' such as Keynes as mere 'tinkering', when in fact it was they who were providing the real choice. It was the failure of the Labour Party to recognise that this was the choice that doomed it to failure and sterility in this crucial period.

In concentrating attention on the Government's handling of the unemployment problem I am conscious of the risk of doing it an injustice. A survey which embraced its conduct of foreign affairs would undoubtedly have shown it up in a better light. Unemployment policy was admittedly its Achilles heel; and a government may fairly claim to be judged, by the historian as well as by the electorate, on its whole record rather than on one issue, however important that issue.

Nevertheless, unemployment was the key issue of the 1929 election campaign, and was so regarded by all the three parties. Moreover, with the onset of the world depression, all other problems came to be linked to, or submerged by, the rising numbers of the unemployed. All policies came to be judged by the single question: how will they affect the unemployment figures? Hence this book, which starts with a narrowly defined problem — that of the 'intractable million' who could not secure permanent employment in the Britain of the nineteen-twenties — gradually comes to embrace virtually the whole field of domestic and international politics; and it ends, as did the Labour Government itself, on a note of international drama and crisis.

Inevitably much of the study is taken up with a comparison of the Labour Government's *performance* with other Parties' *promises* which, understandably, is to the disadvantage of the Government, since performance rarely lives up to expectation. It may also plausibly be argued that the British Labour Cabinet fared little worse in its handling of the unemployment problem than did Governments in other countries.

Nevertheless, if a real choice existed, that fact compels a harsher judgment. In the United States and Germany economic crisis followed suddenly on years of prosperity and relatively full employment. But in Britain the problem of the 'intractable million' was nine years old when Labour took office. A formidable body of dissenting opinion had grown up in opposition to the orthodox Treasury and banking views. Since the pressures of orthodoxy were less in Britain than elsewhere, a progressive Government should have enjoyed more scope for manœuvre. In addition most countries which fared badly during the depression — and few did not — had Governments of the Right which might be expected to be unresponsive to 'progressive' opinion, or to the electoral pressure of the poor and the unemployed. In the Labour Party, willingness to help was there in plentiful measure, but the ability to translate moral fervour into constructive policy was woefully lacking.

Since the nineteen-thirties mass unemployment has, fortunately, become a thing of the past — or so we suppose. But the economic problem, of which it was simply the most painful and dramatic symptom, has still not been solved: it is merely that the specific symptoms of the maladjustment have changed. Today, as then, people talk of the need to renovate an obsolete industrial structure, to cut costs and increase productivity. Now, as then, they argue that industry is being sacrificed to the City of London, that Britain should attempt to regroup its world-wide trading and financial commitments on to a smaller group of countries which might, in effect, become one huge domestic market. As I write, Britain is applying, for the second time, for membership of the Common Market. This book attempts to show the efforts of one age to cope with problems that are very far from being solved today.

I

THE ECONOMIC BACKGROUND

i. INTRODUCTION

THE economist Pigou coined the phrase the 'intractable million' to describe that 10 per cent of the working population unable to find regular employment in the Britain of the nineteen-twenties. There had, of course, been unemployment before 1914, but it had fluctuated heavily, falling to 3 or 4 per cent in good years, and rising to 10 per cent and over in years of depression. The novel feature of post-war unemployment was that it continued at a permanently high level.

There was little hint of this as the immediate post-war boom, based on a universal desire to replenish stocks, got under way in 1919–20. The boom was helped by the Government's decision not to restore the gold standard, suspended during the war. This would have involved violent deflation,[1] and to start the peace with a depression seemed an appalling prospect. However, the Government took fright at the rapid inflation which on the Continent foreshadowed the collapse of most Central European currencies. The Bank Rate was put up to 6 per cent in November 1919, and to 7 per cent the following April. The boom was cut short and deflation started in earnest to prepare for a return to the gold standard. In 1921 unemployment in Britain rose to 19 per cent. Recovery when it came was slow and limited. The 1913 level of production was not regained till 1927. Unemployment from 1922 to 1929 remained about 10 per cent.

Mass unemployment was initially explained by the dislocation of the

[1] Between 1913 and 1918 the British wholesale price level had more than doubled. A. C. Pigou, *Aspects of British Economic History 1918–1925*, 1947, p. 234.

international trading monetary systems caused by the First World War. Hence the aim of British Governments was to restore as swiftly as possible the pre-war trading and monetary structure. This involved currency stabilisation (via a return to the gold standard) and the reduction of tariffs put up during and immediately after the war.

However, as the decade wore on it became increasingly apparent that Britain's leading export industries were being hit, not only by post-war dislocations, but also by long-term changes in demand which the war doubtless accelerated. 'Back to 1914' would not solve the problems facing the coal, textile, and heavy engineering industries, where the bulk of the unemployed were concentrated. Moreover the return to the gold standard in 1925 hindered the development of new industries and the rationalisation of old ones by creating monetary stringency at a time when plentiful credit was needed for adaptation to the new conditions.

Though government intervention in the economy had to some extent been legitimised during the war, the climate of opinion in the nineteen-twenties favoured a swift return to *laissez-faire*, and this dictated the course of British economic policy. Nevertheless an important section of influential opinion had, by the end of the decade, come round to the view that traditional remedies would not meet the new economic facts; thus by 1929 there had developed a vigorous debate on economic questions which formed the staple of the election campaign of that year.

ii. THE RETURN TO NORMALITY

The gold standard was a device for keeping the national currencies of different countries at a fixed relative value, thus generating the confidence required for international trading. Imbalances in trading accounts between nations were supposed to lead to gold movements which *automatically* set in motion corrective forces designed to adjust relative prices and incomes to the required level. As Sir Dennis Robertson put it, 'the case for the old gold standard was not simply that it was a device for keeping step; it was also that it was a rough and ready device . . . for regulating the volume of home activity'.[1] Departure from it was supposed to lead to uncontrollable inflation with a subsequent collapse of trade,

[1] Quoted in A. J. Youngson, *The British Economy 1920–1957*, 1960, p. 230.

repudiation of debts and destruction of savings. This supposition appeared vindicated by the experience of the European inflation of 1920 to 1923.

Britain as the world's leading trading nation was anxious to take the lead in re-establishing the gold standard system. It was especially anxious to go back to gold at the pre-war rate of parity. The pre-war rate was a symbol of normality; it was also a symbol of London's financial strength and it was thought that nothing short of return to the old parity would restore confidence in London's ability to resume her former role.[1] Britain's economic strength and London's financial position had both in fact served to make the pre-war gold standard a 'British managed standard'.[2] By 1925, when Britain formally returned to gold, her position had been gravely impaired. A large portion of her assets had been sold to pay for the war; her exports could no longer produce a surplus sufficient to finance international growth on the pre-war scale. Hence after 1925 London was increasingly forced to finance its operations with short-term funds attracted by high interest rates. Yet these very rates were liable to discourage domestic enterprise. In addition, the 'gold exchange' system whereby countries were permitted to keep their reserves in sterling rather than in gold imposed a further strain on Britain's slender gold holdings. These factors made the restoration of the gold standard system an extremely precarious undertaking, almost an act of faith.

The position would have been greatly eased had the new powerful creditor nations, the United States and France, been prepared to play their full part in the maintenance of international investment. But New York and Paris had neither the expertise nor the willingness to lend abroad on a scale commensurate with their economic strength. It is true that New York did so up till 1928, but in that year American lending began to dry up as funds were diverted to a boom on the New York exchange which the Federal Reserve Board proved initially unwilling and later unable to control. France, which became a major creditor with

[1] Reginald McKenna, former Chancellor of the Exchequer, said 'I cannot imagine that our credit would have survived if we had not [gone back to the pre-war parity].' Quoted Youngson, *The British Economy 1920–57*, p. 236.

[2] David Williams, 'London and the 1931 Financial Crisis', *Ec. H.R.*, April 1963, p. 513.

the stabilisation of the franc at a fraction of its pre-war parity in 1927, adopted a policy of deliberately adding to its gold reserves and discouraging foreign investment by stamp duties and coupon taxes. Thus after 1928 it was left to Britain to try to make the gold standard work. Not surprisingly the task ultimately proved impossible.

Although the British return to the gold standard has been described as an 'employment policy'[1] it could not do much to help the declining export industries, especially as the pound was over-valued in relation to other currencies.[2] Moreover the monetary stringency, dictated by the need to build up reserves, sustain the volume of foreign lending, and attract short-term funds, depressed the level of domestic investment and thus slowed down the development of new industries and the rationalisation of old ones. A lower rate of parity would not of itself have ensured the prosperity of the domestic economy — but it might have made easier that restructuring of British industry which was urgently required.

Free trade was an integral part of the gold standard system, for it was only under conditions of free trade that the sanctions of gold standard morality could be relied upon to operate. For clearly the gold standard system in its pure form would break down if a country could escape into protection as an alternative to making the price readjustments required by a trading imbalance. As the world's leading trader, Britain benefited from a free market, both at home and abroad. To the nineteenth-century Victorian optimist free trade also had an important political function. An ever-increasing network of intricate commercial connections between nations, each freely exchanging the goods it was best adapted to produce, would gradually remove political frictions and inaugurate an age of international co-operation. For Britain's competitors, late starters in the struggle for markets, and less dependent upon exports for their prosperity, free trade was less attractive; and in the second half of the nineteenth century, manufacturers destined to compete with those of

[1] R. S. Sayers, 'Return to Gold', in *Studies in the Industrial Revolution*, ed. Pressnell, 1958, p. 317.

[2] Keynes argued in *The Economic Consequences of Mr. Churchill*, 1925, pp. 5–6, that the pound was over-valued by 10 per cent in relation to the dollar. This price gap was probably eliminated by 1928 (see Youngson, *The British Economy 1920–1957*, p. 35), but only by further deflation. However, as France and Belgium stabilised their currencies at a fraction of the pre-war parity, they both enjoyed competitive advantage over Britain.

Britain grew up behind tariff walls in the U.S.A., France and Germany.[1]

The McKenna duties of 1915 marked the first serious breach with free trade at home.[2] They were designed to save shipping space and foreign exchange rather than to protect industry; but they proved so valuable a source of revenue that they were not repealed after the war. In 1921 came the Safeguarding of Industries Act, designed to protect certain key industries and also shelter others against the effect of currency depreciation abroad and dumping. Some of the highly specialised manufactures thus protected — precision scientific instruments, electrical parts, synthetic organic chemicals — were destined to play a much greater role in Britain's export trade in the future. In 1925, 1926 and 1928 the list of 'safeguarded' maufactures was extended, the notable addition being artificial silk. However, although the safeguarded industries expanded throughout the nineteen-twenties the numbers of people employed in them were very small compared with the major export staples. By 1929 Britain's average tariff level had only reached 5 per cent. For all practical purposes, free trade remained intact.

There were three main obstacles to any general expansion of tariffs. First, Britain's prosperity had always depended on international trade. Tariffs disrupted it; therefore Britain regarded the early restoration of general free trade as a prime political objective in the nineteen-twenties. After the currency collapses and market dislocations of the early nineteen-twenties, many impressive international conferences called for a reduction of tariffs.[3] Although resolutions to this effect were solemnly endorsed by the participating countries, they were never given practical effect. There was no real confidence in the revival of trade, and rather

[1] Average tariff levels of the U.S.A., France and Germany in 1913 were 33 per cent, 18 per cent and 12 per cent respectively. W. A. Lewis, *Economic Survey, 1919–1939*, 1949, p. 48).

[2] Customs duties were imposed on motor-cars, motor-cycles, films, clocks and musical instruments.

[3] The chief of these were (i) the Genoa Conference of 1922, (ii) the Geneva Conference of 1927 which reported that 'Europe remains today with its tariffs higher and more complicated, less stable and more numerous than in 1913'; urged that the time had come 'to put an end to the increase in tariffs and to move in the opposite direction'. Twenty-nine Governments ratified this declaration. League of Nations, *Commercial Policy in the Inter-War Period*, 1942, pp. 22, 37 ff.

than venture forth unarmed into the international arena many countries aimed to secure at least their home base for their existing industries. Britain, with apparently the most to lose from the extension of tariffs, could not afford to take a lead in the dismantling of her nineteenth-century trading system, and therefore waited vainly for tariffs to come down.

Secondly, tariffs suggested not only economic but also political nationalism, which would endanger the Versailles settlement, create new rivalries, and ultimately lead to a revival of militarism. The London Congress of the International Chambers of Commerce in 1921 condemned them as 'obstacles to peace and the progress of civilisation'. To the internationally-minded British statesmen of the nineteen-twenties free trade offered one of the main guarantees of peaceful co-existence between countries.

Thirdly, free trade was the political platform of two of the major political parties. The rejection of protection, both in 1906 and 1923, had fortified it as a political force.[1] For the Liberals, turbulently led by the unpredictable Lloyd George, it was a powerful unifying factor. Many Labour leaders, also, had graduated to socialism via liberalism and had inherited liberalism's international outlook. So free trade was an important plank in their policy also.

Thus there was little demand for protection in the nineteen-twenties. Beaverbrook's commitment to empire free trade remained as fervent as ever, but the economic situation was unfavourable during the partial recovery between 1922 and 1929. The Conservatives under Baldwin's leadership were content to add to the list of 'safeguarded industries'. Everyone paid lip-service to the advantages of an all-round reduction in tariffs. But the protectionist feeling was far from dead. It was bound to make itself immediately felt in the event of economic crisis.

iii. THE PROBLEM OF THE EXPORT INDUSTRIES

Commentators in the nineteen-twenties distinguished between normal and abnormal unemployment. Normal unemployment, based on pre-war experience, was reckoned to be about 4 per cent. The problem therefore

[1] 1923 had also showed strong surviving free trade elements in the Conservative Party, e.g. Lancashire, Glasgow (areas of exporting industries).

centred on the remaining 6 per cent — 600,000 men and women who could not be reabsorbed by industry. It was this problem Lloyd George had specially in mind when he talked in 1929 of 'reducing unemployment within one year to normal proportions'.

Despite the relative stagnation of the British economy in the nineteen-twenties, abnormal unemployment was confined to certain sections of the country and associated particularly with a few big export industries. Mowat describes the 'two Britains of the inter-war years: chronic depression in the north and in the Celtic fringe, moderate prosperity in the south'.[1] This regional concentration of unemployment, far away from London, helps to explain the relative indifference of Governments to the plight of the 'special areas' in the inter-war years.

The north and the Celtic fringe were the homes of the ailing industrial giants, especially coal and cotton which together accounted for about 60 per cent of abnormal unemployment. Other industries with heavy unemployment were the dock and harbour trades, shipping and iron and steel.

Textiles and coal were Britain's chief export industries. In 1913 their exports formed 55 per cent of the total value of Britain's physical exports. The single most important item in the textile industry was cotton. In 1913 cotton alone provided a quarter of the total value of Britain's physical exports. After the war these two industries were unable to re-establish their former position.

In 1913 Britain had exported 73m tons of coal. By 1921 this had shrunk to 25m and, although there was a recovery, exports between 1925 and 1929 (excluding 1926) averaged about 50m tons. This decline in exports caused a fall in coal production from 287m tons in 1913 to 258m tons in 1929. There was a similar pattern in cotton. In 1912 exports of cotton piece goods amounted to about 7,000m sq. yards. By 1929 they were about 3,500m sq. yards.

The causes of this decline are varied. In coal the switch to new forms of power — oil, gas, electricity — was important, though not decisive. The main explanation was the increase of coal exports by Germany, the loss of the Baltic markets to Poland, and the virtual elimination of the Russian trade following the Bolshevik Revolution. Not only did German and Polish miners work at lower wages than their British counterparts, but the industries of both countries established powerful cartels for

[1] C. L. Mowat, *Britain Between the Wars*, 1955, p. 274.

marketing and distribution, while improvements in technical efficiency produced a marked rise in output per man-shift.

Cotton faced a similar problem. Partly as a result of the war, when British exports dried up, many countries which had relied on British cotton began to expand their own production, generally under tariffs. In India, Britain's main market, production trebled between 1913 and 1929, and the British Government could not refuse the Indians protection against British maufacturers. Another major factor in the decline in Britain's cotton exports was the emergence of Japan as a leading competitor. Starting from virtually nothing in 1913 Japan had by 1929 captured 19 per cent of the world's trade. Here again the cost was decisive: Japanese workers earned less than a fifth of the British wage, and the new producers installed automatic looms, while British mills were still largely equipped with hand looms.

The wartime expansion in shipping increased employment in the dock areas which was not maintained after the war. The decline in exports accentuated what would in any case have been a difficult position. Shipbuilding likewise contracted after the war. Iron and steel was particularly dependent upon the prosperity of those industries which it supplied. During the war steel capacity had increased by 50 per cent owing to the demand for munitions. It was estimated in 1920 at 12m tons; only twice between 1920 and 1929 did output exceed 9m tons.

The concentration of unemployment in the major export industries, coupled with the fact that the export trade had traditionally provided the dynamic of the British economy, suggested that the way back to prosperity was to restore those industries to their former position. There was very little disposition, especially earlier in the decade, to accept the contraction of the export industries as permanent. Even in the case of cotton, manufacturers argued that a decline of sales in the cheaper grades of cloth might be offset by exporting more high-quality fabrics. Owners tended to explain losses in terms of costs. 'If the other competing countries have increased their production and captured our markets it is because British coal has been too dear', wrote Sir Adam Nimmo, vice-president of the Mining Association.[1]

The two main methods of reducing costs were wage cuts and rationalisation. Rationalisation was a word used loosely in the inter-war period to

[1] *The Observer*, 24 July 1927.

describe two distinct processes — the institution of economies of scale by concentrating production and marketing into larger units, and the installation of more up-to-date machinery. Both were designed to reduce labour costs by increasing productivity. Wage reductions, however, provided they could be enforced, promised quicker results.

Between 1920 and 1926 the coal owners were twice able to impose substantial wage reductions on the miners, and in 1926 a longer working day also. The social, economic and political costs, however, were enormous. In 1926 the industrial struggle was lifted to a new level of intensity; and though the General Strike failed in its immediate purpose, it made the Government and owners in other industries alive to the probable consequences of any general attempt to lower wages. (It was about this time that the phrase 'rigidity of wages' came into general use.) After 1926 the wages struggle was tacitly abandoned. Money wages remained stable for three years, despite a further drop in the price level. In other words, unemployment came to be generally accepted as an alternative to wage reductions. This meant that the unions became more interested in increasing the rate of unemployment benefit than in increasing employment, an unfortunate shift of attention since it reinforced the belief of the political wing of the Labour movement that unemployment could not be cured under capitalism.[1]

Rationalisation, the other method of cutting costs, proved similarly unpalatable to both owners and workers. It required capital, management reorganisation and enforced liquidation: the benefits were bound to be long-term. Capital was not easy to find. Industries such as iron and steel had over-invested immediately after the war, expecting boom conditions: now they were expected to find money to liquidate their bad debts. Profits were not sufficient to enable them to reorganise out of reserves. The investing public were apprehensive: interest rates were high through the need to defend the gold standard. Besides, as we have seen, the depressed industries were not prepared to accept contraction as permanent. Indeed the Samuel Report, the main rationalising document for the coal industry, was criticised by the owners for its defeatist outlook.[2] Lancashire was not prepared to renounce its great

[1] See below, pp. 27–8.

[2] e.g. Sir Adam Nimmo, *The Observer*, 24 July 1927. 'There is not a suggestion of expansion. There is no note of adventure. The industry is not told to

achievements,[1] nor were the iron and steel and shipbuilding industries prepared to reduce, till the nineteen-thirties, the surplus capacity which they had inherited from the war. Finally, from the workers' point of view rationalisation implied redundancy at a time when alternative jobs were hard to find.

Thus it is not surprising that rationalisation, though much discussed, was hardly ever undertaken by the heavy industries in the nineteen-twenties. Instead they tried to solve their problems in a number of ways. Coal maufacturers tried experiments, such as the Five Counties Scheme, whose basic objects were to maintain the domestic price of coal by means of quotas and output restriction and to promote exports by centralised selling agencies and levies on members designed to cut the export price.[2] The textile and shipbuilding industries relied largely on short-time working to ease the burden of unemployment: this was to become a major issue in 1930.

iv. THE ECONOMIC ESTABLISHMENT

Economic orthodoxy in the nineteen-twenties was not the creation of contemporary economists; rather it was the product of traditional views held by the most powerful institutions and interests in the economic community concerning their own functions and the proper role of government. They did not all speak with the same voice. In particular there developed in the post-war decade a sharp conflict of interest between industry and the City. But in general the degree of consensus was remarkable, and represented a body of opinion that no government would lightly challenge. We shall consider briefly the attitudes of business men, bankers and the Treasury.

Businessmen were imprisoned conceptually in the world of the firm. From their point of view the expectation of profit was the main stimulus to investment and production. The main variable factors in the expecta-

go and fight it out with competitors, wherever found, in the spirit of courage and daring. The outstanding note is — cut it down.'

[1] As late as 1926 Sir Charles Macara, a leading textile maufacturer, was confident of regaining 'our former supreme and prosperous position in the cotton trade of the world' (*The Export World*, Special Number, April 1926).

[2] J. H. Jones and others, *The Coal-Mining Industry*, 1939, pp. 88–107.

tion of profit were labour costs and taxation. When a firm's profits were declining the correct remedy was to reduce the labour costs; the restoration of profit would stimulate production and thus employment. The economic health of the nation could only be measured by the aggregate profits of the business community. When aggregate profits were declining the correct remedy was to reduce the burden of taxation. In generalising from the experience of a single firm, businessmen viewed wage earners simply as producers, not as consumers.

Taxation was regarded as a burden on productive enterprise. It was, of course, necessary to pay for the upkeep of government, the service of the National Debt and the provision of various basic services. When profits were large, it might even be justifiable to use its proceeds for social services. When profits were poor, however, every additional item of taxation would reduce not only the capital stock available for investment, but also the incentive to earn and to save. Throughout the first quarter of the twentieth century businessmen grumbled at rising taxation imposed in part to pay for expanding social services — education, pensions, and various types of insurance to which the State contributed.[1]

When a business was threatened with insolvency it instituted economies: men were laid off, wages were cut, directors' salaries were reduced and so on. Often bank loans were made conditional on such economies, which were regarded as indicative of a firm's resolve to set its house in order. A government was expected to take similar measures if the nation was threatened with insolvency, i.e. was unable to balance its accounts.

Businessmen took a jaundiced view of government interference in the economy. In part, of course, this stemmed from classical theory which held that *laissez-faire* was the most perfect system of economic management devised by the genius of man. But it had more practical roots. Governments, especially Labour Governments, were thought to be composed of men who, having had no practical experience of business affairs, could be relied upon to make a mess of any business enterprise they touched. Direction from Whitehall was supposed to destroy initiative, efficiency and the urge to innovation. More fundamentally,

[1] In fact the biggest increases in taxation were due to the vast expansion of the national debt following the war which, being a fixed obligation, made it virtually impossible for Governments to reduce taxation; hence the interest in 'conversion' which we shall note later.

businessmen realised that government intervention in the economy was increasingly likely to be directed against them in the interests of the working class. They were not averse to state interference when they felt such interference would be to their own advantage. In the big depression of the last quarter of the nineteenth century they were the first to demand government protection against foreign competition. The campaign for tariffs, quite as much as the radical reforms of the Asquith administration, marked the real end of *laissez-faire*. It was intervention of the 'socialistic' kind to which they were opposed.

The decision to return to the gold standard was, of course, a political one. But it was taken at the behest of financial rather than industrial interests. Industrialists were perfectly well aware of the probable consequences of a return to the pre-war parity in 1925, but their warnings were brushed aside.[1] The main protagonists of an early return were the Bank of England and the merchant banks; both, in different ways, were bound to benefit from the re-emergence of London as the world's financial centre and both assumed, if they thought about it at all, that industry would benefit in equal measure.

The Bank of England was traditionally responsible for the monetary management of the nation. It claimed the right to carry out this task without political interference. During the war, however, government control had been established in emphatic manner in 1917 when Bonar Law, the Chancellor of the Exchequer, forced the resignation of the Governor of the Bank, Lord Cunliffe. In the early post-war years, the Bank was in eclipse, as the Government chose inflation rather than deflation in the first flush of post-war optimism. The financial crises in central Europe caused a change of policy and when deflation was started in 1920 to prepare for a return to the gold standard the Bank was ready to resume its traditional role as custodian of the nation's financial conscience.

Like the business community which generalised from the practice of

[1] Written evidence presented to the Committee on Currency and Bank of England Note Issue by the F.B.I., 30 July 1924, para. 5. In forecasting a gap of 10 per cent, the F.B.I. Memorandum analysed accurately the consequences that would follow from an attempt to close the gap by further deflation. (Quoted in Macmillan Committee, *Minutes of Evidence*, vol. i, 1931, pp. 190–1. For the Macmillan Committee see below, p. 117.)

an individual firm, the Bank of England generalised from the practice of an individual bank. It saw its relationship with the Government as 'the ordinary duties of banker to client'.[1] Its task was to ensure that the client did not live beyond his means; the task of the gold standard, managed by the world's central banks, was to ensure that nations did not live beyond their means. The restoration of the gold standard, in short, gave the Bank the whip hand over the Government, as long as the Government chose to keep Britain on the gold standard. In 1927 it was able to reject a request by Winston Churchill, the Chancellor, to postpone a rise in the bank rate,[2] and by 1930 Sir Ernest Harvey, the deputy governor, was stating in the strongest terms the doctrine of the Bank's independence from political control.[3]

We have seen that the return to the gold standard involved the sacrifice of domestic enterprise. The need to attract short-term funds to re-establish London's role as a major lender and financial centre, coupled with the desire to restrain domestic prices in order to preserve the restored currency value, entailed a policy of high bank rates and consequently dear money. The repercussions on industry were hardly realised. At one point in his evidence to the Macmillan Committee Montagu Norman, the powerful governor of the Bank, denied the connection between bank rate movements and the volume of credit available to industry:

Keynes: If you had to-day to raise bank rate, say, by 5 per cent for international reasons, do you think that you could make that bank rate effective without altering the volume of credit at all?

Norman: I do not say that you could for certain, but you might be able to do so.

Keynes: Would the curtailment of credit by £50,000,000 have no effect of any importance on industry?

Norman: I do not think it would. . . .

Accused by Keynes of repudiating orthodox bank rate theory, Norman admitted that

[1] Macmillan Committee Evidence, 3.

[2] P. J. Grigg, *Prejudice and Judgment*, 1948, p. 193.

[3] Macmillan Committee Evidence, 3.

'the internal situation would have been much easier over the last few years if the rate had been . . . say 4 per cent instead of 6 per cent'.

Keynes: You mean there would have been less unemployment?
Norman: I think there would.[1]

The ignorance of the Bank of England about the effects of its monetary policy was matched by the unwillingness of the joint stock banks to take any active part in the initiation or management of enterprise. As Norman explained, 'I have never been able to see myself why, for the last few years it should have been impossible for industry *starting from within* to have readjusted its position'.[2] There was no tradition of industrial banking in England as there was in the United States and Germany where the banks, being closely associated in the management of the concerns in which their money was invested, were naturally interested in maximising their profits.

If the Bank of England had a vested interest in maintaining the international position, no less did the London financial houses which formed 'the City'. Their prosperity depended on the volume of world trade and the extent to which it could be credited or financed in London. To the City there could be no antithesis between the prosperity of London and that of the whole nation. Not only did its connections bring England much business; the services performed by the merchant banks were an important item in Britain's 'invisible exports'. Above all, as in the case of the big export industries, there was a reluctance to renounce the great achievements of the nineteenth century. The mystique of the City, or as Norman put it 'the faith that is in us', continued to exercise its powerful sway on Britishers and foreigners alike. As Wade noted in 1926, the City provided an example of

> the most amazing success in the world's financial organizations. A better case of adaptation to the needs of a great financial and trading nation has never been known . . . a wider study and understanding of its functions and operations will show both employers and employed in our industries how our future industrial success, like that of the past, must be interdependent with this perfect machine which liquefies credit and irrigates trade from day to day.[3]

---

[1] Macmillan Committee Evidence, 3379, 3388, 3492, 3493.

[2] Macmillan Committee Evidence, 3339.

[3] A. S. Wade, *Modern Finance and Industry*, 1926, p. 40.

The Treasury was the natural ally of the City. Its main function was to regulate fiscal policy and control government expenditure. Its main aim was to balance the Budget and reduce government spending.

The Treasury, like the banking institutions, had a very restricted view of its role in the economy. It did not view itself as a ministry of economic affairs: indeed, economic affairs were not regarded as a unified field. The Treasury concerned itself with two matters: purely financial questions — loans, conversions, relations with the Bank of England, the presentation of estimates to Parliament, the control of exchequer issues and so on — and control of the expenditure of other departments. Sir James Grigg, principal private secretary to five successive Chancellors, recalls how as a very junior clerk he was sent on missions to other government departments 'to lay down the law' to officials very senior to himself.[1] Monetary policy was in the hands of the Bank of England. Industrial policy, such as existed, was in the hands of the Board of Trade and the Ministry of Labour, both of junior Cabinet status. Thus the Treasury, which was in the best position to gain an overall picture of the national economy, was not responsible for anything but fiscal matters; while the departments directly concerned with labour, industry and trade were too specialised and unimportant to acquire an overall view or to exercise any control.

The principle of the annual balanced Budget was once again a generalisation from the budgetary maxims thought to apply to an individual. Sir James Grigg declared in his autobiography:

> I distrust utterly those economists who have with great but deplorable ingenuity taught that it is not only possible but praiseworthy for a whole country to live beyond its means on its wits and who . . . teach that it is possible to make a community rich by calling a penny twopence, in short who have sought to make economics a *vade mecum* for political spivs.[2]

The importance of the Budget was political rather than economic[3] —

[1] P. J. Grigg, *Prejudice and Judgment*, p. 36.

[2] Ibid., p. 7.

[3] For, of course, the Chancellor's Budget did not clearly reveal the true economic position of the public finances. What was included and what was left out was largely a matter of custom and arbitrary choice. Further, no distinction was drawn between the capital and current account. (See U. K. Hicks, *The Finance of British Government, 1920–1936*, 1938, pp. 279–83.)

never more so than during a depression.[1] Just as the individual was supposed to reduce his standard of living in response to a reduced income, just as a firm was expected to economise in a bad period, so was the Government expected to reduce its spending when faced with a fall in receipts from taxation and customs duties. Any failure to give the expected lead would undermine the confidence in the offending Government of both domestic and foreign businessmen and bankers and thus confidence in the nation's currency, its creditworthiness, its investment possibilities and so on. This would hit especially hard a big trading nation which was also a major financial centre.

It might be necessary to balance a Budget by economies in depression; but the consistent predilection of the Treasury for economy at all times stemmed from the view that government expenditure was basically unproductive. Taxation was necessary to pay for the upkeep of administration, the service of the national debt and such basic public services as the armed forces but was, all the same, a burden on 'productive enterprise', i.e. it deprived businessmen of resources which they would have used for investment. It was these reasons that prompted Gladstone to try to abolish the income tax first instituted by Pitt and which made all Governments feel guilty about increasing expenditure. However, classical theory had always recognised as legitimate government expenditure on certain public utilities which would not be sufficiently profitable to attract private capital. As it became increasingly important for Governments in the late nineteenth and early twentieth centuries to woo working-class voters, this collection of necessary public utilities was extended to include social services — education, housing, pensions and various types of insurance — thus forming a range of public enterprise that would have amazed Adam Smith and his followers.[2]

[1] Thus, for example, Churchill was allowed to use devices of unprecedented ingenuity to balance his Budgets, such as raids on the road fund, use of capital assets to balance current revenue, anticipation of future receipts by altering instalment dates, etc, without producing any general apprehension, simply because the economy was moderately prosperous. It would have been quite different in a depression.

[2] In 1913 national income was estimated at £2000m. Public expenditure (both government and local authority) at £325m accounted for about 16 per cent. In 1924, with national income at £4000m, public expenditure amounted to £1110m, or nearly 30 per cent. (U. K. Hicks, *The Finance of British Government, 1920–1936*, p. 25.)

Throughout the nineteen-twenties Governments were prepared to exploit, to a greater or lesser extent, this loophole in the traditional view to ameliorate unemployment, but not without opposition from a Treasury firmly wedded to Gladstonian principles and a business community that resented depredations on the 'stock of capital'.

The greatest single budgetary burden in the nineteen-twenties was the interest and sinking fund payments on the national debt which amounted to about £400m a year. This wholly unproductive item of expenditure which constituted a grievous and increasing burden on industry as deflation continued was largely the result of loans enthusiastically subscribed by a patriotic public to pay for the war. There was considerable support early in the decade for a 'capital levy' to help pay off the war debt, but this came to nothing. The two main forms of war debt were the 'floating debt' consisting of treasury bills, and the long-term debt. The size of the debt had deflationary consequences because the enormous cost of servicing it entailed a high level of taxation, while the efforts to renew treasury bills pushed up the short-term rate of interest. Hence it became a primary aim of treasury policy to reduce the interest charges on the long-term debt by converting the big war loans (especially the 5 per cent issue of 1917) to a lower rate of interest and secondly to reduce drastically the outstanding volume of treasury bills. The first objective was admirable; the second, however, meant that borrowing for any purpose was likely to be discouraged. Indeed one of the melancholy consequences of the war was that borrowing acquired a hopelessly bad reputation, and the phrase 'piling up burdens for future generations' was often to be heard on the lips of politicians during the nineteen-twenties. The almost unanimous feeling that the war debt ought to be reduced as quickly as possible was also responsible for the provision in the Budget for a high sinking fund of about £60m, without which it was not considered to be truly balanced.

V. THE ROLE OF THE GOVERNMENT

A powerful impetus to state interference in the economy was given by the war. Not only did the Government exercise a general control over the economy unknown in peacetime, but it also took over the management of a number of key industries — notably coal and railways. With the post-war cry of 'back to normal' the Lloyd George coalition once more gave free enterprise its head. But state responsibility for the economy had to some extent been legitimised, and with the start of the depression in 1920 it was considered almost natural for the Government to step in to remedy the deficiencies of capitalism. We have already referred to the McKenna duties and the gradual extension of 'safeguarding' during the nineteen-twenties. But the Government went further than this. The dislocation of the export trade prompted it to devise financial incentives for exporters. The onset of mass unemployment brought with it government-inspired public works programmes and other measures designed to increase the level of employment; it also forced the state to extend and improve the wartime structure of unemployment insurance. These steps were intended to be temporary — to tide over the abnormal phase of post-war readjustment. But it is doubtful whether they could have been taken by any peacetime Government before the war.[1] As post-war unemployment continued much heavier than previously, practice lent them a certain familiarity. But it would be wrong to conclude that they came to be regarded as normal.

Export credits were first started and developed between 1919 and 1921 with two Overseas Trade (Credit and Insurance) Acts which allowed the Board of Trade to guarantee bills drawn by traders for exports up to an amount outstanding at any time of £26m. By 1925 the scheme was open to all countries except Russia. In its mature form exporters were able to obtain short-term guarantees under this scheme of up to 75 per cent of the price of the exported goods without enquiry into their financial position; and up to 100 per cent if they were prepared to provide security. Between 1926 and 1929 guarantees were given for up to £12m altogether. When it is remembered that the total value of Britain's physical exports was about £700m a year it can be seen how limited was the use of the scheme.

Trade Facilities came into existence in the autumn of 1921. Their object was to overcome the restrictive effects on investment of the very high interest rates ruling immediately after the war. The Treasury was empowered to guarantee loans towards capital development which were

[1] Though the 1911 Insurance Act was regarded as capable of extension even at the time.

designed to relieve unemployment. Applicants might be governments, municipalities and companies in Britain, the Empire or foreign countries. The original Act provided for guarantees not exceeding £25m. Subsequent Acts raised the maximum to £75m and in fact £74½m worth of guarantees were given during the lifetime of the scheme before it was wound up in 1927.

The main beneficiaries of Trade Facilities were foreign firms and municipalities, but this was not considered objectionable as capital development abroad was supposed to promote employment at home. A treasury report of 1930 noted:

> In other cases, notably in connection with shipping and industrial enterprises in this country, the Act had less favourable results and may have involved the Treasury in heavy losses. . . .[1]

It was partly because of these losses that the scheme came to an end in 1927.

In December 1920 the Unemployment Grants Committee[2] was set up under treasury authority 'for the purpose of assisting Local Authorities in the United Kingdom in carrying out approved schemes of useful work other than work on roads and on housing schemes'.[3] The setting up of the Committee coincided with the onset of mass unemployment. At first it was hoped that conditions would quickly revert to normal and the Committee could soon be disbanded. Gradually as this hope faded it came to be accepted as permanent.

The Committee was allowed to spend a maximum of £3m a year. The favourite form of finance was to help the local authorities with their loan repayments, though in some cases there was a direct subsidy of wages. The proportion of the total capital cost met by the Committee grant on all the schemes averaged about 35 per cent. Between 1920 and 1928 the total of approved schemes came to £106m. At an average of 35 per cent the exchequer liability was £33m. Spread over fifteen years (the average

[1] *Treasury Report on Trade Facilities* prepared for the Two Party Conference on Unemployment, June 1930; see below, p. 201. Lord Lothian's Papers, Box 214.

[2] Generally known as the Lord St. Davids Committee from the name of its chairman.

[3] *U.G.C. Final Report*, June 1933, Cmd. 4354, p. 3.

period of a loan) liability came to just over £2m a year — well within the limits laid down by the original terms of reference.[1]

Between 1925 and 1928 there was a sharp tailing off in activity owing to stringent conditions imposed in 1925.[2] But in 1928, following the report of the Industrial Transference Board, the Government introduced more favourable terms for local authorities willing to employ 'transferred labour'. If authorities in the more prosperous areas were willing to take at least 50 per cent of the men required for the works from the depressed areas, the Government would be prepared to increase their grant to 63 per cent of the total cost and also to drop the five-year acceleration condition. These were the 'premiums' to be paid to these authorities for importing the unemployed into their own areas. The disadvantage of this new provision was that prosperous authorities were now able to get higher grants than depressed ones, but the Government

> considered that the more generous grants were justified because of the national advantage which would follow from the grants by the absorption in the more prosperous district of men from depressed areas where industry was in a state of stagnation.[3]

This new policy did have some effect in stimulating new applications. Between July 1928 and June 1929, £6m worth of schemes were approved, as compared with only £1m in the previous two years.

The most important feature of the public works programmes of the nineteen-twenties was that primary responsibility for them rested with the municipalities and other semi-autonomous public authorities (such as the Central Electricity Board). The obligation of the Government was limited to providing financial incentives for the authorities in question to expedite and enlarge the scale of their own works. Even in the case of road building, greatly expanded in 1920 with the establishment of the Ministry of Transport and for which government help was provided out of a special tax levied on car owners which went into a road fund,

[1] *U.G.C. Report*, Cmd. 4354, p. 22. In fact the public works programme was even less impressive than that. 'Schemes approved' and 'schemes carried out' were by no means identical.

[2] A local authority was only entitled to help if (i) its area had 15 per cent unemployment, (ii) it was prepared to 'accelerate' work by five years, and (iii) its proposed schemes qualified as 'public utilities'.

[3] *U.G.C. Report*, Cmd. 4354, p. 7.

responsibility for submitting schemes rested with the local authorities. It was not until the Liberal proposals were produced in 1929 that any serious thought was given to a national public works programme, mounted and financed directly by the Government.

The 1911 Unemployment Insurance Act had established the principle of compulsory insurance against unemployment. But only a small minority of trades which were thought to be the least susceptible to unemployment were included. Benefits were paid out of an insurance fund composed of 'equal thirds' contributions from the state, employers and employees. In order to obtain benefit a workman had to have paid at least ten contributions and established that he was unable to obtain work. Attendance at the employment exchange and readiness to take suitable employment were accepted as *prima facie* proof of a claimant's capacity and availability for work.

During the war, when it was important to maintain industrial peace and when there was little prospect of unemployment, the insurance scheme was extended to cover the majority of trades, the main exceptions being agricultural workers and domestic servants. By 1920 there were 12m insured workers as opposed to 2½m in 1911. The rates of benefit had also been doubled, with a differential rate for women who, as a result of wartime work, came into the scheme in large numbers. Although the 'equal thirds' principle was retained, the war had forced upon the Government a financial commitment never contemplated by the 1911 Act. But this was not all. In 1919, in a modest effort to fulfil its promise to create a land fit for heroes, the Lloyd George Government tacked on to the main insurance scheme an 'out of work' donation scheme, with considerably higher rates of benefit, for demobilised soldiers unemployed pending reabsorption into industry and civilian workers thrown out of work by change from war to peace production. This had three new features. It provided benefits without contributions — it was a genuine 'dole'; it contained dependants' allowances; and finally it introduced as a condition for obtaining benefit the stipulation that a claimant should be 'genuinely seeking work'. This last provision was to discourage people switching over from the main scheme to the rather more attractive 'dole' scheme.

As unemployment continued at a high level after 1920, the 'dole scheme', intended to be purely temporary, was extended to all those who could no longer keep up contributions because of prolonged unemployment, and incorporated, with its special features, into the main scheme. However, the inclusion in the scheme of people paying no contributions, coupled with the abnormal rise in unemployment in 1920–2, meant that the insurance fund ran heavily into debt. A surplus of £22m in 1920 rapidly became a deficit of £15m in 1921. The Government gave the fund borrowing powers of up to £20m to meet the immediate crisis, a sum that was gradually increased to £40m by 1929.

The history of unemployment insurance between 1925 and 1929 is the attempt by the Conservative Government of Stanley Baldwin to restore the fund to a 'sound actuarial basis'. No Government, except the Labour administration of 1924, had accepted the 'dole' or 'uncovenanted benefit' as permanent, for that would deny the insurance basis of the scheme, which was considered vital. If a large number of workers continued unable to pay contributions, then a separate scheme would have to be worked out for them: they should not burden the insurance scheme proper. To examine these problems the Government appointed a committee in 1925 under Lord Blanesburgh. The Blanesburgh Committee sought to reduce the debt of the fund by reducing benefits. It also hoped that within a year of its report, which came out in 1927, employment would have improved sufficiently for all insured workers once more to be paying contributions. The 'dole' scheme was formally to end, then, in 1928. This hope proved illusory and it was extended by a further 'transitional' period to 1929. But its early demise was still confidently expected.

As we have seen, the various devices started by Governments during and immediately after the war to relieve or mitigate the hardship of unemployment were intended to be purely temporary. They survived well into the post-war period because unemployment continued unexpectedly heavy. But their survival was rather uneasy. The Conservative Government of 1924–9, in its pursuit of economy, cut down the work of the Unemployment Grants Committee, abolished Trade Facilities, and attempted to curtail unemployment insurance. Government encroachments into the domain of private industry were never completely accepted, even by the Governments which undertook them. Moreover they were likely to become especially vulnerable to attack when they were most needed, i.e. when unemployment was at its highest. For it was then that industry's clamour to be relieved of taxation burdens would reach its peak and the pressure on the Budget which financed them would be at its greatest.[1]

vi. THE UNEMPLOYMENT DEBATE

It was widely accepted that the unemployment problem of the nineteen-twenties was 'permanent' rather than 'cyclical', that it was independent of the trade-cycle. It was inevitable that some conflict of opinion should develop about how to deal with it. We will consider the attitude of the Labour Party in the next chapter. Within the confines of orthodox economic opinion, two distinct views emerged.

The conservative view maintained that, as abnormal unemployment was concentrated largely in the traditional export industries, the starting point of any solution to the unemployment problem should be an attempt by the export industries to recapture their former markets — by rationalisation or by wage reductions or by a combination of both. The restoration of the gold standard and the campaign for tariff reductions were seen as attempts to create a psychological climate beneficial to the general revival of a world trade dislocated by the war. The choice of the pre-war parity was an attempt to restore the position of London, whose continued pre-eminence was thought to be indispensable to this process. Deflation was regarded as the temporary price to pay for the return to normality. By forcing the required reduction in money costs it would restore the competitive position of the big export staples.

Against this view were those who argued that the declining export

[1] Some interesting statistical information about the retreat of the Government from intervention in the economy after the war is provided by Abramovitz and Eliasberg in their book *The Growth of Public Employment in Great Britain*, Princeton University Press, 1957. The number of civilian personnel employed by the Government in the 'economic regulatory agencies', such as the Boards of Trade and Agriculture, the Ministry of Labour, the Departments for Overseas Trade and for Scientific and Industrial Research, which rose from 11,000 in 1914 to 50,000 in 1918, had declined to 23,000 in 1928, despite a considerable expansion of the Ministry of Labour to cope with unemployment benefit (pp. 41, 46–50).

industries could never be restored to their former position. New industries would have to be developed to replace them, both for export and for supplying the home market with goods previously imported. The working of the gold standard made it impossible either for the newer industries to obtain the credit to expand or for the older ones to rationalise. Deflation damaged business confidence by reducing expectations of profit and by increasing the burden of debts fixed in money terms. This view, especially as expressed by Keynes,[1] was opposed to the restoration of the gold standard at the pre-war parity. After 1925, recognising that a normal operation of the gold standard in the new conditions made inevitable a policy of dear money and deflation, it came increasingly to the conclusion that a definite act of Government was necessary to raise the level of investment.

The fundamental difference between these two views was one of priority. The 'economic establishment' was prepared to pay the price of unemployment for the sake of other benefits — a stable international monetary system, and the restoration of the position of London — though it doubtless hoped that these benefits would in the end lead to a diminution of unemployment.[2] The opponents of this policy saw its disadvantages as more than temporary, its compensations unduly delayed. They were not prepared to go on sacrificing industry and employment indefinitely for the sake of problematic benefits which might accrue at some point in the future.

Underlying the policy and interests of the 'economic establishment' was a substratum of simplified economic theory which was known as the 'treasury view'. Briefly this view ignored the existence of unemployment, and maintained that existing resources of capital and labour were being fully utilised. (This would generally be the case at full employment). It followed that any attempt to increase the level of investment would be either inflationary or diversionary. If the Government created more money without a prior increase in demand to justify it,

[1] e.g. in his *Tract for Monetary Reform*, 1923.

[2] For example, T. E. Gregory argued that 'the question of deflation is not to be disposed of by showing that it will lead to unemployment. For it may be worthwhile to pay this price, not merely to "do justice to the rentier" but, e.g., to get back to a sound currency.' (Quoted in Keith Hancock, 'Unemployment and the Economists in the 1920's', *Economica*, xxvii, 1960, p. 306.)

manufacturers would merely raise their prices. Employees would demand higher wages and a wage-price inflationary spiral would force Britain off the gold standard, disrupt the international currency structure, wipe out savings, and lead to the type of economic collapse that had overtaken European countries after the war. Alternatively, if a Government raised an investment loan it would merely divert funds from normal employment in productive enterprise. Thus while the Government would be providing employment on the one hand it would be diminishing it on the other: and by rather more, for it was held that government-sponsored projects were by definition less profitable than ordinary manufacture. It can be seen that this theory appealed alike to businessmen, resentful of government interference and contemptuous of government inefficiency, to the City, concerned to defend London's international position, and to the Treasury, with its traditional predilection for economy and 'sound finance'.

We have called the 'treasury view' a simplified one because it completely left out the observable and recurring phenomenon of mass unemployment. Quite apart from the experience of the nineteen-twenties there had in the past been prolonged periods of depression. It was surely implausible to maintain that in these periods existing capital was being fully employed on productive manufacture, for if this were the case it would be difficult to account for depression. Nor was this the position of the economists. They assumed that during the downswing of the trade cycle entrepreneurs deliberately refrained from investment in the expectation of prices falling even further. After the depression had run its course, investment would start picking up again and boom conditions would supervene. It the meantime money was hoarded or retained in 'idle balances'.

There is no doubt that the 'treasury view' was rejected by all the leading economists, quite apart from Keynes, who was its principal critic. Pigou subjected it to detailed analysis in 1927 and found it to be fallacious. It was perfectly possible, he claimed, for the State to raise money in a depression without diverting resources from private enterprise.[1] Henry Clay wrote in 1929:

The fundamental objection in principle, then, that public enterprise would

[1] Pigou, *Industrial Fluctuations*, 1927, pp. 289–96.

merely divert without increasing employment, does not appear to be well-founded.[1]

Hawtrey wrote in 1928:

> If the Government comes forward with an attractive gilt-edged loan, it may raise money, not merely by taking the place of other possible capital issues, but by securing money that would have otherwise remained in idle balances.[2]

Robertson argued that the desire of the public to invest could well be obstructed by a banking system tied to international considerations, in which case there would be idle savings waiting to be employed.[3] Other public figures, prominent in banking and industrial circles, similarly attacked the 'treasury view'.[4]

It should be noted that few economists in the nineteen-twenties actually advocated a government investment loan. The normal trade-cycle, they held, was self-correcting. There was no necessity for the Government to 'prime the pump'. Others, however, argued that the position in the nineteen-twenties was abnormal and unprecedented. It displayed most of the characteristics of a trade-cycle depression except that it appeared to be permanent. In such circumstances there was a strong case for the State attempting directly to find use for 'idle balances'. It is this view that formed the basis of the Liberal unemployment proposals in the 1929 election.

[1] Henry Clay, *The Post-War Unemployment Problem*, 1929, p. 133. He supported the theory of idle balances with statistical information from pre-war depressions (p. 15).

[2] R. G. Hawtrey, *Trade and Credit*, 1928, p. 110.

[3] D. H. Robertson, *Essays in Monetary Theory*, 1946, p. 44; Macmillan Committee Evidence, 4714.

[4] e.g. Reginald McKenna, former Liberal Chancellor of the Exchequer and chairman of the Midland Bank (*The Economist*, 29 January 1927, p. 231); Sir Josiah Stamp (Macmillan Committee Evidence, 3959).

2

SOCIALISTS AND UNEMPLOYMENT

i. INTRODUCTION

To Socialists unemployment was the most vivid manifestation of permanent working-class poverty. Any attempt to cure unemployment within the capitalist framework was bound to fail, for unemployment was part of the fundamental problem of poverty, and the only solution to poverty was socialism. This is why the Socialists objected to the 'reformist' capitalism of Lloyd George and ignored the work of 'advanced' capitalist economists such as Keynes, Henderson and Robertson.

By 1900 all Socialists were equipped with some kind of analysis of poverty in the midst of plenty. In its simplest form, they attributed it to the fact that a small class of landlords and capitalists was in a position to deprive the worker of a fair share of the value of his labour. They were able to do this through their ownership of two scarce resources — land and capital. As they thus controlled the means of production they could 'exploit' the worker by paying him just enough wages to enable him to live and work. The difference between these wages and the product of the worker's labour was the 'profit' of the capitalist. Now clearly part of the profit was invested in new machinery and in expanding production. But part of it the capitalist spent on himself and his family. This was the part, Socialists claimed, that should go towards increasing the wages of the workers. There was no economic necessity for the capitalist at all: the State could take over all his functions without loss and thereby release to the people that section of the capitalist's profits that went into his personal consumption.

There were many more sophisticated versions of this analysis. In particular a number of writers, such as Marx, saw mass poverty not only as the product of private ownership but as the cause of the periodic slumps to which the capitalist system was subject. For low wages, they argued, meant that the people would lack purchasing power to consume the goods the capitalist placed on the market. Periodically therefore he would be unable to sell his goods at prices profitable to him.

This over-production or under-consumption analysis brought socialist thought into line with that of 'capitalist' economists who were investigating the causes of the trade-cycle. But whereas the latter attached key importance to regulating the cycle, Socialists were more interested in eliminating poverty. Hence they were not really concerned with trade-cycle analysis: they wanted a total solution, not palliatives.

Theoretically they were equipped to deal with poverty but only in terms of total solution. Would they ever be in a position to impose such a solution? The answer depended on the power they would possess in government. The question of how much power was required and how it could be obtained was endlessly debated between the 'revolutionary' and 'democratic' Socialists. The revolutionary Socialists took their stand on Marx. The way in which this debate was resolved in England, therefore, depended in large measure on how English Socialists reacted to Marx and Marxism.

ii. THE REJECTION OF MARXISM

The novelty of Marxism for English Socialists consisted not of those propositions which it held in common with other criticisms of capitalism but in its unique analysis of the problem of power. Briefly, the Marxist argument was that the ideas and attitudes of a class are determined by its self-interest. The interest of the capitalist class was to maximise its exploitation of the working class; hence it could never be brought to accept socialism by reason, for it defined reason in terms of its own interests; and the only 'reasonable' economic organisation was one that upheld its own interests. It followed that capitalists would never allow themselves to be dispossessed peacefully of their right to exploit: they had to be dispossessed by force. It was the task of a revolutionary leadership to rid the masses of their capitalist ideology in preparation for the revolutionary struggle.

Now most English Socialists found this doctrine extremely strange. For one thing they were not disposed to accept the theory of a class struggle that could be resolved successfully for the working class only by the forcible and bloody dispossession of the owning class. To them the doctrine of bloody revolution was quite alien: a typical import from the Continent where revolutions were frequent. In England the ruling class had just conceded something approaching universal franchise in the Reform Bills of 1867 and 1884 and it was natural for politically minded Socialists to turn to Parliament to achieve their aims. Being less dogmatic and doctrinaire in argument and placing far greater stress on compromise than their Continental counterparts, English Socialists could never really believe that ideas were mainly the product of class interest. Convinced that socialism was a superior idea, they persuaded themselves that capitalists would likewise become convinced; hence many of them, especially the Fabians, devoted themselves to preparing documentary evidence of the malfunctioning of capitalism and permeating the capitalist parties with socialist ideas. Nor did English socialists take kindly to Marx's strictures on religion. In England there was no powerful and reactionary Church, no fierce tradition of anti-clericalism to strike a responsive chord. In fact many prominent early Socialists were active nonconformists and regarded socialism as the political realisation of the Christian faith.

The most common way in which Marxist ideas influenced English socialist thought was in company with other socialist writings which focused attention on the injustices of the capitalist system — its inhumanity, its wastefulness and its toll on human happiness. Marxist concepts of 'class war' and violent struggle were unacceptable to reformist Socialists. The working-class was certainly to be made conscious of its oppression. But the aim of a 'socialistic' party was also to make capitalists conscious of the possibility of a superior economic organisation. The revolution was to be one of reason and not of violence.

Ramsay MacDonald and the other Fabian theorists did not think that in the end the capitalist classes would prove unreasonable. But their conversion would almost certainly take a long time, and a belief in the 'inevitability of gradualness' did not offer any clear guidance about what to do in the interim. For, with the acceptance by the Labour Party of democratic responsibilities, the possibility arose of a Socialist Government coming into office but without any mandate to attack the whole problem of poverty along socialist lines, i.e. by taking over the ownership of the industry.

Besides, it was not obvious that taking over industry little by little would at any single point produce a notable improvement in the living conditions of the mass of the workers, or indeed much alleviation of the problem of unemployment. What were clearly needed, therefore, were supplementary policies for the period of the 'transition', designed to effect improvements in the conditions of the poorest workers and the unemployed in a situation in which the structure of capitalism remained largely intact. The trouble was that such policies might be seen as alternatives to socialism rather than as stages in the advance towards it. In particular, they might remove the *grievances* of the working class which gave the socialist alternative its political support. MacDonald discusses these problems rather unhappily without coming to any conclusion.[1] Nevertheless, there were two thinkers in Labour politics who attempted to work out 'transitional' policies which would have been particularly useful to a Labour Government called upon to deal with mass unemployment. They were John Hobson and Beatrice Webb.

iii. JOHN HOBSON AND BEATRICE WEBB

Hobson was a Liberal economist and lecturer who had early become dissatisfied with some aspects of traditional economic teaching. His 'heresy' dated from the publication of *The Physiology of Industry*, 1889, written in collaboration with A. F. Mummery. This book was an early statement of the 'over-saving' theory, though without any analysis of income distribution which he was to stress in later works. His attack on the classical school led to his exclusion from the academic establishment. 'Even then', Hobson later wrote, 'I hardly realized that in appearing to question the virtue of unlimited thrift I had committed the unpardonable sin.'[2] Denied an academic sanctuary, he plunged actively into the

[1] e.g. in *Socialism and Society*, 1905, pp. 59, 60 n.

[2] Hobson, *Confessions of an Economic Heretic*, 1937, p. 31.

'progressive' politics of the period, and thus his ideas became known to many who were active in building up the Labour Party.

Hobson's analysis of income maldistribution was not really very different from that of the socialist under-consumptionists. Like Marx he makes use of the concept of 'surplus value'. His central proposition is that the unequal bargaining power between buyers and sellers of labour provides the buyers (or capitalists) with a 'surplus' beyond that which is necessary to evoke production. The consequence is an unequal distribution of the national income. As the small group who possess the 'surplus' cannot possibly spend it all, they save it and thus disrupt the correct saving-spending ratio. The capitalists use their excess savings to invest in more production facilities turning out more goods than the remaining income for consumption can absorb at prices sufficient to recover the investment.[1] Periodically there will be a glut of commodities, producing the familiar depression characteristics of congestion, contraction of production and unemployment.

Now this was all common ground with much more generalised socialist thought. The difference between Hobson and the Socialists was that Hobson did not regard the maldistribution of income as being the cause of permanent poverty, but merely that of periodic economic breakdowns. Hence his remedies were directed not towards eliminating poverty but towards evening out the trade-cycle. In other words he was first and foremost a trade-cycle theorist.

However, he was the only trade-cycle theorist whose analysis and remedies were likely to prove valuable additions to the socialist armoury. For Hobson advocated the taxation of the 'surplus' in order to restore the correct saving-spending ratio, the proceeds of this taxation to be redistributed as purchasing power to the workers, either in the form of wages or as social benefits.[2] His proposals, therefore, if not socialist, were indubitably socialistic.

There was, however, one fatal defect in the Hobson plan. As it was

[1] Hobson, *Economics of Unemployment*, 1923, p. 8: 'there exists at any given time an economically sound ratio between spending and saving. . . . The current distribution of income throughout the industrial world tends normally to evoke a rate of saving and capital creation that is excessive. . . .' Hobson regarded 'saving' and 'capital creation' as synonymous, i.e. the surplus of the rich 'accumulates automatically to form an investment fund of capital'.

[2] Ibid.

hardly plausible to suppose that capitalists accumulate a surplus in this sense during the down-swing of the trade-cycle, the Hobsonian remedy of taxation was to be applied on the up-swing when, on his argument, the 'surplus' was being made. Progressive taxation emerges as a weapon to be used in prosperity but not in depression.

Thus, although Hobson provided Socialists with a valuable short-term or transitional instrument for alleviating poverty, it was one that could only be used in time of relative prosperity. To use it during a depression would not only rob it of its economic significance, but, with capitalism still intact, would lead to the kind of showdown which no democratic Socialist Government cared to face.

Beatrice Webb was the eighth of nine daughters of the Liberal railway and industrial magnate, Richard Potter. Born in 1858, she led a conventional upper class life until the 1880s when her friendship with Herbert Spencer made her aware of social injustices. Reading the first collection of Fabian Essays she was attracted by the approach and style of Sidney Webb. They married in 1892 and established the famous 'firm of Webb' whose writings and activities were destined to have such a profound effect on social thinking and on the Labour Party. At first, however, neither Sidney nor Beatrice thought that their ideas would be put into practice by a new political party: they were more interested in permeating existing political parties with 'socialistic' thinking. Thus they served assiduously on public commissions and enquiries, amassed a huge body of evidence on various social problems and entertained at their house the leaders of both the Conservative and Liberal Parties. One result of their friendship with the Conservative Balfour was that he appointed Beatrice to the Royal Commission on the Poor Law which he set up just before he left office in 1905.

The Commission was not an enquiry into the causes of unemployment but into its manifestations, though the minority report, which was largely the work of Beatrice Webb, expressed the belief that

> The investigations that we have made into the *manner* in which persons become Unemployed, and the results on these persons of such Unemployment, would necessarily form the starting point for any useful inquiry into more ultimate causes of social and industrial disorganisation.[1]

[1] Report of the Royal Commission on the Poor Law, vol. iii, *Minority Report*, 1909, p. 570 n.

By this time Beatrice Webb, like most other socialists, was convinced that the causes of 'social and industrial disorganisation' lay in the very structure of capitalist society and could only be overcome by the collective ownership of the means of production. Despite this, the minority report did not hesitate to make suggestions for reducing unemployment within the existing framework of society. The starting point of these suggestions was the recognition that 'abnormal' unemployment was the product of the trade-cycle.

Beatrice Webb recognised that cyclical fluctuations have 'sent up the percentage of unemployed workmen to three, four, and even five times as many as in the better years'. What she envisaged was a deliberate attempt by government departments so to place their orders for work as to counteract the normal ebb and flow of labour. Departments, she thought, should have a ten-year programme of constructional work. When the National Labour Exchange reported that the percentage of unemployed was rising above 4 per cent, the departments would begin to accelerate their programmes. The Admiralty would order 'a special battleship', the War Office 'additional barracks', the Post Office more post offices and extensions of telegraph and telephone services, the Stationery Office 'would get on two or three times as fast as usual with the printing of the volumes of the Historical Manuscripts Commission' and so on. The decisive feature of these proposals was that the works 'would be started before unemployment became acute'.[1] They were to be in the nature of prevention rather than cure.

It was, in fact, this 'decisive feature' that enabled the minority report to distinguish the 'counter-cycle' policy from a public-works policy. Public or relief works were tainted in the eyes of the Labour movement by association with Poor Law navvy work. This work was based on the 'less eligibility' principle, both as regards conditions and pay. When it came to an end there was nowhere to go save back to the Guardians, and as the work undertaken had done nothing to promote the general prosperity of the country, it did not, so the argument ran, promote the creation of jobs for the future. The 'counter-cycle' policy, on the other hand, was intended as a commercial venture. Departments would contract for work, and labour would be hired in the normal way, for standard wages. There was also a recognition that the construction

[1] Ibid. pp. 657–9.

work — to which the report added some schemes for afforestation and land reclamation — was useful, not only in the sense that it gave workmen engaged in it a feeling of purpose, but that it also contributed to the general economic welfare of the country.[1] These factors distinguished it further from traditional relief work, and to make the point explicit the report was careful to state that 'counter-cycle' schemes would have 'absolutely no connection . . . with whatever provisions were made for the men in want or in destitution'.[2]

How were these counter-cyclical proposals to be financed? There is some ambiguity, but basically two methods are suggested, depending at which point in the trade-cycle it is proposed to start the policy. If the policy was started during a depression the money required would be borrowed.[3] Here we have an early statement of the theory of 'idle balances' which was to be used by the Liberals in the nineteen-twenties. The report states that it is characteristic of a depression that 'capital is unemployed and under-employed to at least as great an extent as labour'. This 'unemployed capital' could be drawn out at fairly low interest rates.[4] The 'loan' would be repaid in the good years following the depression — 'the charge falls . . . largely on the years of good trade and high profits'.[5] In the second case, where the works would be started before the depression, there could be no argument against financing them out of taxation or normal budget surpluses. Here the reasoning is based on Hobson. The money would accumulate in a fund to be spent once unemployment had reached a level of 4 per cent. In both cases the report anticipated an expenditure of £40m in ten years for this purpose, the bulk of the expenditure falling in the two or three years of the depression. To reconcile these proposals with the theory of the 'balanced Budget' the report suggested aiming for a balanced account over a ten-year period and criticised 'Treasury book-keeping' for its insistence on an annually balanced account.[6]

Taking the short-term unemployment policies of Hobson and Webb in conjunction we can see clearly their value to Labour Party thinking

[1] Ibid. p. 660. [2] Ibid. [3] Ibid. p. 661.

[4] The assumption here is that interest rates would be very low during a depression: in the later 1920's interest rates were kept high through the need to defend sterling.

[5] Ibid. p. 662. [6] Ibid. p. 661.

and also the limits of their practical utility. Hobson's policy could most plausibly be applied in 'boom' conditions; its whole justification would disappear if applied during a depression and it would moreover have the important practical consequence of depressing the business community and arousing intense opposition. The Webb proposals could in theory be applied both in a boom and a depression. In boom conditions they resembled Hobson's — the taxation of the rich, not to be immediately disbursed in the form of working class consumption power or social benefits, but to be held in reserve for the 'bad times'. In conditions of depression they depended upon a theory of 'idle balances', then relatively novel. It was, in fact, in this latter aspect that the proposals would have proved most useful to the Labour Party in the nineteen-twenties — had they been taken up. Instead it was left to the Liberal Party, guided by Keynes, McKenna and others, to draw practical conclusions from the concept of 'idle balances'. The Labour Party's lack of interest may be readily explained. Progressive taxation was at least 'socialistic' in intent and effect. Drawing out 'idle balances' on the other hand seemed to be mere capitalist tinkering.

iv. THE LABOUR PARTY'S UNEMPLOYED BILL, 1907

Before the minority report came out the Labour Party had introduced in the House of Commons its own Bill for dealing with unemployment. It was the first major policy statement of the parliamentary Labour Party on this subject and was presented four times between 1907 and 1911, each time failing to secure a second reading.

It was this Bill that first gave concrete expression to the concept of 'work or maintenance'. The argument was that every man had the right to work. If society could not guarantee this right because of imperfect economic organisation then it had an obligation to maintain the unemployed decently and humanely. The implications of this theory were far-reaching. It was assumed that capitalist society could not guarantee this 'right to work'. Neither would a Labour Government be able to do so if called upon temporarily to 'run' a capitalist society, though it would of course make great efforts to mitigate unemployment. Hence the first task of a Labour Government in such circumstances would be to provide humanely for the unemployed. Its failure to provide work would be excusable: not so its failure to provide maintenance. This emphasis on maintenance rather than work as the first obligation of a Labour Government played an important part, as we shall see later, in shaping the events of the years 1929–31. In discussing the 1907 Bill, however, we shall consider the proposals for providing work, since the detailed application of the principle of maintenance had not yet been worked out.

The inspiration of the Bill was humane. The right to work was proclaimed as the recognised basis. Local councils were to replace the Poor Law Guardians and distress committees as the 'unemployment authority' for their areas. The primary function of the unemployment authority was to obtain a 'census of unemployed' in its area. Once the unemployed had been registered, it was the duty of the unemployment authority to provide them with work or maintenance. For work, standard rates of wages were to be offered — this was a recurring proviso in Labour's unemployment policies and sprang from a fear of the unemployed being offered to employers as blackleg labour. In addition to the local unemployment authorities, a 'central unemployment committee' was to be established for framing schemes of work, advising the local authorities, and co-ordinating their programmes. The central committee would have 'special commissioners' to 'keep in personal touch with what is being done'. These commissioners and the central committee 'will be ears listening to every complaint from the localities. They will fashion a national policy of education and relief'. It was clear that the central committee would work mainly through the local authority schemes; but it was suggested that in times of 'exceptional distress' — such as when unemployment exceeded 4 per cent — the central committee 'in conjunction with the Local Government Board' should devise schemes of 'national utility', such as afforestation and land reclamation, which were to be carried out centrally.

Finance for the local schemes was to come mainly from rates; but the national schemes were to be paid for by parliamentary grant. 'The solution of the unemployed problem', Ramsay MacDonald wrote, 'is the beginning of the Socialist State'.[1]

[1] *The New Unemployed Bill of the Labour Party, 1907*, published by the I.L.P., with explanatory notes by MacDonald.

In Labour's first Unemployed Bill are to be found many of the features of the policy of the 1929 Government. There is the 'central unemployment committee' without any real powers: executive responsibility for starting national schemes, it is made clear, is to lie with the departments. The initiative for the local schemes is to come from the local authorities, subject to 'approval' and 'modification' from the Local Government Board. But such approval, while it may carry with it a central grant, does not of itself confer the statutory authority for local authorities to proceed with their schemes. Finally, the question of finance is left vague. No definite sum is specified and there is no mention of how the money is to be raised. Presumably it was anticipated that it should come out of current national income.

V. POST-WAR UNEMPLOYMENT POLICY

Democratic socialism reached the peak of its confidence in the years immediately following the First World War. The blending of humane revolt with economic analysis, apparently successfully accomplished, seemed to provide an irresistible combination for the suppression of capitalism. It was in the confident expectation that history was on its side, that socialism alone had the answer to the problems of society, that the Labour Party drew up its constitution in 1918 and challenged the Conservatives and Liberals to a debate on the breakdown of capitalism in 1923. This debate was one of the parliamentary highlights of the year and the attention it attracted seemed to bear out MacDonald's proud assertion that 'There are only two Parties in politics to-day. There is the Capitalist Party and the Labour and Socialist Party.'[1]

The Labour Party was not the only one that pledged itself to a brave new world. But the nineteen-twenties were unkind to such claims and as the decade unfolded Labour's confidence was eroded by the harsh facts of post-war existence. The two 'socialistic' policies it had inherited from before the war — the taxation of the 'surplus' and the counter-cycle policy — became irrelevant: there was little surplus and no cycle. For its major solution, nationalisation, there was no mandate and besides it was not clear that taking over one or two declining industries would have

[1] 166 H.C. Deb. c. 2010.

the slightest effect on unemployment. There is no evidence of any fresh research in the main body of the Party which was dominated by the visionless orthodoxy of Snowden and Graham, Labour's two financial 'experts'. The 'firm of Webb' provided no new ideas; Cole produced many books but not one with any original insight. The only important breakthrough was on the fringes — in the Independent Labour Party, now controlled by the Clydesiders, and in a small group of young men who gathered round Labour's new and glamorous recruit, Oswald Mosley.

Labour's post-war unemployment policy got off to a good start with a plea for a just and generous peace. The Versailles Treaty was neither just nor generous and 1921 was the first full year of mass unemployment. The Labour Party was not alone in attributing the exceptional unemployment to the dislocation of the international trading structure or in criticising the Versailles settlement for making matters worse. Its pamphlet *Unemployment, the Peace and the Indemnity*, declared in 1921 that 'as the result of the war, the blockade and the peace, the entire continent of Europe had been impoverished'. It was the inability of the 'impoverished millions' to buy our goods that went far to explain unemployment at home. 'The decline of our trade with Germany, Russia and Austria would alone account for most of our present unemployment.'[1] The 'fantastic indemnity' which had been imposed on Germany, besides opening up the prospect of 'unending disturbance and perpetual militarism', meant that Germany could only meet her reparations bill by sweating her workers to produce export surpluses. The depression of internal standards of consumption meant that Germany would buy almost no British goods but that at the same time Britain would have to face intensified competition from German workers producing at starvation level. A similar situation existed in the defeated countries of the Austro-Hungarian empire. The Labour proposals envisaged the rapid re-establishment of trade with Russia by the granting of long-term credits, the cancellation of war debts and the rationing of the world's raw materials by an international authority.[2]

The generous internationalism of the Labour Party is greatly to its credit, but it did mean that it was committed to what we have termed the 'conservative case', namely, that abnormal unemployment could only

[1] *Unemployment, the Peace and the Indemnity*, p. 5. [2] Ibid. pp. 11–12.

be remedied through the revival of the major export industries. This in turn committed it to a return to the gold standard at the earliest possible opportunity — an aim which Snowden endorsed in emphatic terms[1] — and to support of the ensuing policy of deflation. This internationalist outlook fitted in with MacDonald's personal interest in foreign affairs. The success of his efforts to secure a revision of the peace treaties and of his conciliatory foreign policy in 1924 confirmed the leadership in its view that it was through international co-operation that unemployment would be mitigated. The party's pamphlet, *Work for the Workless*, commenting on the 1924 achievement remarked:

> It is not upon the programme of public-works and relief schemes, useful as these may be in an emergency, that the Labour Government challenges comparison with anything that any previous Government has done in a similar period. . . . So far as these eight months in office are concerned, it is on its *International policy*, that factor which lies at the very root of the present Unemployment problem, that it confidently asks for the continued support of the nation.[2]

But disillusionment was in store. The return to the gold standard did not produce the expected recovery and was accompanied by a further bout of deflation. Tariff competition increased, despite the pious resolutions of international economic conferences. MacDonald's interest in foreign affairs remained, but by 1929, although economic co-operation had been elevated into a 'Pillar of Peace', it looked much less plausible as a short-term solution to the unemployment problem.

A policy of international co-operation was undoubtedly 'socialistic' in intent, presaging the eventual establishment f a socialist world commonwealth. A public works programme was not. It was a mere palliative measure which did not touch any fundamental causes and moreover stood damned in most socialist eyes by association with nineteenth-century 'relief work'. The attraction of Beatrice Webb's counter-cyclical policy was that it seemed to avoid such associations. Men were to be employed by government departments in the normal way, before they had become unemployed, at standard wages and as far as possible in their normal occupations. By 1921, with mass unemployment a reality, it was implausible to call counter-cyclical what was bound to

[1] On 24 May 1925, 183 H.C. Deb. c. 629. [2] pp. 12–13.

be in effect a public works policy. In advocating such a policy, the Labour Party laid great stress on the need for finding 'socially productive' work and persisted with the counter-cyclical terminology.

The 1921 party pamphlet *Unemployment: A Labour Policy* advocated government contracts of the kind proposed in the Poor Law Commission's minority report, to be arranged over a ten-year period and accelerated in depression. The terminology here is still one of 'anticipating' a slump, of using the 'foresight commonly exercised by an intelligent house-keeper'. Other works to be started were road-building, housing, afforestation and foreshore reclamation. Railway companies were expected to provide an 'enormous amount of work' by arranging the building and repair of locomotive engines, railway coaches, trucks and lines. Local authorities were urged to 'undertake a bold policy for the building and equipment of educational institutions and the erection of new public buildings'.[1]

Nine months of office in 1924 convinced the Labour Party just how difficult it was to start a public works programme. Its exertions in this field were so unrewarding that the party pamphlet, *Work for the Workless*, remarked:

> Labour had realised all through, and never more vividly than now, after some experience of administering the Government of this country, that schemes of work of the character mentioned can never solve the real unemployment problem, even though they may be of some use as stop-gap aids.[2]

The next policy statement on unemployment, *On the Dole or Off*, published in 1926, reflects the more pessimistic reappraisals following the 1924 experience. The aim, strangely enough, after five years of mass unemployment, is still that of 'preventing unemployment . . . [by] deliberately . . . placing our orders for commodities and services in such a way and at such times as will keep the wheels of industry revolving'. The vestiges of this counter-cycle policy are linked for the first time to the idea of a limited market. 'The effect of this policy would be to reduce purchasing power during good years and increase it in bad times.'[3] There is noticeably less emphasis on public works proposals.

It might be thought that one of the chief objections to public works — their association in the minds of Labour supporters with local authority

[1] pp. 24–26. [2] p. 10. [3] pp. 12–13.

relief works of the nineteenth-century kind — could have been met by the transfer of responsibility to the Government. This, indeed, was one of the purposes of the counter-cyclical policy, which envisaged an expansion and contraction in the orders placed by government departments. Unfortunately government departments could undertake very little. The only ones with the authority to provide employment on any scale were the various service departments, the Post Office and the Ministry of Labour, which employed several thousand officials to look after the unemployed.[1] Any determined counter-cyclical policy, therefore, involved increasing the responsibility of the central Government at the expense of the local authorities, at least for emergency periods. But to the Labour Party local government was sacrosanct. Its proposals envisaged no encroachment on it. Yet it was this very absence of government responsibility that made it so difficult to start unemployment projects on a big scale. As *Work for the Workless* noted, the local authorities

> have by reason of the long depression in trade and the consequent burden on the rates become unable to finance new schemes . . . to the extent to which such schemes are desirable.[2]

We look in vain for any proposals to remedy this in Labour's Prevention of Unemployment Bill of 1925. An impressive-sounding National Employment and Development Board is to be set up under the Minister of Labour to 'make advances out of the funds at their disposal' to local authorities, government departments, colonial and Dominion Governments and public utilities for any purpose calculated to increase employment.[3] All this, of course, was already being done by the Unemploy-

[1] In 1928, the various service ministries provided employment for 400,000 men (mainly the armed forces); the Post Office employed 200,000; Inland Revenue and Customs and Excise accounted for 30,000; and the Ministry of Labour 14,000. Altogether the central Government employed well under a million. By 1950 the number of persons in central government employment had risen to 1,700,000; in addition the nationalised industries employed 2,380,000 — some 10 per cent of the labour force. Since 1950, with the ending of war-time controls and partial transport denationalisation, there has been some contraction. (Abramovitz and Eliasberg, *The Growth of Public Employment in Great Britain*, pp. 25, 40–3, 85.)

[2] p. 9.

[3] Reprinted as an Appendix to *On the Dole or Off*, p. 23, Clause 2 (1).

ment Grants Committee and Trade Facilities. There is no suggestion for transferring *initiative* to the Government itself: responsibility for submitting schemes is still vested with the authorities in question.

The Party's 1925 pamphlet, *On the Dole or Off*, proposed the 'scientific manipulation of credit', but as the Party had no ideas on this subject it was relegated to further enquiry. Finance, indeed, was the big stumbling block to any vigorous unemployment policy. As we have seen, the minority report sought to finance its counter-cyclical proposals by establishing a fund into which the Government would pay money out of revenue surpluses in good years to be used in lean ones. This was almost orthodox budgeting, except that the Treasury would have wanted to use revenue surpluses for reducing the national debt or taxation. Labour expected to finance its post-war proposals in similar fashion. Unfortunately in 1921 there was no surplus; the aim was to economise and the Geddes Axe fell in 1922. There was, however, every hope that prosperity would soon return, and so Labour's 1921 proposals could still anticipate future surpluses as a source of finance. Clynes used this argument in the Commons in 1922:

> This period of depression clearly will pass away . . . let us look to the days when we shall be in a more solvent state, for have we no credit to pawn?[1]

As real prosperity failed to return, this argument became progressively less convincing. Labour was indeed in a dilemma. Taxation would expose it to the charge of adding to the burdens of industry; borrowing, to the charge of diverting resources already profitably employed. In 1921 the Labour Party called for 'the issue by the Exchequer during the present year of a sum which will not amount to even a hundredth part of the cost of the war'.[2] About this time there was much support in the Party and elsewhere for a huge 'capital levy' to pay off the war debt and provide some surplus for unemployment projects: Labour speakers liked to conjure up a picture of millions of pounds being spent by the idle rich in riotous living while the poor starved. By 1925, however, taxation was abandoned as a means of raising the money. It would 'in the main only

[1] 159 H.C. Deb. c. 956.

[2] *Unemployment: A Labour Policy*, 1921, p. 33. It apparently thought this sum would be partially offset by retrenchment on military expenditure, saving on the insurance fund and future revenues from a revived economy.

transfer purchasing power from one body of people to another'.[1] So Hobsonianism had been found lacking. The 1925 proposals envisaged the raising of £10m a year by 'bank borrowings'.[2] But why were bank borrowings any less diversionary than taxation? A theory of 'idle balances' such as the Liberals developed would have provided an answer, but this theory nowhere appears in any of Labour's proposals. Neither the Labour leaders nor any established party intellectuals showed the slightest interest in Keynes or any other progressive economist, although the General Council did devote a pamphlet to the eccentric views of Major Douglas, founder of 'social credit'.[3] Indeed the lack of any monetary theory was Labour's most serious weakness.

All Labour's financial proposals in the nineteen-twenties bear the depressing imprint of Snowden. He accepted the 'treasury view' in all its essentials. He had an absolute horror of inflation, writing in 1920 'Government borrowing in this country has reached a point which threatens national bankruptcy', and advocating drastic deflationary measures.[4] To Snowden borrowing was contrary to every dictate of sound finance. Socialism would be paid for out of taxation, as all unremunerative projects should be. If it was not possible to raise taxation, then socialism would have to wait. Speaking in the House of Commons in 1922 he laid it down as a 'principle' for public works that 'no scheme should cost more than it is likely to bring back into the national purse'. Non-remunerative schemes ought only to be undertaken in times of prosperity.[5] On the possibility of expanding credit he wrote to the General Council in 1927:

> The microbe of inflation is always in the atmosphere. . . . An expansion of the currency issue must respond to a genuine demand arising out of real purchasing power and not be used to create a demand.

On the Bank of England he noted 'control of credit is an extremely dangerous weapon to place in anybody's hands, and political interference would be fatal'.[6] Writing in the *Morning Post* early in 1929 Snowden concluded 'there is a good deal more orthodoxy in Labour's financial policy than its critics appear to appreciate'.[7]

[1] *On the Dole or Off*, 1925, p. 12. [2] Ibid. p. 13.
[3] *Labour and Social Credit: A Report on the Proposals of Major Douglas*, 1923.
[4] *Wages and Prices*, pp. 112–13; 120–3. [5] 159 H.C. Debs. c. 1079.
[6] General Council Papers: Mond–Turner Conference. [7] 13 February 1929.

Graham, Labour's other expert, agreed with Snowden. Commenting on a speech by the Liberal McKenna to the shareholders of the Midland Bank in 1927, he wrote, 'Nor need we go so far as Mr. McKenna in criticism of the existing system'[1] — the socialist critique of capitalism! In 1929 he was advocating raising the sinking fund to £100m in order to pay off the war debt quicker and announcing that 'Labour has no desire to increase expenditure, but to decrease it'.[2] These views would doubtless have come as a surprise to the mass of active Labour supporters had they realised their full implications.

The Labour leaders thus accepted the 'conservative' remedy for post-war unemployment on all its essentials. The traditional export industries were to be revived by deflation and rationalisation; the return to the gold standard at the pre-war parity would assist the recovery of world trade. On the question of public works, whereas the Conservatives regarded them as no substitute for capitalism, the Labour Party regarded them as no substitute for socialism. Both were therefore agreed in assigning them a very limited role. The fact that the leaders of both Parties supported the 'treasury view' meant that in any case they were not prepared to spend much money on them. Thus in the big unemployment debate at the end of the nineteen-twenties Labour Party leaders, insofar as they were aware that a debate was in progress at all, came down on the traditional side. They rejected a Government investment loan for national projects. There was no discussion of a possible diversification of industry, the role of banking institutions, or the effects of the gold standard on credit.[3] On all these points Snowden led the Labour Party unthinkingly along the paths of strict orthodoxy.

The differences between the Conservative and Labour Parties arose not over unemployment, but over the unemployed. Labour laid much greater emphasis on decent maintenance than did the other Parties, who

[1] General Council Papers. McKenna said: 'With a reduced total of money available for spending there is a diminished demand for commodities, prices at once tend downwards, and shopkeepers, merchants, and manufacturers curtail their orders. The result is depression and unemployment.' (The *Economist*, 29 January 1927, p. 229.)

[2] *Morning Post*, 15 February 1929.

[3] An exception was provided by the Mond–Turner conversations, which proved highly educative to some members of the General Council, especially Ernest Bevin (see A. Bullock, *The Life and Times of Ernest Bevin*, i, 1960, pp. 403, 426).

believed unemployment was transient, not permanent, and that private enterprise could normally be expected to find work for everyone, and who were anxious not to burden industry with unemployment payments so large as to prevent it from fulfilling its primary purpose — keeping men in work. The Conservatives and Liberals were uneasy about the post-war extensions to unemployment insurance; in particular they never accepted the 'dole', or benefit paid without contributions, as a permanent feature of the system.

The Labour Party on the other hand wanted the State to take complete responsibility for all the unemployed. Benefit would be financed by taxation and be paid of right. Yet in the 1911 debates on Lloyd George's Insurance Bill most members of the parliamentary Labour Party were found to be in favour of the Lloyd George scheme: in particular MacDonald, speaking as leader of the Labour Party, welcomed the contributory as opposed to the 'free gift' principle.[1] The main protagonists of state responsibility in the nineteen-twenties were the trade unions, who, in effect, wrote out party policy on this point, with only lukewarm support from the parliamentary leaders.[2]

The Party pamphlet *Unemployment: A Labour Policy*, produced in 1921, laid down the principle that every unemployed person ought to have a *right* to unemployment benefit, irrespective of contributions, and that payment of benefit should be continued so long as he or she remained unemployed. It therefore proposed bringing into the scheme all those workers excluded from it — agricultural workers, railwaymen and domestic servants — and paying all a standard rate of benefit, almost double the existing one, on uniform conditions. Although complete state responsibility was declared to be the aim, the tripartite structure was retained for the time being, except that the State's contribution was to be raised out of all proportion to the others, to pay for the increased benefits and easier conditions.[3] It was an untidy

[1] 26 H.C. Deb., 29 May 1911, c. 725.

[2] In fact, though the unions advocated financing benefit by taxation on socialist grounds, there were excellent capitalist grounds for doing so: for taxation would spread the cost of maintaining the unemployed to the rentier, thus reducing the 'burdens on enterprise' (see Hicks, *The Finance of British Government, 1920–1936*, pp. 305–6).

[3] p. 19.

scheme: once again the question of finance was left vague, but apparently the additional exchequer charges were to be met by the issue of new money.

The Labour Government of 1924 raised benefits by a small amount but was not prepared to take any further responsibility for financing unemployment payments. However, in the quest for standard conditions to apply alike to those who had paid and those who had not paid contributions, the Government extended the 'not genuinely seeking work' clause, which had hitherto applied only to those on the dole, to all claimants for benefit. The effect of this muddled piece of egalitarianism was to increase the number of disallowances, causing the unemployed great hardship. A few years later Labour speakers were vigorously demanding the abolition of the 'not genuinely seeking work' clause, having forgotten that it was they who first let the monster loose.

The memorandum of evidence submitted jointly by the General Council and the national executive of the Labour Party to the Blanesburgh Committee in 1925[1] demanded higher benefit rates, to be paid irrespective of the number of contributions standing to a person's credit and under the same conditions for everyone.[2] The 'not genuinely seeking work' clause should be abolished[3] and the waiting period reduced from six to three days.[4] The memorandum proposed to continue with the tripartite system for the time being, but with smaller contributions from employers and employees and a much larger one from the Exchequer up to 'whatever sum may be necessary to maintain the proposed benefits'.

The new Labour proposals were identical with those of 1921, except that the scales of benefit were adjusted to the fall in the cost of living that had taken place since then. The proposals contained the same mixture of insurance and dole which the Conservative and Liberal Parties found objectionable and which the Blanesburgh Committee hoped would end of its own accord with the revival of trade. The Blanesburgh Report, which rejected the most important Labour suggestions, was signed by all the three Labour representatives on the Committee, including Miss Margaret Bondfield, who became Minister of Labour in 1929.

[1] See above, p. 22.
[2] *Memorandum of Evidence*, para. 7.
[3] Ibid. para. 64.
[4] Ibid. para. 62.

vi. THE LIVING WAGE AND REVOLUTION BY REASON

The intellectual bankruptcy of Labour's leaders was evident to all who cared to see. They expected to build the temple of socialism on the foundations of a 'correct' financial policy, and were quite unaware that those foundations were being busily undermined by the best capitalist economists. The leadership's hold on the rank and file was secure. MacDonald mesmerised party conferences; Snowden's obvious mastery of financial minutiae baffled his critics; while Henderson, Clynes and Thomas had no independent opinion on these matters: like their party leader they accepted Snowden's authority. Some sections of the Independent Labour Party were not so subservient: though their influence was never very great, their proposals deserve mention because they offered the only challenge within the Party to Snowden's orthodoxy. Moreover, it was from the ranks of the I.L.P. that the chief rebels against the 1929 Labour Government were to spring.

From the I.L.P. stables came two similar policy statements by two different groups. The first, *The Living Wage*, was produced in 1926 by one of Clifford Allen's[1] study groups in search of 'socialism in our time', which consisted of Brailsford, Creech Jones, Wise and Hobson himself. The second, *Revolution by Reason*, 1925, was the work of Oswald Mosley, then twenty-nine, and two young collaborators, John Strachey, just down from Oxford, and Allen Young, an I.L.P. organiser from Birmingham. *The Living Wage* rather than *Revolution by Reason* was the policy officially adopted by the I.L.P. Not only was it produced by their official study group, it was much more 'socialistic' in tone.

The Living Wage devoted itself entirely to the task of increasing purchasing power as the way out of depression, apologising to its predominantly left-wing readership for relegating nationalisation to a supporting role. The way to cure unemployment was through redistributing wealth — the standard Hobsonian analysis — and *The Living Wage* proposed to inaugurate a big scheme of family allowances

[1] Clifford Allen was chairman of the I.L.P. from 1923 to 1925 when he was ousted by a left-wing, proletarian coup which gave control of the I.L.P. machine to the Clydesiders — Maxton, Wheatley, Kirkwood, Buchanan and Campbell Stephen.

to be financed by taxation.[1] But its authors recognised definite limitations to taxation during a depression, a point often forgotten by the political exponents of *The Living Wage*, and therefore proposed to inject further purchasing power by imposing statutory wage minimums throughout industry to be sustained by the printing of new money.[2] This was frankly inflationary as inflation was then defined. But the I.L.P. pamphlet was confident that the added purchasing power of the workers would soon absorb surplus industrial capacity leading to a rise in production. A battery of Socialist controls was proposed to assist the scheme. Credit control was to be secured by the nationalisation of the Bank of England. Industries that refused to raise wages would be nationalised. Attempts by employers to counter higher wages with higher prices would be met by bulk government purchase of raw materials, especially foodstuffs, to enable reserve stocks to be built up.[3]

Whereas most Socialists, even the authors of *The Living Wage*, laid the greatest stress on fiscal policy, Mosley focused attention on monetary policy. Hobson's main concern was to redistribute income by progressive taxation. Mosley perceptively challenged this approach:

> At present Socialist thought appears to concentrate almost exclusively upon this transfer of present purchasing power by taxation, and neglects the necessity for creating additional demand to evoke our unused capacity which is at present not commanded either by the rich or the poor.[4]

Industry was in a dilemma. Although a capacity existed for greater production which would utilise idle plant and men, manufacturers would not expand production until there had been an increase in effective demand, while 'correct' financial policy opposed any increases in effective demand until production had expanded. What was the solution?

The first step in Mosley's remedy was the nationalisation of the banks.

[1] *The Living Wage*, 1926, p. 23.

[2] *The Living Wage*, pp. 15–16, 34. The authors seem to have regarded inflation as a temporary measure pending redistribution. e.g. E. F. Wise, 1 April 1929: 'There was a residue of several hundred million pounds which could be transferred to the working class. While this money was being obtained by taxation, the Government would establish a "minimum wage". . . .' (*The Times*, 2 April 1929).

[3] *The Living Wage*, pp. 19, 38, 42–3.

[4] Mosley, *Revolution by Reason*, a pamphlet read to the I.L.P. summer school at Easton Lodge, August 1925, pp. 16–17.

The state banks would then give industry a clear lead by the 'bold and vigorous expansion of the national credit':

We propose first to expand credit in order to create demand. That new and greater demand must, of course, be met by a new and greater supply of goods, or all the evils of inflation and price rise will result. Here our Socialist planning must enter in. We must see that more goods are forthcoming to meet the new demand.[1]

Socialist planning would be carried out by an Economic Council whose ambitious task would be to

estimate the difference between actual and the potential production in the country and to plan the stages by which that potential production can be evoked through the instrument of working-class demand. The constant care of the Economic Council must be to ensure that demand does not outstrip supply and thus cause a rise in price.[2]

As in *The Living Wage* proposals, the additional working class demand would be created through minimum wages to be financed by the new money, in the form of government subsidies to industry. If the 'great Capitalist monopolies' tried to restrict output to force a price rise, they would be subject to 'summary socialisation'.[3] The bulk purchase of raw materials was also advocated. Finally, Mosley was prepared to abandon the gold standard and let the currency depreciate to its true value, which he reckoned to be about 4·40 dollars to the pound.[4] In a larger exposition of the 'Birmingham proposals' as they came to be known, Strachey advocated a fluctuating exchange to secure an automatic adjustment to the balance of payments. In circumstances of mass unemployment, Strachey argued, the stability of the currency is a 'gigantic irrelevancy'.[5]

Mosley's attempt to 'weld together the socialist case with modern monetary theory'[6] produced a strange mixture. He was not prepared simply to rely on lower interest rates and a fluctuating exchange to secure credit expansion. Like all Socialists he suspected, possibly with justification, that wicked capitalists would sabotage an expansionist

[1] Mosley, *Revolution by Reason*, p. 12.
[2] Ibid. pp. 14–15.
[3] Ibid. pp. 19–20.
[4] Ibid. p. 26.
[5] Strachey, *Revolution by Reason*, pp. 200–1. The book was dedicated to 'O. M. who may some day do the things of which we dream'.
[6] Mosley, *Revolution by Reason*, p. 5.

credit policy initiated by a Socialist Government. In order to ensure that the additional credit was, in fact, utilised, he, like the authors of *The Living Wage*, was prepared to erect a whole scaffolding of socialist controls — statutory minimum wages, nationalisation of the banks and key industries if necessary, bulk purchase of raw materials and so on. Keynes saw the problem rather differently. He did not doubt at this stage that a cheap money policy would revive industry. However, he doubted whether such a policy would be possible with the existing gold standard parity: hence he advocated a programme of autonomous government investment in public works to be financed by drawing out idle balances. There is little doubt that such a programme was, in those circumstances, a more practical and speedier method of securing a rapid expansion of demand than printing new money and then trying to translate it into higher industrial wages through socialist controls.

The Living Wage was debated at the 1927 Labour Party conference, where it was killed by the simple expedient of referring it to the executive, after MacDonald had condemned it as a collection of 'flashy futilities'.

3
LABOUR TAKES OFFICE

i. THE 1929 ELECTION

Unemployment dominated the 1929 election; and dominating the unemployment debate was the Lloyd George pledge, given on 1 March 1929, to reduce unemployment within one year to normal proportions. It was a supreme attempt by the Liberal leader to wrest the initiative from his political opponents and never was such an effort sustained by a more impressive array of publications and policies — intellectually the most distinguished that have ever been placed before a British electorate. It was the Liberal Party that provided the nation with a real choice in 1929: the choice between a vigorous, 'new frontier' economic policy, and 'safety first' from both the Conservative and Labour Parties.

The majority of the electorate did not see the situation in this light. They saw the election as a fight between the 'capitalist' parties on the one hand and the 'Labour and Socialist Party' on the other.[1] It was in the interests of both Conservative and Labour Parties to foster this illusion. The Conservatives hoped to capture the Liberal centre by portraying the issue as democracy versus bolshevism; the Labour Party hoped to capture it by proclaiming that it had taken over the progressive mantle of liberalism. Both were united in dismissing Liberal intervention as irrelevant; and both attacked each other with a vehemence belied by the close resemblance of their programmes.

The Liberal unemployment policy was the product of a remarkable collaboration between politicians and economists, inaugurated in the Liberal Industrial Enquiry of 1925.[2] The fruit of this was the first

[1] The words are those of MacDonald in 1923; see above, p. 37.

[2] Members were: W. T. Layton, E. D. Simon, Lloyd George, E. H. Gilpin, Hubert Henderson, Philip Kerr, J. M. Keynes, Ramsay Muir, Major H. L. Nathan, B. S. Rowntree, Herbert Samuel, John Simon.

'Yellow Book', *Britain's Industrial Future*, published in February 1928, an exhaustive and penetrating survey of the British post-war economy, with far-reaching proposals for government planning, well in advance of anything in existence at the time. Occupying a central place was a big programme for government investment. Subsequently a special committee headed by Lloyd George, Lord Lothian and Seebohm Rowntree, was set up to work out in detail various schemes of national development, and its report, *We Can Conquer Unemployment*, issued in March 1929, was the cornerstone of the Liberal election campaign. Its opening expressed both its mood and determination:

> The word written to-day on the hearts of British people, and graven on their minds is *Unemployment*. For eight years, more than a million British workers, able and eager to work, have been denied the opportunity. . . . What a tragedy of human suffering; what a waste of fine resources; what a bankruptcy of statesmanship.

The central assumption of the Liberal policy was stated on page 9:

> At the moment, individual enterprise alone cannot restore the situation within a time for which we can wait. The state must therefore lend its aid and, by a deliberate policy of national development, help to set going at full speed the great machine of industry.

The Liberal 'emergency' programme was to be concentrated into two years. Pride of place was given to road construction. The British road system was seriously out of date: as Mrs. Hicks remarks, the last government that had taken any interest in motorways was the Roman government. There was a much higher accident rate than in the United States and there were 50 per cent more vehicles per mile of road than in that country. Bottlenecks, blind corners, level crossings, dangerous bridges and narrow streets through market towns were reinforced by such more refined obstructions as bad gradients and inadequately banked corners. The Liberals were going to put all that right. There was to be a big programme of trunk roads, to be built directly by the State, costing £42m and employing 100,000 men.[1] A programme of ring roads was expected to cost £20m and provide employment for 50,000 men.[2] Special attention was to be paid to buying sufficient width of land 'to

[1] *We Can Conquer Unemployment*, 1929, pp. 13–16.
[2] Ibid. p. 16.

allow for any reasonable future growth'. There would be adequate footways, no restricted bridges, no avoidable level crossings, efficient signposting, visible by day and night, no dangerous corners and crossroads, and sufficient parking space along the roadside.[1] District and rural roads were to be reconstructed, old bridges widened and strengthened and new ones built, and level crossings abolished, at an estimated cost of £83m and employing 200,000 men.[2] At a cost of £145m and by employing 350,000 men for two years, the Liberals reckoned that Britain would be equipped with the most modern system of highway communications in the world, with inestimable benefit to the economy and the motorist.

Housing was given high priority. Heavy unemployment in the building industry was attributed to Neville Chamberlain's 1927 cut in the Wheatley housing subsidy. Broadly, the Liberals proposed to restore the Wheatley subsidy, but to concentrate much more than before on building low-rent houses. They estimated that 200,000 houses of this kind could easily be built each year, giving employment to an extra 60,000 men.[3]

Finally, there were plans for telephone installation, the extension and standardisation of electricity, land drainage and the development of London passenger transport which were expected to cost £80m and provide work for 180,000 men annually.[4] Altogether about 600,000 men a year were to be employed for two years at a cost of £250m.

The money was to be raised by loan. The road fund would borrow £145m on its income of £25m a year. The local authorities would borrow money in the normal way for house building with the backing of the government subsidy; the various public authorities concerned would borrow money for the development of London transport with government contributions to interest and sinking fund payments; the Government itself would borrow for the residue of the schemes. Whether these borrowings were to be undertaken separately or lumped together in a big national development loan was not made clear in the pamphlet, though if the Liberals had formed a Government, the big war loans would have been an obvious precedent, dear to the heart of Lloyd George.

[1] Ibid. p. 13. [2] Ibid. pp. 16–21. [3] Ibid. pp. 31–2. [4] Ibid. pp. 34–46, 52.

The Liberal policy was based on the calculation that £1m set 5,000 men to work, half on the actual job and half manufacturing the materials required for that job.[1] But the effect of the expenditure would not end there; as Lloyd George told the Liberal candidates in March 1929:

> If instead of an allowance of one pound or twenty-five shillings a week a man brings home three pounds a week from his job, you double and treble his purchasing power. The mills, the factories, the workshops will derive benefit from it, and the result will be you will start a round of prosperity.[2]

Keynes and Henderson, in an explanatory pamphlet, *Can Lloyd George Do It?*, developed this theme further:

> In addition to the indirect employment with which we have been dealing, a policy of development would promote employment in other ways. The fact that many workpeople who are now unemployed would be receiving wages instead of unemployment pay would mean an increase in effective purchasing power which would give a general stimulus to trade. Moreover, the greater trade activity would make for further trade activity; for the forces of prosperity, like those of trade depression, *work with cumulative effect*.[3] [italics mine.]

Here, then, was the theory of the multiplier, though without the precise calculations which were later to make it an effective instrument of government policy.

To defend the loan against the charge of diverting resources which were already being fully utilised, the Liberal pamphlet made use of the theory of idle balances. It produced figures from McKenna's 1929 address to the shareholders of the Midland Bank showing that between 1919 and 1928 the ratio of 'time deposits' to 'demand deposits' had risen from 28·6 per cent to 44·7 per cent. Time deposits represented money awaiting investment for which no trading use could be found at the time: demand deposits were essentially money in active business use.[4] In a general attack on the 'treasury view' the Liberal pamphlet made the obvious point that

[1] *We Can Conquer Unemployment*, p. 12.

[2] Reprinted in Liberal Pamphlets and Leaflets: *The Liberal Pledge*, 1929, p. 28.

[3] *Can Lloyd George Do It?*, 1929, p. 25.

[4] *We Can Conquer Unemployment*, p. 55.

To begin with, it proves too much! If it were true of the new State enterprises, it would be true of enterprise everywhere, in which case it is difficult to see how trade could ever improve or progress take place.[1]

Keynes and Henderson followed this up in more detail. The objection to the State borrowing money must apply equally to Morris or Courtauld's borrowing money.

We should have to conclude that it was virtually out of the question to absorb our unemployed workpeople by any means whatsoever (other than the unthinkable inflation), and that the obstacle which barred the path was no other than an insufficiency of capital. This, if you please, in Great Britain, who has surplus savings which she is accustomed to lend abroad on the scale of more than a hundred millions a year.[2]

Snowden had it laid down as a 'principle' that public works 'should be . . . prospectively remunerative and that the scheme should cost no more than it is likely to bring back into the national purse'.[3] To satisfy this test of financial soundness the Liberal pamphlet had to prove that the works undertaken would repay the cost of the loan. It saw no difficulty about this. Savings on the unemployment fund would amount to £30m a year.[4] As a result of the restoration of 600,000 workers to industry, exchequer receipts would go up by between £8m and £10m a year. Telephone and electrical development could be justified 'over a due period . . . as an ordinary commercial proposition'. Much of the road expenditure would produce no direct financial return,

but to meet the interest and sinking fund on the loan . . . we have a steady increase in receipts from motor vehicle taxation year by year, which increase alone at the present level of taxation, together with receipts from betterment, is likely to be sufficient to meet interest and repay the whole State expenditure within a comparatively short period of years.[5]

'Betterment' was defined as the principle that 'persons whose property has clearly been increased in market value by an improvement effected by the local authorities should specially contribute to the cost of improvement'. This was the old tax on the 'unearned increment' reappearing in this new setting to help pay for the road programme.[6] On these calculations, the Liberal statement concluded that 'all this

[1] Ibid. p. 54.
[2] *Can Lloyd George Do It?*, pp. 34–5.
[3] See above, p. 43.
[4] *We Can Conquer Unemployment*, pp. 58–9.
[5] Ibid. p. 60.
[6] Ibid. pp. 24–7.

work, therefore, makes no drain on the exchequer'.[1] Keynes and Henderson estimated that, taking the most favourable view of the economic yield of the Liberal programme, the annual budgetary charge would be less than £2½m a year.[2]

We Can Conquer Unemployment created a sensation. The Lloyd George plans were supported by the *Economist* on 18 May 1929; a hundred representative businessmen and industrialists produced a manifesto in favour; Keynes, challenged about earlier quarrels with the Wizard, replied: 'The difference between me and some other people is that I oppose Mr. Lloyd George when he is wrong and support him when he is right.'[3]

The Government of Stanley Baldwin took the unusual step of pressing civil servants and treasury officials to issue a reply, in May 1929, entitled *Memoranda on Certain Proposals Relating to Unemployment*. There were six memoranda altogether, five issued by departmental officials under the signatures of the responsible Ministers and a sixth 'prepared by the Treasury on the direction of the Chancellor of the Exchequer'. The departmental memoranda dealt with the administrative problems of carrying out the Liberal scheme, while the treasury memorandum considered its financial aspects.

The Liberal pamphlet had considered road work to be 'peculiarly suitable for a time of unemployment' because a large variety of labour could be employed all over the country and because work could be started fairly rapidly — 'we consider that within three months of a decision to proceed with this scheme an *effective Government* could have men already working upon those roads' (italics mine).[4] The Ministry of Transport did not agree. It was quite wrong to employ men, often with specialised skills, on what was essentially navvy work; besides, the Liberal expectations of an early start were hopelessly optimistic. Preparation for the road programme would require 'complete engineering surveys, consultation with valuers in order that the cheapest land might be acquired, the comparison of estimates for alternative proposals'. Compulsory purchase would probably be required and also legislation to give the Government the necessary powers. Recruitment

[1] Ibid. pp. 60–1. [2] *Can Lloyd George Do It?*, pp. 29–30.

[3] See Thomas Jones, *Lloyd George*, 1951, p. 229.

[4] *We Can Conquer Unemployment*, p. 16.

and accommodation by the roadside would have to be arranged. Then there were the country lovers to consider: would sufficient regard be paid

> to the preservation of beautiful and interesting buildings, old cottages and natural features of the countryside . . . great assets which natural beauty and historical association afford?

This section concluded that to compress a road-building programme of 'at least a decade' into two years would require dictatorship.[1]

The Ministry of Health commented on the difficulty involved in the large-scale building of uneconomic houses and concluded 'it is only by the ordered progress of recent years that these obstacles have been overcome'.[2] The Post Office stated that there was no reason to suppose that in the following years people would want the telephones that Lloyd George proposed to build.[3] The Ministry of Labour thought that the Liberal estimates of the numbers of unemployed people who would be available for the various projects was wildly exaggerated. The Liberal figure of 60,000 to be absorbed by housing was reduced to 20,000. The claim that 180,000 altogether could be used for housing, telephones and electricity was 'fantastic . . . 80,000 would be an overstatement'.[4] It would be quite wrong to employ juveniles in work 'which carries with it so little prospect of advancement as road construction, land drainage, etc. . . . In the interest of the boys themselves it is better that they should attend the Juvenile Unemployment Centres when unemployed. . . .'[5] The Ministry concluded that only 250,000 men would be available for 'direct employment in State-aided schemes of road work and land drainage and other public works'.[6]

It made great play with conditions of labour. 'Regular conditions of employment . . . including the right to dismiss for inefficient work and laziness' would have to be waived;[7] there would be friction over wages:

> the miner will not be prepared to drain a farmer's land at the agricultural wage, but what will the agricultural labourer, a skilled man, say if the miner, who is wholly unskilled at his work, is to obtain higher wages?[8]

---

[1] *Memoranda on Certain Proposals relating to Unemployment*, pp. 10, 20–3.
[2] Ibid.p. 36.
[3] Ibid. p. 39.
[4] Ibid. p. 9.
[5] Ibid. p. 5.
[6] Ibid. p. 9.
[7] Ibid. pp. 11, 13.
[8] Ibid. p. 10.

The treasury objections involved the familiar restatement of the 'treasury view'. There were no idle balances. Money on time deposit was not idle. It was regarded by industry as an essential liquid reserve which would not be available in any case for long-term investment, and, in addition, it might be used for 'commercial advances or credits and in taking up bills or acceptances for traders as well as in loans to the short-term money market'.[1] Insofar as the loan was raised by diverting money from foreign investment it would have unfavourable effects on foreign trade which had largely depended on the volume of foreign investment.[2] Even if the loan could be raised it would require a very high rate of interest to compete with foreign issues.[3] Commenting on the treasury section of the memoranda, Keynes said:

> Mr Baldwin had invented the formidable argument against the scheme that you must not do anything because it will mean that you will not be able to do anything else.

He added: 'There is not a single economist in the country who will come forward to support the White Paper's arguments.'[4]

What was the Conservative alternative to the Liberal programme? Baldwin's election address took pride in Conservative achievements. Safeguarding had increased employment in every one of the safeguarded industries and had put to work 'directly and indirectly' thousands of men. The De-Rating Act of 1929 had relieved productive industry of three-quarters of its rates, thus adding £27m to its resources; the reduction of railway freight rates had been specially beneficial to the basic industries; there had been a steady expansion of electricity development through the Electricity Supply Act, which had led to the setting up of the Central Electricity Board; road development had been pursued and would continue, though a Conservative Government, if elected, would eschew 'hasty and ill-considered schemes which could only lead to wasteful and unfruitful expenditure'. In the sphere of social reform the 1925 Pensions Act for widows, orphans and old people had already

[1] Ibid. p. 49. Henry Clay, *The Post-War Unemployment Problem*, p. 133, rejected the 'treasury view' that a large proportion of time deposits would not be available for public loans because they were cash reserves of firms by arguing that they would be equally liquid in government securities.

[2] *Memoranda on Certain Proposals relating to Unemployment*, p. 51.

[3] Ibid. p. 50.

[4] *The Times*, 29 May 1929.

benefited 175,000 people; 930,000 houses had been built since 1925; slum clearance was continuing; the network of ante-natal clinics had been greatly extended and infant mortality had been reduced from 75 to 65 per 1,000.[1]

For the future, the Conservatives proposed to continue this policy. An editorial in *The Times* on 1 March 1929 summarised the Tory attitude to state intervention. The Conservative remedies for unemployment were 'the absorption of the unemployed into productive industry' and 'their transference from areas of distress'. The implication was that public funds should be used only very sparingly on schemes outside the expansion of normal productive industry — hence the curtailment of the work of the Unemployment Grants Committee and the ending of Trade Facilities — and that taxation and the total national burdens should be reduced to a minimum, leaving industry to work out its own salvation. Examining the relationship between public relief expenditure and work provided, *The Times* concluded that 'relief schemes demand a colossal financial effort and produce comparatively small result'.

On the contentious issue of protection, Baldwin was forced to steer a middle course between those who wanted merely an extension of safeguarding and those who wanted full-blooded protection, stating at the 1928 party conference that 'no industry will be barred from taking its case before the appropriate tribunal'.[2] Cautious support was given to Imperial preference.[3]

We must now turn to Labour reactions to the Lloyd George programme. The party leaders were in a quandary. On the one hand the Liberal policy looked like the policy they had been advocating for a long time; on the other hand they had no wish to carry out such a policy. They were therefore forced into the unfortunate position of claiming both that the Liberals had stolen their own plans and that those plans were unworkable. At the Free Trade Hall, Manchester, Lloyd George made the most of this dilemma:

> The Labour Party could not make up its mind whether to treat the Liberal plan as a freak or to claim its paternity. (Laughter) Mr. Thomas said it was an

[1] *The Times*, 13 May 1929.

[2] E. A. Rowe, 'The British General Election of 1929', unpublished B.Litt. thesis, Bodleian Library, p. 100.

[3] *The Times*, 13 May 1929.

absurd abortion, but Mr. Henderson said it was the child of the Labour Party. (Laughter) Mr. MacDonald, as usual, tried to have it both ways. He said — often in the same speech — 'This is a stunted thing'. Then looking at it fondly, he said, 'This is my child'. (Laughter).[1]

In reply to *We Can Conquer Unemployment*, the Labour Party produced a counter-blast of its own: *How to Conquer Unemployment: Labour's Reply to Lloyd George*, written by G. D. H. Cole, with a foreword by MacDonald. It was a slovenly document, totally devoid of the insights that lent distinction to the Liberal pamphlet. The Lloyd George proposals are attacked on two counts. First, it is argued that he 'has not a single proposal in his pamphlet that will bring about the reconstruction of industry on a sound and permanent basis'. It is admitted that his measures 'might, for a couple of years, greatly reduce the number of the unemployed. But what is to happen . . . when those years are over?'[2] Road-building in particular is criticised. It is 'less productive of further employment . . . than the more diversified plans' of the Labour Party.[3] The second objection to the Liberal plan is summed up under the heading 'madcap finance', probably a Snowden inspiration. Lloyd George is up to his old games of borrowing recklessly as he did during the war and piling up huge debts that will burden industry in the future. No attempt is made to meet the Liberal argument that the loan will be self-liquidating.[4] Labour apparently proposes to finance its own proposals by taxation, though once again the section on finance is left vague.[5]

On paper, Labour's 'diversified schemes' look impressive. Everything was included — housing, electricity, roads, drainage, land reclamation, afforestation, agricultural improvement, 'comprehensive schemes for restoring prosperity to the cotton and iron and steel trade', coal nationalisation, a national employment and development board, a national economic council, industrial training and so on. MacDonald's vision was equally sweeping:

Roads will be built as a system, bridges broken and reconstructed, railways reconditioned, drainage carried on, afforestation advanced, coasts protected,

---

[1] *The Times*, 13 April 1929.

[2] *How to Conquer Unemployment: Labour's Reply to Lloyd George*, 1929, pp. 5–6.

[3] Ibid. p. 12. [4] Ibid. pp. 9–10. [5] Ibid. p. 18.

houses built, emigration dealt with, colonial economic expansion planned and carried out. . . .

A Labour Government would set up a 'brain for thinking and acting for an industrial State', on the lines of the Committee of Imperial Defence.

At the present moment the Home Office is an independent Department; the Board of Trade is the same. Your spending Departments spend practically independently of each other. I say the time has come for us to co-ordinate these by a Committee over which the Prime Minister himself must preside . . . [with] eyes and ears of its own. It will be really the centre of seeing, thinking, and investigation, gathering together information about unemployment and employment.[1]

Everything was there, but the only definite promise was to set up a committee. It was a policy without a time-limit. The *Liberal Magazine* of April 1929 said:

The mere mention in abstract and general terms of one or more forms of work . . . does not constitute a policy. All these works had not only been thought of but regularly carried out, long before the publication of the various Labour programmes. . . . But what distinguishes the Liberal policy from all previous statements is that it lays down the definite details of the schemes to be undertaken, with estimates of the cost and the amount of employment to be provided by them.

Impressive though the Liberal programme was, it could not restore the fortunes of the Liberal Party. The general election of 30 May 1929 returned to Westminster 287 Labour M.P.s, 260 Conservatives and 59 Liberals. The Conservatives with 8,656,000 votes (38 per cent) polled most in the country; but the combined Labour and Liberal percentage implied a clear repudiation of the Conservative Government and the policies it had pursued. After some hesitation Stanley Baldwin decided not to face the new House of Commons as he had done in 1924, but to resign immediately. On 3 June the King sent for James Ramsay MacDonald and asked him to form his second administration.

ii. THE NEW GOVERNMENT

Born in the fishing village of Lossiemouth in Morayshire, MacDonald was sixty-two years old when he became Prime Minister for a second

[1] MacDonald at the Albert Hall (*The Times*, 29 April 1929).

time. Of all men who have held that office this century, MacDonald is the most difficult to understand. There are two common, contrasting stereotypes of him: a fraud, whose hollowness was for years obscured by a glittering façade of voice, presence and manner; and a sincere, if not always lucid, Socialist of great ability and courage, whose integrity was finally undermined by the 'aristocratic embrace'. Certainly the clue to MacDonald's impact on his generation, and on the Labour movement in particular, lay in what might be called his 'star quality', something impossible to analyse, but irresistibly felt. Beatrice Webb called him the 'greatest artist of British politics'; Mary Agnes Hamilton discerned in him a quality 'distinct from, additional to, achievement', and remarked that 'the whole is more than the sum of its parts'.[1] He struck many rather as does a great singer or actor, whose voice is imperfect or whose technique is flawed, but whose performances go on electrifying audiences. Even those who knew him best debated for years whether this quality was the genuine expression of personality, or whether it was external and accidental. Beatrice Webb, in a malicious phrase, called him 'a magnificent substitute for a leader'. Lord Francis-Williams wrote: 'The more one knows of MacDonald the less one knows him.'[2]

Thus MacDonald's attraction for many existed independently of anything he might do or say. This made him, throughout his life, an extremely controversial figure, for there was never sufficient tangible evidence for an agreed judgment. Even the great political commitments of his life were curiously equivocal. During the First World War and for three or four years after, when he was execrated for his anti-war stand, he was sustained by the Independent Labour Party and in return carried them with him to the forefront of national politics in 1922. Yet neither his anti-war stand nor his relationship with the I.L.P. was quite what it

[1] M. A. Hamilton, *J. Ramsay MacDonald* (including *The Man of Tomorrow*, 1923), 1929, pp. 97, 160. Mrs. Hamilton went through three stages in her — often close—relationship with MacDonald: hero worship, critical admiration and disillusionment, the final one coming after the break of 1931. Her writings, on which I have drawn heavily, offer by far the most perceptive analysis of MacDonald's character and appeal. The most important are: *J. Ramsay MacDonald*, 1929; 'J. Ramsay MacDonald: An Atlantic Portrait', *The Atlantic Monthly*, February 1938; *Remembering My Good Friends*, 1944, pp. 120–30; and *Up-Hill All the Way*, 1954, pp. 56–9.

[2] Francis Williams, *A Pattern of Rulers*, 1965, p. 97.

appeared on the surface, and though the Clydesiders supported him in his bid for the Labour leadership in 1922 and many of them remained attached to him personally till his death, long after he had severed his connection with the Labour movement, they always sensed that he might betray them.[1] Similarly his commitment to constitutionalism, to parliamentary procedure, was offset by a romantic utopianism, far removed from the unimaginative pragmatism of those who, for most of his career, were his political allies, and contributed, far more than most people realise, to the gulf that was eventually to open up between them.

It was the romantic strain in MacDonald that made him the greatest and most inspiring orator in the Labour movement, that gave to his meetings that 'odd special note of passion' which observers noted. He was, of course, helped by a magnificent physical presence, and a 'baritone voice of rare beauty with notes in it as moving as those of a violoncello'.[2] Yet he thrilled less by his affirmations than by his presence. 'On the platform his personality, his face, his voice, suggest the heroic aspect of politics, even when he hesitates to strike that note.'[3] With all the public equipment of an authoritarian leader, he consistently harnessed demagogism to the ends of parliamentary democracy.

His socialism, as one critic unkindly described it,

> is that far-off Never-Never-Land born of vague aspirations and described by him in picturesque generalities. It is a Turner landscape of beautiful colours and glorious indefiniteness. He saw it, not with a telescope, but with a kaleidoscope.[4]

There is little doubt that in 1929 MacDonald was a Socialist; but he was also a conservative. His socialism was romantic, a vision of a better

[1] MacDonald's love-hate relationship with the I.L.P. is one of the most curious episodes in modern British politics. All the Clydesiders started off as MacDonald's men, and in 1923 MacDonald could write, apropos of a Maxton outburst:

'A recent speech by Maxton in Glasgow is really terrible. . . . It is fearful nonsense. And Maxton is such a good fellow.' (Quoted in R. K. Middlemas, *The Clydesiders*, p. 131). Paradoxically, MacDonald was far more tolerant of I.L.P. dissent than Arthur Henderson, the party manager, who would have brought things to a head much sooner. It is not entirely a coincidence that MacDonald's own departure from the Labour Party was followed within a year by the departure of the I.L.P.

[2] Hamilton, *J. Ramsay MacDonald*, 1929, p. 102. [3] Ibid. p. 144.

[4] L. Macneill Weir, *The Tragedy of Ramsay MacDonald*, 1939, p. xi.

life expressed in terms that inspired his followers; but he had too real a sense of history, too great a respect for convention and constitutional forms, to believe that Utopia was within easy reach. While his oratorical manner suggested the dramatic, rather than the gradual, arrival of socialism, in his writings it was described as an evolutionary process. The spirit of socialism was a constant adaptation to new conditions, 'producing new organs when new functions have to be performed, substituting new vitalities for spent ones'.[1] It is hardly surprising that his discourse on socialism produced contradictory impressions. It made the militants and the under-privileged eager for the great day; on the other hand it reassured the anti-socialists that the great day would be long postponed, at any rate so long as MacDonald remained at the helm.

We can appreciate how MacDonald was able to turn the warring elements in his own character — wayward and responsible, romantic and pragmatic — to telling political advantage and in fact to make them the central paradox of the Labour Party itself. He was 'a peg built to hang myths on'.[2] He embodied both its Utopian appeal and the guarantee that it would play the parliamentary game. His ability to hold the ring, by the appeal of his own complex personality, between its revolutionary and constitutional impulses was probably the biggest factor in preventing the emergence, in the nineteen-twenties, of a breakaway revolutionary party on the continental model. Ultimately, of course, he was on the side of constitutionalism, but his great achievement was to keep the extreme left inside the Labour Party until it had spent itself as a major political force. When the I.L.P. finally disaffiliated in 1932 it was no longer a serious contender for working-class allegiance.

As a man, MacDonald was shy and reserved to a fault. The extroverted side of his nature was killed by the death of his wife in 1911. As he himself wrote, in a rare moment of self-revelation, to Mrs. Bruce Glasier in 1914:

> I feel the mind of the solitary stag growing upon me. My fireside is desolate. I have no close friend in the world to share either the satisfaction of success or the disturbance of defeat. So I get driven in upon myself more and more, and I certainly do not improve.[3]

---

[1] MacDonald, *Socialism Critical and Constructive*, 1921, p. 1.

[2] Williams, *A Pattern of Rulers*, p. 68.

[3] Quoted in Lord Elton, *Life of James Ramsay MacDonald*, 1939, pp. 238–9.

It was only in public that he could still unburden himself — 'the platform is his confessional, the crowd his priest'. His private relationships deteriorated, he became secretive, suspicious, aloof. Egon Wertheimer, a German political correspondent, wrote in 1929 that although he was the outstanding figure of international socialism, in the higher circles of the Labour Party 'his personal unpopularity is almost unexampled', the chief complaints being his inaccessibility, his deliberate isolation from his colleagues, his hyper-sensitivity and his vanity.[1] J. H. Thomas, the railwaymen's leader, alone of the 'big five' possessed the gift of intimacy necessary to break through his reserve: the rest of his colleagues MacDonald found rather pedestrian and unsympathetic, and his relations with them remained formal and correct. The most common examples cited of his vanity were his determination not to appear ignorant of any topic under discussion, which meant that experts who came to brief him more often than not went away with the sound of his own diffuse discourse ringing in their ears, and his tendency to disparage achievements of others which threatened to diminish his own pre-eminence. Whether these traits are properly described as vanity is doubtful: rather they reflect a certain lack of self-assurance, the tortured suspicions of a withdrawn mind. Vanity is often the expression of insecurity and in MacDonald's case the reasons are not, perhaps, difficult to find. In the opinion of one commentator surely in an excellent position to judge[2] his illegitimacy was the central influence on his life. His career may be regarded as a triumphant struggle to escape from this stigma; but the price he had to pay was a certain lack of self-honesty which was to prove a great political handicap.

His aloofness from his senior colleagues was particularly resented in view of the fact that he seemed to enjoy the company of the well-born, both inside and outside the Party.[3] Beatrice Webb noted in 1930 that the Prime Minister's itinerary included visits to the King, the Marquess and the Marchioness of Londonderry and the Duke and Duchess of Sutherland.

[1] Wertheimer, *Portrait of the Labour Party*, pp. 174–5.

[2] His daughter, Mrs. Peterkin, better known as Ishbel MacDonald.

[3] Inside the Labour Party among his closest associates were General Thomson and the de la Warrs; the Mosleys, too, were frequent companions.

Alas! Alas! Balmoral is inevitable; but why the castles of the wealthiest, most aristocratic, most reactionary and by no means the most intellectual of the Conservative Party? . . . He *ought* not to be more at home in the castles of the great than in the homes of his followers. It argues a perverted taste and a vanishing faith.[1]

One of the reasons MacDonald welcomed the 'aristocratic embrace' was because it offered him affectionate personal relationships in a world whose conventions automatically excluded both private and political exposure. For despite his pre-eminence in the politics of the Labour movement, MacDonald was not an obsessive politician. Indeed Wertheimer found it easier to imagine him in 1929 'sitting and dreaming by his fireside or wandering with a knapsack on the moors . . . '.[2] Not only did he love being in the countryside, but he was also a patron of the arts, though it is characteristic of people's reaction to him that they always doubted whether his culture was genuine or put on for show. Thus he enjoyed relaxing with those whose background and education had given their lives a non-political dimension. This was, and doubtless is, something which the obsessive politician, who lives and breathes politics the whole waking day, finds it difficult to understand or even forgive.

Like many men who are forever conscious of the passage of time, MacDonald was incapable of organising his own time properly. He found it difficult to delegate responsibility, fearing blunders on every side, which was not altogether unjustifiable considering the calibre of some of his colleagues and their inexperience of parliamentary or administrative procedure. This is one of the reasons why he doubled the offices of Prime Minister and Foreign Secretary in 1924 and why he kept 'Anglo-American relations' under his own control in 1929. Such commitments overtaxed his energy; in his exhaustion he was liable to serious errors of judgment — as in 1924—and exhaustion undoubtedly contributed cumulatively to the breakdown of his health and capacity after 1931. His favourite form of escape, which became a ritual, was to

[1] Beatrice Webb Diaries, 5 September 1930. The quotations throughout are taken from the manuscript in the Passfield Papers at the L.S.E.

[2] Wertheimer, *Portrait of the Labour Party*, p. 175. Herbert Morrison considered his 'great hindrance was an inability to revel in the atmosphere of Westminster. He once . . . shocked me by saying savagely, "Herbert, I hate this place!" ' (*An Autobiography*, p. 103.)

The Labour cabinet, 1929

Standing, from left to right: G. Lansbury, A. V. Alexander, Sir Charles Trevelyan, Miss Margaret Bondfield, Lord Thomson, Tom Shaw, A. Greenwood, N. E. Noel-Buxton, Willie Graham, W. Adamson
Sitting, from left to right: J. R. Clynes, Lord Parmoor, J. H. Thomas, Philip Snowden, J. R. MacDonald, A. Henderson, Lord Passfield, Lord Sankey, W. Wedgwood Benn

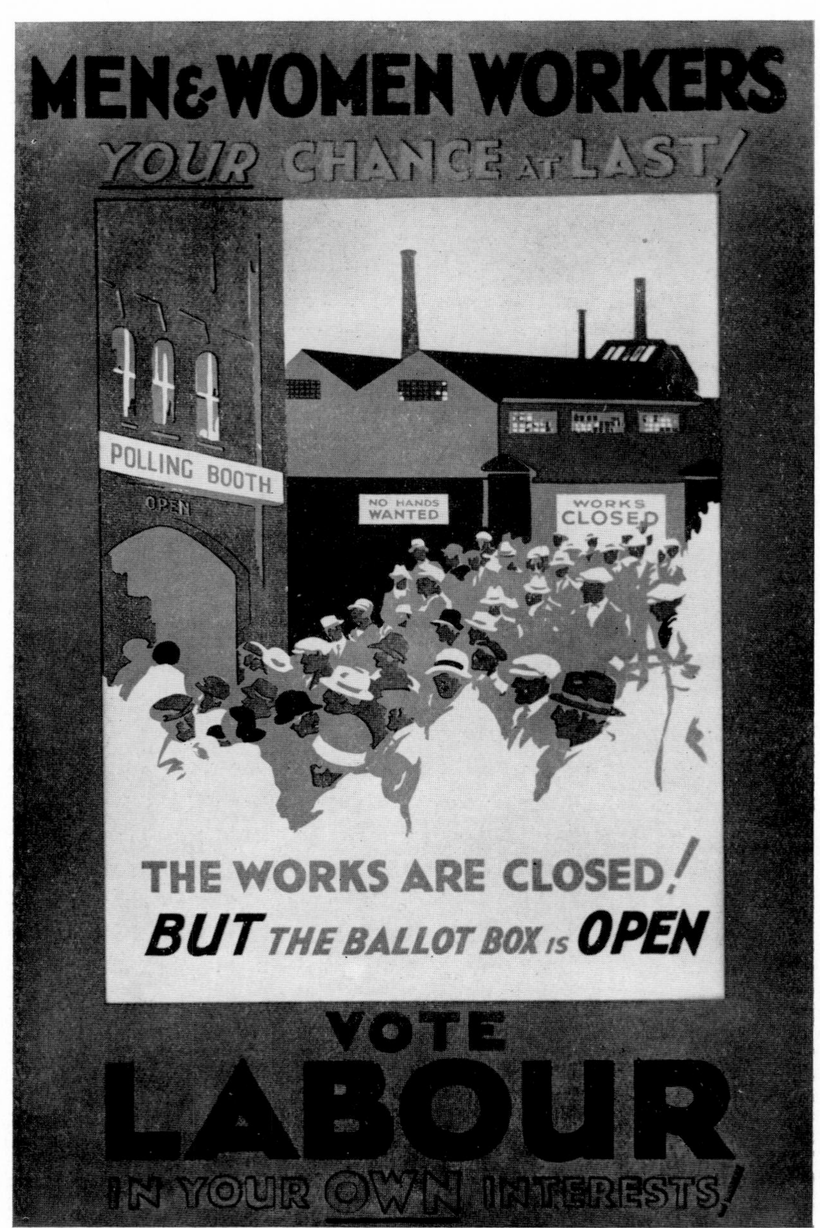

Labour election poster, 1929

spend the week-end with his family at his birth-place: the 4.15 from King's Cross on Friday afternoon carried him overnight to Lossiemouth, where the peace of mind and rest that eluded him in London beckoned and where

> in the long dark nights of the . . . late autumn and winter . . . [he] would go out silently to the shore or the moors in quest of something which haunts life like a dim vision of a strange beauty or a confused echo of a far-away melody.[1]

What that 'something' was MacDonald never revealed.

There was little reason to suppose, in 1929, that the policy and course of his second administration would be vastly different from that of his first. As Prime Minister, his own major preoccupation would continue to be foreign affairs and he would be likely to treat every problem as far as possible within an international framework. Gradualism would mark the Government's approach, and priorities and achievements, as in 1924, would be dictated less by an overall design than by the initiative, ability and drive shown by individual Ministers.

Arthur Henderson, the Foreign Secretary, and by 1929 generally regarded as MacDonald's second in command, was the Labour equivalent of Stanley Baldwin. He was three years older than MacDonald and like him a Scotsman, though his family had moved to Newcastle upon Tyne when he was ten. He had come into the Labour Party from the trade union side, though he early abandoned union for parliamentary politics, entering the House of Commons in 1903. MacDonald worked closely with him for thirty years, yet consistently under-rated him, mistaking his stolidness for stupidity. Arthur Henderson in turn came to despise MacDonald as a person, though recognising until the end that he was indispensable as national leader. Henderson had the genius for political relationships which MacDonald lacked. He was in his element with the party worker, whether it be at the National Labour Club, where he could often be seen at lunch sitting between the shorthand-typists and burly officials from Transport House, or at the party conferences, where

[1] MacDonald, *Margaret Ethel MacDonald: A Memoir*, 1924, p. 113. I have substituted 'he' for 'she', for in many passages about his dead wife, MacDonald describes himself as he liked to see himself, e.g. (on the death of their son) 'Outwardly she was wonderfully calm. But here again, that terrible inability to let the floodgates of grief loose and throw oneself on the neck of a friend was evident' (p. 125).

he did much to smooth MacDonald's passage and make it possible for him to retain the leadership after the fiasco of 1924. Like Baldwin, Henderson devoted enormous time and attention to taking the pulse of his Party, so that he always knew what it was thinking and how it would react: and this in turn determined his own outlook. His constructive ideas were limited to a vague gradualism, his speech-making was mediocre, he wrote nothing. He was dull, practical, teetotal and deeply religious, with all the sterling qualities and limitations of his type. Above all, he was utterly devoted to the Labour movement, which he came to regard as an end in itself. He was, as his biographer has written, 'the incarnation of the Party as a Party'.[1] It is hardly surprising that when the Labour Party recovered from the trauma of MacDonald's 'betrayal' it should come to venerate a man who was, in most ways, his complete antithesis; and this partly explains the fact that Arthur Henderson's reputation today stands higher than that of his more brilliant leader.

Dominating economic policy was Philip Snowden, Chancellor of the Exchequer for a second time. He was a product of working-class Yorkshire with the 'special brand of humour, the special kind of gritty strength, and the easy equalitarianism proper to the children of that county'.[2] He solved the problem of his early poverty 'by the simple process of reducing his own wants to so rigorous a compass that upon thirty shillings a week . . . he was able to . . . lead a life of proud independence'.[3] Borrowing he always regarded as evil. A cycling accident, leading to the inflammation of the spinal cord, crippled him for life in 1891. Thereafter, his thin-lipped, suffering face, his crippled gait and his vituperative invective, which barely hid a kind and tender heart, made him, in Wertheimer's phrase, 'more eloquent of tragedy than any other politician of the British Left'.[4] His earliest hero was Gladstone; from the Liberal tradition he inherited a hatred of drink and gambling; and free trade was in his blood. His political views brought him close to MacDonald, but he always distrusted his leader's subtle personality and habit of vague exposition, and tried to replace MacDonald

[1] Hamilton, *Arthur Henderson*, 1938, p. 266.
[2] Hamilton, *Remembering My Good Friends*, p. 109.
[3] W. S. Churchill, *Great Contemporaries*, 1939, p. 297.
[4] Wertheimer, *Portrait of the Labour Party*, p. 178.

by Henderson in the aftermath of 1924. As he himself lacked any aesthetic taste or real intellectual curiosity, there was little basis for personal contacts between the two men.

His biggest handicap in the Labour Party was his wife Ethel, who epitomised the social climbing of Labour ladies. She is reported to have said that she needed no friends in the Party, as she was so intimate with the Royal Family.[1] Snowden never forgave the I.L.P. for its attacks on her, and after 1922 virtually severed his connection with the party of which he had been chairman, although formally remaining a member till 1927. His narrow, lucid intellect could not abide the woolly emotionalism of the trade union leaders, so he never worked sympathetically with them either. Thus by 1929 he not only lacked a secure power base in the Labour Party but, unlike MacDonald, had no great hold on its affection either.

The tremendous anger of the disinherited spoke through him when he was young and made him one of the most passionate orators of the early I.L.P., but later his scorn was more often than not turned against what he regarded as the facile optimism of the left. His socialism was gradualist: he dismissed Marxism and wrote that 'extremism on one side inevitably begets extremism on the other . . . if progress is to be permanent moral development must proceed parallel with economic change'.[2] But his strongest political feelings were radical rather than socialist. 'Good at figures' at school, he had early established a reputation as the party's financial expert, but his views on public finance were Gladstonian in their severity. When he became Chancellor for the first time, as Churchill remarks, 'The Treasury mind and the Snowden mind embraced each other with the fervour of two long-separated kindred lizards'.[3] His gift for clear and orderly exposition, however, hid from the Labour Party the uncreative nature of his economic thought. 'To every outworn shibboleth of nineteenth century economics', Boothby has written, 'he clung with fanatic tenacity. Economy, Free Trade, Gold — these were the keynotes of his political philosophy; and deflation the path he trod with almost ghoulish enthusiasm'.[4]

[1] B. Webb Diaries, 19 May 1930.

[2] *An Autobiography*, ii, 1934, p. 541.

[3] Churchill, *Great Contemporaries*, p. 293.

[4] R. Boothby, *I Fight to Live*, 1947, p. 90.

With Snowden at the Treasury, the prospect of a vigorous unemployment policy began to look rather remote. Before the election, MacDonald had proposed if Labour won to set up a 'brain' to deal with unemployment, which in structure and function would resemble the Committee of Imperial Defence. He even seems to have envisaged a Ministry of Employment headed by himself, just as Churchill was later to take on the Defence Ministry. The new ministry failed to materialise. Instead J. H. Thomas was appointed Lord Privy Seal with special responsibilities for unemployment, with Lansbury, Mosley and Johnston to help him. Four Ministers of greater contrast could scarcely be imagined.

'Jimmy' Thomas was the most picturesque figure in the Labour movement. 'This painful but disarming personality', as Wertheimer called him, was every capitalist's reassurance that the Labour Party did not take its socialism too seriously. He himself was wont to pay glowing tributes to a 'constitution that enables an engine-driver of yesterday to be a Minister of to-day'. 'He has created round him', Wertheimer continues, 'an atmosphere of vulgar cordiality and a hail-fellow-well-met manner which appears to have taken in the whole of the British Empire with the exception of about a dozen Communists'.[1] Not without considerable courage — he had stood loyally by MacDonald during the war at the height of the latter's unpopularity, though he himself supported the war — he had gained a reputation as a skilful and flexible union negotiator. Totally devoid of constructive ideas, intimate with the City and big business, the boon companion of half the House of Commons, the jingoistic upholder of imperial and national unity, his appointment gladdened the conservatives and dismayed the radicals.[2]

The Cabinet appointment of George Lansbury was MacDonald's gesture to the left. As First Commissioner of Works, with special responsibility for ancient monuments, he was expected to have plenty of time left over to assist on unemployment. Already seventy, he had

[1] Wertheimer, *Portrait of the Labour Party*, pp. 178–9.

[2] Lord Birkenhead, speaking at Liverpool on 24 May 1929, had remarked: 'There is not a man in the present Labour party, with the possible exception of Mr. J. H. Thomas, whom I would entrust to let out push bicycles.' Beatrice Webb makes the same point another way: 'If frequently on the booze, he is sound on the sanctity of property and the free initiative of capitalist enterprise.' (B. Webb Diaries, 31 May 1930.)

always been an inspirational, rather than a practical, Socialist, though he was interested in land settlement and in rehabilitating criminals. Rather strangely, the *Morning Post* of 8 June 1929 saw him as 'perhaps the most resolute revolutionary in the whole of the Socialist Party'. A more daring appointment, to the Chancellorship of the Duchy of Lancaster, was that of the thirty-two-year-old Mosley. Intelligent, handsome, hard-working and arrogant, already a brilliant public speaker, he had joined the Labour Party in the expectation that it would build a land fit for heroes, and he had equipped himself to promote that objective by reading Keynes. Thus he emerged as an opponent of the gold standard and deflation. The hero himself of a small group of adherents who looked to him to 'do the things of which we dream', he was already being talked about as a future party leader. Thomas Johnston, Under-Secretary of State for Scotland, was one of the Clydeside I.L.P. M.P.s, though by now moving towards the centre. He had been a brilliant editor of the Glasgow newspaper, *Forward*, the most influential left-wing journal in the country, and had it not been for a blunder in 1923, he would have gained office the following year.[1] He, like Mosley, was regarded as one of the coming men.

Herbert Morrison, a MacDonald man, went to the Ministry of Transport. Born in 1888, son of a Brixton policeman, he became an errand boy at fourteen, thereafter rising through local politics to become mayor of Hackney in 1920 and in the process creating the powerful London Labour machine which dominated the L.C.C. for over thirty years. 'Is there not a great future in the Party for the self-sacrificing, simple, honest and retiring devotion of Herbert Morrison?' asked Wertheimer in 1929.[2] Certainly, the handling of the road construction programme would be an enormous test of the new Minister's administrative and intellectual capacity.

Miss Margaret Bondfield, Minister of Labour and the first woman ever to obtain Cabinet rank, started work as a salesgirl in a ladies' underwear department at Brighton. Typical of a certain class of spinsters who thronged the world of philanthropy, she records that from 1900 she 'just lived for the Trade Union Movement' with a concentration

[1] He had refused to withdraw a charge against Asquith when requested to do so by MacDonald (see Middlemas, *The Clydesiders*, p. 127).

[2] Wertheimer, *Portrait of the Labour Party*, p. 188.

'undisturbed by love affairs'.[1] Her trade union connection brought her into contact with the Women's Industrial Council, and her investigations on their behalf into the wages and conditions of women textile operatives converted her to socialism.[2] A humourless and somewhat priggish person, with long black skirts and a voice that emitted a harsh cascade of sound, Miss Bondfield was not a particularly sprightly example of the emancipated woman. As Minister of Labour she would have the management of the problem of unemployment insurance, which aroused especially strong emotions in the Labour movement. Much would depend upon her success in handling the trade unions, a task for which she was deemed to be particularly fitted by virtue of her membership of the General Council for much of the preceding decade.

J. R. Clynes, whom MacDonald had replaced as leader in 1922, became Home Secretary. Starting work as a 'little piecer' at the age of ten, he too had entered politics from the union side. An elegant speaker and a likeable personality, he remained, in Wertheimer's words, one of Labour's 'gilt-edged securities',[3] but his value had dropped somewhat and his place in the inner circle was challenged by Willie Graham, another of Labour's Scotsmen, who went to the Board of Trade, and was widely regarded as the successor of Snowden, whom he idolised.[4] Like Snowden 'he possessed an extraordinary gift of lucid exposition', and though he spoke at length, it was always without notes. He was greatly liked, but was not a forceful personality. Arthur Greenwood, the Minister of Health, had formerly lectured in economics at Leeds University, but made no contribution on this subject to Labour Party thinking, though he wrote a vigorous pamphlet urging the socialisation of the liquor trade.

Sidney Webb, the Colonial and Dominions Secretary who went to the Lords as Lord Passfield,[5] had founded and inspired the Fabian Society and was one of the Party's leading thinkers, but at seventy his

[1] Margaret Bondfield, *A Life's Work*, 1948, p. 36. [2] Ibid. p. 45.

[3] Wertheimer, *Portrait of the Labour Party*, p. 183. Morrison described him as 'a Trade Union official pure and simple' (*An Autobiography*, 1960, p. 98).

[4] 'Philip Snowden was Willie's political ideal . . . [who] commanded from [him] a respect amounting almost to awe'. (Thomas Graham, *Willie Graham*, p. 199.) Graham's economic orthodoxy matched Snowden's; see above, p. 44.

[5] His wife refused to be known as anything but Mrs. Webb.

creative period was over and he looked forward to an early retirement. Equally aged was Willie Adamson, twenty-seven years a miner, who went to the Scottish Office; while A. V. Alexander began his apprenticeship for what was to prove a long career at the Admiralty. Tom Shaw, a pacifist, went to the War Office. Most of these men justified Beatrice Webb's strictures on the quality of leading party personnel.

More able, but lacking any firm base in the Labour Party, were the recruits from other parties: Lord Parmoor, almost eighty, who became Lord President; Lord Sankey, the Lord Chancellor; Noel Buxton, Minister of Agriculture; Lord Thomson, Minister for Air; Sir Charles Trevelyan, Minister of Education; and W. Wedgwood Benn, Secretary of State for India. None of them were to have anything to do with unemployment.

The second Labour Governement did not compare unfavourably, in terms of all-round competence, with many other Governments of this century. On the other hand it lacked any Ministers of real intellectual flair, such as Joseph Chamberlain, Lloyd George or Churchill. It was, in short, a Government likely to acquit itself reasonably well in normal times, but fail before the sternest challenges. Nor were the Ministry's somewhat scanty intellectual resources supplemented by the insights of Labour and Socialist academics thinking hard about contemporary problems. Few parties in any age can boast a Keynes: but Ramsay MacDonald did not even have Professor Kaldor or Dr. Balogh to advise him.

The lack of distinction in the leadership reflected the nature of the Labour Party at that time. The Party had originated as a 'grand alliance' between trade unionists and socialists, but the trade union element always predominated and this is reflected in the composition of the parliamentary Party in 1929. Of the 287 Labour M.P.s, 40 per cent were sponsored by the unions, 44 per cent by the divisional Labour parties, 13 per cent by the I.L.P. and 3 per cent by the Co-operative Party.[1] Of the 114 trade-union-sponsored M.P.s, fifty were miners, by far the largest

[1] G. D. H. Cole, *A History of the Labour Party from 1914*, p. 223. A comparison with the 1923 results shows a drop both in union-sponsored Members (from 51 per cent) and in I.L.P.-sponsored Members (from 24 per cent), which reflects the growth of the Party at the expense of its federal parts (ibid. p. 171).

group.[1] Yet these figures mask the true extent of trade union influence, since many of the divisional parties sponsored manual workers, while hardly any unions sponsored what Beatrice Webb was wont to call 'brainworkers'. Against this solid phalanx of union strength, the opposition Parties mustered about a hundred lawyers and ninety-six company directors.[2]

The high union percentage was reflected in the low level of education. J. F. S. Ross has calculated that 72 per cent of all Labour Members between 1918 and 1935 had only elementary education, contrasted with 4 per cent of Conservatives and 14 per cent of Liberals; while only 11 per cent had been to university, contrasted with 69 per cent of Conservatives and 21 per cent of Liberals.[3] Finally, the preponderance of trade union officials made both the average age of entry to the Commons and the average age of the M.P. considerably higher in the Labour Party than in the other two Parties, and Ross wondered how far 'the relative elderliness of the Labour Party in the House is reflected in its policy and its vigour (or lack of vigour)'.[4]

The two most distinct sections of the parliamentary Labour Party were the trade unionists and the I.L.P. Members. The former met regularly as the Trade Union Group to discuss industrial questions. Their leading member was Arthur Hayday, M.P. for Nottingham West, who had been a trimmer and stoker in the merchant service and who in 1930 was to become president of the T.U.C. With one or two exceptions, the parliamentary trade unionists were the second-rankers, the powerful general secretaries, such as Ernest Bevin, preferring to remain outside. Although in theory the I.L.P. group comprised the 142 M.P.s who were members of the I.L.P. (including MacDonald), in practice the only I.L.P. M.P.s who worked closely together were the dozen or so who accepted the intellectual leadership of John Wheatley and James Maxton. These were the Clydesiders, plus one or two others, such as Fenner Brockway, who had captured control of the I.L.P. machine in the mid-twenties and who advanced the distinctive policy of *Socialism in Our Time*. Wheatley had been a successful Minister of Health in the 1924 Government, but his personal reputation was ruined by a lawsuit in 1927 which probably caused his exclusion from the 1929 Government,

[1] J. F. S. Ross, *Parliamentary Representation*, 2nd ed., 1948, p. 61.
[2] Ibid. p. 76. [3] Ibid. pp. 45, 54. [4] Ibid. p. 27.

while the extraordinary-looking Maxton with his long black hair and his cadaverous features was the conscience of the left, highly emotional, unbalanced, but universally loved. Owing to its political extremism the I.L.P. had steadily lost ground within the Labour Party in the nineteen-twenties, and the only question in 1929 was whether it would leave the Party altogether. The Clydeside caucus was likely to prove an embarrassment to any Labour Government.

Education in the 'school of life' rather than the universities had many advantages, but also made for great weaknesses. The parliamentary debating skill of the trade unionists was hardly likely to be a match for that of the lawyers, though it might prove more than equal to that of the company directors, while the formidable talents of the I.L.P. were as likely as not to be deployed against the Government. This meant that the parliamentary oppositions, with the skill of a Lloyd George, Churchill, or Simon at their behest, were likely to triumph in debate, which would be cumulatively damaging to ministerial and parliamentary morale. A lack of administrative experience, mental training and social poise meant that many Labour Ministers were likely to prove less competent and assured in running their departments and establishing their authority over their civil servants than their political opposite numbers, though this might to some extent be counteracted by greater reforming zeal.[1]

[1] In 1924 MacDonald had gone quite unashamedly outside the Party to fill important government posts, especially legal ones, for which special qualifications were required, and although this need did not arise to the same extent in 1929, there were still many ex-Liberals and non-party figures in the 1929 Government. The most spectacular capture was that of Sir William Jowitt who had been elected for Preston as a Liberal in May 1929, accepted the office of Attorney-General in June and got returned that month by the same constituency as Labour Member. The *Morning Post* commiserated with the Liberals in verse:

> Oh, Jowitt; I am lost in grief
> That Ramsay should be gainer —
> How could you take his proffered brief
> Who held my own retainer?

4

THE CHOICE

i. INTRODUCTION

When Labour took office the economic omens seemed favourable. Exports for the first five months of 1929 were up by £8m on the comparable period for 1928; employment which had taken an exceptionally bad turn at the end of 1928 had recovered in the spring of 1929 and unemployment figures for May and June were lower than in the same months the previous year. There was some prospect that the steady rise in exports from 1926 onwards would be maintained and that *pari passu* employment would improve. There was as yet little hint of the sharp fall in the prices of primary products that was to begin in the late autumn. The one disturbing factor was the stock-piling of gold by France and America. But there were signs that France was about to remove some of her restrictions on foreign lending; while the Federal Reserve Bank might be persuaded to call a halt to the speculative boom on the New York Exchange. In these circumstances there was a good case for not interfering with the economy, for not taking any action that might prejudice the quite hopeful prospects for a trade revival.

This course was urged on the Government by the leaders of industry. In their view the two prevailing characteristics of the British economy were excessive costs and lack of confidence. Both could be traced back to government interference. The Government had raised costs of production by constantly increasing taxation, largely to pay for such social services as unemployment insurance, pensions etc. What industry required from the Government was 'a definite pronouncement that enterprise will not be subjected to new anxieties and handicaps by additional legislative enactments'. In particular this meant 'a holiday from social legislation'.

But the Government were not alone to blame. The trade unions had increased costs by their closed shop policy and resistance to wage reductions. Business would look to a Labour Government 'to obtain from the T.U.C. an announcement that their contribution to the new effort would be a declaration of greater flexibility in labour practice'. In return employers might be able to offer 'a truce in wage rate reductions for the next eighteen months'. As part of the stabilisation of trade union-employer relations the Government should make no attempt to change the 1927 Trade Disputes Act.

Finally, manufacturers wanted an assurance that there would be no tampering with the existing Safeguarding Duties.[1]

The City, as we have seen, was curiously insensitive to the problems of industry, being mainly concerned with the international position. But its conclusions were the same. Financial rectitude was essential to maintain confidence in the pound, upon which the City's own prosperity largely depended. In this task the Government's own attitude was of the greatest importance. Any tendency to toy with unsound expedients such as raising a huge loan for development purposes would seriously undermine international confidence. This was especially true, it was held, if the offending Government were a Labour one.

We have already seen why the Labour Party was in no position to offer a serious challenge to these views. Socialist analysis provided no short term alternative; but adherence to socialism precluded the consideration of radical non-socialist analysis of the Liberal Yellow Book type. Snowden's personal ascendancy in matters of finance was also of paramount importance. To him socialism was a luxury that had to be financed out of revenue — like roads and other public utilities. If the revenue were not available there could be no socialism. This was the case for minimum interference. But there was a strong case to be made in the opposite direction. By 1929 there was little prospect that the basic industries would recapture their former markets. The rationalisation of old, and the development of new, industries required capital and confidence. But money was dear and confidence was low after the years of bad trade. A gap had developed between the rate of interest at which

[1] Memorandum to the Prime Minister by the Council of the Federation of British Industries, Autumn 1929 (MacDonald Papers, Unemployment File 8).

people were prepared to lend and the rate of interest at which industry was prepared to borrow. There was at least a case for arguing that the Government should bridge that gap by raising a development loan.

There was a further point. The free market of the classical economist no longer existed. There was no wage flexibility, no free trade; taxation was increasing to support a welfare state. The retreat from *laissez-faire* might be regretted, but it could not be reversed. The important point was to recognise that with its disappearance many of the objections to government interference disappeared likewise.

The other two Parties to some extent accepted this. The Liberals realised that the classical precepts no longer applied to the home market but they insisted on their application to the international market. The Conservatives realised that they no longer applied to the international market but insisted on applying them to the home market. Here political pressures and traditions pulled the Parties in opposing directions. Industry wanted protection against foreign competition but non-interference at home: the Conservative Party was prevented only by electoral considerations from adopting this doctrine in all its rigour. Free trade, on the other hand, was almost the only thing that held the Liberal Party together: it was politically impossible even for the flexible Lloyd George to renounce it. Thus Labour might get Liberal support in pursuing an ambitious policy of home development, but not if that meant interfering with foreign trade. It might get Conservative support for an extension of safeguarding or an all-round tariff, but not if this were for the purpose of starting an active policy of home development.

Faced with a number of choices, all of them involving some risk, a minority Labour Government compromised. In retrospect, it can be seen that it decided to follow Conservative policy with two main modifications. Conservative unemployment policy had been based on non-interference at home plus international action to revive the export trades, implied by the return to the gold standard and lukewarm efforts to secure tariff reductions. This internationalism was common to all Parties and stemmed from the belief that the difficulties of the export industries were caused by the war. On the domestic front, the Labour Government decided, without challenging the basic Conservative view that industry must work out its own salvation, to step up the volume of public works, out of deference to Liberal pressure and its own desire to 'do something' for the unemployed. It determined to give the 'international' approach more coherent form by reversing those 'nationalistic' aspects of Conservative policy which appeared to threaten it — safeguarding, gunboat diplomacy and antagonism to the League of Nations. This meant more vigorous efforts to secure tariff reductions, pacification, and universal disarmament; for it was the great nineteenth-century Liberal premise that political tranquillity and trade went together. However, it would be quite wrong to suggest that this policy was 'worked out beforehand' or even that any real effort was made to estimate its chances of success. The Government merely stepped into the groove vacated by its predecessor and made the minimum adjustments compatible with its own traditions, the interests of its leaders and the political position. Nor was it apparent for quite a long time, even to Ministers, what the Government's intentions were, for such declarations of intent as were handed down were coloured by the need to allay the apprehensions or satisfy the expectations of different groups. Thus to business representatives the non-interventionist aspect of the policy would be stressed; while Labour supporters and Liberals were given to understand that small beginnings presaged more impressive developments in the future. Underlying everything was muddle and confusion.

ii. THE ANNOUNCEMENT OF THE POLICY

The King's Speech of 3 July 1929 promised schemes 'for the improvement of the means of transport, for the stimulation of the depressed export trades, for the economic development of My Overseas Dependencies, for the improvement of the condition of agriculture, for the encouragement of the fishing industry, and for the improvement of the facilities for the marketing of farm and fishery products'. Increased emigration was 'being considered'. Commissions of Enquiry were to look into the cotton and the iron and steel industries. The reorganisation of the coal industry was 'under consideration'. Unemployment insurance was to be the subject of 'a general survey'.[1]

The general design was clear enough. Everything was to be surveyed,

[1] 229 H.C. Deb. c. 48–9.

with the aim of making every branch of industry, especially those connected with exports, a little more efficient: how, it was not made clear. Meanwhile, the Government would maintain the unemployed as decently as possible.

This was the general framework. Within the framework was a small area of specific unemployment policy, barely mentioned in the speech ('improvement of the means of transport'), which was to be a direct government responsibility under the supervision of J. H. Thomas, Lord Privy Seal. Thomas outlined his attitude in the debate of the Address (3 July 1929):

> 'I never hesitated to point out', he declared, 'that, in my judgment, the real and ultimate solution of the [unemployment] problem could never be separated from the trade, commerce and industry of the country.'[1]

Nevertheless, there was something the Government could do:

> I said to myself, first of all: 'There is to be no consideration of schemes that merely mean spending money without regard either to consequences or benefit to the community.' Anyone can spend money. There is a large number of people who construe work as filling a barrow and then emptying it. I do not forget, and I do not intend to forget, that there is no bottomless pit from which money can be drawn. I will not forget that fact. But, on the other side, anyone who knows the feeling in the country and who knows the demoralisation . . . of our people will realise that to do nothing on that side is equally dangerous. My difficulty as between these two extremes is to look at schemes . . . that will not only give work to the unemployed, but will also stimulate trade at home and abroad and add, in the end, to the economic equipment of the country.[2]

Here then we have the justification, in Thomas's characteristic language, for the 'enclave' of government-assisted schemes that had become an accepted part of government policy. His speech marked an advance on the rather negative policy of the Conservative Government, but it fell disappointingly short of Liberal aspirations. In one respect in particular its approach was identical with that of the Conservatives. The Government would undertake no work directly, but limit itself to offering terms, leaving it to the authorities concerned to take up the offer or not as they chose.

[1] 229 H.C. Deb. c. 91. [2] 229 H.C. Deb. c. 93.

This principle underlined the three definite promises that Thomas made. First, he announced that the Government had sanctioned in principle a five-year programme of trunk and classified roads up to £37½m. Secondly, he promised to ask Parliament for power to guarantee, up to £25m, loans raised by public utilities; or alternatively for power to pay interest charges on such loans. Thirdly, he announced that in the Budget each year there would be set aside £1m to be used to pay interest charges for a limited period on loans raised for colonial development.[1]

The remainder of Thomas's speech produced a crop of small ideas thrown out for consideration, some of which were followed up, others not. Perhaps railway carriages and wagons and telegraph poles might be built of British steel instead of imported timber; Charing Cross and Waterloo bridges might be widened and rebuilt; Liverpool Street might be electrified, traffic congestion in London might be met by getting goods carried round the periphery in special tube goods trains; there might be a tube extension from Finsbury Park; it might be possible to encourage industries to move into the depressed areas. The Government would try to introduce more elasticity into the Unemployment Grants Committee. Finally Thomas undertook to appoint a committee to consider 'the hundred and one factors' connected with the problem of removing juveniles and the aged from the labour market.[2]

This was Thomas's *potpourri*: the framework in which his department would work and from which it would not depart. Active government 'unemployment policy' in the next nine or ten months consisted of exploring, accepting or rejecting, and carrying out the ideas and proposals advanced in this speech. There was nothing else — except the Lord Privy Seal's trip to Canada.[3]

[1] The last two promises were given legislative effect in the 'Home Development' and Colonial Development Acts, both introduced on 15 July 1929 and passed before Parliament broke up for the summer. The essential feature of the first was that it made it easier for the railway and electricity companies to borrow money; a treasury advisory committee known as the Duckham Committee was set up to vet schemes. The second was intended to make it easier for colonial governments to start schemes, such as the Zambezi Bridge scheme, which, in a roundabout way, were expected to stimulate employment at home.

[2] For the speech as a whole see 229 H.C. Deb. c. 91–110.

[3] See below, p. 101.

Nor in that period did the Government's overall view change in the least. In July Thomas told the House that the only ultimate solution to unemployment lay in more trade. In November he was pinning his hopes on the 'development of our export trade'.[1] In March 1930 he was writing that, valuable though the work of his department might be, 'it is to the increased provision of ordinary industrial employment through the revival of our trade and industry that the Government attach primary importance'.[2] There was no hint that the work of his department might contribute to that happy outcome.

The Labour Party had promised the unemployed higher rates of benefit obtainable on easier conditions. The King's Speech, however, had promised merely 'a general survey'. It is perhaps hardly surprising that the Government's first proposal on unemployment insurance — the first of many — fulfilled no pledges. Miss Bondfield, introducing it on 11 July 1929, described it as a 'stop-gap motion to enable us to tide over the present emergency in regard to the financial position of the fund'.[3] The fund had, by June 1929, borrowed £36½m of the £40m it was allowed, and there was clearly a risk that its borrowing powers would be exhausted during the summer. Either its borrowing powers or its income could be increased. The Government chose to do the latter, but rather than increase contributions from employers and employees, it simply increased the Treasury's contribution by £3½m, thus raising the fund's income from £43m to £46½m and at the same time destroying the 'equal thirds' principle upon which the fund had rested.

The I.L.P. was extremely critical. There was not a word of hope in the Bill for the unemployed, said Campbell Stephen. It was simply a matter of book-keeping. What about the 'not genuinely seeking work' clause and the increased benefits?[4] Miss Bondfield appointed, on 25 July, a small committee under Sir Harold Morris, K.C., to consider the former; she would make no promises at all about the latter. The first debate on unemployment insurance set a pattern which was to recur throughout the Government's lifetime — Ministers worried about the finances of the fund; backbenchers worried about the finances of the unemployed.

[1] 231 H.C. Deb. c. 670.
[2] Cmd. 3519.
[3] 229 H.C. Deb. c. 1127.
[4] Ibid. c. 1123–6.

James Ramsay MacDonald

'A peg built to hang myths on.' (*Lord Francis-Williams*)

Philip and Ethel Snowden

'He trod the path of Deflation with ghoulish enthusiasm.'

Stanley Baldwin

'Mr. Baldwin has invented the formidable argument that you must not do anything because it will mean that you will not be able to do anything else.' (*J. M. Keynes*)

David Lloyd George

'If only Ll.G. had preserved himself as a National man of emergency.' (*J. L. Garvin*)

iii. POLITICAL REACTIONS AND THE POSITION OF THE GOVERNMENT

MacDonald's opening statement in the debate on the King's Speech was to give rise later to many conflicting interpretations of his motives. Baldwin, for the Opposition, had taunted the new Government with the charge that the Speech could be summed up in the sentence 'My Ministers are going to think'. The Prime Minister accepted this without embarrassment and appealed for help in the thinking process from all sections of the House in words that have often been quoted:

> I wonder how far it is possible, without in any way abandoning any of our party positions, without in any way surrendering any item of our party principles, to consider ourselves more as a Council of State and less as arrayed regiments facing each other in battle . . . so that by putting our ideas into a common pool we can bring out from that common pool legislation and administration that will be of substantial benefit for the nation as a whole.[1]

Bassett has effectively dealt with the charge that MacDonald was already plotting a National Government.[2] But in disposing of this sinister interpretation he falls into an opposite error. He writes: 'MacDonald's plea in 1929 was simply one that the more serious problems of the day should not be discussed in a partisan spirit', and elsewhere: 'a minority government . . . dependent upon the support of another party or other parties for its necessary majority in the House of Commons, is bound, if it is to endure, to enter into some form of collaboration, some kind of informal coalition'. This is undoubtedly true. Nevertheless, if MacDonald's words were not sinister, they were certainly weak. It is true that the Government had to establish some minimum form of collaboration with one of the other Parties: but there was no need to offer to do so with both at the same time, especially as a Labour Government's natural ally in these circumstances would seemingly be the Liberals rather than the Conservatives. Further, to expect a coherent policy on unemployment — or anything else — to emerge from a 'pooling' of Labour, Liberal and Conservative ideas was naïve to say the least. By offering to pay as much attention to Conservative as to Liberal

[1] 229 H.C. Deb. c. 64–5.

[2] R. Bassett, *1931: Political Crisis*, 1958, pp. 40 and 417.

views on unemployment, MacDonald was deliberately spurning the opportunity created by a 'progressive' majority.

It should be noticed that it was the Labour Government that rejected the support of the Liberals, not the Liberals who refused to support the Government. Lloyd George had made his position clear in a speech to the National Liberal Club on 13 June:

> If the [Government] tackle the [unemployment] problem promptly, boldly, energetically and wisely they will have no more hearty and steady supporters than the Liberal Party. We shall be prepared to afford them every support in securing the necessary power to avoid delay and to overcome refractory and selfish interests.[1]

Here was an unequivocal offer of support for a bold unemployment policy. Why did the Government not take it up?

First, there is little doubt that important members of the Government thought the Liberal policy far too radical. Snowden had attacked its 'madcap finance'. It proposed to raise a large sum by borrowing. To Snowden all government borrowing was evil: improvements had to come out of revenue. Taxation to raise £100m was out of the question. That was the end of the Liberal plan as far as he was concerned. Even if these overwhelming grounds for rejection were not considered sufficient, had not the civil servants pronounced the whole scheme impracticable?

Thus the Liberal plan itself offered no satisfactory basis for co-operation between the two Parties. Nor was any other basis easy to find. The Liberals were sure to demand their price for keeping the Government in power — electoral reform. The bulk of the Labour Party were opposed

[1] *Daily Telegraph*, 14 June 1929. Lloyd George was, of course, aware of the dangers of this stand. In a letter to C. P. Scott, editor of the *Manchester Guardian*, written on 30 April, before the election, he declared:

> An agreed programme would not save the situation if the Socialists make a mess of the job.... The consequence would be that the discredit would fall more hardly on the Liberals than the Socialists. They would always have a solid trade union vote to fall back on....
>
> On the other hand, if you can convince me of the possibilities of the Socialists doing the job well, the young men of our Party would leave us and join the Party which was carrying through a Liberal programme successfully.
>
> Either way the Liberal Party would be done for.

(Quoted in Frank Owen, *Tempestuous Journey*, 1954, p. 710.)

to proportional representation and extremely dubious about the alternative vote. MacDonald's views appeared to vary with the results of particular general elections; but after 1929 there appeared to be no compelling reason for upsetting the existing electoral system. Thus the Government were not prepared to promise electoral reform, though they were prepared to set up a committee.[1]

In the Labour Party there was a massive mistrust of Lloyd George. Labour supporters recalled the string of broken promises that marked his premiership, of which the one that rankled most was his treatment of the Sankey Report on coal mines. Labour Members felt that his unemployment programme was just a 'stunt' in a desperate effort to regain power. He was regarded as tricky, unprincipled and unreliable—the last person upon whom one wanted to depend.

Finally, there was always the nagging question: could Lloyd George deliver the Liberal vote? A number of prominent Liberals, in and out of Parliament, were by no means committed to his leadership, though they had campaigned under him for party unity. They would look for the earliest opportunity to break away. Others, though prepared to accept him as leader, disliked his programme and were anxious once the election was over to tone it down.[2] The old divisions between Asquithians and Lloyd Georgians, conservatives and radicals, continued to threaten Liberal unity.

In the last analysis, though, *had* the Government really wished to carry out a bold unemployment policy it would have turned to the Liberals despite Lloyd George. If the Liberals refused to support it in carrying out their own policy, MacDonald could have appealed to the country at any time in the first six months of Labour Government with good prospects of winning an absolute majority. But it would scarcely have come to that, for the Liberals could not afford another early election, especially on such an unfavourable issue. It was lack of belief, not lack of a majority, that determined the initial unemployment decisions taken by the Labour Government.

[1] Known as the Ullswater Committee; promised on 10 July 1929, finally set up in December. See D. E. Butler, *The Electoral System in Britain, 1918–1951*, 1953, pp. 59–62.

[2] Thus, by 15 July, the pledge 'we can conquer unemployment' had, in the eyes of Sir Herbert Samuel, become a 'tentative suggestion' (230 H.C. Deb. c. 485).

One of the paradoxes of the position was that the left wing supported MacDonald in his refusal to enter into any combination or informal understanding with the Liberals. To them such collaboration would have meant a betrayal of socialism; whereas in fact it offered them the best chance of getting the kind of unemployment policy they wanted. In being resolute for socialism the left were unwittingly condoning the MacDonald–Snowden retreat from the spirit of Labour's policy.

Thomas's speech, to which we have referred, bore more resemblance to the speeches of the previous Conservative Minister of Labour, Sir Arthur Steel-Maitland, than to the Liberal Yellow Book. It was hardly surprising that it received a warm welcome from the Conservatives. Churchill, replying for the Opposition, said that he found Thomas's proposals so sensible, attractive and moderate that he could not see any serious differences about them arising between the Government and the Conservative Party. The real difference, as Churchill rightly pointed out, was between the Government's proposals and the 'very expensive and audacious plans' of Lloyd George which he commended Thomas for rejecting.[1] Other Conservatives spoke in similar vein. The Conservative Press joined in the chorus of approbation. In particular the *Daily Telegraph* noted that Thomas happily combined the 'instincts of the capitalist' with the 'sedulously cultivated idiom of one of the proletariat' and made great play with the disappointment of the left — 'jam yesterday and jam tomorrow, but never jam today'. The *Daily Express*, always optimistic, thought that Thomas's plans 'constitute a great triumph for the policy advocated by the *Daily Express*'.[2]

The Liberals were not so pleased. Lloyd George said he was disappointed with Thomas, especially since his speech seemed to meet 'with the wholehearted approval of the late Chancellor of the Exchequer'. He hoped it would not be the Government's last word on unemployment policy.

Labour comment was far from enthusiastic, but there was a general willingness to accept Thomas's programme as a first instalment; James Sexton, for instance, said he would accept it as a beginning 'while, Oliver Twist-like, demanding more'. This interpretation was fostered by Ministers. MacDonald, speaking at Durham on 7 July, admitted that there had been things left out of the King's Speech but went on:

[1] 229 H.C. Deb. c. 112. [2] 3 July 1929.

I did not ask you to give me power for three weeks. I said give me power for five years. . . . You turned out the old Government but you have no idea of the old furniture and rotting wall-paper . . . that they have left behind.[1]

The *Daily Herald* made a reference to the lack of a parliamentary majority.[2]

The I.L.P. was more critical. Maxton said 'frankly, I should be dishonest . . . if I did not express very plainly my complete dissatisfaction with the King's Speech, and the speech of the Right Hon. Gentleman the Lord Privy Seal';[3] but a more telling attack on the policy of 'instalments' came from the one first-class mind on the left, John Wheatley.

This is the day of the Government's power. To-day the Government could do anything. To-day the Government are not showing the courage that their supporters on these benches expect. If they displayed that courage and went on with their own policy, the parties opposite would not dare to wound them, however willing they might be to strike; but, after the Government have disappointed their friends, by 12 months of this halting, half-way legislation, as one of my friends described it, and have been discredited in the country, then, 12 months from now, there will be no party in this House poor enough to do them honour.[4]

The *New Leader* on 12 July summarised the I.L.P. position on unemployment:

This scheme here and that credit facility there will improve things, but somehow this one simple truth has got to be borne in mind (and stated) — that unemployment is a by-product of capitalism and you can't solve it, or even appreciably lessen it, within that system.

So far we have been discussing what might be termed orthodox party reactions to the Government's policy. But there were hints in this early period of a new approach to unemployment which cut right across party and established doctrine, whether of the right or the left. This approach emphasised that unemployment was basically caused by the lack of demand. Boothby, a young Conservative M.P. for East Aberdeenshire,

[1] *Manchester Guardian*, 8 July 1929.

[2] 5 July 1929. [3] 229 H.C. Deb. c. 164.

[4] 230 H.C. Deb. c. 98. Wheatley was protesting against the Government's decision not to restore in full the housing subsidy of 1924, cut by Neville Chamberlain in 1927.

argued that deflation prevented any possibility of a trade revival. W. J. Brown, secretary of the Civil Service Clerical Association, and Labour M.P. for West Wolverhampton, launched a strong attack on the 'treasury view' and advocated an embargo on foreign lending to make available more money for home investment. Both proclaimed irrelevant the old controversy between free trade and protection; the ideas of both bore the strong imprint of Keynes. Boothby was a close friend of Mosley, with whom he had spent a summer in Venice when the latter was working on *Revolution by Reason*, a book similarly influenced by Keynesian thinking.

5
THE FAILURE OF IMAGINATION

i. INTRODUCTION

'WHEN the House of Commons has ceased to meet', said the Prime Minister in July 1929, 'then we have got a free field for work and I want that free field.' The 'work' MacDonald had in mind was work to further his grand design for reducing political tension in the world and eventually stimulating employment at home. He himself spent the summer immersed in foreign affairs. At Lossiemouth he conferred with General Dawes on naval disarmament; early in September he was addressing the Assembly of the League of Nations at Geneva; on 12 September it was announced that he would visit America for a month to discuss naval disarmament with President Hoover; he left for America on 28 September. Unfortunately this programme of pacification was rudely upset by his own Chancellor's heavy touch in dealing with the French. Snowden considered the French were doing too well out of reparation payments, at the British expense. So he went over to the Hague to claim an increase in the British share, sat there implacably for a month refusing to compromise, almost wrecked the conference by his rudeness, earned the plaudits of the British press, and received a hero's welcome on his return to London.[1] Meanwhile, Henderson preached disarmament at Geneva, while Graham expounded there his plan for tariff reductions,[2]

[1] The Hague conference met to consider the Young Report which had scaled down the annual German reparation payments from £125m to £100m. It had also scaled down Britain's share by £2,400,000 — from £22,800,000 to £20,400,000 — and had limited her share of the 'unconditional' annual payments to £1m, France benefiting in both cases. Snowden insisted on restoring the cut of £2,400,000 and also wanted £6m a year instead of £1m.

[2] See below, p. 150.

and Thomas spent nearly six weeks in Canada. It is hardly surprising that at the Liberal Party Conference in October, Sir Charles Hobhouse described the Government as a subsidiary of Cook's Tourist Agency.[1]

In the specific area of unemployment policy assigned to Thomas's organisation, the Retirement Pensions Committee worked steadily throughout the summer: but that was all the thinking or planning which took place. The remainder of Thomas's programme called for non-government initiatives. The Government had announced conditions and terms for loans and grants; there was nothing to do except encourage applications and wait for them to come in. The Morris Committee, appointed by Miss Bondfield, Minister of Labour, investigated changes in the administration of unemployment insurance, and on the wider front of domestic policy, Graham's Cabinet committee on coal mines negotiated with the miners and owners for a Coal Bill.

Reactions to the Government's unemployment policy over the summer recess followed the lines established in July. The I.L.P. was critical and became increasingly so. At its summer school at Digswell Park, Maxton asked: 'Has any human being benefited by the fact that there has been a Labour Government in office in the last two months? I can think of nobody except two murderers who were reprieved.'[2] I.L.P. comment urged the Government to concentrate on increasing mass purchasing power rather than exports. The Liberal Party was also critical. At the Party Conference in October, Samuel said that Thomas had not risen to the level of his great task. Nathan argued that after four months the Government had not produced a single new idea. Thomas had joined the Government with an inflated reputation as an astute negotiator; he seemed likely to leave it as a pricked balloon.[3] The Conservatives continued to express approval, though in language that must have jarred on Labour supporters. Baldwin noted with satisfaction on 27 September that the Government had found it impossible to introduce any schemes that had not been devised by previous Governments.[4]

In the Labour Party there was a general reluctance to pass censure and

[1] The National Liberal Federation, *Report on the 46th Annual Meeting*, 2–4 October 1929, p. 5.

[2] *Morning Post*, 5 August 1929.

[3] *Liberal Conference Report*, 1929, pp. 10, 26–7.

[4] *Gleanings and Memoranda*, June–December 1929, p. 408.

instead an urge to take pride in the Government's positive achievements, especially in foreign affairs. At the T.U.C. Conference in Belfast general enthusiasm was expressed for Snowden's stand at the Hague and there was little discussion of unemployment, though fears were expressed about rationalisation.[1] At Labour's annual conference at Brighton, Thomas added Canada to his House of Commons mixture of July, but the mixture remained unimpressive. Even so, there was no criticism, except from Wheatley, a few questions only from Bevin and others.[2] On the whole, the Labour Party was prepared to suspend judgement and wait for the further official statement of government policy scheduled for the House of Commons in November.

ii. THE UNEMPLOYMENT COMMITTEE

The Unemployment Committee, consisting of Thomas, Lansbury, Mosley and Johnston, got off to an uncertain start, typifying the lack of preparation and unsureness of aim that characterised the Government's domestic unemployment policy. No one appeared to know whether or not Johnston was a member of the Committee, least of all Johnston himself. As late as October he was writing to Lansbury:

> I'm not sure whether I have any right upon that committee [Thomas's Committee], or whether I only form part of an interested audience. Adamson [Secretary of State for Scotland] pleads with me to attend, or I should have gone long ago.[3]

The four Ministers formed what was known as 'Thomas's Committee'. But it was hardly a committee in the proper sense. It had no precise function or terms of reference. Thomas, as Lord Privy Seal, had a personal function — to co-ordinate unemployment policy — and his office was given an extra complement of civil servants to help him to do this. But the three other Ministers were not an integral part of this organisation. Rather they were thought of as being available to assist Thomas on specific problems — working out a particular policy,

[1] *T.U.C. Annual Report*, 1929, p. 424.
[2] *Labour Party Annual Report*, October 1929, pp. 176–87.
[3] Lansbury Papers, 19.d.193.

receiving deputations, or speaking for the Government on unemployment questions in the House of Commons. Winston Churchill described Mosley as 'a sort of ginger assistant to the Lord Privy Seal and more ginger than assistant, I have no doubt'.

Thomas himself was given no executive authority: his department could not set a single man to work. His task was to co-ordinate the existing instruments of executive authority. He was supposed to 'ginger up' the departments — to press them to submit schemes with an employment content in them to the Cabinet. Likewise his department was responsible for what non-departmental unemployment policy there was. For example, it was he who piloted the 'Home Development' Act, granting assistance to public utilities, through the Commons in July. Local authorities came to him to inquire about the conditions under which they might receive grants from the Unemployment Grants Committee.

Yet even in these fields responsibility remained divided. Thomas's department might have inspired the Home Development Act, but the Treasury administered it. The U.G.C. was placed under the direction of the Ministry of Labour. Finally, road building did not come directly under Thomas's purview, being administered by the Ministry of Transport. Thus Thomas's task was to know what was happening everywhere and to try to fashion some semblance of order amid conflicting and often competing departmental activities.

To help him in this undertaking he was able to make use of two sets of civil servants. First he took over from the Ministry of Labour a group of civil servants who had been concerned there with the work of the Unemployment Grants Committee. These civil servants formed the Lord Privy Seal's secretariat and were there to cope with the expanded work of his department. They were headed by Sir Horace Wilson, who became Thomas's chief of staff. They were not, however, automatically at the disposal of the three advisory Ministers.

Secondly, Thomas formed an inter-departmental committee on unemployment, consisting of the permanent heads of the various departments meeting once a month under his chairmanship. The main purpose of this body was to spread information about unemployment activities in each department and to co-ordinate and order work. It was never designed to have any policy-making or executive capacity, as the political chiefs were absent from its meetings. The advisory Ministers were not members.

In addition, there were a number of *ad hoc* committees which operated at various stages in the lifetime of Thomas's organisation. The Committee on Retirement Pensions was one; for it, Thomas made use of the three advisory Ministers and it was served by his own staff. A Committee on National Schemes was set up in November.

This was the formal structure. The practice, of course, was much more informal. Thomas met whom he liked and when he liked. The composition of meetings and consultations varied with the needs of the moment. The only person who made himself indispensable was Sir Horace Wilson: he was always present whatever the occasion. For the rest Thomas met local authority and trade union deputations, consulted groups of businessmen and financiers, sometimes with Mosley, more often without him. His personal activities ranged far and wide. He appropriated with relish the task of cheering up people, especially the business community, and he stumped the country making optimistic speeches. His trip to Canada was a personal venture and had no real relation to the work of his organisation, though he thought it might have some relation to unemployment.

Why did the organisation set up fall so far short of MacDonald's Albert Hall conception? The main reason was that government unemployment policy created no need for a new economic organisation. For a long time it pinned its hopes on a revival of ordinary business activity. Hence there was no need for an 'economic general staff' or any other institutional innovations.

Nevertheless, it became obvious in the autumn that the unemployment machinery was not working well. Considerable friction began to develop between Thomas and his advisory Ministers. Part of the trouble was institutional: the Ministers were not properly integrated into the unemployment organisation, and within the organisation itself there was not sufficient provision for co-ordinating the various aspects of policy. Part of it stemmed from policy differences. Part of it was temperamental. Human ingenuity can often find a way of overcoming formal defects in structure: but between Thomas and the advisory Ministers there soon developed such a lack of *rapport* as to bring to an end effective co-operation.

As early as 28 July Beatrice Webb was receiving complaints from Lord Arnold, the Paymaster-General, who

is in a great state of discontent with J. H. Thomas's incapacity as organiser of Employment. Oswald Mosley and Lansbury, his lieutenants, report that Thomas does not see them; but he is in the hands of that arch reactionary, Horace Wilson . . . whom he calls 'Orace' and obeys implicitly. That he refuses to sit down and study the plans proposed and therefore cannot champion them in the House. That he gets 'rattled' and when not under the influence of drink or flattery, is in an abject state of panic about his job. Arnold suggests a Governorship in Australia.[1]

Thomas's trip to Canada in the summer[2] did not improve matters. The advisory Ministers regarded it as a joy-ride which would accomplish nothing, an impression which was confirmed on his return. Nor was Thomas impressive as an executive. Committees which had been set up went for months without meeting, and when they did meet the results were often farcical.[3] Thomas gave no help or encouragement to the Retirement Pensions Committee; he rarely saw the advisory Ministers; memoranda went unread or unacknowledged. By 25 October Lansbury was complaining to Mosley:

I am really in despair about the whole business of unemployment. We all seem to be working in such an unco-ordinated way, and although the Privy Seal is looked upon as the co-ordinating authority, I really do not see it operating.[4]

On 2 November Mosley had luncheon with Beatrice Webb. Not surprisingly she found him 'contemptuous of Thomas's incapacity'. She herself noted perceptively that 'there is nothing wrong with the poor man except that there is nothing in him'.

Thomas's failure to produce any 'second instalment' of unemployment policy in the autumn exposed him to a severe attack from his own Party and the Liberals; he could not have been unaware of the opinions of his advisory Ministers. These pressures threatened to produce complete physical and mental collapse. Arthur Henderson, the Foreign Secretary, told Beatrice Webb that

[1] B. Webb Diaries, 28 July 1929. [2] See below, p. 101.
[3] See T. Johnston, *Memories*, 1952, pp. 105 ff. [4] Lansbury Papers, 19.d.177.

he is most concerned about Thomas, who is completely rattled and in such a state of panic, that he is bordering on lunacy.... The P.M. fears suicidal mania. The joy-ride to Canada has brought no result — except discredit ... [He] is too neurotic to take counsel ... regards all suggestions as accusations of failure.

Henderson at this stage was suggesting that the Prime Minister himself should take the matter in hand; should set up a committee of home defence against unemployment; should bring in Cole with a proper research department; should send Thomas away for a long rest and install Oswald Mosley under the committee to carry out agreed plans.[1]

iii. RETIREMENT PENSIONS COMMITTEE

One way Labour proposed to ease unemployment was by

... cutting off supplies to the labour market at both ends by raising the school leaving age and providing maintenance allowances and by giving more ample old-age pensions to men and women of sixty-five and if necessary sixty.[2]

On 29 June 1929 Thomas appointed a sub-committee to enquire into (*a*) retirement pensions for industrial workers and (*b*) the raising of the school-leaving age in relation to unemployment. The 'Old and Young Committee', as Mosley immediately dubbed it, was to consist of Lansbury (Chairman), Mosley and Johnston as its ministerial members, and one representative each from the Treasury, the Ministries of Health and Labour, the Board of Education, and the Scottish Office, plus the Government Actuary.[3] The Committee did not remain 'Old and Young' for long. On 17 July it was decided by the Cabinet 'that the question of raising the school leaving age should be dealt with entirely as an educational matter'. Hence there was no need for the sub-committee to give consideration to the 'Young'. Thomas, taking the cheerful view, concluded that this would give the Committee more time to spend on pensions.[4] In fact, the Ministry of Labour had already submitted evidence claiming that although 400,000 fourteen-year-olds would be withdrawn from the labour market if the school-leaving age were raised,

[1] B. Webb Diaries, 2 December 1929

[2] *Women and the General Election* (Election pamphlet), p. 51. See also *Labour and the Nation*, pp. 19, 27, 38.

[3] Lansbury Papers, 19.d.10.

[4] Ibid. 19.d.54.

the number of vacancies created for the adult unemployed would only number 85,000.[1]

The earliest discussions took place on procedure. The permanent officials prepared for the Committee a comprehensive questionnaire to be sent to two thousand firms and public authorities already known to have pension schemes in operation. Mosley opposed this on the grounds of 'too great a dissipation of departmental energy without any profitable results to justify it'. He prosposed instead 'questions addressed to a few big concerns, such as railways, enquiring the age and conditions of retirement and whether they possess any information of subsequent work undertaken by those retired'. The questionnaire should be short and simple.[2] Mosley's suggestion was accepted.

Meanwhile evidence had been received from the Ministry of Health on the difficulties of removing the aged from industry. If the pension were to be claimed by workers who had reached a certain age by a certain date, the 'sudden shrinkage of work' would cause grave dislocation. If the pension were paid as a flat rate, it would be too low to attract the highly paid and too high for the low-paid workers. It would lead to an agitation to raise the unemployment insurance benefits to the level of the new pensions. There would be countless administrative difficulties.[3]

This was discouraging: but more helpful was the support received from the General Council and other Labour organisations. The Labour Party had long been committed, in a rather nebulous way, to a scheme of retirement pensions. At the fourteenth joint committee meeting of the Mond–Turner group in July, Bevin came out strongly in favour of a retirement pensions plan.[4] The Committee decided to ask C. R. V. Coutts, 'an eminent actuary', to prepare a report on Bevin's proposals. Coutts calculated that to increase old age pensions all round from 10*s*. (the existing level under the Contributory Pensions Act of 1925) to 30*s*. a week would cost the Exchequer £60m a year — a prohibitive amount.

[1] Ministry of Labour, *The Effect of Raising the School Leaving Age to 15 on Unemployment*, Lansbury Papers, 19.d.37.

[2] Ibid. 19.d.32.

[3] Notes by Allan Young on Ministry of Health Memorandum, Ibid. 19.d.48.

[4] He had been urging the proposal since the previous November. (See Bullock, *The Life and Times of Ernest Bevin*. vol. i, pp. 402–3.)

If, on the other hand, the increased pension of thirty shillings a week were to be restricted to those over sixty-five still in employment, about 350,000, the problem would be more manageable. As there were roughly 350,000 unemployed under thirty-five years old, the success of the plan as a solution to unemployment clearly depended 'on how far the employed workers over sixty-five and the unemployed workers under thirty-five are distributed over the industrial field in the same proportions'.[1]

Coutts undertook to examine the distribution of the two groups (hereafter Groups A and B). His conclusions were depressing. Group A consisted largely of agricultural workers. Group B consisted largely of industrial workers. Moreover of the 350,000 in this category who were listed as unemployed a large proportion were 'casual' labourers — in other words they were in regular but not continuous employment, so that they would figure in the unemployment totals for the purposes of insurance, but would not be available for different types of work. Coutts' conclusion was that 'if the whole of Group A workers were to be retired from industry that would obviously create a demand for labour, but not in the industries nor in the areas where there are younger workers now wanting a job'.[2]

From Coutts' memorandum it followed that sixty-five was too late as a starting age. Also it became clear that any proposal for an all-round pensions increase to cover retrospectively all those already receiving pensions and to encompass all those who subsequently reached pensionable age (whatever that might be) would be too expensive. A limited scheme was clearly required; but a limited scheme gave rise to baffling problems of equity.

Throughout August and September Lansbury's committee battled with the problem. Lansbury has recalled the scene in his memoirs:

> The committee . . . met . . . in a sort of semi-dungeon high up in the Treasury offices. We were surrounded by the reputed *elite* of the Civil Service. . . . For the most part these expert gentlemen were dumb. . . . The Ministers did most of the talking. There was, however, always present one faithful watchdog who represented the Treasury.[3]

The composition of the Retirement Pensions Committee was indeed a curious one. It consisted of ministerial and non-ministerial members,

[1] Lansbury Papers, 19.d.71–3.
[2] Ibid. 19.d.75–8.
[3] Lansbury, *My England*, 1934, pp. 142–3.

who were not required to make positive recommendations, but merely to examine the possibilities. But as the summer wore on, a clear difference of opinion developed between the Ministers and the civil servants. The Ministers wanted retirement pensions and were convinced that they had found a feasible scheme. What the civil servants wanted is not clear: but they did not like the scheme the Ministers had hit on. They would not sign a report advocating its adoption. Normally such a situation would never have arisen: the names of the Ministers alone would have appeared on the report and it would have been their sole responsibility; then the civil servants could have drafted anything that the Ministers required of them. But in the circumstances of shared responsibility the civil servants did not feel they could go beyond the terms of reference which were simply to enquire into the matter.

The Committee decided to present two reports. The official report would be drawn up by the non-ministerial members of the committee, giving details of the four schemes considered, facts concerning cost and so on, plus a concluding section of 'general remarks' which would attempt to evaluate the merits of the various proposals. The Ministers would present a separate report, urging the acceptance of one of the four alternative schemes listed in the 'official report'.

This plan was decided upon in the latter part of September; Lansbury then wrote to Thomas explaining what had been agreed and urging him to support the Ministers' chosen scheme in the Cabinet.[1] The official report was ready by 21 October; the Ministers' report, drafted by Mosley, was ready by the twenty-second; once more Lansbury urged Thomas to champion it in the Cabinet. The two reports themselves were before the Cabinet by the end of October and were sent to the Treasury for detailed examination.[2]

The ministerial report recommended to the Cabinet scheme 'C' of the official report as 'an emergency plan to deal rapidly with the unemployment problem'. This scheme provided a pension of £1 a week for a man and ten shillings for his wife for all workers subject to unemployment insurance, plus railwaymen, if they had reached the age of sixty on an appointed day and were willing within a specified period (six months) to retire from industry. Assuming that 390,000 persons out of a possible 677,000 would take the pension, the cost would work out at £21,600,000

[1] Lansbury Papers, 19.d.180–2. [2] Ibid. 20.d.218 ff.

in the first year, falling to £10m in the course of five years.[1] Against this expenditure there would be a saving to the unemployment insurance fund of about £9m a year, leaving a net exchequer burden in the first year of about £12½m.[2] The ministerial report conceded that 'the figures are admittedly susceptible to a certain margin of error', but pointed out a 'happy feature' of the scheme that arose in consequence: 'The more who accept the pensions the more vacancies we create: the fewer who accept the pensions the smaller the cost.'

The estimate as to the number of vacancies that would be created by the retirement of 390,000 men varied as between the Ministers and civil servants. Lansbury in a letter to Thomas described the variation as 'ranging from 220,000, the lowest, up to 310,000 which is the highest'.[3] Mosley's estimate was 280,000.[4] The official estimate was 230,000.

Both the ministerial and official reports pointed to the cheapness of the scheme as a means of providing employment. For public works it was thought that £1m provided employment, direct and indirect, for 4,000 men. This meant that it cost £250 to employ a man for a year. Assuming that 280,000 men would be employed by the pensions scheme, the average net cost per person placed in employment would work out at £43; assuming 230,000 men, £60. Either way, it was less than a quarter of the cost of providing employment by public works. The ministerial report claimed, with some justification, that 'the . . . scheme here suggested is, in fact, by far the cheapest means yet devised of setting the unemployed to work'.[5]

A further point in favour of the scheme, brought out in both the official and ministerial reports, was that it would provide employment for men 'not in temporary artificial occupations outside their own trades (as in relief work), but in permanent occupation with normal industry'.[6] These were the advantages: the main objections concerned the equity of the proposals.

[1] Official Report, General Remarks, Lansbury Papers, 20.d.250.
[2] Ibid. 20.d.256–7.
[3] Lansbury to Thomas, 23 October 1929, Lansbury Papers, 20.d.233–4.
[4] Resignation speech, 239 H.C. Deb. c. 1361–2.
[5] Lansbury Papers, 20.d.223.
[6] Ministerial Report, Lansbury Papers, 20.d.223; also General Remarks, 20.d.257.

Before considering them, it is worth noting an important point brought out by the official report, namely how far a scheme which cut down the numbers of the unemployed, not by creating new jobs, but by increasing the numbers of state pensioners, could be regarded as a solution to unemployment. To this the Ministers merely argued that if some workers had to be maintained in idleness, better it should be the old than the young.[1] This was reasonable as far as it went, but it was difficult to avoid the impression of a mere juggling with figures.

More serious were the objections concerning the fairness of the scheme. Agricultural and domestic workers were to be excluded; so were the small shopkeepers and self-employed workers who were outside the scope of the Contributory Pensions Act. Their exclusion from the Act had been justified on the grounds that they had paid no contributions: but the new scheme was to be non-contributory. To these points, the Ministers made no effective reply.

An even more serious objection concerned the differentials between the old class of pensioner under the 1925 Act and the new class. In 1928 some 80,000 workers over sixty-five had retired on the pension of ten shillings a week offered by the Contributory Pensions Act. 'Are these persons to see their neighbours who remained a little longer in industry now pensioned off with thirty shillings a week?' And what of the claims of men and women who reached the age of sixty after the appointed day? The only answer could be that this was a strictly limited scheme designed to achieve a strictly limited objective, but 'such an answer may not be regarded as conclusive by the man who sees his fellow workman who is just over sixty pensioned off with thirty shillings a week for life while he being just under sixty can only look forward to ten shillings at sixty-five with a further ten shillings when his wife reaches that age. . . .'[2]

Despite these objections, the official report did not end on a critical note. 'The real value of the proposal', it concluded,

> is to be found in the moral and economic advantage of replacing old people in industry, who have passed most of their life in hard work and would now welcome a rest, by young men and women who have been striving for years to find a proper outlet for their energies.

---

[1] Lansbury Papers, 20.d.226.

[2] Ibid. General Remarks, 20.d.255.

These positive merits were not sufficient to recommend the hard work of the Retirement Pensions Committee to the Cabinet. Without Thomas's support and in face of an adverse treasury report, the proposals were doomed. The Cabinet finally rejected them in December.

iv. THE LORD PRIVY SEAL IN CANADA

In his opening statement in the Commons, Thomas announced his intention of visiting Canada shortly after the end of the parliamentary session. The purpose of the trip would be to discuss emigration.[1] The Canadian Government, in welcoming the visit, hoped that it would lead to an extension of the 'three thousand family scheme', a project launched in 1924 with the object of settling British unemployed families on the land in Canada.[2] Speaking at the end of July, Thomas confirmed that he was going to Canada to 'discuss questions of migration on the spot'.[3]

It is hard to see why Thomas so soon after his appointment as 'Minister of Employment' should have been keen to go to Canada to discuss what was, after all, a very marginal problem. Even if migration, as he said, was something that 'has to be negotiated on the spot',[4] a junior Minister or departmental official could easily have been sent. In any case, Australia offered much better prospects for emigration than Canada: not only were more people going there, but emigration was also expanding at a faster rate. Moreover, the 'three thousand family scheme' had not been particularly successful; within a few years, 25 per cent of the families had withdrawn from the scheme, either to drift to the towns or to return to England.

However, it was soon clear that there was more to the trip than just emigration. Whether fresh objectives developed after the original decision had been taken, or whether Thomas was just keeping quiet about them, is unclear. Just before he left he said he was going to 'improve the trade relations between Great Britain and Canada and to investigate the subject of emigration'. It would be a mission, he announced, which would 'benefit the Empire as a whole'.[5]

[1] 229 H.C. Deb. c. 109. [2] *The Times*, 5 July 1929. [3] Ibid. 29 July.
[4] 229 H.C. Deb. c. 109. [5] *The Times*, 10 August 1929.

It was natural, in view of its analysis, that the export trade should be uppermost in the Government's mind. It was also natural that Thomas should have the Empire in his. His party included three Welsh coal manufacturers, a shipowner from Cardiff and the deputy manager of the Great Western Railway.[1] He went to try to improve Britain's exports to Canada of coal, steel and motor cars. Yet Britain's trade with Canada as a whole was negligible. Her exports to the Dominion amounted to less than 5 per cent of her total exports. It is true that they had risen by almost 1 per cent between 1926 and 1929, but this was largely due to increased sales in alcohol consequent upon American prohibition. Perhaps it was the negligible quantity involved that impressed Thomas with the possibility of expansion. But the reason why Canada did not buy goods from England was simple: America was much nearer and it cost much less to get goods from America than from England. Rarely was there a less promising outlook for a mission.

Thomas reached Quebec on 16 August. On arrival he said, 'I am going to see everybody who is worth seeing and talking to'. His passage had been pleasant — 'on board ship they tell of the witty speeches he made during the crossing'.[2] Arriving at Ottawa next day he revealed for the first time 'an ambitious scheme for expanding the market for British coal in Canada'.[3]

In Ottawa Thomas met Forke, Minister of Immigration. The outlook was unpromising. Union leaders objected to increased immigration. However, Thomas did arrange for 3,000 single men to go to Canada to work on the land the following spring, after suitable training in England. This was the sum of his achievements in the field of emigration. After a further morning of conferences with the Finance and Trade Ministers, he left for Montreal.

By this time he had abandoned emigration as 'an unfruitful field for discussion'.[4] Instead he concentrated on trade. In Montreal he had conferences with bankers, railwaymen and businessmen. He pointed out that whereas Britain bought half of Canada's wheat exports, Canada bought three times as many raw materials and manufactured products from the United States as from the mother country. This was unfair.

[1] *Manchester Guardian*, 21 September 1929.
[2] *Toronto Globe*, 17 August 1929. [3] *The Times*, 19 August 1929.
[4] *The Times*, 22 August 1929.

'The problem of our unemployed at home can be helped very materially by larger purchases being made in the Old Country.' Here was an opportunity for Canadians to show 'the old pioneer spirit of Imperialism that made the Empire great'.[1]

On to Toronto and more dinners and more speeches: Canada should buy from Britain 'as good business, not charity'. If the Empire was not worth doing a little to support there was no use waving the flag.[2] John Bull was very far from being down and out, he told the Canadian directors; and Snowden at the Hague had shown that 'patriotism is not the monopoly of a class'.[3]

Early in September Thomas set out west. In Winnipeg he conferred with Sir Henry Thornton, president of the Canadian National Railways, and also with officials of the Wheat Pool. He thought there was a chance of reducing freight charges by guaranteeing two-way cargoes for ships — coal to Canada and wheat to Britain. He arranged for officials of the Wheat Pool to meet him on his return to London. In Winnipeg, Elmer Davis, vice-president of the Canadian Manufacturers Association, struck a chillier note. He wanted to tell the Old Country manufacturers: 'You have got to supply the goods wanted in the form wanted . . . the goods sent out here are not what we require.' He also pointed out realistically that the development of new trade and markets would take a long time.[4]

Thomas was not discouraged. After his heavy travelling he took a few days' holiday with Thornton at Minaki, touring the famous Jasper Park in the traditional cowboy costume.[5] Refreshed, he returned to Winnipeg where he succeeded in getting his first conditional promise, from Beatty, president of the Canadian Pacific Railways, to 'consider the purchase of Welsh coal for use in Canada if its cost compared favourably with that of the United States, but it would not be used to supplant Canadian coal'.[6]

Before sailing home on the *Duchess of Atholl*, Thomas addressed a luncheon of the Ottawa Canadian Club. His parting Imperial appeal was marked by a slight touch of asperity, induced perhaps by its failure to

[1] *Toronto Globe*, 21 August 1929. [2] *The Times*, 2 September 1929.
[3] *Toronto Globe*, 2 September 1929. [4] *Toronto Globe*, 3 September 1929.
[5] Fuller, *The Life Story of the Rt. Hon. J. H. Thomas*, 1933, p. 221.
[6] *The Times*, 10 September 1929.

evoke a practical response. 'Britain', he declared, 'had poured money into Canada when no one would touch her and the opportunity had now come, when the Mother Country was faced by an economic problem . . . for the Canadians to show their gratitude by diverting business to her.'[1] Thus ended the Canadian visit of, in Thomas's words, 'the first British Cabinet Minister to have transformed himself into a commercial traveller'.[2]

Thomas had been absent from Britain for nearly six weeks, at a time when the Government might have been expected to exert its maximum effort to find work for the unemployed. What exactly had he accomplished?

To the press on his return he announced that he was 'completely satisfied' with the results of his trip. 'Definite negotiations on prices, both for steel and coal' had taken place 'with those directly concerned'. Trial cargoes had been ordered. Questioned about steel Thomas replied waggishly, 'I have got a lot of things up my sleeve'.[3] A few days after his return he was more explicit:

> I am happy in the knowledge that some of [the unemployed] will earn their Christmas dinner this year. That will be my best reward. I have created an atmosphere for the Old Country in Canada.[4]

Asked for definite information he replied that nothing could be revealed publicly before he had reported to Parliament. In the meantime he received deputations of coal, steel and motor-car manufacturers, anxious to know what the Lord Privy Seal had accomplished on their behalf. They came and went in conditions of 'highest secrecy'. Then they went and came no more.[5]

V. THE PUBLIC WORKS PROGRAMME

The Government's public works programme rested upon the initiative of the local authorities: it was their responsibility to initiate and to

[1] *The Times*, 11 September 1929.

[2] On his return he was asked to become an Honorary Associate Member of the National Union of Commercial Travellers.

[3] *The Times*, *Manchester Guardian*, 19 September 1929.

[4] *The Times*, 24 September 1929.

[5] *Manchester Guardian*, 24, 27 September and 23 October 1929.

execute schemes. The Government merely provided a proportion of the cost.[1] Two government agencies were mainly responsible for the administration of this assistance: the Unemployment Grants Committee and the Ministry of Transport. The latter dealt with roads; the former covered everything else. The scale of the works, and hence the employment they would provide, depended upon the rate of grant, and the conditions on which the grant was made available. The speed with which they could be started depended upon how long it took the U.G.C. and the Ministry of Transport to 'clear' the schemes presented and the local authorities to obtain the necessary legislative powers to start them. The Labour Party, as we have seen, believed that the local authorities should retain some share of responsibility for public works in the interests of local democracy.

The U.G.C. was almost moribund when the Labour Government took office. Between 1926 and 1929 it had sanctioned only £6m worth of schemes, compared to over £100m in the previous six years. The starting of 'transfer' grants in 1928 had produced a small revival, but far short of what the Labour Government hoped to achieve. Nevertheless, the Government scarcely improved the rate of subsidy. Between 1920 and 1928 the treasury contribution, mainly in the form of contributions towards loan repayment, had averaged 35 per cent of the total cost. Between June 1929 and July 1930 it averaged 38 per cent.[2] This set a firm limit to any expansion of the public works programme. On 1 July 1929, Snowden had sanctioned a road programme of £37½m to be spread over five years. £9½m was for trunk roads and £28m for all other roads, locks, bridges, canals, etc. In addition there was a small 'annual' programme of miscellaneous road works. The government contribution

[1] The Government also assisted public utilities through the Duckham Committee; here the initiative was to come from the public utility in question.

[2] The details of the treasury contribution to U.G.C. schemes was as follows:

		%			%
Non-Revenue Schemes:	transfer	63	*Revenue Schemes:*	transfer	33
	non-transfer	44		non-transfer	26
				others	40

Non-revenue schemes were defined as those producing a negligible return on investment (e.g. cemeteries, wash-houses, sewers); hence local authorities were given more generous help with their loan repayments.

was met from the road fund which accrued from motor vehicle licences. It was more generous than for U.G.C. works, amounting to about 50 per cent of the total cost: for trunk roads, the proportion was as high as 75 per cent. The main change from previous practice was that the Government was committed for five years instead of for one; but the actual amount it was prepared to make available in any one year differed little from the annual sums being spent on roads under the previous Conservative Government, and again there was a sharp limit on any expansion of the road programme.

What the Government did do was to ease the conditions for receipt of grants: this applied equally to U.G.C. and road schemes. From 1925 grants which did not involve importing labour — 'non-transfer' grants — could be made only to those areas where unemployment averaged 15 per cent in any one year. This requirement was now reduced to 10 per cent. The requirement of 50 per cent imported labour for 'transfer' grants was also dropped in favour of a more flexible approach, though a certain proportion of imported labour was still insisted on. By these means the Government hoped to stimulate applications. But a large number of authorities where unemployment did not come to 10 per cent, but which could not contemplate importing 'transferred' labour, still remained ineligible for grant.

Nor did the Government do much to speed up the start of the schemes. The existing procedure was that the local authority first of all had to submit its plans to the U.G.C., or the Ministry of Transport, or occasionally the Ministry of Health, who would consider them in the light of the conditions on which grants were made and from the point of view of their social and economic utility. A scheme which had passed this hurdle would then be considered from the constructional and engineering point of view. Plans might require modification: and a lengthy correspondence might hold up matters for weeks or months. Even final sanction did not lead to immediate commencement. For many of the larger schemes, the local authority did not have the statutory power to employ additional men or requisition land. In order to secure this power it had to promote a parliamentary private Bill. The only time it could do this was in December. Thus between June and December 1929 the U.G.C. sanctioned about £12½m worth of schemes; but practically no additional work could be provided for the winter. By 30 November

£25m of the £37½m promised for the road programme had been sanctioned, £9m for trunk roads and £15½m for the remainder. Yet by February 1930 less than four thousand men altogether were employed on road schemes, and most of these were on schemes taken over from the Conservatives. The Government made little effort to improve this: the most Thomas would do was to speed up a little the private Bill procedure. The activists in the Ministry chafed at these obstacles. Sir Oswald Mosley first of all tried exhortation. Throughout the summer he was busy seeing deputations from local authorities, explaining to them the new terms and conditions, urging them to present schemes. He was appalled by the ignorance and lethargy of the local officials. In September he set off on a speaking tour to 'ginger up' the localities. Speaking at Newport on 8 September he urged electors to enquire what the local authorities were doing. 'Every citizen', he urged, 'should enrol himself in the great national army that is fighting unemployment.' He asked local councils to 'formulate and expedite their plans for the consideration of the Committee'.[1] With an eye to the forthcoming municipal elections of 1 November, he advised electors to 'return councillors who are energetic and prepared to support large local plans for dealing with unemployment'.

He was, however, compelled to admit that local authority apathy was merely one, and possibly the least important, reason for delay. It was very difficult for local authorities to borrow money, even with the Government promising to help with repayment. In the depressed areas where unemployment was highest, their credit had already been exhausted. The only solution to their problems was for the Government to increase the rate of subsidy.

For example, the Government might have stepped up the *standard* rate of grant to the *maximum* — 63 per cent for non-revenue 'transfer' schemes. But this was prevented by the need to offer an additional inducement to local authorities to accept 'transferred' labour into their areas. This dictated the maintenance of a differential between 'transfer' and 'non-transfer' grants. As it was, the local authorities, even in relatively prosperous areas, were very reluctant to import unemployed men from the depressed areas. Lansbury complained to Thomas on 7 November that the London authorities 'absolutely refuse to consider

[1] *Labour Press Service Bulletin*, 19 September 1929.

transfer to London in any circumstances'. But Thomas was adamant: in that case they would not get the grant.[1] A possible solution might have been to increase the 'transfer' grant to, say, 80 per cent, thus enabling the 'non-transfer' grant to be upped to 60 per cent. But this, it was felt, would be encroaching too far on local authority responsibility for 'local works'.

It became increasingly plain that there could be no solution to this dilemma within the structure of a local authority public works programme. The omnibus solution favoured by Mosley was to take a bloc of the public works policy — road construction — right out of local authority competence and make it a state responsibility. Mosley, like Lloyd George, was impressed by the employment possibilities offered by a big road programme. The Government would assume complete financial responsibility which would increase the scale of the programme. As each local authority would no longer have to acquire special powers in order to construct its own few miles of road, there would be much less delay in getting the schemes started. Transferred labour would be employed directly on the national road plans, thus removing local authority fears of having to support additional unemployment in their own areas. At the same time, because there would be no need to pay the wealthier authorities a 'transfer premium' the level of grant to the depressed areas could be raised as high as was necessary to evoke an expansion of the remainder of the public works programme.

As early as 24 September Mosley was writing to MacDonald:

> the present non-transfer terms . . . entail a big burden on the rates which depressed areas cannot support and have led to a virtual cessation of schemes in South Wales.

In a memorandum of 17 October written jointly with Johnston he stated that 'on the basis of present policy no substantial improvement leading to a further acceleration of work plans [can] be achieved'. The only solution was to employ transferred men on national schemes.[2]

Three objections were advanced to national road schemes. First, government responsibility might cut out some of the delay, but not all that much. This point was to be put forcibly by Sir Henry Maybury, chief engineering consultant to the Ministry of Transport, and others

[1] Lansbury Papers, 20.d.267–72. [2] Ibid. 20.d.212–4.

throughout the life of the Government. It echoed the objections to Lloyd George's trunk road programme.[1] Second, if the Government started and financed national schemes, would the local authorities be prepared to proceed with their own works and continue to find a share of the cost? Third, national road schemes would destroy the delicate division of responsibility between the Government and local authorities. Herbert Morrison, the Minister of Transport, who was himself pressing for an expansion of the road programme within the existing local authority framework, was already worried by the large government contribution to the local authority road schemes: pushing the burden entirely on to the Exchequer, he argued, would be bad for 'good government'.[2] Sir Horace Wilson suggested that this third objection might be met by constructing roads nationally and then handing them over to the local authorities for maintenance. This was the argument adopted by Mosley but with little effect.[3]

Mosley's demands irritated Morrison, who wrote a little later to Thomas of

> the interesting but rather wearisome debates and cross-examinations on the Committee on National Schemes. Clearly Mosley suffers somewhat from L.G.'s complaint: the road complex. A road is a means of transport: road work can assist, but it cannot possibly be a principal cure of immediate unemployment. Road transport must be considered in relation to other forms of transport. There should be and there is no bias in the department.[4]

vi. PREPARING THE COAL BILL

The King's Speech assigned priority to the need to reorganise the coal, iron and steel, and cotton industries in order to 'improve their position in the markets of the world'.[5] This followed from Labour's analysis that the solution of the unemployment problem lay in the revival of the basic export industries, and that rationalisation was the only way to secure this revival. Yet rationalisation as a solution for unemployment was bound to

[1] See below, pp. 218, 222–3.
[2] 231 H.C. Deb. c. 720–1.
[3] Mosley to Thomas, 3 September 1929. Lansbury Papers, 19.d.132–4.
[4] 2 February 1930. Thomas as a railwayman was equally opposed to the Mosley 'complaint'.
[5] 229 H.C. Deb. c. 48–9.

be long-term; its short-term result was likely to be more unemployment. Hence it was regarded with great suspicion by the trade unions who tended to attribute unemployment itself to the inexorable replacement of men by machinery. The trade unions were not opposed to *rationalisation* provided it was coupled with *nationalisation*, or with government provision for displaced labour.[1] Nationalisation was ruled out by the political position; while the provision of alternative jobs was not something the Government was prepared to contemplate.

The coal industry provides an interesting case study of the difficulties in imposing government 'reorganisation' as part of an unemployment policy. Coal and cotton were the mainstays of the export trade before the First World War. Both had suffered heavily in the post-war struggle for markets. The loss of coal markets produced the most bitter industrial clashes of the nineteen-twenties. The owners were determined to recover their position by cutting wages. Despite the failure of the General Strike the miners resisted with surprising success: although wages came down, it was not by much. In the late nineteen-twenties neither side was prepared to face a repetition of the struggle, and there was a tacit acceptance of a wages *status quo*. One consequence of the General Strike, however, the miners were not prepared to accept as permanent. This was the addition of one hour to the working day. Labour came to office in 1929 pledged to restore the working day to seven hours. It was thus bound to become involved in the affairs of the coal industry.

Yet it was clear that cutting the working day would only add to the difficulties of the industry. The King's Speech recognised this. The relevant paragraph promised to consider 'the question of the reorganisation of the coal industry, including hours and other factors, and of the ownership of minerals'. In other words reorganisation would be the offset to the shortening of hours.

The question was, what type of reorganisation? There were two possible models. On the one hand, the Government could follow the advice of the Samuel Report to concentrate production into larger units, eliminate the inefficient pits and rationalise transport arrangements. This would have gained the support of the Liberals, but not of the coal owners, a number of whom would certainly suffer in consequence. The alternative was to give statutory recognition to regional experiments

[1] See *T.U.C. Annual Report*, 1929, pp. 424 ff.

of groups of owners started in 1928, of which the Five Counties Scheme was the most extensive. These relied mainly on quota systems to avoid overproduction at home and maintain internal prices, and on a levy to subsidise export prices, the levy being in effect a tax on the domestic user of coal. Of the two alternatives, only the first really represented 'rationalisation'. Yet its difficulties were apparent. The miners did not want pits to close, thus throwing more people out of work; the owners resented the idea of compulsory amalgamations which might eventually improve the efficiency of the industry but would do nothing immediately to help exports and profits.

A Cabinet Committee was set up under Graham, President of the Board of Trade, to prepare the necessary legislation. Members included Thomas, Miss Bondfield and Ben Turner, Secretary for Mines. The Prime Minister also attended from time to time. The Committee negotiated with two sets of people — the Miners Federation, led by Herbert Smith and A. J. Cook, and the employers' Mining Association represented by Evan Williams, Adam Nimmo and W. A. Lee. The two groups, with bitter memories of industrial strife behind them, refused to meet the Cabinet Committee together or even to see each other, which did not help matters. In addition, Herbert Smith was notoriously inflexible in discussion — a characteristic also shared by the employers' representatives. Only A. J. Cook proved unexpectedly pliable.[1]

At the first meeting of the coal committee with the Miners Federation MacDonald bluntly explained the situation. The employers had told him that the cost of restoring the working day to seven hours would mean 2*s.* on each ton of coal, which would force them to ask for 20 per cent wage reductions. Any attempt to restore the pre-1926 working day would probably bring down the Government. 'Would that help us or you?' the Prime Minister asked.[2]

The intractable nature of the problem confronting the Cabinet Committee emerged only too clearly. The Miners Federation were holding out for a seven-hour day and a guarantee against wage reductions in the form of national agreements and a National Wages Board. The

[1] For an account of the discussions see MacDonald's statement in the House, 233 H.C. Deb. c. 1772; for Cook's attitude, the *Annual Conference Report of the Miners Federation*, 1929, pp. 67–70, 101.

[2] Miners Federation *Annual Conference Report*, pp. 67–8.

owners would accept at most a half hour reduction in the working day; and that only at the price of national quota systems, an export levy and freedom to reduce wages if necessary. They would have preferred no government legislation at all. The Liberals, on the other hand, were pressing rationalisation of the Samuel Report type.[1]

The summer and autumn passed by in long and tedious negotiations, as repeated efforts were made to frame a measure to please everyone. Whatever his other virtues, Graham was not a forceful personality, and there was almost no progress. From time to time Thomas assisted, but he proved to be a broken reed. The only person who could have resolved the deadlock was MacDonald; but he was otherwise occupied during the summer, and at the end of September he left for a month's journey to America and Canada in search of naval disarmament.

The original intention had been to introduce a Coal Bill in mid-November and take it through all the committee stages before the Christmas recess; but by the end of October agreement was no nearer. The main difficulty between the miners and owners was the wages problem. The miners wanted national agreements; the owners' representatives argued that the Mining Association 'existed merely to arrange certain legal matters connected with the industry' and had no power to negotiate a national agreement.[2] On 29 October the Government circulated a draft Bill to both sides for comment. It proposed (1) the reduction of hours to seven and a half from 6 April as a first instalment of a gradual reduction to seven hours, (2) national and district quota schemes, (3) a national levy to subsidise exports. There were also proposals for the nationalisation of minerals and the gradual acquisition of royalties, which would form a separate Bill. It omitted all reference to the points at issue between the miners and owners: there was no safeguard for miners' wages, and no promise of national agreements. As envisaged in the government draft the Bill was to be a deal between the miners and the owners: the miners got their reduction, and in return the owners' marketing schemes were to be put on a statutory basis. There was no mention of rationalisation or compulsory amalgamations; yet presumably Liberal support would be needed to get the Bill through the Commons, as the Conservatives were bound to oppose those sections shortening hours.

[1] *Manchester Guardian*, 25 July 1929. [2] *Morning Post*, 27 August 1929.

The draft proposals were considered inadequate by both sides. The owners were against the reduction in hours, but were determined to reduce wages if it came into force. The miners wanted protection for wages and a reduction in working time (some of them, led by Herbert Smith, would settle for nothing less than seven hours). There seemed little hope of agreement. The *Manchester Guardian* confessed to 'serious disappointment that the Cabinet should take such a limited view of its opportunity and the uses to which a progressive majority in the House of Commons can be turned'. It realised that the quota schemes were directly opposite in tendency to the Samuel Report's plea for concentrating production in larger units; rather they would preserve the life of the inefficient pit.[1]

vii. UNEMPLOYMENT INSURANCE

The 'not genuinely seeking work' clause was proving just as intractable as miners' hours. In 1924, as we have seen, the Labour Government had misguidedly applied it as a test to all claimants for unemployment benefit, not just those on the 'dole' scheme. In the next few years its administration had been so tightened up that the number of disallowances had risen from 27,000 in 1927 to 251,000 in 1929: hence Labour clamour for its abolition.[2] The new stringency had been dictated by the Government's economy drive in 1926–7 and had been made possible by the administrative changes recommended in the Blanesburgh Report, introduced in 1928. The effect of these was to transfer the adjudication of doubtful claims from the local committees to the Chief Insurance Officer's department at Kew: thus no considerations of local sentiment or compassion were to upset the application of the stricter policy. From 1928 onwards, the applicant had to set out on his claim form the 'steps he had taken to find work' so that the officer could judge the 'genuineness' of his claim to be seeking work. These steps had to include going the rounds of the factories and firms applying for jobs, even when the unemployed worker knew that there were no jobs available. For in the

[1] *Manchester Guardian*, 14 November 1929.

[2] Ministry of Labour, *Annual Reports*, 1927–9, pp. 113, 113–15, 124–6.

nineteen-twenties, only a minority of employers were in the habit of notifying job vacancies at the local Labour exchanges.

Miss Bondfield had appointed the Morris Committee to consider what legislative changes were necessary to give effect to the Government's promise to abolish the 'not genuinely seeking work' clause. In the meantime she tried to soften its administration by reverting as far as possible to the procedure before 1928. On 9 September 1929, she reintroduced a local assessors' board to consider doubtful claims, on the discretion of the local insurance officer. In her autobiography Miss Bondfield noted: 'I had greatly softened the impact of a cruel and troublesome method.'[1] Further than this she could not go. In a letter to her constituents at Wallsend she wrote: 'I soon discovered that there was practically nothing I could do without breaking the law.'[2]

The Morris Committee, appointed on 25 July, had two Labour representatives: Arthur Hayday, M.P. for Nottingham West and soon to be president of the T.U.C., and Mrs. A. Adams, a Labour councillor. It held six sittings and presented its report on 24 October.

In its evidence, the General Council of the T.U.C. made it clear that it was entirely opposed to the 'not genuinely seeking work' provision. It rejected the principle that an applicant 'having established unemployment and availability for work, should also be called upon to prove that he is not a malingerer'. An investigation into the 'state of the applicant's mind' was a a task for a psychologist, not the Chief Insurance Officer. The sole ground for disqualification should be the exchange's proof that a claimant was 'definitely offered suitable employment and had refused it'. This came to be known as the Hayday Formula.

The employers' organisations, on the other hand, argued that the N.G.S.W. clause was an essential part of the unemployment insurance system, preserving it from the abuse of the work-shy.

The Morris Committee inclined to the General Council's view but was reluctant to accept the Hayday Formula as the sole test, for it did

[1] *A Life's Work*, p. 281.

[2] *Manchester Guardian*, 21 October 1929. Miss Bondfield also set up retraining schemes. Her efforts to train the unemployed to be hairdressers, waiters and domestic servants were the subject of a biting and amusing attack by John Scanlon, in *The Decline and Fall of the Labour Party*, 1932, pp. 145–6.

not cover the possibility that the claimant might *know* of the existence of suitable work even if he had not been offered it. So in addition to the Hayday Formula it recommended that a claimant should be disqualified if there was 'evidence that suitable work was available and [the claimant] fails to prove that he had made reasonable efforts to obtain such work'.[1] *Industrial News*, the organ of the General Council, observed that the new formula was 'very indefinite and might lead to all sorts of difficulties'. The *New Leader* of 1 November was more explicit. The report's recommendation on the fourth statutory condition was 'of such a character as to make it inevitable that the worst features of the present system will continue'.

[1] *Morris Report*, para. 43. The two Labour members signed a minority report.

6

FIRST FALTERING STEPS

i. INTRODUCTION

By the autumn of 1929 there were signs that all was not well with the international economy. American lending which had largely financed German recovery and which largely enabled debtors all over the world to maintain a precarious stability, was greatly reduced in 1929 as more and more funds were diverted to the New York stock exchange boom.[1] The reparations tangle at The Hague demonstrated to the world the extent to which France was prepared to use its powerful creditor position to pursue political aims. A French-engineered 'flight from the mark' in the spring and summer of 1929, clearly designed to secure German compliance with French demands, threatened the structure of German finance; and French withdrawals from London between July and October may perhaps be partly explained as a reaction to Snowden's anti-French stand at the Hague, though there were perfectly legitimate seasonal causes. The exodus of gold to New York and Paris underlied the weakness of London's exchange position and nearly forced Britain off the gold standard.[2] On 20 September, following the Hatry scandal,[3] Bank Rate was raised to 6½ per cent and there were

[1] Exports of capital from the U.S.A. declined from $1099 million in 1928 to $206 million in 1929; France which had exported $503 million in 1927 and $237 million in 1928 became a net importer in 1929. (League of Nations, *World Economic Survey*, 1931–2, p. 39.)

[2] Montagu Norman told the Committee of the Treasury on 5 August that unless there was a change, especially in France and the U.S.A., part of Europe, including the U.K., might be forced off the gold standard. (Clay, *Lord Norman*, p. 252).

[3] Clarence Hatry was a London financier who controlled a number of investment trusts and had interests in slot machines and cameras. The

rumours that American credits were to be obtained to defend sterling. The New York stock exchange crash of 23 October 1929 ended the monetary crisis by bringing back to Europe the funds that had sought large killings across the Atlantic, though it inaugurated the far more serious world economic crisis that was to dominate men's thoughts and lives for the next five years.[1] However, although Bank Rate was able to come down to 3 per cent in gradual stages, the obvious vulnerability of sterling, even to moderate capital movements, increased the difficulties of attempting to combine a bold domestic unemployment policy with the maintenance of the gold standard; while the short, sharp crisis itself was a dress rehearsal for the larger one of 1931.

Nevertheless, the fright caused by these financial happenings did prompt Snowden to expedite that authoritative enquiry into monetary practice which had been urged from the time of the Mond–Turner conferences in 1928. On 4 November he announced the setting up of the Macmillan Committee on Finance and Industry

> to enquire into banking, finance and credit, paying regard to the factors both internal and international which govern their operation, and to make re-

---

immediate cause of his collapse was his decision to buy United Steel and use it as the basis of a financial merger of the British steel industry. Unable to raise the whole of the £8m needed to complete the purchase, Hatry resorted to issuing scrip certificates in excess of the registered shares of his companies and used these as collaterals to obtain loans. This fraud failed to secure the solvency of his group, and shares finally collapsed on 20 September. Investigations revealed the extent of the fraud — over £2m was involved — and Hatry and his leading associates received heavy prison sentences.

[1] The Stock Exchange collapse was both effect and cause. Indices of American industrial and factory production had begun a steady decline from June 1929, following the end of the building boom. This recession was bound to have an effect on the stock market, the prosperity of which was itself an exaggerated symptom of the industrial boom of 1927–9. The fairly orderly reduction of share prices which took place throughout September and early October was probably sufficient to destroy the almost invincible confidence in ever rising share prices upon which the market boom had been based. However, the crash also accelerated and deepened the depression by frightening investors, and bankrupting financial institutions as debtors defaulted. A wave of bank failures increased hoarding, slowed down the rate of transactions and thus reinforced the other factors dragging down the economy. For the best account of the events of October 1929, see J. K. Galbraith, *The Great Crash*, 1955.

commendations calculated to enable these agencies to promote the development of commerce and the employment of labour.

Although the composition of the Committee was such as to ensure a fairly authoritative report, its terms of reference suggested that it would be long in coming out: and so it proved.[1]

ii. PARLIAMENT REASSEMBLES

Parliament reassembled at the beginning of November and on 4 November Thomas gave the House an account of his stewardship. The U.G.C. had approved schemes totalling £11m; the Duckham Committee (advising on the Home Development Act), £7m; of the £37½m allowed for the road programme, £21m had been sanctioned; finally there had been a grant of £3m for building a bridge across the Zambezi; making in all a total of £42m. This, Thomas calculated, would provide 1,400,000 man-months of employment.

Thomas then referred to Canada. 'As a result of the visit', he declared, 'a contract for five 7,000 ton ships to deal with the coal next year alone is being negotiated'.[2] There was no mention of trial cargoes or definite orders for coal; just one or two vague remarks such as

> I say without fear of contradiction that, whatever may be said to the contrary, the difficulty about hard coal next year will not, so far as Canada is concerned, be to get customers, but will be to supply the demand.

Negotiation for five 7,000-ton ships was thus the sum of Thomas's achievements. In time even they came to be mentioned less and less. As Wheatley finally put it they were 'the ships that pass in the night'.[3]

To be fair to Thomas, he could hardly have accomplished anything

[1] Lord Macmillan was a judge; there were two professional economists, Keynes and T. E. Gregory; four bankers, R. H. Brand, Reginald McKenna, C. Lubbock and A. A. G. Tulloch; three industrialists, L. B. Lee, Sir W. Rume and J. Frater Taylor; two Labour representatives, Ernest Bevin and Sir Thomas Allen; Lord Bradbury, ex-Treasury, and J. Walton Newbold, ex-Communist.

[2] 231 H.C. Deb. c. 675.

[3] 233 H.C. Deb. c. 1808.

more, especially since he did not carry imperial preference, the one thing that would have interested the Canadians, in his traveller's bag. He was not criticised for what he accomplished or failed to accomplish, but for going on such a small errand in the first place. As Lloyd George put it on 4 November, he was:

> like a commander-in-chief at the beginning of a campaign leaving his head-quarters and the campaign to be thought out and directed by subordinates on the staff, whilst he goes off to some remote corner in order to attend to some minor operation. . . .[1]

Thomas had claimed that the £42m worth of unemployment schemes would provide 1,400,000 'man months' of work. What he meant was that if the £42m were spent in one month 1,400,000 men would be employed. However, no one intended that it should be spent in one month or even one year; rather it would be spread over three to five years, possibly even more. In other words, taking four years as an average, the employment provided, on the Government's own estimate, would be just under 30,000 men a year out of an unemployed population of 1,200,000.[2] When Thomas made his announcement none of the schemes had actually been started, nor would most of them be for months to come.

This time Thomas's proposals failed to win the assent of either of the opposition Parties. Broadly, while the Conservatives accused him of spending too much money, the Liberals said it was not enough — a discrepancy which was to furnish the Government with an easy debating point, but little parliamentary comfort.

We have seen that the Government had taken advantage of the loophole in the 'treasury view' that justified expenditure on public projects. Sir Laming Worthington-Evans for the Conservatives now attempted to plug it. The Government, he argued, were committed to the view that public expenditure must be productive; otherwise it would be money down the drain. The test then was whether Thomas's schemes were productive (i.e., would yield an economic return). It was perfectly true that the building of roads was in some sense productive as it facilitated traffic and reduced costs. But it was nothing like as productive as the manufacture of goods. This applied to Thomas's other

[1] 231 H.C. Deb. c. 693. [2] See *The Economist*, 9 November 1929.

schemes. Thomas had considerably over-estimated the amount of productive work that could be financed by public money; it followed that he was pouring away money which manufacturing industry would be only too happy to use. This was the orthodox 'treasury view' which the Government had never challenged.[1] Other Conservatives attacked the Government on different lines. Sir George Penny argued that the decline in the export trade was due to high costs caused in part by the burden of unemployment insurance and union restrictive practices. The Government should be dealing with these problems and also making every effort to expedite rationalisation.[2] Other Conservatives argued from the position that costs were too high relative to Britain's competitors to the remedy of protection to safeguard wages and profits from sweated labour and dumping. Among those who adopted this position was W. E. D. Allen, later to join Mosley's New Party.[3]

For the Liberals Lloyd George was at his brilliant and provocative best. Thomas had taunted him because he had said that the proposals were not sufficiently bold. 'Bold! They are timid, pusillanimous and unintelligent.'[4] The *Manchester Guardian* was to reinforce him on his charge of unintelligence. Unemployment was 'an intellectual problem first and an administrative one only second'.[5] A month later, with the publication of the government White Paper on unemployment, the *Manchester Guardian* elaborated this theme. Thomas 'did not speak like a man who has any grasp of the problems involved'. No one was asking for miracles but a *plan*, but 'his survey is mist and his future plans even more nebulous than his immediate ones'. 'When a Minister does not himself understand a problem he is helpless in the hands of very loyal, but it may be uncreative, officials.'[6] Both in public and private Liberals were saying that Thomas ought to be replaced.

There is little doubt that Thomas's statement was a disappointment, not only to the Liberals, but to government supporters likewise. As was to be expected the most bitter criticism came from the I.L.P. In the Commons on 4 November Maxton said:

[1] 231 H.C. Deb. c. 678–87.
[2] Ibid. c. 697–700.
[3] Ibid. c. 728, 740, 748–50.
[4] Ibid. c. 691.
[5] *Manchester Guardian*, 5 November 1929.
[6] *Manchester Guardian*, 11 December 1929.

One of my enthusiastic colleagues on these benches said that Labour was in for twenty years. Well, I hope so. God knows that at the rate of progress indicated in the Lord Privy Seal's speech they will need every minute of it![1]

The *New Leader* of 8 November stated that 'it is no use concealing any longer the fact that Mr. Thomas is coming to grief over his handling of unemployment'. The Glasgow *Forward* of 9 November noted: 'Could there have been anything more fiddling or footling than Mr. Thomas's expedition to Canada and the boasting of it as a great adventure to find the solution of the unemployment problem?' J. C. Welsh, M.P. for Paisley, Renfrew, summed up moderate Labour reactions:

It is admittedly a difficult problem. But why all the timidity when the country is expecting that something bold and big can ease the situation . . . I do feel there will be disappointment in the country over this statement by the Lord Privy Seal.[2]

The disappointment is easy to understand, the surprise less so. The Government, true to their analysis that unemployment could only be solved through the revival of the basic export industries, were pursuing the policy they had announced in the summer. That policy did not embrace a big government investment programme. 'Anybody can spend money', Thomas was fond of saying, 'but spending money is no cure for unemployment'. Thus there would be no attempt to provide employment 'artificially'. What the Government would do was to encourage the basic industries to make themselves more efficient: the Government's Coal Bill was due shortly and Thomas had plans to encourage rationalisation. The Government would also try to provide decently for the victims of capitalism: the Unemployment Insurance Bill was about to be published. For the mass of Labour M.P.s who saw no possible solution to unemployment except 'socialism', this was a far more legitimate concern for a Labour Government than the provision of 'artificial' work. It was by providing decently for the unemployed that Labour's leaders would show their practical commitment to socialism; for more constructive socialist legislation was clearly ruled out by the minority position. With this simple and *simpliste* analysis most Labour M.P.s were satisfied.

[1] 233 H.C. Deb. cc. 701–3. [2] *The Miner*, 9 November 1929.

iii. THE UNEMPLOYMENT INSURANCE (NO. 2) BILL

With the Morris Report ready, Miss Bondfield started to prepare her Unemployment Insurance (No. 2) Bill. There were two motives behind it. Firstly, there was the desire to give effect to the Labour pledge to improve the rates and conditions of benefit for the unemployed. Secondly, there was the need to put the unemployment fund on a more secure financial basis. That these two motives were ultimately to prove contradictory was not as yet apparent.

The proposed legislation was of great concern to the General Council of the T.U.C., and on 7 November a joint deputation from the General Council and the national executive committee of the Labour Party called on the Minister of Labour to hear her views and to put forward views of their own. They wanted the standard rate of benefit increased from seventeen to twenty shillings and the various dependants' allowances increased also; they asked for the inclusion within the scheme of agricultural workers and domestic servants, a reduction of the waiting period from six days to three, and — of course — the repeal of the obnoxious clause four (the N.G.S.W. clause). In addition, they wanted an investigation into 'the problems associated with casual, seasonal and part-time employment'.[1] Had the Government agreed to do this, it would have protected itself in advance from what was later to prove the most vulnerable point of attack on the structure of unemployment insurance.

Miss Bondfield replied that on financial grounds a Bill was immediately necessary and the financial situation limited what she could do. It was unthinkable to raise the contributions of employers and employees in the existing circumstances and the question therefore was: how much could she get out of the Treasury? The Bill was bound to be limited in scope, but the unions should not regard it as the last word of the Government. Larger questions concerning the structure of unemployment insurance would be the subject of a more comprehensive Bill later on.

Hayday then requested that the General Council be allowed to take part in the drafting of the Bill. This request was rejected by Miss Bondfield, who said that the responsibility for preparing legislation rested

[1] General Council Papers, File 157.83 d.

with the Government alone, and also that joint drafting would merely delay matters. The General Council's claim to partnership in the formation of industrial policy gives some ground for the opposition contention that any Labour Government would be subject to dictation from the trade union movement. Miss Bondfield was plainly embarrassed by Hayday's request, but in reality the General Council were not seeking such sweeping powers. They felt that the Labour movement was a partnership between the industrial and political wings and that such a partnership should continue when the political wing formed a Government.

After rejecting the General Council's request, Miss Bondfield relented to the extent of agreeing to the formation of a joint consultative committee to meet with her from time to time to discuss the progress of the Bill through the Commons.[1]

The text of the Unemployment Insurance (No. 2) Bill was published on 15 November. Like the Coal Bill which was to follow, it was a feat of balancing between conflicting claims and pressures. To satisfy in part Labour pledges, rates of benefit for certain categories were increased, though the standard rate of benefit for adults over twenty-one — the chief element in the unemployed worker's pay packet — was left unchanged: Snowden simply refused to produce the money.[2] The increases were expected to cost £2m.[3]

The new Bill followed the Morris report on the 'not genuinely seeking work' condition, embodying its two tests in the first section of the revised clause four:

[1] General Council Papers, File 157. 34.

[2] The new Bill increased the rates of benefit to men and women aged nineteen to twenty from twelve shillings and ten shillings to fourteen shillings and twelve shillings per week; for those aged eighteen to nineteen from ten shillings and eight shillings to fourteen shillings and twelve shillings; for those aged seventeen to eighteen from six shillings and five shillings to nine shillings and seven shillings and sixpence. For those aged sixteen to seventeen the rates remained at six shillings and five shillings. For those coming into insurance when the school-leaving age was raised to fifteen, the rate was fixed at six shillings and five shillings. Adult dependants' allowances went up from seven shillings to nine shillings. The children's allowance remained at two shillings.

[3] 232 H.C. Deb. c. 750–1.

If on a claim for benefit it is shown that the claimant, knowing that a specific situation in any employment, being employment which is suitable in his case, was or was about to become vacant, refused or neglected to apply for the situation or refused to accept it when offered to him, he shall be disqualified for benefit.

The Hayday Formula section of this clause was straightforward: a claimant would be denied benefit if he refused an offer of suitable work. But what test was to be applied to establish that a claimant 'knowing that a specific situation in any employment . . . was or was about to become vacant, refused or neglected to apply for the situation'? Section two of the new clause attempted to supply the answer:

If . . . it is shown that employment in the usual occupation of the claimant and of a kind suitable in his case was available . . . and that the claimant could reasonably have been expected to know that such employment was so available, the claimant shall, unless he shows that he has taken all such steps as (having regard to the means usually taken for such a purpose and to the extent to which such employment was available) he could reasonably be expected to take for the purpose of obtaining such employment, be disqualified from receiving benefit.[1]

This looked suspiciously like the old clause four in a new disguise. For the phrase 'means usually taken for such a purpose' could only be a reference to the type of test demanded as a proof of genuinely seeking work under the old clause: the number of calls made on firms in a given period, the names and addresses of such firms and other similar details. Nevertheless, Miss Bondfield undoubtedly believed that a considerable concession had been made; and the Government Actuary estimated that it would cost £3,250,000 per annum.[2]

The great concession had, in fact, been made not by the wording of the new clause, which was little improvement over the old one, but by the administrative changes in the method of adjudicating claims which came into force on 9 September.[3] The new Bill strengthened these changes, making it mandatory for the exchange officer to refer all disputed claims to the local court of referees (as the board of assessors was now called), whose decision would be binding. Having thus largely removed the grievances occasioned by the fourth statutory condition, why did Miss Bondfield prove so obdurate about the wording of the new

[1] A Bill to Amend the Unemployment Insurance Acts, 1920 to 1929. Ordered by the House of Commons to be printed 12 November 1929 (Bill 63).

[2] Cmd. 3437, para. 8.

[3] See above, p. 114.

clause itself? The Ministry of Labour was probably anxious to retain some test other than the Hayday Formula as a kind of residual power that could be evoked, by tighter administration, if it became obvious that people were claiming benefit as a soft option to seeking work. It was to prevent this that the unions were so anxious to fortify the administrative changes with legislative enactments.

The increases in benefit and changes in the method of judging claims were expected to cost £5½m. This was the additional money that would find its way into the pockets of the unemployed *from national funds*.[1] It was, in fact, an additional charge upon the unemployment fund. To enable it to meet that charge and also to give it an extra margin of security, the fund was relieved of its obligation to pay benefit to those who had fallen out of benefit, i.e. who no longer contributed to its income. As we have seen, it was this obligation that was the main cause of the fund's growing indebtedness. Under the new Bill, payment of 'transitional' benefit was transferred from the fund to the Exchequer. This was expected to save the fund and cost the Exchequer £8½m in the full financial year 1930–31.[2]

The Act of July 1929 had raised the income of the fund to £46m. This remained its income under the new Bill. The relief from £8½m of its obligations was partly offset by the £5½m of new obligations. Thus the fund's position was improved by £3m which, it was hoped, would enable it to balance with a live register of 1,200,000 unemployed as opposed to a live register of 1,000,000 under the previous system.[3] The total exchequer charge for a full year was increased by £12½m made up of £8½m for transitional payments, £3½m under the July Act and a further £500,000 for administrative costs. As the Treasury was already paying £12m to the unemployment fund, the total cost to the Exchequer of unemployment benefit in 1930–31 was estimated to be £24½m.[4]

[1] The qualification is important, for those who had previously been disqualified under the fourth statutory condition would have received part of the money from local funds (Poor Law).

[2] Cmd. 3437, para. 11. [3] Cmd. 3437. para. 12.

[4] Ibid. para. 13. The finances are somewhat complicated. The important point of the new arrangements was that Miss Bondfield was budgeting, by means of an increased treasury contribution, both for new expenses and for expenses that had previously been met by borrowing. The new Bill was worth £5½m to the unemployed out of national funds. All the rest was book-keeping.

The new financial arrangements were designed to satisfy two conflicting interests. Labour supporters would be pleased by the increased money handed to the unemployed and by the increased exchequer contribution. Opposition Members would be pleased by the attempts to restore the fund itself to a 'sound actuarial' position. Both sides could read what they wished into the promise of further comprehensive legislation.

The publication of the Unemployment Insurance Bill provoked sharp criticism from within the Labour Party. The I.L.P. were the most vocal in their denunciations. Campbell Stephen announced the same day, 15 November, that the I.L.P. would fight it 'tooth and nail' for 'we feel that it does not in any way improve the situation of the unemployed'. He also gave notice of a 'reasoned amendment' on the second reading.[1] Perhaps more disturbing to the Government was the reaction of the General Council. In an editorial dealing with clause four the *Daily Herald* of 16 November wrote:

> It is sincerely to be hoped that there will be no ambiguity on this point when the Bill passes into law; and the Trade Union Movement, at any rate, will certainly endorse the view its representatives expressed in their reservation to the recent Morris Report, that the only disqualification under this head should be the definite refusal of an offer of suitable employment.

With evidence of disappointment and anger coming in, it was widely expected that there would be revolt of Labour M.P.s at the P.L.P. meeting on 19 November, but this failed to materialise. MacDonald, putting in a rare appearance, made a strong plea for acceptance 'not as something they desired, but as the best they could get under the circumstances'. He argued that the pledges made were part of a programme to be carried out in the lifetime of a normal Parliament, not to be redeemed within a few months. The Labour Party should therefore regard the Bill as an instalment only. The Premier also warned I.L.P. Members that the national executive would appeal over their heads to their constituency parties if they voted against the Bill. MacDonald's syrup as usual sweetened what might have been an ugly situation and party support was secured. Even so, thirteen M.P.s voted against presenting the Bill for a second reading, and the P.L.P.'s official statement supported it 'subject to any amendments on points of detail which the Minister of

[1] *Daily News*, 16 November 1929.

Labour may find herself able to accept'.[1] Maxton immediately announced that he would not consider himself bound by this decision. Nor apparently did he feel bound by a decision taken by the I.L.P. Members who by forty-one to fourteen decided to support the Bill. These fourteen rebels who consisted of the Clydeside and extreme I.L.P. Members were soon to drive out of their party all those moderates who disagreed with them.[2]

The Bill had its second reading in the House on 21 November. Miss Bondfield gave moderate Labour opinion its cue when she remarked: 'I am not ashamed of having done too much. I only regret that, called upon to administer a bankrupt estate, I have only been able to do so little.'[3] The official party view was that the Bill was the best that could be managed in the circumstances and was to be regarded as an instalment of a larger measure to follow later — a familiar theme of all the Government's legislation, and cumulatively damaging to morale. However, it did enable moderate Labour speakers to support particular improvements within the general framework of disappointment.[4]

The Conservatives had no wish as yet for a general election, and so front-bench comment was restrained. Tory backbenchers were more forthright. Viscount Lymington accused the Bill, rather obscurely, of 'over-throwing the whole contributory principle' and condemned it as an 'attack on the independence and the moral fibre of the people' which would 'eat into the stubborn endurance of our English character'.[5] W. S. Morrison thought it better to equip the young with 'spiritual armour' than material sustenance.[6] Lieutenant-Colonel Moore argued that the Bill would 'turn this country into a community of subsidised paupers and pauperised employers'.[7] Earl Winterton deplored the de-

[1] *Manchester Guardian*, *The Times*, 20 November 1929.

[2] *Manchester Guardian*, *The Times*, 20 November 1929. For an account of this 'defeat' of the I.L.P. dissidents see Robert E. Dowse, 'The Left Wing Opposition During the First Two Labour Governments', *Parliamentary Affairs*, Spring 1961, pp. 234–5. However, the date of this meeting should be 19 November not 21 October.

[3] 232 H.C. Deb. c. 752.

[4] e.g. the Rev. Gordon Lang, who welcomed the increased rates for single girls of eighteen on the grounds that it would make them less likely 'to supplement that meagre income in the most deplorable and most regrettable way' (232 H.C. Deb. c. 1040).

[5] 232 H.C. Deb. c. 789–90. [6] Ibid. c. 1049. [7] Ibid. c. 1168.

struction of the spirit of adventure in the young.[1] The one point of substance made by Conservative speakers, later to be echoed in non-Conservative circles, was the effect of the measure in obstructing the mobility of labour, by making it more attractive for the unemployed to stay in the depressed regions.[2]

The Liberals, on the whole, welcomed the Bill, including the proposals to abolish the 'not genuinely seeking work' clause, but, following Lloyd George, argued that it placed the emphasis in the wrong place: far better to provide money for putting men to work than for keeping them in idleness.[3]

The main threat to the Unemployment Insurance Bill came not from the Opposition Parties but from Labour's own supporters. Two strong lobbies in the Party were determined to press amendments on the Government. The more powerful was the trade union group who followed the lead of the General Council. They accepted, with reluctance, the Chancellor's veto on higher scales of benefit, but were determined to make sure that the new fourth statutory condition really did involve the end of the 'not genuinely seeking work' clause. Outside Parliament, the joint consultative committee sought to press an acceptable formula on Miss Bondfield. In the Commons, Arthur Hayday emerged as the lobby's chief spokesman. The trade unionists relied on influencing the Government behind the scenes rather than through a frontal attack in the House which might cause a Government defeat. No such inhibition restrained the Maxtonite group. They mounted an attack on a broad front, demanding the full Blanesburgh scales, abolition of the 'not genuinely seeking work' condition, and reduction of the waiting period from six days to three, and making it clear that they were determined to press amendments on these matters in committee. Their very intransigence alienated the bulk of the Party who sympathised with their general aims, but disapproved of the embarrassment and risk of defeat to which they were exposing the Government.

Miss Bondfield's resistance to the Hayday Formula, which the unions were determined to have, made the position very difficult. The General Council and the parliamentary trade union group were anxious not to be associated with I.L.P. attacks on the Government, but it would be impossible to maintain the front of loyalty unless Miss Bondfield were

[1] 232 H.C. Deb. c. 2028–9. [2] Ibid. c. 786. [3] Ibid. c. 768, 775.

prepared to give way. It was decided to appeal to the Prime Minister, and on 3 December he received the following letter:

An Energetic Plea

Dear Prime Minister,

All members of the Trade Union Group in the House of Commons numbering about 100, the Chairman of which is Col. Watts Morgan, M.P., Mardy Jones, M.P. (Secretary) and James Sexton, M.P. (Treasurer), are very much concerned because the Cabinet up to the present time do not feel inclined to allow the Minister of Labour to accept what is known as the 'Hayday Formula' to Clause 4 in respect to 'Genuinely Seeking Work'. Also, why they are [*sic*] not prepared to reduce the waiting period from six days to three.

For the sake of approximately £4,000,000 per annum, the Cabinet is making it most difficult for us, and I am firmly convinced that even now at the eleventh hour if the Cabinet could see its way clear to accept these two propositions, we should be able to kill the opposition that has been going on for some days in the House by John Wheatley, Kirkwood and Co. *What we have seen and heard pains us all I am sure*. We, at any rate, are anxious to support the Government in every way, but on the foregoing two points we feel strongly. [italics mine.]

Will Thorne (signed)[1]

Apart from the evidence afforded of strong trade union feeling about clause four and of a desire, verging on the subservient, to remain loyal to the Government, this letter is interesting for the light it sheds on Miss Bondfield's negotiations with the joint committee. Apparently she told the committee that the chief obstacle to her conceding the Hayday Formula was the opposition of the Cabinet. This may possibly be true, but in that case we have to ask how far the opposition of the Cabinet was based on the opposition of the Minister herself? The General Council formed a very strong impression that the Minister was 'tenaciously resisting' the abolition of the fourth statutory condition. In view of this her advocacy for its abolition before the Cabinet must have been less than compelling. Moreover, one would have expected to find in the Cabinet at this stage a comfortable majority for the Hayday Formula. Perhaps, then, it was the opposition of Snowden, on financial grounds, that was the delaying factor? It is doubtful whether Snowden's opposition would be more decisive than the opposition of the Minister herself. Had she been keen on the abolition of clause four, Snowden would not have been able to resist popular cabinet clamour.

[1] MacDonald Papers, File 6, Unemployment Insurance.

It appears that the appeal to the Premier had some effect, for Miss Bondfield announced on 5 December, after a very confused Commons debate, that the Government would accept the Hayday Formula as the sole test of disqualification. She conceded with bad grace; but the Attorney-General, Sir William Jowitt, was even more put out, remarking: 'Are we to legislate on the lines that these people should think that they need do nothing themselves; that they should wait at home, sit down, smoke their pipes and wait until an offer comes to them?'[1]

The next day, Snowden told a meeting of the P.L.P. that the limit of concessions had now been reached and no amendments involving additional expenditure could be considered. The trade unions accepted: having won what they considered to be the major point on clause four, they were now prepared to retire gracefully from the struggle. Not so the Maxtonites. They had put down a reasoned amendment for the second reading which obtained thirty-four signatures, although twelve later withdrew, having signed by mistake. Maxton declared rhetorically:

> Two shillings for a child! The price of a pint of milk is 3d. Give the baby a pint of milk each day for a week — 1s. 9d. gone; — 3d. left for all that the wee tot needs. Would you demoralise that baby if you gave its mother 5s.?'[2]

In committee the Maxtonites moved four amendments, despite the decision of the P.L.P. meeting of 6 December to facilitate the passage of the Bill with all speed. Altogether forty Labour M.P.s voted against the Government on one amendment or other, indicating considerable resentment from outside the Maxtonite group itself.[3] MacDonald was furious. 'If every one or two', he declared at a dinner of the London Scots Labour Club, 'set themselves up to be wiser, to be more honest, to be more energetic and to be more determined than everybody else, every movement in which we are engaged will dissolve in the end into anarchistic fragments.'[4]

[1] 232 H.C. Deb. c. 2686. [2] 232 H.C. Deb. c. 777.

[3] Brockway proposed that the Act become operative on 1 February, not 13 March 1930; McKinlay tried to increase adult dependants' allowances from nine to ten shillings; Jennie Lee, to increase children's benefit from two to five shillings. Finally Maxton tried to get the waiting period reduced from six days to three.

[4] *Manchester Guardian*, 7 December 1929.

James Henry Thomas

'There is not a man in the present Labour Party, with the possible exception of Mr. J. H. Thomas, whom I would entrust to let out push bicycles.' (*Lord Birkenhead*)

On the dole

'Are we to legislate on the lines that people should sit down, smoke their pipes and wait until an offer comes to them?' (*Sir William Jowitt, Labour Attorney-General*)

The Government Actuary in a memorandum issued on 10 December 1929 estimated that at least another 150,000 people would come on to the register as a result of the abolition of clause four. This estimate was derived from a simple comparison between the periods 1925–7 and 1928–9.[1] However, other increases were likely which could not be definitely calculated. They would come from people 'not really in the market as competitors for employment, but [who] may hold themselves out as such if they are thereby enabled to qualify for benefit'. He had particularly in mind married women who had not worked since marriage and seasonal workers during the off-season.[2] His inability to provide any estimate of the numbers of such new claimants made his statement all the more disquieting. Neither the Actuary nor the Ministry of Labour liked the new arrangements; both were determined, by pointing out their disadvantages, to get them reversed as quickly as possible. The frequency with which the Actuary's unsupported assertions were used by the Opposition in the days ahead to weaken public confidence in the new Insurance Act provides an example of the way in which hostile officials can undermine government policy.

iv. THE COAL MINES BILL

Two days after the Actuary's bombshell, the Coal Bill, having been through twelve drafts, was finally published. Its main points were a reduction in miners' hours to seven and a half per day in eight-hour areas; a National Industrial Board to protect wages; provision for national and district marketing and output schemes; national and district levies for exports; and a National Committee of Investigation to protect consumer interests. The Bill was a patchwork of compromises to placate the divergent interests involved. The miners got a small reduction in hours, plus an Industrial Board to protect wages with powers so limited as to make it ineffective. The owners received statutory protection for output restriction, price maintenance, and export subsidies. The consumers got an Investigating Council with powers of recommendation. There was no mention of amalgamations. Nor was there any reference to the nationalisation of royalties.

[1] See above, p. 113.

[2] Cmd. 3453, paras. 8–9.

The Conservative position was plain: the owners having rejected the reductions in hours, the Conservatives would oppose the Bill. This placed the onus squarely on the Liberals. They were totally opposed to the quasi-protectionist output restrictions and export bounties: they were disappointed that there was no mention of amalgamations. The Bill was not a rationalising measure at all. Consistency and honour demanded opposition. On the other hand the combined votes of the Liberals and Conservatives could bring down the Government. This was not a prospect the Liberal Party relished. The Government was still popular and had gained much prestige in international affairs. It would be in a position to mount a highly effective attack on the Liberals for obstructing its first major item of legislation, the product not of rash socialist promises but of months of careful preparation. Its position could hardly be much worse as a result of a general election. The Liberals, on the other hand, might well suffer a crippling reverse, as in 1924.

The obvious tactics for the Liberals were to try to amend the Bill in such a way as to meet their requirements. In practical terms this involved adding to it 'rationalising' clauses giving government power to institute amalgamations, and deleting from it the levy and output restriction provisions. The only question was — should they press for a promise from the Government to amend the Bill before the vote on the second reading or after? If the Government promised before the vote to accept committee amendments they would be able to abstain with a clear conscience: on the other hand they would be less free to oppose subsequently in committee. If the Government refused to make such a promise the Liberals would be obliged to vote against the Government. This would then leave them a free hand in committee, but only if the Government won the vote. The best tactics of all might be a Liberal vote against the Government on the second reading, sufficiently finely calculated to enable the Government to survive, but sufficiently close to frighten them into making big concessions in committee.

Before the second reading three prominent Liberals, Runciman, Maclean and E. D. Simon, announced that they would not vote against the Government. Other abstentions were rumoured. Speaking for the Liberals in the debate, Sir Herbert Samuel said that the message of the Bill ought to have been concentrate your industry, work the pits full-time, adopt modern methods of coal getting, eliminate waste in transport and the great waste in the cost of retail distribution.[1]

Would the Government promise to insert clauses providing for compulsory amalgamation, Samuel asked? The Government would not, and the majority of the Liberals went into the lobby against them on 19 December. The Government had a majority of eight, 281 to 273.

The figures were deceptively close. Neither of the Opposition Parties wished to bring down the Government. Although Labour were only nine short of their full complement, nearly thirty Conservatives were missing. Similarly, only forty-four Liberals voted against the Bill. Two voted for it and six abstained. Thus both Conservatives and Liberals could make their gesture of opposition without much fear of a government defeat. Lloyd George's tactics on this occasion were closely analysed in a letter from Jules Menken to Lord Lothian:

... On the second reading of the Coal Bill the division which so nearly resulted in a defeat for the Government was, of course, the direct consequence of Lloyd George's speech, and that was, I think, unquestionably designed, by goading the Government with personal taunts, to prevent the announcement of concessions during the second reading debate, which might have induced the Liberal Party to vote for the Bill or abstain, and which would certainly have given the Government a stronger position, and a less conciliatory attitude, in the subsequent Committee stage. This extremely clever manœuvre succeeded remarkably well. Incidentally it has irritated the P.M. almost beyond endurance, and a recent message of his to one of the Scottish papers expressed a petulance which is in direct ratio to the extent of the strategical defeat which the Government suffered.[2]

It may be questioned whether Lloyd George's 'extremely clever manœuvre' was really as clever as all that. Although its effect was doubtless to make the Government more anxious to compromise on the Coal Bill, by reviving all the old distrust of Lloyd George in the Government ranks it actively hindered the prospect of alliance between the two progressive parties on the basis of a 'bolder' unemployment policy, which was the declared aim of the Liberal leader. Lloyd George's

[1] 233 H.C. Deb. c. 1309.

[2] A reference to MacDonald's article in the Glasgow *Forward*, 4 January 1930, see below, p. 162. The letter (dated 14 January) is from the Lothian Papers, Box 191.

tactics in fact gave the Government a wonderful excuse for inaction. To all accusations of failure it could reply that it lacked a parliamentary majority; to all suggestions for a 'progressive alliance', it could point to the Coal Bill and argue that Lloyd George would dish Labour whenever it suited his purpose. The real stupidity of the Liberal tactics was not in wanting to change the Bill — for it was a bad Bill which needed improvement — but in trying to squeeze an extra tactical advantage out of a difficult situation. The Party thereby lightly surrendered the very strong moral position which it had built up in the previous six months and which up to that time constituted the strongest single argument for a 'progressive alliance'.[1]

V. MACHINERY OF GOVERNMENT — THE ECONOMIC ADVISORY COUNCIL

The malfunctioning of Thomas's committee led to a number of suggestions for improvement, the most important of which was contained in a memorandum by the Ministry of Labour official, H. B. Butler, British representative on the International Labour Organisation, which was passed on to MacDonald in November.

Butler had argued that there had been no systematic effort under government guidance to reorientate and rebuild British industry and commerce to meet the difficulties of post-war conditions. The efforts of Thomas might be good in themselves but they were 'unsystematic and unco-ordinated'. A great deal of valuable information never came before a single body charged specifically with unemployment functions. The Ministry of Labour had much specialised and detailed knowledge; in the Home Office were lodged reports of factory inspection staff dealing

[1] The Bill eventually became law in August 1930, six months behind schedule. It was much mutilated. The one provision that might have had an immediate effect on exports — the levy — was deleted in committee. The Lords' amendments on the hours question held up the Bill for two months; eventually the Government agreed to a 'spreadover' of the reduction over a fortnight. The Liberals inserted amalgamation clauses to promote rationalisation: they were so weak that they were never used. The quota schemes on the other hand ensured that little was done in the nineteen-thirties to make the industry more efficient.

with rationalisation and factory management; the Board of Trade had much information on production, salesmanship, commercial possibilities abroad; the Balfour Committee had accumulated a mine of information on industry; there were inquiries on foot relating to coal, steel, cotton and credit policy. There was no machinery for bringing all this together and viewing it as a whole, collating and focusing it so that it might serve as a basis for action.

Butler proposed three new pieces of machinery. First, an *economic general staff*, with the Prime Minister as chairman, consisting of all the Ministers connected with unemployment, which would take all the important decisions on policy. Under its auspices, *standing committees* would be set up to advise on each of the main branches of economic policy; they would all be interlocking through some degree of common membership and would include representatives of departments and experts and academics brought in from outside. Each one would be presided over by a member of the economic general staff and each would become part of the permanent machinery of government. Finally, Butler proposed a *secretariat* consisting of twelve higher civil servants of first-rate ability, who would hold the machine together. It would prepare the work of the economic staff and standing committees by collecting all the information available in the various departments on each subject for discussion and presenting it in lucid, manageable form. It would handle all the secretarial work of the committees; finally it would keep itself informed of the executive actions by the departments to carry out decisions, so that at any moment a complete record of what was being done in any field would be immediately available.[1]

Among other things Butler's memorandum urged the Government to make more use of expert advice from outside the civil service. MacDonald, who saw Parliament as a laboratory, was all in favour of proliferating experiments provided they produced no definite results; and on 1 December he lunched with a group of economists at 10 Downing Street. Those present included Clay, Cole, Keynes, Layton and Tawney. The *Manchester Guardian* commented that he was 'in the process of developing an idea he has long had of associating expert advisers with the machinery of government'. This and subsequent conversations were crystallised in the Prime Minister's announcement in the Commons on

[1] MacDonald Papers, File 17 b, Unemployment.

22 January that the Government intended to set up an Economic Advisory Council under his chairmanship. The membership and staff were announced on 12 February. There were fifteen full members, including Bevin, Citrine, Cole, Keynes, Stamp and Tawney; five permanent officials consisting of Thomas Jones, A. F. Hemming, Hubert Henderson, H. V. Hodson and Colin Clark (statistics); finally, the Prime Minister announced that 'we have a list of distinguished industrialists and economists to assist on specific points'; all of which prompted Hore-Belisha to ask MacDonald whether he was satisfied he had left out no one of note.[1]

Hore-Belisha's comment was shrewd. The list of names might sound impressive, but the Council need be little more than a ceremonial body — at best a discussion group. Past experience tended to support this. A Committee of Civil Research had been in existence for a number of years. It had dealt with miscellaneous topics of marginal importance which no department was prepared to consider, such as locust control and the ravages of the tsetse fly. This Committee in fact formed the nucleus of the new E.A.C. Unfortunately the legacy of the Committee of Civil Research hung over the early meetings of the E.A.C. and agendas were full of the same topics of marginal importance that had exercised the earlier committee.

Moreover, the exact status of the Council was not clearly defined. It was to be presided over by the Prime Minister, often accompanied by two or three leading Cabinet colleagues, including the Chancellor. But the advisory Ministers were not members. There was no direct liaison with the departments; it was not integrated into the general machinery of unemployment in the way Butler had suggested. Also, at first, there was little for it to do. The Government was still pursuing the policy announced the previous summer: the search for alternatives had not yet begun. In its first shadowy period of existence it threatened to become as Mosley put it, 'a discussion group revolving ideas in a void'. It was only the break-up of Thomas's committee, the worsening economic position that forced on the Government a reappraisal of its unemployment policy, and the release of the Prime Minister from his foreign preoccupations, that enabled it for a few months in the summer of 1930 to move into the centre of affairs.

[1] 235 H.C. Deb. c. 409–10.

vi. THE POSITION OF THE GOVERNMENT

In its first six months of office the Labour Government undoubtedly made a good impression in the country. At any time up to the end of 1929 it could have faced the electorate with every prospect of winning an absolute majority. Labour candidates did well in the municipal elections of 1 November, making a net gain of a hundred seats in eighty of the larger boroughs, contrasted with a net loss of fifty seats by the Conservatives and fifteen by the Liberals.[1] In the four by-elections between August and December 1929 — at South-East Leeds, Twickenham, Kilmarnock and Tamworth — the average swing to Labour was 1·4 per cent.[2]

Quite apart from the 'honeymoon' effect there were solid reasons for the Government's success. MacDonald had once more made a very good initial impression as Prime Minister, especially in foreign affairs. He received an extremely flattering press in the opening months of his premiership and opinions were confirmed by the outstanding success of his American visit in October. Snowden had earned admiration for the obstinate and aggressive way in which he had defended Britain's financial interests at the Hague; Arthur Henderson, too, made a good start as Foreign Secretary and was applauded in the 'liberal' press for getting rid of that troublesome proconsul, Lord Lloyd, High Commissioner of Egypt.[3] On the home front there were fewer successes, but both the Widows', Orphans' and Old-Age Contributory Pensions Bill and the Unemployment Insurance (No. 2) Bill, taken in the autumn session, promised to benefit considerable numbers of people.

The high point in the acceptance of the second Labour Government by the nation came on 20 December 1929 when MacDonald and Snowden received the freedom of the City of London at a luncheon at the Mansion House. Beatrice Webb who was present has given us her impressions:

[1] *Manchester Guardian*, 2 November 1929.

[2] I am indebted to Mr. Michael Steed for this calculation.

[3] Lord Lloyd had resigned on 23 July 1929 after receiving a telegram from Arthur Henderson 'of such a character that I think most people would have accepted it as an invitation to terminate their position' (230 H.C. Deb. c. 1301). The resignation was due to policy differences over the question of non-interference in Egypt's domestic affairs.

J.R.M. is the greatest political *artist* (as distinguished from orator or statesman) in British political history. . . . His handsome features literally glowed with an emotional acceptance of this just recognition . . . a glow which enhanced his beauty — just as a young girl's beauty glows under the ardent eyes of her lover. . . . His yarn about his old Scottish schoolmaster might be considered a wee bit shoddy to cynical listeners, but his delightful voice redeems the tale.

Thomas made a 'pitiful contrast . . . his ugly and rather mean face and figure made meaner and uglier by an altogether exaggerated sense of personal failure'. He was almost 'hysterical in his outbursts of self-pity'; everyone was against him, his 'damns flowed on indiscriminately'.

He takes no counsel with Mosley and Lansbury re staff appointments or remedial measures. Terribly vain — he panics when flattery turns to abuse. For years he imagined himself as a future P.M.; today the question is whether he will drink himself into helpless disablement.

Beatrice Webb concluded: 'Jimmy is a boozer, his language is foul, he is a Stock Exchange gambler, he is also a social climber. He is, in fact, *our* Birkenhead.'[1]

Unemployment was, in fact, the Achilles heel of the Labour Government; and Thomas slumped over the Mansion House table was the symptom of its failure to grapple with it. He could hardly have succeeded, since the whole analysis of the Government was that unemployment would only diminish through a revival of normal trade and industry. At the end of 1929 it was still too early to come to a definite judgment on that point: employment was no worse and no better than it had been in the previous year. The Government's uninspiring policy, however, made Thomas peculiarly vulnerable. The Conservatives though largely agreeing with him taunted him on the contrast between his performance and the expectations held out by the Labour Party before the election; the Liberals, who wanted a bolder unemployment policy, accused him of running away. His most important function — that of creating confidence in the Labour Government among businessmen and financiers — was hardly calculated to make him a hero in his own Party; his Unemployment Committee was disaffected, with the three advisory Ministers in almost open revolt.

This contrast between the public and private performance of the

[1] B. Webb Diaries, 21 December 1929.

Labour Government extended to other spheres. The preparation of the Unemployment Insurance Bill had threatened to produce a rift between the political and industrial wings of the Labour movement, owing to Miss Bondfield's monumental tactlessness. The negotiations between Graham — 'able and assiduous, but timorous and unimaginative'[1] — and the miners and owners, had again exposed the Government's failure of nerve at crucial moments. Even with the expectation of Liberal support for a strong rationalising Bill, the Government continued to flounder hopelessly in a vain attempt to square competing interests.

The Government resolutely turned its face away from the Liberals. Even before the shocks of 19 December it had rejected a Liberal offer of an 'informal understanding'. This had originated, strangely enough, in a suggestion made by that inveterate political busybody, Mrs. Ethel Snowden, wife of the Chancellor. On 12 November she urged Thomas to admit that no individual Party could settle the unemployment problem and to invite all Parties to get together and deal with it as a non-political issue. This was not quite what the Liberals wanted, but it provided a convenient starting point. On 15 November the *Daily News* published the following statement made to its representative by Lloyd George:

> Certainly I agree with Mrs. Snowden that unemployment is a matter above party and above considerations of purely party advantage. I am sure that I can speak for the Liberal Parliamentary Party when I say that it would most willingly take part in such an all-party conference with the object of contributing to the solution of this great human tragedy. . . .

In the Commons six days later Lloyd George renewed his pledge of support for any strong unemployment policy in the following words:

> You have here people who are prepared to assist the Government in any great projects they put forward for handling this topic; you have an assurance from myself and my friends that we will support the Government in any well considered enterprise . . . but you really cannot go on much longer unless you do something more to deal with the unemployed than the proposals of the Lord Privy Seal. . . . You cannot expect the House of Commons to tolerate it, and I cannot understand why hon. Members opposite tolerate it.[2]

In the meantime two Liberal M.P.s asked the Prime Minister whether

[1] B. Webb Diaries, 9 November 1929.

[2] 232 H.C. Deb. c. 776–7.

he was prepared to set up an all party conference to discuss unemployment. MacDonald was non-committal, but despite the fact that it was his wife who made the suggestion, the stumbling block to an all-party conference was the Chancellor himself. The Conservatives would come with safeguarding which was anathema to him; the Liberals would produce their Yellow Book which was also anathema to him. In the event nothing came of the tentative November probings. Lloyd George commented:

> I have done all I can. I have told the Prime Minister in my speech in the House of Commons that the Liberal Party is prepared to co-operate with him in solving unemployment to the full limit of its power. I cannot do more than this. The next step must come from him.[1]

---

[1] *Daily News*, 25 November 1929.

7

THE IMPACT OF THE SLUMP

i. INTRODUCTION

In April 1930 MacDonald coined a new phrase — 'the economic blizzard' — to describe the world depression which had developed at the end of 1929. He blamed this 'blizzard' for the rapid rise in British unemployment figures and suggested that fresh thinking was needed to work out new policies.

The Great Depression, as it has been called, was the most important event of the inter-war years. It killed the bright hopes of the nineteen-twenties. It brought ruin and poverty to millions and wreaked havoc with their political faiths. Countries emerged from it at last, embittered and suspicious, sometimes with new and frightening regimes, as men renounced leaders who had failed them. Centuries of progress seemed to have been swept away as the world, a prey to new fancies and terrors, drifted steadily towards war.

How and why did it happen? There is no easy answer. It is generally agreed that it was the American recession in the summer of 1929 that started the downswing; also that it could scarcely have gone so far had the world monetary system, fashioned in the nineteenth century, been functioning better. W. A. Brown, in his monumental study, *The International Gold Standard Reinterpreted*, explains why it was not functioning, citing as reasons the decline of London, the failure of the new 'nucleus' of London, New York and Paris to co-operate effectively, and the post-war debt problem. A third influence was the over-production of agricultural and primary products, leading to a constant downward pressure on prices which became irresistible once the foreign lending which supported the various valorisation schemes dried up in 1929. In combination, these factors produced a collapse in world commodity prices at the end of 1929. The price of wheat fell by 19 per cent; cotton by 27 per cent; wool by 42 per cent; silk by 30 per cent; tin by 29 per cent; rubber by 42 per cent; sugar by 20 per cent; coffee by 43 per cent; copper by 26 per cent. The serious reduction in purchasing power entailed by collapses of this magnitude diminished the export markets of the industrial nations. From the start of 1930 unemployment rose rapidly in England and Germany and to a lesser extent throughout western Europe.

Undoubtedly this depression was a severe set-back to the Government's plans. It had staked everything on a trade revival; it had spurned the bolder measures of Lloyd George and Mosley in the conviction that better times would come of their own accord. The failure of the gamble on returning prosperity provided the Government both with an excuse and an opportunity. It could blame its failures on the blizzard and it could start again. But which direction would it take?

For an understanding of the worsening economic position it turned to the newly formed Economic Advisory Council. At its first meeting in February a committee was set up under Keynes to indicate the 'principal heads of investigation' to be undertaken in order to arrive at a proper 'diagnosis' of the 'underlying economic situation'. The other members were Sir Arthur Balfour, Sir John Cadman, Walter Citrine and G. D. H. Cole.[1]

For the information of the committee and also of the Prime Minister, Hubert Henderson, the E.A.C.'s secretary, wrote regular progress reports on the world situation. They afford interesting evidence of how the crisis was 'presented' to the Government by its advisers. Written in April 1930, the following is typical of four or five such reports:

> Until last autumn, [Henderson wrote] the centre of the British economic problem was the decline in the volume of our export trade, both absolutely and relatively to the foreign trade of the outside world. Several of our old-established exporting industries had lost an important fraction of their export business, and there were no export developments in newer trades of a comparable order of magnitude. This loss of export trade gave rise directly to the problem of 'surplus labour' attaching to old-established industries like coal and cotton, and, indirectly, to various maladjustments which impeded the development of internal trade.

---

[1] Citrine later became ill and was replaced by Bevin.

Meanwhile, general business activity, both in Great Britain and throughout the world, was prejudiced by a steady deflationary trend resulting from something in the nature of a world scramble for gold following on the general return to gold standards. The fall in gold prices between 1924 and 1929 was heavy, the rate of fall exceeding that of the long deflationary period from the late 'seventies to the middle 'nineties. This necessarily acted as a brake upon the expansion of business, and in the case of Great Britain, increased the difficulty of absorbing the 'surplus labour' of the distressed exporting industries in other expanding occupations. For some time, however, the buoyant condition of the American and European stock markets gave rise to repercussions immediately favourable to business activity, and no serious world depression made itself felt until the Wall Street collapse last autumn.

Since then a severe world-wide trade depression has been superimposed on our special national difficulties, and this constitutes the dominating fact in the immediate situation. Stimulated by the sense of impoverishment resulting from Stock Exchange losses, the 'vicious circle' of reactions which characterises the typical trade depression is now in full play. With commodity prices moving downwards, purchasers have become increasingly reluctant to buy, until they feel sure that the bottom has been reached. Thus the volume of business is further restricted, and this in turn accentuates the fall of prices. This condition in one market communicates itself to others, until practically every trade in practically every country is affected in some degree. . . .

Although Henderson thought that unemployment would get worse before it got better, he was not pessimistic about the long-term prospects. He thought that the depression would of itself 'set forces in motion which ultimately effect a cure, notably cheap money'. In Henderson's analysis, just as dear money was the main cause of the depression, so cheap money would generate a recovery. On the other hand, such 'hopeful possibilities' as existed 'are very far from being certainties, and depend for their realisation on the monetary policies pursued throughout the world'.

There is an inconsistency about Henderson's analysis which well illustrates the dilemma of the classical economist in this period. On classical assumptions the depression itself generates forces making for recovery, such as low interest rates. But Henderson also realised that cheap money depends on the 'monetary policies pursued throughout the world' — which far from being automatic depend on conscious decisions by Governments. In other words, the 'real world' no longer necessarily corresponded to the classical model.

Under the heading of 'Remedial Measures' Henderson discussed four possible methods of increasing employment. It might be possible to expand the export trade, but he did not consider that this offered any hope for the immediate future. He discussed a number of protectionist or pseudo-protectionist devices for diverting home consumption from imports, without pronouncing any opinion. In mentioning the 'stimulation of total consumption' he drew attention to 'the possibility of developing the system of instalment buying which had done so much in recent years to maintain a high volume of consumption in the United States' and also wondered whether it would be possible to bring down retail prices by the 'rationalisation of distribution'. Finally, he considered the 'development of capital assets at home', pointing out that this would entail a large programme of government investment in housing, transport and public utilities. Whether such a programme would unbalance the budget or retard the fall in interest rates, thus curtailing ordinary industrial expansion, were matters for enquiry.[1]

Meanwhile, the E.A.C. committee under Keynes was running into difficulties. The 'intellectuals', Keynes and Cole, were soon at loggerheads with the 'practical men', Balfour and Cadman. Balfour, a steelmaster from Sheffield, who had previously headed the Committee of Enquiry into Trade and Industry, and Cadman, a mining engineer and Chairman of the Anglo-Persian Oil Company, held definite views about the consequences of state intervention. Having seen the draft report that Keynes laid before them, they determined to produce one of their own.

Although the committee's task was limited to preparing heads of discussion, both Keynes and Cole on the one hand and Balfour and Cadman on the other made their own position perfectly plain. Keynes and Cole took Henderson's view that there was no hope of absorbing the unemployed in the foreseeable future by increasing exports. They calculated that it would need an increase in exports of £100m to provide work for merely 300,000 men — yet there were a million and a half unemployed on the register. The only alternatives Keynes and Cole could see were a combination of tariffs, import controls and home investment or 'a policy of inactivity in the hope of something favourable turning up'.

Balfour and Cadman disagreed. They declared that the 'fundamental object of our enquiry is to discover the reasons for Great Britain's failure to secure her share of such improvements in world trade as are

[1] E.A.C. (Economic Outlook 4), April 1930, Henderson Papers, Box 1.

taking place'. They had little doubt that the explanation was to be found in a combination of high taxation, excessive wages, the cost of the social services, trade union restrictive practices, the decline in emigration, and the advent of a Labour Government. All these matters, with the exception of the last, should be the subject of careful enquiry. In the meantime the Government should avoid embarking on any expenditure which would further damage confidence. Balfour and Cadman made it clear that the unemployment problem could only be solved by the revival of the export trade and hinted that tariffs were probably indispensable.[1]

Predictably enough, Snowden found the businessmen's analysis more 'weighty' than that of the economists, though he could hardly have relished the hints of protection in either. However, he was not at all pleased that the E.A.C. should be discussing these matters at all. He regarded the Council as a fanciful whim of MacDonald's which, if not carefully watched, would encroach on his own responsibility for financial policy. He now sternly warned it to have no further discussion on these questions. The reason he gave was that they were already being considered by the Macmillan Committee (whose report would clearly be a long time in coming out) and that any separate investigations would prejudice the work of that Committee. He also rejected the 'pessimism' of Keynes and Henderson about the export trade. Their view 'was not shared by many of the people acquainted with the *practical problems of industry*'[2] (italics mine).

ii. THE PRESSURE OF UNEMPLOYMENT

As the world depression deepened, unemployment in Britain rose. Some seasonal increase was of course to be expected during the winter months. What was completely unforeseen was that the figures would continue to rise in the spring. Whereas in March 1929 1,204,000 men and women had been registered as unemployed, in March 1930 the number was 1,700,000.

The unexpected rise almost immediately upset the financial calculations of the unemployment insurance fund and forced Miss Bondfield to increase the borrowing powers of the fund — to £50m in March 1930

[1] Ibid. 1, 2 May 1930. [2] Ibid. 12 May 1930.

and to £60m in July. She might have increased contributions and/or decreased benefits; she might have increased the exchequer contribution as she had done in her previous Acts. However, there was a natural reluctance to upset the arrangements just completed: far better, if the crisis were temporary only, to take temporary measures to meet it. The problem of paying back the borrowing could be postponed till matters improved. The Government's decision to embark on a career of borrowing, rather than reorganise the fund on sound 'actuarial principles', was eventually destined to destroy it.

The coincidence between the passing of the new Unemployment Insurance Act and the rise in unemployment figures presented the Opposition with its first target. It was immediately claimed that the relaxation of conditions had been the chief cause in swelling the numbers of the unemployed. Churchill delivered a characteristic onslaught on 28 March:

> An avalanche of new claims is pouring in. The numbers mount continually; the expenses rise by leaps and bounds; heavy further increases . . . are in prospect. . . . They are coming upon us simply owing to the relaxation of official safeguards. . . .

The Government Actuary had suggested that a 'considerable group of new claimants' not in the labour market at all would claim benefit when the conditions were relaxed. It was the married women and the part-time workers, the Opposition claimed, who were swelling the numbers. Miss Bondfield, on the other hand, stressed that the world depression was the major cause.

One of her greatest embarrassments was the failure of Thomas to relieve the pressure on the unemployment fund as he was expected to. The numbers of unemployed rose steadily throughout the year, forcing her repeatedly to seek fresh borrowing powers. She was unable to offset the bad impression this caused by promising better things in the future. Had she possessed Thomas's ability to see a silver lining in every cloud she might have contrived to make her grisly tale more palatable. As it was she conscientiously produced the facts and figures supplied by her department and warned the House that she would soon be back for more. She did feel keenly, though, that she was being let down by the 'constructive' side and later noted in her autobiography:

The Clydeside Revolution

Cart before the Horse

. . . the persistent attempts of the Opposition to talk irrelevancies on the general subject of my strictly limited bills were due to the fact that Thomas was not satisfying the House.

There can be no doubt that this was one of the strategic points in the Government's position which let in the Opposition.[1]

The criticism, then, of Opposition spokesmen was not that any particular measure produced by Miss Bondfield was unnecessary but that the psychologically depressing effect of repeated borrowing was not being countered by a constructive policy, either to provide work, or radically to reorganise unemployment insurance, or both.

The Liberals were strong protagonists of providing work. Why was it immoral, they asked, to borrow money to put men to work, and perfectly moral to borrow to keep men in idleness? There was no difference in principle, the Treasury would have replied. The sole criterion was whether there was any prospect of the loan being repaid. But in practice a Chancellor might well prefer borrowing for the unemployment fund to borrowing for public works. First, pending major legislation, borrowing was the only way of ensuring that unemployment payments would continue to be made. Second, it was cheaper to give a certain number of men unemployment pay than to set them to work; besides it took far less time. For these reasons the analogy of borrowing for the unemployment fund was unlikely to impress any Chancellor as temperamentally averse to borrowing for any purpose as was Snowden.

The Conservatives, on the other hand, laid the chief stress on reorganising the finances of the fund. Financial orthodoxy demanded that when there was no hope of repaying loans expenditure should be met out of current revenue. Throughout the nineteen-twenties the theory that the unemployment fund would one day be able to repay its borrowing appeared just credible. By 1930 it seemed less so.

It is interesting that in the first two Unemployment Insurance Acts passed by the Labour Government — in August 1929 and March 1930 — borrowing was rejected as a means of restoring the fund to balance. Indeed Miss Bondfield repudiated it in the most emphatic terms, stigmatising it as a 'dishonest course, because it would be contracting a debt that you saw no possible way of paying off'.[2] When subsequently she asked the House to increase the fund's debt to £50m, then £60m,

[1] Bondfield, *A Life's Work*, p. 297. [2] 232 H.C. Deb. c. 1103.

and later on by even more, it was easy for Opposition speakers to point out that she stood condemned out of her own mouth.

When Miss Bondfield first asked for more money, the Conservatives held their fire, as Baldwin's Government had itself borrowed for the unemployment fund. But when she came to the House again in July, with unemployment standing at two million, they went over to the attack. As Walter Elliot, leading for the Conservatives, put it on 23 July:

> If we are to accept the right hon. Lady's figures as normal . . . raising the contribution or lowering the benefit will become an . . . urgent necessity.[1]

The only way of escaping Elliot's dilemma was to opt for a completely non-contributory scheme, to be financed entirely out of taxation. This was Labour's own policy. However, in view of the tremendous pressure mounted during the year for a reduction in taxation, it is clear that a proposed increase of £70m to £80m a year would have brought down the Government. The politically easiest course was to go on borrowing in the hope that something would turn up.

This was precisely what Miss Bondfield seemed to be doing. Nevertheless we must not suppose her policy to be as completely negative as she made out in the House of Commons. Early in March 1930 she tried to get Cabinet acceptance for a scheme to bring agricultural workers within the ambit of unemployment insurance. Such a move would satisfy a long-standing Labour demand. It would also be cheap, for there was comparatively little agricultural unemployment. The fund might even be able to make a small profit.[2] There was some support in the Cabinet, but Snowden warned its members not to overlook the psychological effect on industry of a proposal that would undoubtedly be represented as another 'dole' and his objection proved decisive.

By May Miss Bondfield was proposing more comprehensive legislation designed to 'bring to an end the continuous procession of Bills to provide finance'. She suggested raising the contribution of employers and employees by *2d.* each, with the Exchequer providing an additional sum equal to the increase in contributions, thus raising the income of the fund from £46m to £62m. In addition, Miss Bondfield wanted the

[1] 241 H.C. Deb. c. 2197.

[2] MacDonald Papers, File 6, Unemployment Insurance. Memorandum from Miss Bondfield to the Cabinet, 6 March 1930.

borrowing power raised by an extra £20m to £70m. Her suggestion was discussed in Cabinet, but once more the decision went against her. Snowden argued that to add to the burdens of the employers would be psychologically disastrous; for this reason he also opposed raising the borrowing power by £20m and bid Miss Bondfield be content with £10m.[1]

Snowden's decision cut both ways: the shock to industry may have been minimised, but the Opposition were given an extra opportunity to undermine the Government's position by the opportunity afforded for further debates in the autumn and early new year; and the decision increased the Government's dependence on Opposition goodwill to make available the further sums required.

iii. THE CONSTRUCTIVE SIDE

If Miss Bondfield's policy at least offered a hope of solving the problems of the unemployment fund, Thomas's offered none of reducing the numbers of unemployed. In public he was as confident as ever. On 12 February he declared: 'I think the bottom has been reached.' At Derby on 12 March he thought that 'things could only improve'. By 20 March he announced with something of his old confidence that 'the worst is past'. Two months later the prospect of recovery was as unpromising as ever, but Thomas was still able to take comfort in the thought that 'there is less suffering in our country than in any previous period in our history'. More significant was the lack of any new ideas. Instead of thinking he fell back increasingly on traditional wisdom. Speaking at Manchester on 10 January he said: 'All that Government can do, when all is said and done, is infinitesimal compared with what business can do for itself.' At Birmingham on 24 February he said: 'The problem boiled down to how the Government can help the export trade. . . . I am convinced that the spending of millions of pounds instead of solving the problem will aggravate it.' On 1 March he was saying that 'quick remedies are quack remedies'. By 18 March he was advising his audience 'not to make the mistake of looking for short cuts . . . in the history of the world short cuts had proved disastrous'. Reviewing his performance on 20 May, the *Manchester Guardian* wrote: 'Mr. Thomas's

[1] MacDonald Papers, File 6, Unemployment Insurance.

principal charm was once his vivacity and unexpectedness. He is getting sadly stereotyped. He has become a man of single speech, and not a very good speech at that.'

As we have seen, the Government believed that only a trade revival would mop up unemployment. Its policy, both international and domestic, was designed to promote this end.

The political highlights of the international policy were MacDonald's visit to the United States, recognition of the Soviet Union,[1] signature of the Optional Clause,[2] the Naval Disarmament Conference in London from January to March 1930, and vigorous support of the League of Nations. On the economic side Willie Graham, the President of the Board of Trade, proposed at Geneva on 9 September 1929 that all nations should agree to a tariff truce for two years, while they planned phased reductions in tariff levels. The Assembly made warm noises of approval, as it had on the occasion of every previous suggestion of this kind, and referred the matter to a special conference. This conference which met on 17 February 1930, under the grandiose title of Preliminary Conference with a View to Concerted Economic Action, was attended by twenty-seven nations. Discussions were started in an atmosphere of the utmost gloom. People were just starting to register the world depression. None of the British dominions turned up: they were planning to increase, not reduce, their tariffs. Nevertheless eleven countries signed a conven-

[1] Although a Labour Government was expected immediately to resume diplomatic relations with the Soviet Union, the issue once more threatened to become immersed in the dreary and sterile wrangling over the payment of Tsarist debts. Henderson's initial note of 17 July 1929 invited the Russians to send a representative to discuss 'outstanding questions' prior to any exchange of ambassadors. The Russians refused to negotiate about debts or anything else until Ambassadors had been exchanged. Notes passed to and fro until, under pressure from his own left wing and the Liberals (see *Manchester Guardian*, 2 August 1929), Henderson backed down and relations were formally resumed in November. However, the debt question still prevented the granting of long-term credits to Russian importers which would have helped Britain's exports. The Government's suspicion of communism went to the length of forbidding Trotsky to visit England (11 July 1929).

[2] On 19 September 1929, the Government signed the Optional Clause of the Statute of the Permanent Court of Justice at the Hague, whereby it agreed, subject to certain safeguards and exceptions, to refer all disputes with other countries to arbitration.

tion and a protocol. In the convention they agreed not to increase their tariffs until April 1931; in the protocol they agreed that tariff reductions were indeed desirable.[1] The convention was to be ratified by the Governments concerned by 1 November 1930: it would thus be a six-month, not a two-year, truce. The British dominions promptly denounced it and proceeded to increase their tariffs.[2] By November most of the big names had dropped out. Britain ratified on 14 September, but when the final count was made it was found that she had been joined only by Belgium, Denmark, Finland, Latvia, Norway, Sweden and Switzerland. By that time the deepened depression had effectively prevented the spread of Graham's scarcely infectious optimism; America had put up the Hawley–Smoot tariff in July and most countries were anxiously seeking to strengthen further their defences against the economic blizzard. Nevertheless throughout 1930 the tariff truce negotiations were given as the primary reason why Britain could not put up tariffs of her own.

So much for the international policy. On the domestic front the Government's chief aim was to secure rationalisation of the major export industries. The chief obstacles to rationalisation lay in the structure of the basic industries and their relationship with the banks. Nineteenth-century industry had grown up on very individualistic lines, with innumerable small units of production which combined only occasionally and for specific objectives — e.g. to force wage reductions. Hence it was virtually impossible to get these industries to formulate *any* policy for their future, let alone a rationalisation policy which was exceptionally complicated and involved numerous individual reappraisals. The banks who might have been able to provide the initiative did not regard it as their function to urge policy on their clients, even when those clients were heavily in debt to them.

The King's Speech had promised enquiries into the iron and steel and cotton industries with a view to discovering means 'to improve their position in the markets of the world'. The appropriate committees were

[1] The details of both convention and protocol are to be found in the *Board of Trade Journal*, 27 March 1930.

[2] The new Australian tariff which came into force on 4 April 1930 added 50 per cent to the duty on numerous classes of goods; India had raised its tariff on cotton piece goods from 11 to 15 per cent in February.

duly set up under the auspices of the Committee for Civil Research.[1] In the meantime Thomas, with his wide industrial and financial connections, tried to bring industry and the City together in an attempt to provide finance for rationalisation projects. His discussions with the representatives of industry had convinced him of the widespread feeling in industry that the City was not interested in its problems. Thomas put this matter to Montagu Norman, who assured him that 'no sound scheme had been held up for lack of finance'.[2] This was probably true as far as Norman was concerned, but, of course, all hinged on the definition of 'soundness'. No one opposed 'sound' government expenditure; unfortunately most of it was considered unsound by definition. Armed with the Governor's assurance, Thomas told Manchester businessmen on 10 January that the City was ready to give 'financial advice and backing to sound schemes of financial reconstruction'.[3]

Thomas's announcement quickened interest in rationalisation and both he and Norman felt it would be advantageous to form a new institution to promote it further. Accordingly they announced, on 15 April 1930, the formation of the Bankers' Industrial Development Company, under Norman's chairmanship, 'to receive and consider schemes submitted by the basic industries of this country for the purpose of their rationalisation'. The new company was to be supported by many of the most influential banking and financial institutions in the country. It was not, however, to finance anything itself; as Norman put it, 'arrangements will be made for the provision . . . through *existing agencies* of such moneys as may seem to be essential' (italics mine). Equally, it was made plain that no government money was involved. In other words, the City houses were determined to get their commission. The B.I.D.C. was to be nothing more than a vetting and guaranteeing body —

[1] Two committees, on cotton and iron and steel, headed respectively by Clynes, the Home Secretary, and Graham, President of the Board of Trade, were set up at the end of July 1929, with identical terms of reference: 'to consider and report upon the present condition and prospects of the . . . industry and to make recommendations as to any action which may appear desirable and practicable in order to improve the position of this industry in the markets of the world'.

[2] Board of Trade memorandum presented to the two-party conference on unemployment, June 1930. Lothian Papers, Box 214.

[3] *Manchester Guardian*, 11 January 1930.

it would vet applications and guarantee the financial institutions against loss. As the money of its own subscribers was involved in this second function, it was bound to make sure that none but the very 'soundest' schemes received its *imprimatur*. The essentials of the traditional industrial/banking relationship were preserved.[1]

With these terms of reference, it is not surprising that the B.I.D.C. achieved almost nothing. After almost a year only one small scheme had actually been submitted and approved,[2] and S. Hammersley, Conservative M.P. for Stockport, who was closely connected with the cotton industry, wrote in August 1930:

> I feel that the intervention of the Bankers' Industrial Development Company, under its present auspices and with its present directing heads, is not only of no use to Lancashire — it is a positive hindrance.[3]

By this time the two committees of enquiry into the cotton and iron and steel industries had reported. Lancashire, the first one stated, had to choose between losing her trade by continuing as before or reorganising with modern methods to reduce costs and improve marketing: the organisation of the industry was still the same as in the nineteenth century.[4] The report on the iron and steel industry was considered 'too damaging . . . to publish in this country'.[5] Both reports stressed the urgent need for amalgamations, financial reorganisation, and more modern machinery; but the Government, considering that coercion would raise too many problems, preferred to leave these industries to work out their own salvation with the doubtful assistance of the B.I.D.C.; though it did give one of its officials, Sir Horace Wilson, the status of Chief Industrial Adviser, as a sign of its continuing interest in the problem.

If the rationalisation policy failed to make much headway, the public works programme fared little better. Morrison, the Minister of Transport, was fighting hard to get more money out of Snowden, but with very limited success. The Government had authorised a five-year road pro-

[1] The above details of the B.I.D.C. are taken from the statement made by Norman, published in the *Financial Times*, 16 April 1930.

[2] Macmillan Committee Evidence, 9038.

[3] Quoted in the *Liberal Magazine*, September 1930, p. 426.

[4] *Manchester Guardian*, 3 July 1930.

[5] Lansbury Memorandum, Lansbury Papers, vol. 25, n. 1017, para. 8.

gramme of £37½m. Early in December Morrison proposed an increase of £7½m in the trunk road programme, bringing it up to £17m, and an increase of £9m in the ordinary programme, bringing it up to £37m; thus increasing the road programme altogether from £37½m to £54m.

The three months' negotiations between the Treasury and Ministry of Transport revealed in the correspondence between Snowden and Morrison[1] shed considerable light on the formation of government unemployment policy. The Treasury appears in its familiar role as the watchdog of the national finances, reluctant to sanction any expenditure that might create budget difficulties; the Ministry of Transport was eager to press ahead with a more ambitious programme.

Snowden vetoed the Ministry's suggestion on 19 December, but Morrison renewed his proposals, on 16 January 1930, in modified form, asking now only for an increase in the trunk road programme. Once more Snowden remained obdurate and Morrison, in an effort to break the Treasury bottleneck, compromised by proposing an increase of only £4m in the trunk road programme, to be met by a deduction from the rest of the five-year programme. The question of restoring the £4m cut would be held over for the time being. The effect of this change would be not to increase the road fund liability, but to concentrate more money on trunk roads, at a rate of grant designed to attract local authorities. Snowden finally accepted this solution on 27 March.

The debate between Snowden and Morrison revolved round the question of the economic value of road-building and how this value was to be assessed. Snowden argued that the test of the economic utility of further road construction must be 'the help it will afford to productive industry in the near future'.[2] He was not satisfied that Morrison's new proposals satisfied this 'test': Britain's roads were already the best in the world. Morrison interpreted 'economic utility' in a looser sense:

I do not see [he wrote] how you can expect to get specific proof of immediate help to productive industry in respect of particular lengths of road improvement and construction. Must not the argument rest on the enormous growth of traffic, including commercial and industrial traffic, which uses roads and will continue to increase, and on the fact that a highway system designed for quite other conditions cannot without radical reconstruction and realignment give that growing traffic the facilities to which it is entitled?[3]

---

[1] MacDonald Papers. [2] Snowden to Morrison, 19 December 1929.
[3] Morrison to Snowden, 13 March 1930.

This issue was, in fact, central to the whole public works debate. The Liberals had admittedly argued that public works should be undertaken, irrespective of economic return, because they increased demand — an anticipation of the developed Keynesian theory. Nevertheless, they staunchly maintained that their proposals would 'pay for themselves'. When Snowden and the Treasury applied narrow business accounting techniques to this claim they found, not surprisingly, that it could not be sustained. But it was not the claim itself that was wrong: simply the methods used to test it. Modern cost-benefit analysis has developed a much wider concept of economic utility, embracing, in the case of public services, an idea of 'social utility'. This development is foreshadowed in Morrison's argument: it is entirely absent in Snowden's.

The terms of the agreement bore little relation to the arguments deployed on both sides. Because Snowden was chancellor he got the best of the bargain; but the fact that he was forced to compromise is a tribute to Morrison's pertinacity.

In sum, the Government's response to the first six months of the world depression was the borrowing of £20m for the unemployment insurance fund, Willie Graham's speeches at Geneva, the Bankers Industrial Development Company, and an extra £4m for a five year trunk road programme. It is hardly surprising that its stock in the country began rapidly to decline and that internal disaffection reached the point of open revolt.

iv. SNOWDEN'S FIRST BUDGET

We have already referred to the businessman's attitude to government expenditure: the F.B.I. memorandum handed to the Government in the autumn of 1929 had urged it to 'take a holiday from social legislation'.[1] One of the problems facing a Labour Government was that it had to prove itself more virtuous than a Tory Government in order to generate an equivalent degree of confidence; for it was bound to be widely suspected of having evil designs on industry and profits. Early in 1930, F. A. Macquisten, Conservative M.P. for Argyllshire, argued in the Commons that a Conservative Government could embark on much

[1] See above, p. 76.

'socialistic legislation' without creating a crisis of confidence, for the holders of capital realised that the Government was basically on their side; but when Labour undertook the same legislation to the accompaniment of

> displays of temper and indignation whenever the question of anyone making profits is mentioned . . . then, of course, you get capital slipping away, and there is no enterprise.[1]

It is, therefore, hardly surprising that Labour's Unemployment Insurance (No. 2) Bill, so bitterly attacked by its own supporters for being too timid, should have aroused widespread alarm in business circles. R. H. Brand, a leading banker, expressed these fears in general terms, in a letter to Lord Lothian, a leading Liberal, dated 5 December 1929:

> I regard the frame of mind of the ordinary Labour Socialist as hopelessly wrong. The more he puts his ideas and principles into practice the more we shall have unemployment and every other kind of trouble. The difficulty is that he can then turn round to an ignorant electorate and point out how badly private enterprise is working when, in fact, the troubles are largely produced by his own interference with it. It is quite possible, therefore, that we may have to go a good deal further along the downward path. I confess I look with alarm on the spirit that the Labour Party is inculcating into the rising population that they need not rely on their own efforts, but can always rely on the State assisting them. The burden of all this kind of legislation will ultimately, I think, be too great for active industry to bear.[2]

In the light of such misgivings it is unfortunate that the Government should have given the impression of having capitulated to its own left-wing and trade union elements over the 'not genuinely seeking work' clause. It would have been far better had it introduced the final clause itself right at the outset. As it was, some credibility was given to the view that MacDonald and Snowden, moderates though they were, would be unable to resist the pressure of their own left wing.

During the first few months of 1930 Conservative pressure was aimed particularly at influencing the forthcoming Budget. In London on 5 February Baldwin said: 'The first thing to which . . . I should devote myself if I were returned, is economy and the stoppage of fresh expenditure of any kind until employment is better'.[3] At Belfast on 14 February

[1] 237 H.C. Deb. c. 846.
[2] Lothian Papers, Box 191.
[3] *The Times*, 6 February 1930.

he went on: 'It is the dread of increased taxation . . . that is destroying confidence.'[1] Conservative business pressure groups took up the same refrain. A special report of the Federation of British Industries argued that British industry was 'handicapped by a load of taxation which not only far exceeds that of any other important commercial country, but, so far from . . . decreasing, has actually grown cumulatively more burdensome' and went on to advocate a reduction in 'unproductive' expenditure.[2] Businessmen all over the country called for reduced taxation and spoke or wrote of the 'crippling burdens' on industry. Even the Archbishop of Canterbury thought that the cost of the social services was becoming 'a severe strain upon the industries of the country' and wondered whether they might not be 'undermining the very sources of wealth as well as the independence and individual responsibility of our citizens'.[3]

Amid these gloomy pronouncements Snowden had to find an extra £47m to balance the Budget. The increase in anticipated expenditure was due mainly to four items. Firstly, the Conservatives had made insufficient provision to pay for the cost of the De-Rating Act and Snowden was obliged to find an extra £15m under this head. Secondly, there was an additional £14m for unemployment insurance; thirdly, the Government's Widows', Orphans' and Old Age Pensions Act which received the Royal Assent in December 1929 would cost £5m; and fourthly, Snowden felt obliged to set aside £5m for part repayment of the deficit of £14½m on the accounts of the previous year. It was this last provision that drew from the *Manchester Guardian* of 15 April the comment that the Budget displayed 'a puritanical rigour such as has not been seen since the days of Gladstone'. Snowden proposed to find the additional revenue largely by taxation. The income tax went up by 6*d*., there was an increase in surtax and death duties, and finally an increased tax on beer in the best traditions of temperance legislation. By these devices Snowden announced proudly he would leave his successor 'no bills to pay'.

It will be seen that of the additional estimated expenditure only £11m was devoted to increasing the social services, although the I.L.P.

[1] Ibid. 15 February 1930. [2] Ibid. 17 February 1930.
[3] Ibid. 29 January 1930.

clamoured for £200m.[1] Nor did Thomas's schemes cost very much. The total exchequer grants under the Home Development Act passed the previous July totalled £1,185,000.[2]

Liberal reactions to the Budget were friendly: they were pleased by Snowden's promise to value land preparatory to a land tax which would secure 'to the community a share in the constantly growing value of land';[3] and also by his decision not to renew many of the safeguarding duties due to expire shortly, though he regretted that he could not afford as yet to renounce the revenues of the McKenna and silk duties.[4] The Liberals voted solidly with the Government. Conservatives on the other hand denounced the increases in taxation on the grounds that they depleted the stock of capital, weakened the will to save and 'killed off the goose that lays the golden egg'. The I.L.P. accused Snowden of 'following with admirable consistency principles of finance which must bring disaster to our social purposes'.[5]

V. THE POSITION OF THE GOVERNMENT

On 23 December a leading article in *The Times* reviewed the Government's position. It reported that whereas as recently as October Labour had stood well in the country, by December its position was 'weak and shaken'. It attributed this deterioration largely to the Government's own fumblings, especially its handling of the Coal Mines Bill. The Coal Mines Bill was certainly a factor. It was universally regarded as a bad Bill, and it brought the Liberals for the first time out in the open against the Government, significantly enough because they regarded it as insufficiently radical. This, however, was not its only consequence. It took up an inordinate amount of parliamentary time and thus threw the whole of the Government's legislative programme out of gear. On 25 June 1930, MacDonald announced that the Government would be forced to postpone the Education (School Leaving Age), Consumers'

[1] Of the £14m for the unemployment insurance fund, £8m was a book-keeping transaction.

[2] 237 H.C. Deb. c. 2667.

[3] Ibid. c. 2680. This Bill was postponed till the next session.

[4] Ibid. c. 2671–2.

[5] *New Leader*, 18 April 1930.

Council, Land Valuation and Industrial Hours Bills, all of which had passed their second reading in the Commons, till the following session. It had not been possible even to introduce a Bill to repeal the 1927 Trade Disputes Act.

Meanwhile unemployment rose dramatically. The Government's modest programme had unluckily been overtaken by the deepening world crisis, but as Mosley was to remark later this should have been a spur to doing more, not an excuse for doing less. Thomas's incapacity and obvious bewilderment brought a general lowering of morale and increasing dissension. On 31 January 1930 Henry Snell, chairman of the consultative committee, wrote to MacDonald:

> The spirit of the party is quite good and they are happy on most things, but full of anxiety about the present position of the unemployment question and there may be some danger of the more restive spirits making their feelings public. Of course there are always complaints of this kind but they appear to me to be more than usually numerous and keen at the present time.

During the spring Conservatives and Liberals took advantage of the Government's decline to intensity their criticisms. Wheatley's prophecy of the previous July that 'after twelve months of halting, half-way legislation' no Party in the House would be poor enough to do it honour was being rapidly fulfilled, though he himself did not live long enough to see its final vindication. In these circumstances Passfield wrote to his wife: 'I have a feeling that there will be a general election within the next three months. But who can tell? Threatened governments, like threatened men, are apt to survive beyond expectations.'[1]

Within the Party, the I.L.P. had long been dissatisfied with Thomas's policy. In the autumn session their main energies had been concentrated on the Government's Unemployment Insurance Bill; now they turned their attention to the lack of an unemployment policy. Their opportunity for attack was provided by rumours of the Mosley memorandum that began to circulate early in February.[2] The I.L.P.'s position on unemployment remained true to the proposals of the 'Living Wage' enunciated in 1926. The *New Leader* of 27 December said in an editorial:

> The fact is that Mr. Thomas cannot, or will not, see that the development of the home market, the increase of purchasing power among the masses, the

[1] 6 March 1930; Passfield Papers, II.3.1.

[2] See below, p. 171

undertaking of huge development schemes, and investment therein of a huge amount of national money are the only hopes.

The 'huge development schemes' were to be paid for by taxing the rich. Thus Maxton said on 7 February that 'a Socialist Chancellor of the Exchequer should have no compunction in taking the greater part of the money on which supertax was paid and using it for national services'.[1] Brockway a few days later urged Snowden to raise £200m by taxation for the purpose of raising mass purchasing power.[2] In its desire to finance socialism out of taxation the I.L.P. position was the same as that of Snowden. The only difference was that he thought the moment was inopportune. In a broadcast address in April he acknowledged that 'the happiness of the people can be vastly improved by great schemes of social reform and national reconstruction' but believed that

these vital improvements are only possible out of revived and prosperous industry from which our national revenue is derived. In the present circumstances the first concern must be to restore and maintain a spirit of confidence and enterprise among those responsible for the conduct of our trade and industry.[3]

Neither the I.L.P. nor Snowden saw borrowing as a short-term alternative.

However, the dissatisfaction of the I.L.P. was real enough, and in the first few months of 1930 steps were taken which were eventually to lead it outside the Labour Party. On 20 April at the I.L.P. annual conference, the London central branch moved a resolution instructing the National Administrative Council 'to reconstruct the I.L.P. Parliamentary Group on the basis of acceptance of the policy of the I.L.P. as laid down by decisions of annual conference, and as interpreted by the N.A.C., and to limit endorsements of future I.L.P. candidates to nominees who accept this basis'. This motion was accepted. Its purpose was to enable the I.L.P. to function as a more coherent group in Parliament and in the country; its effect was to limit membership to those who supported Maxton's leadership. Of the 140 M.P.s who belonged to the I.L.P. only eighteen accepted the Maxton 'whip', and between this smaller group and the rest of the Labour Party relations became increasingly strained.[4]

[1] *The Times*, 8 February 1930. [2] *The Times*, 24 February 1930.

[3] *Manchester Guardian*, 16 April 1930.

[4] See Mowat, *Britain Between the Wars*, p. 363.

The formation of an organised 'enclave' within the Party was a direct challenge to the leadership which for some months had been inveighing vigorously against disloyalty. Faced, as they saw themselves, by a menacing Conservative–Liberal majority, Labour leaders tried hard to secure unity within their own ranks. MacDonald himself took the offensive when he criticised 'those who prefer propaganda to building and criticism to responsibility and who see no difference between a friendly Government battling with circumstances and a hostile one battling with right'.[1] On 17 February he made his displeasure plainer still by resigning from the I.L.P., of which he had been a member since 1894. He was quoted as saying: 'In view of what is going on it was impossible for me to keep up my association. The I.L.P. has lost both its grip on socialism and its sense of the meaning of 'comrade'. If the salt has lost its flavour, it is henceforth good for nothing.'[2] Snowden had resigned his membership in 1927. MacDonald's action, though he had been only a nominal member for many years, symbolically affirmed the capture of the I.L.P. by the Clydesiders from its old respectable, pacifist leadership of the First World War. Within the Labour Party, MacDonald, with the loyal support of Arthur Henderson, managed to isolate the I.L.P. rebels from the bulk of the Party and prevent the spread of disaffection. Henderson was indispensable during this period. When MacDonald shirked the task of bringing the parliamentary Party to heel, Henderson was always there to do it for him. And, unencumbered by sentimental attachments, he had even less sympathy for the rebels than the Prime Minister. At the party meeting on 19 March he asked bluntly: 'do the I.L.P. mean to accept the decisions of the Party and behave as a loyal element of it, or go outside it?'[3] As yet the I.L.P. leaders did not know the answer.

To its own supporters, the Labour Party's failure to stem the rise in unemployment and its generally poor showing on the home front proved a grievous disappointment, especially after the high hopes of 1929. A scapegoat had to be found; and the Liberals were ready to hand. Labour speakers at this time made much of the impossibility of passing 'socialist' legislation from a minority position and accused the Liberals of plotting

[1] Glasgow *Forward*, 4 January 1930. [2] *Daily Herald*, 18 February 1930.

[3] *Daily Telegraph*, 20 March 1930. He once said: 'The plural of conscience is conspiracy.'

to destroy the Government at the earliest possible opportunity. Thus MacDonald argued that 'Mr. Lloyd George and Mr. Winston Churchill seem to have decided that at all and any cost they are to defeat us', and went on to accuse Lloyd George of having made an 'outrageous personal attack' on Graham in the course of the coal debate which 'was plainly designed to prevent any co-operation in the lobby between Liberals and the Government'.[1] Herbert Morrison took up this line with gusto. On 4 January he warned the Liberals that they must decide whether they wanted to facilitate 'constructive legislation' or whether they wanted to destroy the Government.[2] Speaking at Middlesbrough on 19 January he claimed that the parliamentary situation made it impossible for the Government to follow 'those clear and definite socialist paths which were dear to the hearts of all of them'.[3] R. C. Morrison, the Prime Minister's parliamentary private secretary, speaking at Keswick on 1 February, said: 'If Lloyd George remains leader of the Liberal Party there is going to be a general election this year'.[4] In blaming the Liberals the party leaders and the I.L.P. were at one. The leadership needed a scapegoat; the I.L.P. could not credit the party leaders with the conservatism they displayed and concluded that this could only be due to a 'capitalist' conspiracy in the House of Commons.[5] In fact the I.L.P. remained firm against any 'understanding' with the Liberals on the grounds that this would finally mark the abandonment of any 'socialist' programme.

One explanation of the Government's negative attitude towards the Liberal Party was the simple fact that the Liberals were advocating a more radical policy than the Government's. Labour leaders undoubtedly felt guilty about this, which put them on the defensive. Moreover, as they were unwilling to explain to their followers why, in their opinion, it was impossible to carry out a 'bolder' domestic policy, they found the 'lack of a parliamentary majority' a convenient excuse, entirely plausible

[1] *Forward*, 4 January 1930. A reference to the Liberal 'tactics' described on pp. 133–4.

[2] *The Times*, 6 January 1930. [3] *Daily Herald*, 20 January 1930.

[4] *Manchester Guardian*, 3 February 1930.

[5] While Labour was attacking Lloyd George's 'treachery' Neville Chamberlain noted in a letter of 22 March 1930: 'I have no doubt that Ll. G. would make a deal with Labour if he could . . . but I do not believe he has made, or can make any such deal, because the Socialists simply can't afford the discredit of an alliance with him' (K. Feiling, *Life of Neville Chamberlain*, pp. 177–178).

on socialist assumptions. Either they could accuse the Liberals of open hostility or they could argue that they were 'insincere' in their advocacy of radical measures. Underlying and giving strength to the last point was the 'Lloyd George complex' which was a crucial factor in the politics of the inter-war years. Lloyd George, the argument ran, was untrustworthy; and that was sufficient reason for spurning his offers of support.

How far does the record of the Liberal Party during the first year of Labour government bear out the theory either that they were seeking the earliest opportunity to destroy the Government or that they sabotaged government policy? An examination of the Liberal record in the division lobbies from June 1929 to June 1930 reveals the following facts. If we exclude private Members' Bills, free votes and I.L.P. amendments (in which the other Parties generally did not vote), we find that a majority of Liberals supported government motions twenty-five times, voted with the Government against the Conservative amendments or censure motions eight times, abstained eight times, proposed amendments which received Conservative support five times, proposed amendments without Conservative support twice, and supported Conservative amendments four times. They thus voted with the Government or abstained in a possible forty-one divisions out of fifty-two. The two Liberal amendments which did not receive Conservative support were not significant, and so we are left with nine votes where the Liberals combined with Conservatives against the Government.

Of these, four concerned minor, non-party, amendments in the committee stage of the Unemployment Insurance Bill in which the lowest government majority recorded was 89. The remaining five dealt with the Coal Mines Bill. On one occasion Liberal support for a Conservative amendment secured the defeat of the Government, on the proposal to delete a central levy for exports. On the other occasions enough Liberals voted with the Government or abstained to secure a ministerial majority.

Thus the Labour case for arguing that the Liberals were obstructing government legislation rested on the five hostile amendments to the Coal Bill either moved or supported by a majority of Liberals. Yet the Government could hardly argue that the Liberals were preventing the passage of 'socialist' legislation. The Coal Mines Bill was not a socialist measure: but there were grounds for saying that it was a bad one. In fact the main Liberal criticism of it was that it was too weak. Liberal amendments in committee which Graham accepted were designed to strengthen the Government's power to enforce reorganisation of the coal industry.

Concerning unemployment, it cannot be said that the Liberals were obstructive. In all the unemployment debates until the beginning of 1930 the Liberals voted with the Government. In the first six months of 1930 they generally abstained, a measure of their hardening criticism of the Government's failure to produce 'bolder' measures. Here the Liberals were a progressive pressure group attempting to prod the Government, by their criticisms, into more positive action.

The generally co-operative Liberal attitude was maintained despite Labour's refusal to enter into any 'informal' understanding with the Liberal Party or to collaborate on unemployment questions and in face of petulant ministerial criticisms of Liberal 'obstruction' led by MacDonald himself. In an important speech on 20 January Lloyd George renewed his pleas of the previous November for parliamentary co-operation and consultation especially on unemployment policy. However, he was not offering a *carte blanche*. He described the conditions for such co-operation as follows:

> There must also be an understanding that while members of the Liberal Party are engaged in supporting the Government on great measures in the House of Commons they will not be assailed by Government nominees in their constituencies; or, on the other hand, there should be a *bona fide* promise that a measure of electoral reform will be carried by the Government at an early date before a possible General election. . . . Up to the present none of these conditions has been fulfilled. . . . Therefore until we have an honourable understanding with regard to co-operation we must fall back on . . . independent action, deciding each question entirely on its own merits.[1]

Labour reaction to Lloyd George's conditions was hostile, the *Daily Herald* commenting: 'Labour will never consent to any suggestion which has for its purpose leaving sitting Liberal Members to hold their seats without attack.'[2] On electoral reform, the Labour representatives on the Ullswater Committee rejected proportional representation out of hand and were only prepared to consider the alternative vote under certain conditions beneficial to the Labour Party.[3] Further suggestions for

[1] *Liberal Magazine*, 1930, p. 75.

[2] 21 January 1930.

[3] See D. E. Butler, *The Electoral System in Britain 1918–51*, p. 60.

co-operation met with scant response. As the *Liberal Magazine* of June noted in an editorial '[the Government] are helpless. But they appear to be also stubborn: like a certain aged and drunken Scotsman, they would rather go to hell than be saved by a "meenister of the wrang Kirk".'

Following Sir Laming Worthington-Evans's attack on Thomas in the House of Commons on 4 November the Conservative Party had moved over to a position of uncompromising hostility to the Government, tempered only by a marked inability to get Conservative M.P.s into the lobby to oppose government policy. So bad had absenteeism become that the Central Council of the National Union passed a resolution in March deploring the 'slackness of the attendance of the Conservative Members in the House of Commons. It would remind the Conservative Members that they owe a duty to their leader, Mr. Stanley Baldwin, and to those who elected them. . . . The meeting further urges that His Majesty's Government should be defeated on every possible occasion with a view to decreasing their prestige.'[1]

Lord Passfield's prediction that the Government would be turned out within three months was proved wrong. One reason for this we have already noted: the Liberals were not, in fact, as hostile to the Government as Labour leaders were wont to pretend; besides, they were not prepared to defeat the Government to put in the Conservatives, especially as the Conservatives stood for a general extension of safeguarding. Although many Liberals were unwilling to keep the Government in office solely in order to achieve a more dynamic unemployment policy, they were prepared to co-operate with Labour in defence of Free Trade; and Mrs. Snowden's 'Free Trade lunches' of Labour and Liberal leaders were a picturesque characteristic of this period.

Also significant in prolonging the life of the Government was the disunity in the opposition parties. The first few months of 1930 saw an intensification of the attempts of Beaverbrook and Rothermere to commit the Conservative Party to Empire Free Trade. On 18 February Beaverbrook announced the formation of a 'United Empire Party' with plans for contesting three hundred seats at the following general election, adding: 'I am forced to recognise that not only have Free Imports let us down but that the old Parties, slaves of tradition — impervious to any new ideas — have let us down, too, and that out of these old bottles it is

[1] *Gleanings and Memoranda*, January–June 1930, p. 331.

no use looking for any new wine'.[1] Beaverbrook's campaign aroused considerable enthusiasm among the Conservative rank and file, and Baldwin was forced into a series of humiliating concessions, culminating in a promise to hold a referendum on food taxes when the Conservatives returned to power.[2] This concession was but a prelude to a fresh encounter. Soon Beaverbrook and Rothermere were demanding to know the names of Baldwin's Cabinet before they were announced, so as to be able to scan their imperial credentials. This suggestion Baldwin repudiated with contempt in a notable speech at the Caxton Hall on 24 June; but though this strengthened his personal position, the activities of the Press lords continued to menace Conservative unity.[3]

The Liberals also had their troubles. The main issue was the question of the Lloyd George Fund. Viscount Grey, the Liberal elder statesman, made a speech to the Liberal Council on 14 January in which he singled out the fund and Lloyd George's personal qualities for special attack, adding: 'when the election comes, if things are as they are to-day with regard to the leadership, the Liberal Council must fight, not under that leadership, but under its own organisation and its own fund'.[4] A few days later Lady Oxford, widow of Asquith, wrote to *The Times* supporting Grey and stating that there was 'widespread political apprehension' in the Liberal Party about Lloyd George's leadership. Many Liberals were genuinely upset by the Party's reliance on a personal fund accumulated by Lloyd George during his premiership of the Coalition and felt that Lloyd George was placing them in a humiliating position in refusing to make over the fund unconditionally to the Liberal Party. It was useless for Ramsay Muir, chairman of the Liberal Organisation Committee, to point out that the fund had always been available, without conditions, on request: the fund continued to remain an issue between Lloyd George and many members of his Party, threatening to disrupt the Liberals once more.[5]

[1] *Daily Express*, 18 February 1930.

[2] *Manchester Guardian*, 6 March 1930.

[3] See G. M. Young, *Stanley Baldwin*, 1952, pp. 149–55.

[4] *The Times*, 15 January 1930.

[5] For a discussion of the Lloyd George Fund, see *The Times*, 19 January 1930.

8

MOSLEY REVOLTS

i. BACKGROUND TO THE MOSLEY MEMORANDUM

MOSLEY entered Parliament in 1918 at the age of twenty-two. Before that he had had no political experience whatsoever. Moreover, unlike Churchill who had also entered the Commons very young, he did not come from a political background: his family had provided the country with many clergymen, but no politicians. Allied to youth and lack of political background was a temperament particularly suited to action. These three factors produced the first of Mosley's misapprehensions: that a person entered politics to *do* something. What Mosley wanted to do, in common with so many others of his generation, was, quite literally, to 'build a land fit for heroes'. He described his policy to this end in 1918 as 'socialistic imperialism'.

Very early on Mosley became aware of a paradox: the scientific and technological power to produce was constantly growing; the power of the people to consume, however, was lagging behind. The result was under-consumption leading to mass unemployment, the great blight of the nineteen-twenties. To the young Mosley it seemed only common sense that the authority of the State should be brought in deliberately to equate production and consumption. This line of reasoning brought him close to socialist thought — to the theories of Hobson and the I.L.P., who held that the State should raise mass purchasing power by redistributing wealth. Mosley, however, never believed that redistribution would in itself increase general prosperity. Mass poverty was not simply a function of the unequal distribution of income, but of the need to compete in world markets. The I.L.P.'s mistake, in short, was that it viewed England as a closed economic system. If world trade were constantly expanding, as it had been in the nineteenth century, then doubtless the free exchange of commodities between nations would ensure rising standards of living. But if it were not — if, in particular, other countries could now produce at home the goods which Britain had previously sent them — then, Mosley reasoned, internal wage standards would inevitably be sacrificed to increasingly bitter international competition. He rejected rationalisation as an alternative method of cutting costs because in the short run it would create more unemployment and in the long run it would not guarantee a sufficient increase of exports to absorb the unemployed. The question then was: were wages to be forever depressed in order to enable Britain to fight the hopeless battle of world markets?

These speculations were later to lead to the concept of a large free trade area — an enormous home market, capable of supplying all the raw materials necessary for manufacture, 'insulated' against the chaos of world markets. For Mosley in the nineteen-thirties it was the British Empire, in the nineteen-fifties it was Europe-Africa which was to form such an area. Already in the nineteen-twenties the glimmerings of this idea were discernible and led him not to fascism, but to left-wing socialism, with its emphasis on developing the home market under cover of import controls. He also added to the I.L.P.'s preoccupation with redistribution an interest in monetary policy as the means of expanding demand, and he repudiated the gold standard mentality which would sacrifice domestic employment for the sake of the problematic benefits of international trade.

Mosley joined the Labour Party, in Strachey's words, with 'a genuine, unsophisticated desire to do something for the unemployed'. As Chancellor of the Duchy he thought he was going to be given a hand in formulating an unemployment policy. Instead he found that the main lines of policy had been determined without his assistance and that the policy itself was directly contrary to his own views. The new Government had made no attempt to challenge the 'treasury view' that the State should do little or nothing and that the only solution to the unemployment problem lay in a revival of the export industry — a possibility which, as we have seen, he regarded as illusory. For a time he thought that the very modest programme outlined by Thomas foreshadowed a much bolder public-works programme later on: but by the autumn these hopes had been disappointed. During the summer he was kept busy trying to 'ginger-up' the localities and working on the retirement pensions scheme. The first activity yielded meagre returns because of the character and conditions of government grants; the second collapsed before Snowden's opposition. In addition, he had grown increasingly contemptuous of Thomas, and increasingly disturbed by the confusion resulting from the lack of any proper organisation for dealing with unemployment. This, then, was the background of intellect and experience that determined Mosley's actions in 1930.

ii. THE EMERGENCE OF THE MEMORANDUM

On 13 December 1929, Mosley saw MacDonald and mentioned to him a 'memorandum' he was preparing on general questions relating to unemployment. The authorship of the memorandum has been the subject of some dispute. Raymond Postgate alleges that in the 'spring' of 1930, Lansbury

> decided in consultation with Mosley and Johnston to assemble the most obviously useful [plans] into one document and force it on his colleagues' attention. Mosley, the least occupied and the best writer, was the draftsman.[1]

This is quite untrue. Mosley's letter to MacDonald of 27 February states, 'when I talked to you on 13 December, I had not considered sending the memorandum to other colleagues'. Not only, then, was a draft of the memorandum in existence by December 1929, but Mosley makes it clear that it was not a co-operative undertaking, although Lansbury and Johnston certainly knew what was afoot and in part the memorandum embodies the results of the joint experiences of the three advisory Ministers in the summer and autumn. Thomas was as yet ignorant of the project. It was not until after the Christmas recess that Mosley 'casually' told Thomas that he 'had jotted down a number of new proposals on "our special problem" ', and added in the most offhand way: 'Some of these ideas you will agree with and some you'll probably turn down; but, in any case, Jim, I'd like you to see them.'[2]

The sequence of events is reasonably clear. About the middle of January Mosley sent a copy of the now final draft of the memorandum to

[1] R. Postage, *George Lansbury*, 1951, p. 256.
[2] Thomas, *My Story*, 1937, p. 170.

Keynes for his comments, adding: 'I am getting near to my "last word".' Keynes, with Mosley's permission, showed it to Hubert Henderson: they both agreed that 'it was a very able document and illuminating'.[1] Fortified by their opinion, Mosley sent a copy to MacDonald on 23 January.[2] Simultaneously MacDonald received letters from Lansbury and Johnston informing him of their general support for the memorandum.[3]

The question of whether Mosley showed the memorandum to Thomas before submitting it to MacDonald has been disputed. The main confusion arises from Thomas's own narrative, written seven years later, which gives the following account.[4]

At the start of January Mosley told him that he was jotting down a number of ideas on unemployment which he would show to him in due course. Five weeks later (i.e. early in February) without having heard any more from Mosley he received a telephone call from MacDonald asking him whether he knew anything about a memorandum which Mosley had just submitted with the request that it be placed before the Cabinet. Thomas replied that he had received no such memorandum, whereupon MacDonald wrote to Mosley telling him to send a copy to Thomas, who then received it for the first time.

There are two difficulties about accepting this as an accurate version. First, it is certain that MacDonald received the memorandum from Mosley on 24 January, in other words three weeks after Mosley's conversation with Thomas, not five. Secondly, in his covering letter to the Prime Minister dated 23 January, Mosley writes: 'I have already sent a copy to Thomas, whom I have assured that the criticism of the present situation is in no way intended as a reflection upon him.'[5] The only way to reconcile these accounts is to assume that although Mosley posted the two copies of the memorandum simultaneously, or almost simultaneously, MacDonald got his copy first. But then we must reject both Thomas's implication that Mosley never intended him to see it before it reached MacDonald and also that Mosley only sent it to him after MacDonald had told him to. The whole story rather illustrates the extent to which Thomas's organisation had broken down and the lack of contact between him and his advisory Ministers.

The question of which Minister placed it before the Cabinet now be-

[1] Keynes Papers, Correspondence, 1930. [2] Resignation letter.
[3] Appendix IV. [4] Thomas, *My Story*, pp. 169–74. [5] See Appendix IV.

comes irrelevant. MacDonald, Thomas and Lansbury had copies; presumably MacDonald brought the matter up himself. At the Cabinet, held towards the end of January, it was agreed to set up a sub-committee, consisting of Snowden, Greenwood, Miss Bondfield and Shaw, to consider Mosley's proposals and the memorandum was thereupon dispatched to the Treasury for 'thorough examination'.

The memorandum itself went into cold storage, but the etiquette of its presentation came up for lively discussion a fortnight later. There were two points at issue. First, Thomas learnt that both Lansbury and Johnston had seen it before he had; secondly, that Mosley had also shown it to others, including his parliamentary private secretary, John Strachey. At Strachey's house it had been seen (though not read) by journalists, and presumably Strachey had told them what was afoot; at any rate a substantially accurate account of the presentation of the memorandum appeared in the *Manchester Guardian* on 7 February 1930, and in the next few days rumours were rife of a 'mutiny' of the three advisory Ministers.[1] Thomas interpreted these happenings as further evidence of Mosley's 'disloyalty', and brought the matter before the Cabinet on 19 February. On the Cabinet's decision to take no further action, he sent MacDonald his resignation. MacDonald urged him to withdraw and Thomas continued in office.[2] However, MacDonald sent Mosley a strongly-worded reprimand and advised him to see Thomas and try to restore good relations. By that time, however, it had become impossible. Everything now waited upon the sub-committee's report.

iii. THE CONTENTS OF THE MEMORANDUM

Mosley's policy, as outlined in his memorandum and his resignation speech in the Commons on 28 May 1930, falls into four sections. The first deals with the administrative machine; the second, with long-term economic reconstruction; the third, with short-term work plans; and the fourth with finance and credit policy. It is only with regard to the third section that Mosley acknowledges a collective inspiration for his memorandum, writing:

[1] *Manchester Guardian*, 8 February 1930.
[2] Thomas, *My Story*, pp. 170–2.

these proposals will be largely a summary of suggestions which Mr. Lansbury, Mr. Johnston and I have advanced at various times during the last six months, and which have been largely rejected or suspended.

Mosley had become increasingly dissatisfied with the administrative machinery for tackling unemployment. His main criticisms were a lack of any systematic thinking about unemployment which made impossible a rational allocation of priorities (departments were like 'a crowd of bookmakers jostling through a turnstile on the racecourse'), a lack of co-ordination between the various departments dealing with unemployment,[1] and an absence of central executive responsibility for unemployment policy. In his note on 'The State and Rationalisation' Mosley further argued that there was no effective liaison between the various authorities concerned with rationalisation. The Economic Advisory Council discussed it; the banks were setting up an organisation to promote it.[2] The only link between the two came from the fact that Thomas attended meetings of the E.A.C. and was a friend of Montagu Norman.[3]

In an earlier debate, Leopold Amery had attacked the powerlessness of the Lord Privy Seal to initiate any policies.[4] In his speech on that occasion Mosley had made a qualified defence of Thomas's position:

> It has been pointed out that the Lord Privy Seal has no executive authority to provide work. That is perfectly true. He must work through other departments and so must any other Minister in his position. . . . Either you work through those departments or you duplicate the whole machinery of Government. . . . The only way to surmount that dilemma is to have in supreme control a Minister who controls nearly all the major departments of state. That would mean a change in the whole machinery of Government in the country, which has not so far been contemplated by any Party.[5]

It was precisely this change that Mosley now suggested. The mobilisation of the resources of the Government for an attack on unemployment could be made effective only under the direction of the Prime Minister himself. Mosley proposed an *executive committee* meeting weekly under the Prime Minister and consisting of the Chancellor of the Exchequer,

[1] Here he echoed Lansbury's complaint of 25 October; see above, p. 94.

[2] A reference to the Bankers' Industrial Development Company formally established on 15 April.

[3] 'The State and Rationalisation', addendum to the memorandum, 3 April 1930. Lansbury Papers, 20.d.338.

[4] 3 February 1930, 234 H.C. Deb. c. 1627–8.

[5] Ibid. c. 1642.

the Lord Privy Seal, the Advisory Ministers, the Ministers of Health, Agriculture, Transport, the President of the Board of Trade, and the parliamentary secretary of the Department for Overseas Trade. Operating under this committee would be a number of *standing committees*, headed by Ministers from the executive committee, dealing with particular areas of economic policy — credit, agriculture, overseas markets, civil research, rationalisation and so on. Both the executive committee and standing committees would be served by a *secretariat* of twelve higher civil servants under the head of the Treasury whose task it would be to co-ordinate and centralise the body of information dispersed round the departments and prepare agendas and memoranda for the executive and standing committees. Linked with the executive side by overlapping membership would be a central research organisation with its own sub-structure of advisory committees, consisting of economists, businessmen, bankers and representatives of other political parties. To the whole structure would be attached a *development bank* to provide credit for rationalisation, trade facilities, and industrial development.

This, in essence, was the revolution in government proposed in the memorandum and described diagrammatically in an Appendix which is reproduced below:

Prime Minister's Department

Secretariat of twelve higher civil servants Draws from and centralises the body of information now dispersed in departments; provides secretary for each standing committee.	*Research Committee of Economists* Acts as liaison between advisory and executive committees and provides one adviser on each advisory committee.
Executive Committee and Sub-Committees Headed by P.M., Chancellor of Exchequer, L.P.S., Ministers of Health, Labour, Transport, Agriculture; President of Board of Trade, 'unemployment Ministers', Secretary of Dept. of Overseas Trade. Meets monthly.	*Advisory Committee and Sub-Committees* Advisory Economic Council of economists, businessmen, financiers, etc. in which the participation of other political parties may be sought. Meets monthly.

Long Term Planning	*Sub-Committees*
Industrial Production	Industrial Production
Credit Policy	Credit Policy
Agriculture	Agriculture
Overseas Markets	Overseas Markets
Civil Research	Civil Research

Short Term Schemes
Unemployment Grants Committees
Transport
Miscellaneous

To this structure is attached a Finance House or Industrial Bank which will provide credit for (*a*) large scale schemes of rationalisation, (*b*) financing of export trade to countries which need extended credit.

From a comparison with H. B. Butler's proposals (p. 134) it is clear that Mosley drew heavily from that source. Both sets of proposals may be criticised for being unnecessarily formalistic: Mosley especially was obsessed with the need to provide the right machinery, when what was far more important were the right policies and the right men to administer them. A committee headed by MacDonald, Snowden and Thomas would hardly have provided the executive thrust that Mosley wanted. A more formidable practical objection was advanced by Lansbury's private secretary, Auriol Barker, who wrote:

The twelve higher Civil Servants forming a secretariat would, presumably, be wholetime workers in the new department. This would necessarily mean that they would sever connection with their old departments, so that they would cease to form a liaison with them. Furthermore, Sir Warren Fisher, as head of the Civil Service, would never, I think, create a driving force in the matter. The whole tradition of the Treasury is to act as a brake and the Secretary of the Treasury is only looked upon as Head of the Civil Service in the sense that by controlling pay and appointments he controls 'establishment'. No department, I think, looks to the Treasury for 'direction' as to their work.[1]

We now turn to Mosley's long-term policy. It was in this field in particular, Mosley noted, echoing Butler, that there was a real need for clear thinking about the long range problems and prospects of British industry. No such thinking had been done, because there was no body capable of carrying out the type of survey required, armed with the

[1] Auriol Barker to George Lansbury, 17 January 1930, Lansbury Papers, 20. d. 328.

information that lay buried and scattered in the departments and the countless commissions of enquiry. Mosley cited three major problems which required systematic investigation: the future relationship of roads and railways, rationalisation, and the long-term role of the export trade. On the first point he wrote in the memorandum:

We have not yet even considered the balance between railways, roads and canals in our economic equilibrium. Yet everything is subordinated to our promotion of railway development. My constant demands for a big road programme involving employment on a large scale are always countered by the objection that such a programme might damage the railways.

Concerning rationalisation and the export trade Mosley turned his attack on to the fundamental premises of the Government's unemployment policy. The Government maintained that it was through a revival of exports, promoted by rationalisation, that the solution to the unemployment problem would emerge. Mosley derided this supposition as illusory. On rationalisation he said in the Commons on 28 May 1930:

It is held . . . that although at first rationalisation displaced labour, that very soon it so expands the market open to the industry that the labour displaced is absorbed, and more labour in addition, with the result that ultimately the unemployment problem is solved. The only criterion that we can apply to that belief is the evidence which exists in connection with trades which have already rationalised. I have been at some pains to examine the facts in trades which have at any rate partially rationalised. . . . I applied this criterion to . . . four big groups of trades and I found, between 1924 and 1929, an average increase in production of over 20 per cent, but an average decline in insured workers in those trades of over 4 per cent. Over five years you have that immense increase in production — a very great achievement — and over the same long period a steady decline in the employment in those trades, which were ever increasing their efficiency and expanding their markets. It would appear, therefore, on the evidence which exists, that rationalisation in itself is at any rate no short and easy cut to the solution of the unemployment problem.[1]

Nevertheless Mosley did not deny that rationalisation had to take place. 'Socialism', he declared in an earlier debate, 'is not a device for the maintenance of obsolescent plant.'[2] What he did object to was the confusing of the long-term problem of reconstruction and the short-term problem of unemployment. He attacked the Government for having left rationalisation entirely in the hand of the banks. He argued that English banking

[1] 239 H.C. Deb. c. 1351–2. [2] 234 H.C. Deb. c. 101.

institutions, unlike German ones, were unfitted 'by tradition and present practice to play any such part without at least the aid of a general direction by the State'.[1] In the Commons he accused the Government of having abdicated to the banks.[2] To secure government control of rationalisation he suggested setting up a development company in which the Government should have the controlling interest, equipped with an effective research organisation and provided with sufficient capital, to promote reorganisation and modernisation.[3]

In attacking the 'fetish of the export trade' Mosley developed a theme from which he has never since deviated. Broadly, he argued that the rapid industrialisation of underdeveloped countries behind tariffs had virtually destroyed our basic export industries, citing textiles as a prominent example. Further he argued that to attempt to recoup these losses by the development of more specialised industries was ultimately doomed to failure as scientific development had destroyed the free trade argument for specialisation: what one country could produce today another would tomorrow. In these circumstances the goal of securing a surplus on balance of payments in order to export capital to enable other countries to industrialise even more rapidly was foolish. All that was necessary was 'to export sufficient to buy our essential foodstuffs and raw materials'. A vigorous policy of home development, industrial and agricultural, under cover of import controls, would eventually render us less dependent on exports. He concluded:

> If we are to build up a home market, it must be agreed that this nation must to some extent be insulated from the electric shocks of present world conditions. You cannot build a higher civilisation and a standard of life which can absorb the great force of modern production if you are subject to price fluctuations from the rest of the world which dislocate your industry at every turn, and to the sport of competition from virtually slave conditions in other countries.[4]

Subsequent developments, especially since 1945, have rendered these views unfashionable. However, in the circumstances of the time,

[1] Mosley Memorandum. [2] 239 H.C. Deb. c. 1357.

[3] 'The State and Rationalisation', Lansbury Papers, 20. d. 339–40. This was eventually done by a Labour Government in January 1966, when George Brown set up the Industrial Reorganisation Commission with drawing rights from the Treasury of £150m (*The Economist*, 29 January 1966).

[4] 239 H.C. Deb. c. 1355.

Mosley's pessimism about the future of world trade was understandable. Rising standards of living had repeatedly been abruptly reversed by the operation of the trade cycle: in the nineteen-twenties mass unemployment itself was a direct product of the failure of the traditional export industries. The Conservative demand for protection and Beaverbrook's plea for empire free trade were all based on the recognition that free trade could no longer guarantee prosperity in a world of 'fighting' tariffs and political and financial upheaval. Inside the Labour Party a policy of import controls for agriculture had long been advocated. In addition, there was a growing criticism within the trade unions of sending money abroad to equip foreign competitors. Before the Macmillan Committee Bevin asked, 'If you are limited by what you can lend and there is a claim by British steel for finance, aren't you creating unemployment by exporting it abroad?'[1] The world crisis of 1930–1933 was to breach even that most redoubtable stronghold of free trade belief, the Liberal Party.

Speaking immediately after Mosley in the debate of 28 May 1930, Lloyd George described his proposals as 'an injudicious mixture of Karl Marx and Lord Rothermere'. This was shrewd but not quite accurate: they were a judicious mixture of Lloyd George and Lord Rothermere, combining as they did a vigorous policy of home development in line with the Liberal proposals with full protection for the British farmer and the expanding home industries. Here Mosley showed that he refused to be bound by traditional Conservative and Liberal attitudes to free trade and protection. As he said: 'I believe we can leave it to the ghosts of Cobden and his opponents to continue [these] discussions of long ago in whatever Elysian fields they now frequent.'

Mosley insisted on a clear distinction between long-term and short-term schemes. The long-term policy would take many years to bring to fruition, and insofar as it depended on rationalisation, its short-term effect would almost certainly be an increase in unemployment. Yet

> at present we are tinkering with long period reconstruction in terms of short period schemes for the relief of unemployment . . . we are concentrating on Rationalisation schemes and holding out hopes to the country that we are thereby reducing immediate unemployment. We are in fact doing immediately exactly the reverse.[2]

[1] Macmillan Committee Evidence, 1331. [2] Mosley Memorandum.

Mosley's short-term proposals arose from the discussions and experiences of the advisory Ministers in the previous months. To the Commons he outlined the retirement pensions plan and argued that this would reduce unemployment by 280,000 at a cost to the Exchequer of £2½m a year if the cost of the scheme were averaged over fifteen years.[1] Raising the school-leaving age to fifteen would, he estimated, provide employment for 150,000 at a cost of £4½m a year. But it was 'in the interacting spheres of the Ministry of Transport and the Unemployment Grants Committee that the major conflict between my views and those of some other Ministers have arisen'.[2] On the question of roads, 'the first important fact which fortunately has not yet been understood by the House of Commons is that the road programme shows practically no increase on the road programme of the late Government'.[3] He proposed instead a £100m road programme concentrated into three years. Concerning the work of the Unemployment Grants Committee, the 'transfer' condition was holding up work both in the more prosperous areas where councils could not justify to their constituents importing unemployed men and in the depressed areas where the rate of grant was kept lower owing to the need to maintain the higher 'transfer' grant as a premium. The transfer problem would be solved by employing transferred men on national road schemes; this would then enable grants of 100 per cent for the depressed areas. Summarising, Mosley proposed a £100m programme for the Unemployment Grants Committee to be compressed likewise into three years.

This £200m spread over three years would provide employment for 300,000 men a year. If retirement pensions and a higher school-leaving age were added, employment would be provided for over 700,000 men annually.

Mosley estimated that this would cost the Exchequer £10m extra per annum. Retirement pensions and the raising of the school-leaving age would cost £7m. The additional £70m to be raised for the work of the Unemployment Grants Committee would be borrowed at an annual interest of £3m a year. The additional money for roads would be borrowed on the revenue of the road fund, and interest charges would be paid by that fund and not by the Exchequer.[4]

Snowden was later to write that 'the finance of these schemes would

[1] 239 H.C. Deb. c. 1360–2.
[2] Mosley Memorandum.
[3] See above, p. 106.
[4] 239 H.C. Deb. c. 1362–3.

not stand a moment's consideration'.[1] In fact Mosley's only really dubious item in budgeting was his calculation that retirement pensions would cost the Exchequer only £2½m a year. He argued that 'it was right and proper . . . to average the cost of the scheme . . . over the fifteen years of the scheme'.[2] In the first year, he admitted, it would cost £12m — the figure of the two reports of the retirement pensions sub-committee.[3] However, what was right and proper to Mosley was not right and proper to the Treasury, who insisted on annual book-keeping. Yet even with a figure of £12m the total budgetary charge for the proposals would amount to only £19½m in the first year and less thereafter.

Lastly, Mosley dealt with the prospects for raising loans on the scale he envisaged. This point had worried him for some time and on 6 February he wrote to Keynes asking his advice on how to raise £200m over three years 'without undue disturbance of the market and with the minimum charge upon the Exchequer'. Keynes replied encouragingly. The local loans fund, he thought, might support a loan of up to £40m a year for U.G.C. work without making necessary an additional exchequer charge; as to the question of how to raise large funds on the market as cheaply as possible and with the minimum disturbance, 'this is mainly a technical matter . . . primarily a question for inside experts'. The creation of a national investment board would probably be indispensable.[4] Fortified by these opinions Mosley proceeded in his memorandum and resignation speech to launch a forceful attack on the 'treasury view'. If the whole basis of economic policy were the restriction of credit then there was doubtless some force in the argument that it would be difficult to raise large loans for such purposes as contemplated, as it could be said that capital resources were being fully utilised. Given an expansionist economic policy, such as would be implied by a vigorous policy of public works and home development, there could be no force in that view as 'it would mean that every single new enterprise is going to put as many men out of employment as it will employ'. This was equivalent to saying that nothing could ever be done by any Government or Parliament. 'It is a policy of surrender, of negation.'[5]

[1] *An Autobiography*, vol. ii, p. 875. [2] 239 H.C. Deb. c. 1361.
[3] See above, p. 99.
[4] Keynes to Mosley, 8 February 1930. Keynes Papers, Correspondence, 1930.
[5] 239 H.C. Deb. c. 1371.

Mosley countered the argument that raising a big loan for unemployment purposes would destroy confidence in the currency by asking rhetorically,

Do we believe that such expenditure, or anything approaching to such moderate figures, would involve a 'flight from the pound' especially if it be counteracted by the enormous psychological effect of such great reductions in the unemployment figures and be accompanied by a scientific and explicable long-term programme for economic reconstruction?[1]

Finally, there was the treasury argument that raising money for home development would necessarily curtail foreign lending. As we have seen, Mosley was not likely to regard this as decisive. He asked:

Why is it so right and proper and desirable that capital should go overseas to equip factories to compete against us, to build roads and railways in the Argentine or in Timbuctoo, to provide employment for people in those countries while it is supposed to shake the whole basis of our financial strength if anyone dares to suggest the raising of money by the Government of this country to provide employment for the people of this country?[2]

There would be few who would quarrel with the substance of these propositions today. Even the curtailment of foreign lending as a temporary measure had much to commend it, though the treasury argument that in the long term expansion of international credit was indispensable for the development of world trade is doubtless true. The tragedy was that in this period Britain was making a valiant effort to maintain foreign lending on slender reserves at the expense of domestic employment, while the U.S.A. and to a lesser extent France, which were in a much stronger position to do so, were uselessly sterilising gold in their bank vaults.

Mosley concluded a powerful parliamentary speech, lasting over an hour and delivered without notes, with the following words:

You have in this country resources, skilled craftsmen among the workers, design and technique among the technicians, unknown and unequalled in any other country in the world. What a fantastic assumption it is that a nation which within the lifetime of everyone has put forth efforts of energy and vigour unequalled in the history of the world, should succumb before an economic situation such as the present. If the situation is to be overcome, if the great powers of this country are to be rallied and mobilised for a great national

---

[1] Mosley Memorandum. [2] 239 H.C. Deb. c. 1371.

effort, then the Government and Parliament must give a lead. I beg the Government tonight to give the vital forces of this country the chance that they await. I beg Parliament to give that lead.[1]

Following an adverse report by the Cabinet sub-committee, the Mosley memorandum was finally rejected by the Cabinet in May 1930. The precise terms of the report are not known: but the reason for the memorandum's rejection are quite clear. They were stated in their essentials by Thomas in the Commons when he followed Mosley in the debate of 28 May 1930.

First of all, he dismissed Mosley's finance, arguing that 'to talk about providing employment for 800,000 people at a cost of £10m a year is grotesque and absurd'. This point has already been considered; however, it must be remembered that the figure of £10m was given not as the total cost but as the annual exchequer charge, a quite different matter. Next Thomas proceeded to pour scorn on Mosley's pessimism about the export trade, with some justification.

What would the position [be] of any party going to Lancashire and saying to the 32 per cent of the cotton operatives who are out of work. . . . 'There is no hope for you so far as the export market is concerned'. We felt that was not the right policy. We felt that the only real permanent hope is reconstruction at home, re-equipment at home, and rationalisation, which will make the factories more efficient, all with a view to enabling us to compete fairly and squarely and with a fair chance for the export trade in the markets of the world.[2]

Thomas defended leaving rationalisation to the banks on the grounds that if the Government decided to take the matter directly in hand there would be such political pressure that it would 'practically be impossible to reorganise [industries] on a fair, equitable and business-like basis'.[3]

The reason for rejecting the retirement pensions scheme was not that the Government were opposed to pensions as such but because 'they believed . . . that nothing could be so absurd and ridiculous as to assume that because of the accident of birth on a given day one person was entitled to draw from the State one pound a week and in the other case, the person who was a day late, should only draw ten shillings'.[4]

Thomas's rejection of a £200m loan closely followed Snowden's

[1] 239 H.C. Deb. c. 1372.
[2] Ibid. c. 1432–3.
[3] Ibid. c.1433.
[4] Ibid. c. 1453.

argument in his correspondence with Morrison that no expenditure should be sanctioned unless detailed plans had been drawn up.

Thomas said:

I am going to challenge anyone to show that schemes have been held up merely because of the lack of finance. The difference between my hon. Friend and myself and the Government on that point is, that it is sheer madness merely to talk of any sum of money, and after you have raised the money to see how you are going to spend it. The business way is to set about finding the scheme, to examine all the proposals, to test them in the light of practical experience and, when you have done that, to see how you are going to find the money.[1]

The Lord Privy Seal argued that it was impossible to spend £100m on roads in three years. The criteria of schemes, as explained by Thomas in an earlier speech, was whether the work would 'ultimately be remunerative' and 'add to the general efficiency of the nation as a whole'. He had no time for 'merely filling up a hole or loading a barrel'.[2] On this basis 'one of the greatest authorities in the country', Sir Henry Maybury, had told him that it would not be possible to spend more than £20m in addition to the Government's programme over five years.[3] In addition Thomas rejected national road schemes on the now familiar ground that 'you cannot take the responsibility of breaking down local government in this country'.

This then was the Government's case against the Mosley memorandum. Thomas concluded:

For twelve months, I have been battling with this job in most difficult circumstances, not living to-day and forgetting there is a morrow, not believing for one moment that the problem of unemployment is one that can be settled by temporary expedients. I never believed it and never said it, and I do not believe it to-day. But I am entitled to say this: I am up against it. It is not the first time I have been in a crisis. But the more difficult the period the harder I work and the longer I stick to the ship.[4]

A week later Thomas became Secretary of State for the Dominions. He certainly stuck to the ship, but no longer as Minister of Employment.

[1] 239 H.C. Deb. c. 1434. [2] 229 H.C. Deb. c. 101.

[3] A reference to Sir Henry Maybury's memorandum, in Lansbury Papers, 19.d.117.

[4] 239 H.C. Deb. c. 1438.

iv. THE RESIGNATION OF MOSLEY

On 19 May 1930, Oswald and Cynthia Mosley dined with the Webbs. Sir Oswald was at a crisis in his career which could be summed up simply: to resign or not to resign? The Cabinet had definitely rejected his memorandum. As a consequence he, Lansbury and Johnston had refused to speak for the Government in the debate on unemployment on that day, when the Government majority fell to fifteen. The treasury examination of the memorandum had been completed early in May; by 9 May the Cabinet sub-committee under Snowden had recommended to the Cabinet the rejection of the memorandum; during the following ten days Mosley and the other unemployment Ministers vigorously defended it in discussions with the Prime Minister and other members of the Government, but to no avail. The discussions 'only served to emphasise our differences'.[1] The memorandum was definitely rejected.

Sir Oswald and his wife discussed the general situation. She complained that since the advent of the Government, MacDonald had consistently refused to discuss unemployment with her husband. Sir Oswald said that the Party was breaking up in the country; there would be such a débâcle at the next election that it would not recover for a generation. Mosley's comment was given some point by the Fulham by-election of 6 May when the Labour majority of 2,211 was turned into a Conservative majority of 240 — the first Government defeat since the general election. The Conservative candidate, Sir Cyril Cobb, was closely associated with Lord Beaverbrook's campaign for empire free trade.[2] Mosley did not abuse his leaders, with the exception of Thomas. About 'Jimmy' he was contemptuous. The meetings of officials with the Minister to discuss unemployment schemes were 'more discreditably comic than any in the Apple Cart'. Mosley liked and respected Snowden but said he had become a Conservative and anti-socialist without knowing it — largely due to the 'classy' adventures into which Mrs. Snowden had dragged him. About MacDonald 'we agreed that he was a great artist and left it at that'. Beatrice found the Mosleys 'sincere and assiduous in their public aims', though Sidney doubted whether Mosley

[1] Letter of resignation, 21 May, given in full in Appendix IV.

[2] *Manchester Guardian*, 7 May 1930.

had sufficient judgment and knowledge to lead the Labour Party in home affairs. Mosley said that if he resigned he would lead a 'new group' who would vote solidly to keep Labour in but would be critical of the Party's policy both inside and outside Parliament. Finally, he regarded Keynes and Salter as the two men who could really give good advice on unemployment, and said that they ought to be engaged at large salaries.[1]

On 20 May the three advisory Ministers had a long meeting with the Prime Minister, the Lord Privy Seal, Greenwood and Herbert Morrison. The greater part of the talking was done by MacDonald, Thomas and Mosley. 'At times the discussion became heated.'[2] The Prime Minister 'shared the views of Mr. Thomas'. What emerged from the meeting was that Mosley intended to resign, while Lansbury and Johnston agreed to stay on. After this meeting Mosley saw the Prime Minister alone. MacDonald 'who was very friendly with him tried to persuade him to stay on'. There was a rumour of his being offered a Cabinet post to appease him — possibly the Ministry of Agriculture, where changes were impending.[3]

The next day Mosley's resignation was officially announced. *The Times* and *Morning Post* took the view that Sir Oswald was an ambitious careerist, a man on the make who was deserting a sinking ship. The *Daily Herald* on the other hand thought his resignation 'courageous' and predicted that 'he will do big things for democracy'. The *Manchester Guardian* argued that it would be a good thing for the Government to be harassed by a 'critic of the left-centre' and thought that Sir Oswald's influence outside the Ministry would be greater than inside it. Captain Harold Macmillan, a Tory temporarily out of the House, wrote to *The Times*, deploring its 'unappreciative' attitude to Mosley's resignation. Mosley was resigning because he thought the Party should keep its election pledges — apparently an outmoded attitude. 'I hope some of my friends will have the courage to applaud and support his protest.'[4]

On 21 May there occurred the first of the two meetings of the parliamentary Party at which Mosley appealed directly to M.P.s against the Government. Sir Oswald made 'a short personal statement' based mainly on his resignation letter and gave notice of his intention to move a motion of censure on the Government's economic policy'. This was,

[1] B. Webb Diaries, 19 May 1930.
[2] *Manchester Guardian*, 21 May 1930.
[3] Ibid. 9, 21 May 1930.
[4] *The Times*, 27 May 1930.

apparently, 'received with cheers'. There was a demand that the motion be discussed immediately. This would have been to Mosley's advantage. The Government had not yet decided what its attitude to such a motion would be. The Prime Minister and Thomas were not at the meeting. In the heat of the moment it was at least possible that Mosley would receive a large vote. In these circumstances, Arthur Henderson saved the day by urging a twenty-four hour postponement. This was narrowly carried by eighty votes to sixty-nine.

Before the meeting scheduled for the following day the Government let it be known that it would resign if Mosley's censure motion was carried at the party meeting. Meanwhile, those who were sympathetic to Mosley's criticisms of the Government, but who wanted to avoid a direct censure motion being put to the vote, were preparing a compromise resolution. This was the 'Thurtle amendment' also put down for discussion. Thus the stage was set for 22 May.

At 8 p.m. Mosley rose to deliver his indictment of the Government. G. R. Strauss, parliamentary secretary to the Ministry of Transport and personally unsympathetic to Mosley, wrote a full account in his diary of what he called 'one of the most dramatic meetings I have ever attended', which is worth quoting in full.

[Mosley] made an extremely eloquent speech which effectively played on the dissatisfaction held by many members of the Party about the Government's policy, and, certainly, won the sympathy of many more. He pitched his speech on a very high note of emotion, and managed to sustain a dramatic fervour throughout his appeal. It was a magnificent piece of rhetoric which I wouldn't have missed for worlds. Mosley's constructive suggestions appear to be weak, remote and unconvincing. His figures were obviously fantastic. But most members of the Party present felt that, in his position, he must know what he was talking about and as something, obviously, had to be done to stem the rising tide of unemployment, his plan should, at least, be carefully considered, and, in view of the apparent failure of the Government to cope with the matter, they certainly — that is, the Government — deserved some censure. The platform was plainly nervous as to the outcome of the meeting after Mosley's fine speech. MacDonald spoke next, but his vague phrases carried no conviction. Arthur Hayday opposed Mosley's attitude in a rather incoherent speech. But John Bromley, who was General Secretary, I think, of the Locomotive Men's Union, to everybody's surprise supported Mosley. Ernest Thurtle moved an alternative resolution in the form of an amendment which, while appealing to the Government to increase the efforts to help with unemployment problems, could, by no stretch of the imagination, be called a vote of censure. J. H. Thomas made a few words in his most lachrymose and emotional vein. 'It was', he said, 'the most humiliating day of his life.' Jimmy turns on this emotional tap much too often nowadays, and at the back of the Committee room, at any rate, his appeal was received with smiles and sniggers. The tenor of the discussion was this: that, while all agreed that more should and could be done to cope with the unemployment problem than had been achieved in the past, it was highly undesirable from the Party point of view, that the censure motion that Mosley had moved, should be put to a vote. This point was stressed by Henderson, in winding up the debate, when he appealed to Mosley in very moving language to take the noble line which would be consistent with the manner in which he had affected his resignation, to withdraw his motion, and allow his various proposals to be discussed in detail at various Party meetings. Everyone assumed that Mosley would agree to do this. He offered to postpone his motion, but this the Party would not have. Whereupon he insisted on putting it to the vote. Instantly, all the support and sympathy he had received deserted him. A vote was taken . . . which showed that he had only 29 votes in his favour and 210 against him. Mosley's action in refusing to withdraw . . . was a grave misjudgment of the feeling of the meeting and a tactical blunder. Had he agreed to do so, Mosley's position in the Party would have been exceedingly strong. Now, as it is, he's looked upon with little sympathy by the I.L.P. group even, who refer to him with disdain, and with complete lack of confidence by the Labour group as a whole. It will take a very long time for him to retrieve his blunder.

Vernon Hartshorn, a Minister in the Government[1] turned to a neighbour at the meeting and remarked 'A pity he didn't withdraw. He would have done himself a lot of good'. Whereupon, Lady Cynthia Mosley, who was in earshot, turned on him in indignation and said, 'He didn't care for his own good, but only just for his Party.'[2]

This very full account of the parliamentary meeting deserves some elucidation. Other accounts of the meeting allege that it was Mosley's 'arrogance' that alienated sympathy. The fact is that he was outmanœuvred by that great tactician Arthur Henderson. The outline of Henderson's plan is clear. The Thurtle amendment, avoiding the language of censure, called for 'intensified efforts on the lines of Labour party policy to reduce unemployment'.[3] The amendment was subsequently withdrawn at the suggestion of Henderson, 'at a time when it looked like being carried'. To Arthur Henderson, with his great 'feel'

[1] Actually Hartshorn became a Minister a week later.

[2] Diary entry read by Strauss to A. S. King, *Nuffield Oral History*, Interview, 19 January 1962. This account is taken from the transcript.

[3] *Manchester Guardian*, 22 May 1930.

for party atmosphere, it must have seemed that the Mosley resolution would easily be defeated by a skilful appeal to party loyalty. But it was not evident that these tactics would work with the Thurtle amendment, for it avoided direct censure. Nevertheless its passing would not help the Government, for despite its moderate language, it was clearly animated by the spirit of Mosley's criticism. And its anti-Government bias would be made explicit if Mosley himself agreed to withdraw his motion in favour of the Thurtle one. Therefore Henderson's tactics were to clear the decks for an unambiguous party appeal by getting Thurtle to withdraw: in this he succeeded. He now appealed to party loyalty and expressed 'sympathy' with the aims of the memorandum, even urging its profitable discussion at future party meetings. This latter proposal could hardly have been meant seriously, since the Cabinet, on expert advice, had rejected it. By these means Henderson hoped to isolate the Mosley supporters from the mass of the Party. Next, in an equally friendly spirit, he called upon Mosley to withdraw. He thus had Mosley beaten both ways. If he persisted he would be crushed by the massive vote of the party faithfuls. If he withdrew, the Government would have escaped without an adverse resolution being put to the vote. This is what Henderson undoubtedly hoped would happen.

Perhaps in retrospect it can be seen that Mosley made a grave tactical error in insisting on a vote. But it would not necessarily have seemed so at the time. From his point of view, he was clearly being subjected to the same tactics that had ensured massive support for the Government at meeting after meeting of the parliamentary Party — the appeal to unity and the promise of further discussions. The latter he regarded as a sham. If the Government escaped unscathed — as they were hoping to do — they could continue exactly as before, perhaps with a few minor adjustments. It was by no means clear that in these circumstances his 'position in the Party would have been exceedingly strong'. It might be strong in the sense that people would say he had acted honourably. In the long term this might improve his party standing. But in the short term it would not help him to force his alternative policy on the Government. The only hope of doing this seemed to lie in his persuading a sufficiently large number of M.P.s to break the stranglehold of party loyalty and vote with him. If he could get forty or fifty openly on his side he would be in a powerful position.

In the upshot he got only twenty-nine. How near he came to getting an extra twenty or thirty can be measured only by the number of abstentions. The parliamentary strength was 286. Strauss records that it was 'a crowded meeting'. Yet only 239 votes were recorded. The attendance is not known. But there were most probably a number of abstentions. Mosley must have come close to getting the forty or fifty votes he wanted.

It is clear from Strauss's account that many M.P.s even then must have thought that Mosley had made a 'tactical blunder'. Yet this interpretation was by no means universally stressed in contemporary comment. A few days later, Beatrice Webb was asking: 'Has MacDonald found his superseder in Oswald Mosley?'[1] The *Daily Herald* 'regretted' that Mosley felt unable to withdraw his resolution, but stressed the 'friendliness' of the meeting: it clearly did not regard the vote as a critical point, though allowances must be made for party bias. Writing in the same paper on 26 May Ellen Wilkinson argued that prior to Mosley's resignation people had said that it was bad manners of left-wing M.P.s that had prevented them from securing greater support in the Party,

> but the courtesy with which Mosley conducted his resignation, both in the Party meeting and in the House of Commons was so exquisite that it ought to be carefully described in a book of etiquette for the chapter on 'How to Resign Nicely'.

At the party meeting, Wilkinson added, 'Mosley made the speech of his life'. There was no mention of his 'mistake' which, surely, would have disturbed the 'exquisite' impression he had created.

In view of the mounting dissatisfaction within the Labour Party, highlighted by Mosley's resignation, and of increasing pressure from the Liberals, unemployment policy could scarcely continue exactly as before. In addition, as MacDonald himself admitted in the House, the dramatic rise in unemployment figures was creating a fundamentally different situation from that which existed when Labour took office. Thomas's position, in particular, had become untenable. In a sense he had merely been carrying out government policy, but this in itself would not have been sufficient to discredit him, had the Party felt more confidence in him as a person — as it still did in Snowden. As it was, on 31 May, the Prime Minister received a petition, signed by sixty Labour

[1] B. Webb Diaries, 29 May 1930.

M.P.s, calling for the dismissal of Thomas as Minister for Unemployment.[1] He himself had announced at the party meeting of 22 May that, following the end of the naval conference, he would give 'personal and complete attention to the unemployment problem'.[2] Now the M.P.s' petition gave him a convenient opportunity to recast the unemployment machinery. On 5 June it was announced that Lord Passfield who had hitherto doubled the offices of Colonial and Dominions Secretary would be relinquishing Dominions to Thomas and that the charge of unemployment policy would be entrusted to a small Cabinet committee headed by MacDonald.[3] A few days later, the Prime Minister finally accepted the suggestion of the previous November for an all-Party conference on unemployment and sent out invitations to Baldwin and Lloyd George. These changes signified that the first phase of the Government's unemployment policy had ended in failure. The search for a new policy now began.

[1] B. Webb Diaries, 31 May 1930. [2] *Daily Express*, 23 May 1930.
[3] *Manchester Guardian*, 6 June 1930.

9
THE PRIME MINISTER TAKES CHARGE

i. INTRODUCTION

FOLLOWING the breakdown of the Thomas experiment certain immediate problems arose. There was need for a new unemployment organisation to replace that which had been wound up. The rise in unemployment figures and the criticisms of Mosley and others suggested the need for a new push on the public works front, both to provide work during the coming winter and to remove the impression of Whitehall indecision which had damaged the 'image' of the Government's unemployment policy. Finally, with the hardening of the attitude of the two Opposition Parties, the Government felt a need to strengthen its parliamentary position. These problems occupied it till the summer recess when there would be more leisure for a fundamental re-thinking of policy in the light of world developments.

ii. THE MACHINE

By moving Thomas to Dominions, MacDonald had brought his unemployment committee to an end. One of its members, Mosley, had, in any case, already left the Government. Moreover, as already noted, the Prime Minister had promised the meeting of the parliamentary Labour Party on 22 May to give 'personal attention' to the problem of unemployment. Many interpreted this as a reference to the long-awaited 'co-ordinating brain' mentioned by MacDonald in his election speeches. The experience of the previous year had produced a stream of criticism of the functioning of Thomas's organisation with plentiful suggestions for its reform. All these factors pointed to substantial changes.

The administrative reshuffle that took place in June produced two new pieces of machinery. In place of Thomas's 'unofficial' committee, a panel of Ministers was formed to discuss and co-ordinate the work of the various departments dealing with unemployment. In place of the civil servants who had been seconded to the office of the Lord Privy Seal, a new secretariat was established to serve the ministerial panel, with rather broader functions.

The panel of Ministers was a Cabinet committee consisting of all the Ministers who were concerned with unemployment, plus the remaining members of Thomas's committee, including Thomas himself.[1] The key figures were MacDonald, who was chairman, and the new Lord Privy Seal, Vernon Hartshorn, who acted as his deputy and was the only Minister working 'full time' on unemployment. Others whose responsibilities and personal standing gave them great influence were Snowden, Graham and Thomas. Greenwood, Miss Bondfield and Morrison, as the Ministers most closely connected with local authority works, played important roles from time to time, as did the new Minister of Agriculture, Dr. Addison,[2] when the Government's agricultural policy came to be announced in the autumn. There is no evidence that Lansbury or Attlee made much of a mark; but Johnston's prestige gradually increased.

The new secretariat of civil servants was headed by Sir John Anderson, the permanent under-secretary at the Home Office, and contained three other officials seconded from the Treasury, the Ministry of Labour and the Board of Trade respectively.[3] Attached to it were Hubert Henderson of the Economic Advisory Council and also representatives from various departments who were not seconded from their normal duties but merely sent along to safeguard their departmental interests.[4] The object of the secretariat was, in MacDonald's words, to enable 'more use to be made of concentrated and co-ordinated experiences from the departments which have been dealing with [unemployment] in a more piecemeal way'.[5]

[1] The new Chancellor of the Duchy, Clement Attlee, was at first excluded from the panel but later brought on (240 H.C. Deb. c. 1138: 244. H.C. Deb. c. 851).

[2] He replaced Noel Buxton on 5 June 1930.

[3] 240 H.C. Deb. c. 432–3.

[4] Ibid. c. 433, 797. MacDonald's account is not quite clear.

[5] Ibid. c. 433.

There were now three pieces of unemployment machinery — the panel of Ministers, the secretariat of civil servants and the Economic Advisory Council which had been set up in January. How far did the new structure meet the criticisms levelled at the old?

On 18 June MacDonald sent Hubert Henderson a copy of Butler's memorandum of the previous November,[1] asking for his comments. Henderson replied as follows:

> I notice that Mr. Butler's Memorandum is dated November 1929. Since then the Economic Advisory Council has been set up. Moreover, in the last few weeks the Panel of Ministers on Unemployment has been created with a special Secretariat of Civil Servants drawn from the various Departments. These bodies cover between them the greater part of Mr. Butler's suggestions. I do not think there is anything to be said just now for creating any further administrative machinery. Time must be given to see how the new machinery works.[2]

The most obvious change at the ministerial level was that instead of one Minister co-ordinating the whole range of unemployment policy, there was now a Cabinet committee. In practice, Hartshorn took over most of Thomas's responsibilities, so the change was one of form rather than substance. What was lost was the feeling that there was one Minister specially charged with providing employment. This change was reflected in House of Commons procedure: hitherto Thomas had answered all unemployment questions; now there was a reversion to the older procedure of departmental answers.[3] The gains lay in a better liaison between Ministers partially concerned with unemployment, and the merging of the unemployment organisation with the decision-making organisation — a change urged by both Butler and Mosley. Briefly, the panel of Ministers, headed by the Prime Minister and senior Ministers, could provide the 'executive thrust' that Thomas could not. As far as improved liaison was concerned, the chief beneficiary was MacDonald; and this was just as well in view of the 'personal attention' he was now giving to the problem.

Thomas's civil servants were primarily an administrative group, charged with carrying out particular projects organised by the Lord Privy Seal's office. The new secretariat had no departmental responsi-

[1] See above, p. 134. [2] MacDonald Papers, File 17b, Unemployment.
[3] 239 H.C. Deb. c. 2355–6.

bilities. Its task was to provide the panel of Ministers with the information, facts and figures, collated from the departments, relevant to any discussion of the panel of Ministers. It was also an 'ideas' organisation which, it was hoped, 'would bring forward . . . new proposals for short and long term methods of dealing with the problem of unemployment'.[1]

In theory, then, the main points of the Butler–Mosley proposals on machinery had been met. The panel of Ministers certainly bore a resemblance to Butler's economic general staff and Mosley's executive committee. The secretariat was very much on the lines envisaged by these two, except that it had fewer officials. There were no ministerial standing committees on various aspects of policy, but it could be argued that this function was performed to some extent by the departments. An expert advisory body had been set up in the Economic Advisory Council. The lines of communication which would enable up-to-date advice to be translated into effective decisions had been opened. Insofar as inadequacy of machinery was at the root of the failure to deal properly with unemployment, that deficiency had largely been remedied. But as Sir John Gilmour said in the House when the new organisation was being discussed: 'It matters not what kind of a committee you have; what does matter is the spirit in which you approach these problems.'[2]

iii. THE EXPANSION OF PUBLIC WORKS

From the autumn of 1929 onwards there was considerable pressure on the Government to expand and accelerate the public works programme. It could do this in several ways — by easing the conditions on which local authorities might receive government help, by making it easier for local authorities to get their schemes started, or even by starting national schemes of its own. The last possibility was ignored, but on the other two the Government made some important concessions in June and July.

[1] H. B. Usher, P.M.'s private secretary, to P.M., July 1930. MacDonald Papers, File 15, Unemployment.

[2] 240 H.C. Deb. c. 525.

Before considering these, however, it will be convenient to summarise the state of the public works programme at the end of June.

	Total value schemes approved (£m)	Average exchequer contri-bution (per cent)	Total value schemes in operation (£m)	Number of men employed.
Home Development Committee	26·7	24	8·3	Just starting
U.G.C.	41·7	41	27·0	37,000
Trunk Roads	13·0	75	2·7	
Five-Year Road Programme	22.0	50–60	3·0	27,000
Annual Road Programme	7.5	–	3·4	
Totals	110·9		44·4	64,000

Note: The method of government finance in almost all cases took the form of interest and/or sinking fund payments on loans raised by the authorities in question over a period of fifteen years.

The compromise reached between Snowden and Morrison in March 1930 was that £4m should be transferred from the five-year programme to the trunk-road programme, thus increasing the latter to £13½m and reducing the former to £24m. This was the most that Morrison could get at the time, but, as we have seen, he did not intend to let the matter rest. On 19 May he saw MacDonald. It was a bad day for the Prime Minister. He had been closeted for three hours with Lansbury, Johnston and Mosley, all bitterly critical of the Government's unemployment policy: he did not as yet know whether all three would resign. Now Morrison came full of complaints about Snowden's refusal to give him more money. MacDonald was in no position to resist and promised to write to Snowden.

Since March Morrison's demands had grown. Earlier he had asked merely for an additional £7½m for the trunk road programme: now he asked for £7½m to be added to the increase of £4m already conceded, bringing the total for trunk roads up to £21m. In addition he wanted the cut in the five-year programme restored. His departmental advisers discouraged any more ambitious proposals. On 27 May he asked Sir Henry Maybury, the Ministry's chief engineer, whether 'vastly greater expenditure, financed by borrowing' was feasible to provide a 'great and immediate volume of employment' in a short time. Maybury replied the same day:

I see no justification for the proposal that a large sum of money should be raised by loan because in my view there is no immediate transport demand.[1]

A day or two after the interview MacDonald wrote to Snowden asking him to give immediate attention to Morrison's proposals. Snowden replied on 30 May as follows:

I am in communication with the Minister of Transport about the Trunk Road schemes referred to in your letter. I need not of course tell you that I have never raised financial obstacles to legitimate road development though naturally I have always required to be satisfied that particular schemes are sound and economically valuable. And I will look into those additional ones you refer to without delay. . . .[2]

At a conference with Snowden on 5 June Morrison got all he was asking for. The trunk road programme was increased to £21m almost without discussion. Snowden demurred about restoring the cuts in the five-year programme, but eventually agreed to this likewise. With MacDonald backing the Minister of Transport, he was in no position to resist.

What the concessions meant was that the Ministry could now go ahead and give approval for a number of works which had been submitted but for which there was then no money available. They did not mean that more men would be put to work on the roads in the immediate future, for both the trunk road and the five-year programmes were phased over five years and would reach their peak, in employment terms, during their second and third years.

In the field of local authority public works the volume of schemes was disappointing. The main reasons for this were the 'transfer condition' and the numerous delays, both administrative and legislative, before work could be started. If there was to be an expansion of public works for the coming winter, some method would have to be found of by-passing these delays.

To overcome these difficulties, the Government invited representatives of the local authorities to a conference in London. This opened at the Guildhall on 17 June with MacDonald in the chair, and Morrison and Greenwood also present. Opening the proceedings, MacDonald

[1] Lothian Papers, Box 214.

[2] MacDonald Papers, File 19, Unemployment.

blamed the 'slow and cumbrous' machinery of many local authorities for the delay in starting schemes. In reply, Sheffield's Lord Mayor blamed government machinery — there were too many departments to be consulted. The grant was also insufficient. Corporations ought to get 75 per cent of the cost for the full period of the loan, instead of 50 per cent for half the period. Representatives from depressed Welsh areas argued that it was impossible to get anything done without 100 per cent grants. There were numerous criticisms of the 'transfer' condition, and speakers also stressed the difficulties of authorities acquiring land for public works projects. The first open meeting was so revealing that the Government decided to hold a series of private round table conferences in the following few days with selected delegates in order to find a way round the problems and 'to make a plan . . . and organise a new drive'. (Greenwood)[1]

With further information from these private gatherings, the panel of Ministers met on 23 June to decide what to do. Before them was a paper prepared by the secretariat giving an admirable survey of the choices and difficulties:

> Authorities which at present are required to accept the transfer condition and as a result qualify for the higher rate of grant will not be satisfied with the abandonment of the transfer condition if it means that they can only receive a lower rate of grant. The alternatives therefore are either to impose on those authorities a lower rate of grant with the result of producing considerable dissatisfaction and discouraging new proposals or to continue to pay to those authorities the present higher rate of grant unconditionally. If the second of these alternatives were adopted the difficulty would at once present itself of the hard hit area which would claim not unreasonably that it should be given more favourable terms, equally of course unconditionally. To meet this demand would involve giving rates of grant, over a large part of the country, representing a very high proportion of the cost, of what are, after all, local works.[2]

However, despite the risks set forth by the civil servants, the ministerial panel did decide to abolish the transfer condition and to make the higher rate of grant — 63 per cent for non-revenue-producing schemes — unconditionally available to all authorities. They also decided that for schemes financed otherwise than by loan, the contribution to the wages

[1] For an account of the opening day of the Conference see *Manchester Guardian*, 18 June 1930.

[2] MacDonald Papers, File 20, Unemployment.

bill would be increased from 75 per cent to 90 per cent. In order to meet the case put forward by representatives from Wales for a 100 per cent grant, it was decided to seek powers to allocate £500,000 for full grants to authorities in such areas, although the execution of the works was to be left entirely to them.[1]

To remedy the legislative and administrative delays, the Government introduced into the House on 7 July 1930 a Public Works Facilities Bill which rapidly passed all its readings and received the Royal Assent in August. It aimed firstly to provide a speedier alternative to ordinary private Bill procedure, by substituting a procedure by ministerial order subject to certain parliamentary safeguards; the new procedure could be initiated at any time, whereas private Bill procedure was limited to fixed dates and could begin only at the end of December in any year. Secondly it applied to land required for public works the simplified procedure for compulsory purchase of land already required for municipal housebuilding — in other words local authorities could make out an order for compulsory purchase which would become immediately effective if the Minister approved, with the safeguard of a local enquiry in case of objections.

What did these decisions signify? The dropping of the transfer condition and the making of all authorities eligible for the maximum grant certainly helped the local authorities; but one of their complaints was that the grant itself was too low. The £500,000 fund, provided by the Necessitous Areas Bill, was an attempt to meet the needs of the really derelict areas, but obviously it would not go very far, if we remember that £1m was supposed to provide employment directly and indirectly for 4,000 men. The government refusal to raise the grant was due not so much to budgetary reasons (for the annual charge was very small) as first, to a growing conviction that these works were useless, and secondly, to the feeling that they were 'after all, local works' and that therefore the local authorities should pay for part of them. As Greenwood told the local authority representatives on the closing day of the Guildhall meeting:

It is essential that some measure of local financial responsibility for such works should remain; and it would be a great disservice to local government to develop a system under which the main responsibility for the inauguration and

---

[1] Statement by Minister of Health, 25 June 1930. Cmd. 3616.

execution of local works should rest not with the local authority who are primarily concerned but with the central Government.[1]

The effect of the Public Works Facilities Bill became apparent only after some time. Its most useful provision was that which conferred the simpler and speedier powers for compulsory purchase. By November twenty-four orders had been submitted to the various responsible Ministers, though it was admitted that most of the schemes were small.[2]

Nothing had been done to meet the local authorities' complaint of departmental slowness once schemes were submitted, and indeed Conservative speakers in the debate on the Public Works Facilities Bill pointed out that this was a far more frequent cause of delay than the private Bill procedure which the Government sought to by-pass.[3]

In sum, the efforts to help the local authorities were useful, but small; they extended the limits of the public works policy, but only through permissive legislation: direct government schemes were still abjured. As a contribution to providing employment for two million men and women they were, of course, insignificant.

iv. LABOUR–LIBERAL RAPPROCHEMENT

Right from the start there had been good reasons for the Labour Government to try to achieve an 'informal understanding' or even a coalition with the Liberal Party. Both Parties appeared to agree on the need for a 'bolder' unemployment policy; both favoured the reorganisation of the coal industry; both were committed to an internationalist foreign policy. Thus Labour could have sought Liberal support without sacrificing the bulk of its short-term policy, and in return would have gained a certain security of parliamentary tenure, and a freedom to carry out its programme without the delays and frustrations inherent in a minority position.

The need for co-operation had become even more pressing after the Government had experienced its first year in office. At any time to

[1] Cmd. 3616, p. 3.

[2] Treasury Note to P.M.'s office, 25 November 1930. MacDonald Papers, File 24, Unemployment.

[3] e.g. Sir Kingsley Wood, 241 H.C. Deb. c. 817.

December 1929 it could have appealed to the country with some confidence of being returned with an increased representation. By 1930 this was no longer so. In fact by-election results suggested a heavy defeat.[1] Hence it became advantageous to try to secure a guaranteed period in office so as to allow sufficient time for the Government's unemployment policies to show some result, or if that was hoping for too much, at least to allow the world crisis to pass. Again, after a year in office as a minority Government, ministerial morale was low. The Liberals, on the whole, had provided reliable support in the lobbies, but there were signs that this would not continue for ever; they had not, on the other hand, been so keen to vote the closure, which meant that debates were often protracted into the early hours of the morning, especially in the case of the Coal Mines Bill, which the Liberals tried to 'improve' in committee.

If the need to secure Liberal co-operation had increased, the difficulties in the way remained apparently unresolved. First, there was the question of policy: the Liberals wanted a much bigger public works programme. Secondly, there was the issue of electoral reform. Thirdly, there was the distrust of Lloyd George. Finally, there was MacDonald's curious attitude to coalitions. In his 'Council of State' speech he had appealed for co-operation from both opposition Parties. This was partly due to his reluctance to rely entirely on Lloyd George. But it also stemmed from his Fabian belief in permeation and consensus. MacDonald kept hoping that if unemployment could somehow be lifted out of the arena of party politics and discussed frankly in a friendly atmosphere with the opposition leaders, agreement would emerge in favour of a certain course of action. Yet any positive unemployment policy was bound to involve attacking some vested interest, whether capitalist or socialist, free trade or protectionist, business or financial. MacDonald's recourse to endless consultation stemmed ultimately from his reluctance to choose between the various alternatives open to him. It was bound to lead to stalemate at the centre. It may be argued that in normal circumstances mediation between powerful conflicting pressure groups is the only plausible role for democratic leadership. But this is rarely the way in which great problems are overcome.

[1] In February the Government majority at Sheffield (Brightside) was reduced from 10,449 to 2,931; and in May the Government lost West Fulham.

Characteristically, then, he turned first not to the Liberal Party, but to both Parties. On 19 May 1930, he wrote to Baldwin and Lloyd George asking them whether they would be prepared in principle to confer with the Government on problems of agriculture and unemployment. He later explained his purpose in making this suggestion in language very similar to that of his 'Council of State' speech:

> The invitation was sent for the purpose of getting the three of us to meet together with such friends and helpers as we might choose, within reasonable limits, putting our ideas into a common pool, and seeing whether from that we could come to a measure of agreement which would enable important legislation to go through the House . . . not under conditions of being blocked or delayed, but under conditions of special facility.[1]

Lloyd George accepted: Baldwin wanted further information. On 4 June MacDonald wrote again making a definite offer. He suggested (1) that the opposition leaders should confer with Ministers specially appointed for that task; (2) that they should bring two or three advisers with them; (3) that papers should be circulated to them giving them all the information necessary to discuss the topic in question. He stressed, however, that the meetings would be advisory and not executive in purpose — responsibility would rest with the Government.

Baldwin replied on 20 June, rejecting the offer and thereby brutally exposing MacDonald's naivety. He wrote:

> We are, in fact, not invited to a Council of State whose decisions will prevail, but to a conference in which you will submit to us your proposals when they are matured with the purpose, *and the sole purpose*, of ascertaining what facilities we will accord for their execution. [italics mine.]

He made it plain that in the opinion of the Conservative Party the only real remedies for unemployment were, first, getting rid of the Labour Government and secondly, extending protection and imperial preference. As neither of these results was likely to emerge from a three-party conference he saw no point in attending one.

Thus MacDonald was left with Lloyd George. The Liberal leader accepted all the conditions. But he did urge that

> in order to secure Parliamentary co-operation free from friction, it is essential the Government should not introduce measures dealing with unemployment . . . without first discussing them in joint conference.

[1] 240 H.C. Deb. c. 431.

MacDonald promised full consultation, adding graciously that Baldwin's refusal 'need not prevent our conferring together'.[1]

Soon after this, on 26 June, the first meeting of the now two-party conference was held at 10 Downing Street. With MacDonald were Snowden, Hartshorn and Greenwood. Accompanying Lloyd George were Lord Lothian and Seebohm Rowntree. Other meetings took place throughout the summer, with results that will be described later.

Thus, belatedly, the two 'radical' Parties came together. Lloyd George still hoped that the fruit of co-operation would be a bolder unemployment policy. He made this clear in an interview with Ernest Hunter, the *Daily Herald* political correspondent, on 16 June. Hunter, playing on Labour fears of Liberal duplicity, said: 'But it is feared that the Liberal Party will not grant the 'guillotine' without which drastic proposals could not be forced quickly through the House of Commons.' 'Nonsense', replied Lloyd George, 'we shall certainly support a reasonable guillotine for agreed emergency measures.' He went on to suggest an 'emergency session' of the House of Commons to pass 'half a dozen first-class Bills', and looked forward to a 'working alliance' between the two Parties for this purpose.[2] In the upshot there was no emergency session and the only two Bills passed — the Public Works Facilities Bill and the Necessitous Areas Bill — were hardly 'first class measures'. Far from the Liberals obstructing 'drastic proposals', the Government showed no intention of introducing them.

If the Government and the Liberals could not agree about unemployment policy, they were united in their hatred of protection. Protection always had the greatest appeal in times of depression: an election in the summer or autumn of 1930 would therefore be the worst possible thing from the Liberal point of view, especially as it looked as though Labour would be defeated. Even if Labour survived, there would be little scope for a distinctive free trade party. Thus the Government's fear of defeat and the Liberals' fear of an early election combined to dictate a policy of riding out the storm.

Strangely enough electoral reform no longer appeared quite the barrier to co-operation it had once seemed. Proportional representation

[1] The correspondence between the three party leaders was published in *The Times*, 2 July 1930.

[2] *Daily Herald*, 17 June 1930.

was out of the question as Labour was firmly opposed, although Snowden was in favour,[1] but the alternative vote offered better possibilities. MacDonald could not have felt too happy about the prospects for the coming election. If the alternative vote could save the day, then it might be worth considering. With this in mind he met Lloyd George a number of times in May to discuss electoral reform. A concrete product of his speculation in this field was revealed in a story published by the *Manchester Guardian* on 23 May. It gave very full details of a memorandum, apparently drawn up by the Prime Minister and other Cabinet Ministers for the consideration of the N.E.C. and P.L.P. The memorandum proposed an electoral pact between Labour and Liberals at the following general election on the basis of the alternative vote, and went into details of how the second preferences would be split. It assumed that the Liberals would win thirty-seven seats and Labour eight from the Conservatives. This document was apparently discussed at the N.E.C. meeting on 20 May, when MacDonald made an eloquent plea for its acceptance; but Henderson opposed it on the grounds that the Party was opposed to the alternative vote, and it was agreed to drop it.

Two days later a statement from Transport House described the story as 'completely untrue'. But, significantly, it did not deny the existence of a document, stating that it had 'merely discussed the various possibilities and results on voting of different types of electoral reform'.[2] On 23 May *The Times* announced a 'breakdown' of negotiations between MacDonald and Lloyd George. Perhaps in view of the adverse party reaction the Prime Minister thought it wisest to desist.

[1] *An Autobiography*, vol. ii, p. 888.

[2] *Manchester Guardian*, 25 May 1930.

10

THE PARTIES AND THE SLUMP

i. INTRODUCTION

As the world depression deepened, the Government were increasingly faced with the demand for positive action to meet the worsening situation. For it was already becoming apparent that, in lieu of any rapid revival in world trade, the policy of negation would inevitably lead to a financial crisis in the not too distant future. The Liberals, as we have seen, were still trying to force upon the Government their 'bolder' domestic policy of public works and capital expenditure, though this policy was to undergo significant modifications in the course of the two-party conversations. More important perhaps was the increasing groundswell in favour of protection which was finally to provide the Conservative Party with a positive alternative to government policy. The decline in business profits produced a predictable clamour in favour of retrenchment in public expenditure, which was focused in an attack on the 'dole' and its alleged 'abuses', but over which already loomed the spectre of an unbalanced Budget and all its attendant evils. Underlying everything was a growing pessimism about the future of world trade, a greater willingness to toy with 'unsound' expedients as a way out of depression. This was the general background to the summer thinking of all three Parties on unemployment questions.

ii. THE COMMITTEE OF ECONOMISTS

For the Government, the summer of 1930 was taken up with the thinking that might have been done in the summer of 1929. By now the

Government had a proper 'brain' at its disposal for the task, or rather two — the E.A.C., and Anderson's committee of civil servants. For the first time since he took office, the whole machinery of government began to hum with the enquiries that MacDonald so loved to encourage. He himself had just taken over from Thomas responsibility for unemployment policy and felt in need of enlightenment. Perhaps he was growing tired of Snowden's lectures; perhaps he felt that the position of the Government needed restoring by a bolder economic policy.

In any event, freed for the moment from his foreign preoccupations, MacDonald seriously applied himself to the economic problem. He intervened more frequently at meetings of the E.A.C. and complained that it was not being very helpful. The E.A.C. itself was hardly to blame, since all initiative rested with the ministerial members and Snowden had warned it not to discuss serious matters. The remedy lay with MacDonald as chairman. On 30 June 1930, Hubert Henderson suggested that the Prime Minister ask the non-ministerial members of the E.A.C., one by one, for their opinion on the economic situation and the policies required to meet it, their replies to be collated and presented in the form of an E.A.C. memorandum. MacDonald concurred, despite Snowden's disapproval, and at the meeting of 10 July read out five questions and asked for replies in writing in time for the following meeting. The questions dealt with the issues raised by Keynes and Cole in their report and Henderson in his April memorandum.[1]

Keynes was unhappy about this method of procedure. The non-ministerial members were numerous and many of them were not economists but 'practical men' who could be relied upon to repeat the advice of Balfour and Cadman. When such replies were set against those coming from the economists the confusion and disagreement would be even greater. As a means of silencing the businessmen he urged MacDonald to abandon his questionnaire and instead appoint a small sub-committee of leading economists

[1] The five questions were: (1) What in your view are the chief causes of our present industrial position? (2) What in your view should be the trade policy adopted by H.M.G. to restore trade? (3) How in your view can the home market be developed thus enabling more people to command effective power to consume? (4) How in your opinion can the volume of exports be increased? (5) What in your opinion would be the framework of a definite Imperial Trade Policy? (Keynes Papers, E.A.C. 4).

to closet themselves together and try to produce, say by the end of October, an agreed diagnosis of our present problems and a reasoned list of possible remedies.[1]

MacDonald, who was all in favour of enquiries, unlike Snowden, whose convictions had become unalterably fixed many years before, immediately agreed. The committee of economists was set up on 1 August with instructions

to review the present economic condition of Great Britain, to examine the causes which are responsible for it and to indicate the conditions of recovery.[2]

Keynes was made chairman and with him were Pigou, Hubert Henderson, Lionel Robbins and Sir Josiah Stamp.[3] The joint secretaries were A. F. Hemming and R. F. Kahn. The Prime Minister asked them to have a report ready by 20 October.

The two leading economists in the group of five were undoubtedly Keynes and Pigou. Although both were Fellows of King's College, Cambridge, they were men of deeply contrasting character. Keynes, in addition to being a brilliant theoretical economist, was also very much a public figure, passionately concerned with the major problems of economic policy, especially unemployment. He had played a leading part in fashioning the Liberal Party's proposals on the subject, and his advocacy of a big public works programme placed him firmly in the ranks of those who desired a 'bold' unemployment policy. Pigou, by contrast, was the epitome of the cloistered academic. He wrote prolifically, but his books and articles, while rigorous and exact, had little general appeal and were not, on the whole, concerned with public policy. He was a theoretician first and foremost and disapproved of Keynes's attempts to popularise economics and his tendency to make fun of classical precepts. While he was by no means a reactionary, his devotion to the neo-classical school as represented by his beloved teacher, Marshall, his relative indifference to public policy, and his profound mistrust of all politicians made his advice less serviceable than it might have been.

[1] Keynes to MacDonald, 10 July 1930. Keynes Papers, E.A.C. 4.

[2] Keynes Papers, E.A.C. 4.

[3] Keynes had suggested, in addition to himself, Sir Josiah Stamp, Hubert Henderson, Henry Clay, Pigou, Lionel Robbins and D. H. Robertson.

Hubert Henderson was an economist who had left academic life to become editor of *The Nation and Athenaeum*, which soon became the leading exponent of progressive economics, with regular contributions from Keynes. Both he and Keynes were identified with an expansionary credit policy, in contrast to the deflation practised by the Bank of England: they wrote a joint article in 1929 endorsing Lloyd George's programme. From 1930 onwards Henderson was secretary to the E.A.C. and as such 'unofficial' economic adviser to the Government. In this capacity he wrote reports on the economic outlook which were models of lucidity and good sense. Lionel Robbins was then just thirty-two, but already Professor of Economics at the London School of Economics, where his passionate and brilliant lectures against all forms of government interference in the economy marked him as a Liberal of the old school, firmly wedded to classical precepts. Sir Josiah Stamp was the only member of the committee who was not primarily an academic economist. He had risen from humble beginnings to a leading position in the Inland Revenue department and his most important book *British Incomes and Property* was based on his intimate knowledge of the taxation system. From Inland Revenue he had proceeded to industry and was in 1930 president of the London, Midland and Scottish Railway, as well as a director of the Bank of England. His inclusion on the committee was perhaps intended to give an air of practical experience to its proceedings, but his contribution was not great. He complained that discussions were dominated by Keynes and Pigou who could not understand each other's terms, while the rest tried to keep the peace between them.[1]

The decison to invite a group of economists to diagnose the nation's ills and suggest remedies to the Government was an exciting and unprecedented attempt to make expert economic theory directly serviceable to government policy. As such it was viewed with grave suspicion by Snowden and the Treasury, who thought it was encroaching on their position. Snowden distrusted both Keynes and Henderson, and did not appreciate the Prime Minister's attempt to arm himself with extra-Treasury opinion, believing that, like a constitutional monarch, he should consult only his official advisers. On Keynes's part, too, it was a considerable act of faith to suppose that a group of brilliant men with differing political convictions might be persuaded to agree on remedies

[1] B. Webb Diaries, 14 October 1930.

that depended as much on value-judgments as on economic theory. Nevertheless, he had promised MacDonald a report by October and with this date in mind the economists set to work.

At the first meeting on 10 August Keynes asked Pigou to prepare a memorandum outlining briefly the heads of evidence for subsequent discussion. It was ready by 6 September and is an extremely lucid and interesting statement of the economic malaise and the various alternative remedies that might be adopted to meet it.

The existing economic situation, Pigou stated, was due to two factors: first, the long-enduring maladjustment dating from the beginning of the post-war slump, on to which had been superimposed the second factor — a downswing of a normal industrial cycle.

Britain's long-term difficulties were due to a combination of three factors. First, the relative demand for labour had altered in different occupations and the necessary readjustments had not been made. Secondly, the aggregate demand for labour had not expanded much. Thirdly, the rate of real wages had risen substantially. If one factor was taken as given, the trouble lay in the failure of the other two to fit in with it. Given the state of demand, excessive real wages were the cause of the trouble; given the state of real wages, the inadequacy of demand was the cause.

Had the classical laws been allowed to operate there would have been no 'intractable' unemployment problem since, according to classical theory, no equilibrium position was possible short of full employment. What would have happened was that the unemployed in the depressed industries would have sought work in the non-depressed industries and forced down real wages there. This would have brought the relative demand for labour into line with the relative demand for products; by cutting costs it would have brightened businessmen's expectations of future profit and thus stimulated investment; by increasing savings it would have reduced the rate of interest, thus cheapening the cost of borrowing. These consequences would have sufficed to restore full employment. The trouble was that these adjustments had not taken place, because of the existence of 'rigidities' in the wage structure caused mainly by the action of the trade unions in preventing a fall in money wages and by unemployment insurance which tied the unemployed to the distressed areas.

Granted these rigidities, there were three ways open to the Government to increase employment. It might try to reduce real wages by monetary measures, such as inflation or devaluation, or by a tariff which would increase the price of consumption goods; it might try to 'alter the conditions of productivity', especially foreign demand, by using rationalisation to lower costs and prices, and thus make exports more competitive; finally it might use 'devices' to stimulate home investment, such as bounties on wages or output in particular industries with elastic demand, selective protection, public works and so on, while leaving the other factors untouched. Pigou justifies 'devices' on the grounds that if there is clear evidence that the economic machine is not working as it should, then measures which in normal circumstances would do harm might, in such a case, do good.

The monetary effect of the depression was a shrinkage in the money supply through people tending to hoard, to leave money on time deposit, to keep more money liquid, etc. Now in circumstances of complete flexibility a temporary contraction in the supply of money, by its effect in reducing incomes, would create the conditions for recovery as already described. However, where the wage structure was inflexible, a contraction of the money supply stream would merely deepen the depression, without generating these forces of recovery. Hence in abnormal conditions, Pigou was prepared to advocate a curtailment of foreign lending as a 'device' to increase the domestic money supply.

Pigou's paper clearly demonstrates the problems facing the economist in this period as he tries to translate economic theory into practical policy. Almost invariably he has to work with two sets of assumptions, one of complete flexibility such as the classical model demands, the other of rigidities which exist in the real world. The policy conclusions which follow from one or the other are diametrically opposed, thus adding to the confusion of politicians. In the first case the correct policy would be one of deflation; in the second, one of 'inflation'. However, the second case simply did not exist in classical theory; hence theory became completely unserviceable and economists were forced back on the concept of 'abnormality' to explain what was happening.

But to say that classical theory had no solution to the problem of 1930 is not to say that economists were thereby bound to give the wrong advice. In fact most of them gave the right advice, hesitant and reluctant though it was. And when some of them did give the wrong advice it was based less on a crude translation of outdated theory into irrelevant precept than on certain value-judgments about the relationship of the individual and society or the function of government, derived from nineteenth-century political economy which of course was concerned with much more than economic theory. And it is only fair to add that the 'wrong' advice was given much more frequently by the business community, the City and the Bank of England than by the professional economists.

Pigou's opening statement produced much discussion on the effects of (i) an increase in investment, (ii) a tariff, (iii) a reduction in money wages. Pigou, Henderson, Robbins and Stamp all agreed that an increase in home investment would probably increase employment, but added that much depended on the way it was done. Thus Henderson laid great stress on the utility of the investment and warned that a certain type of government investment — such as a public works programme — might actually diminish overall investment by alarming businessmen. Pigou thought that if the extra investment was a purely 'monetary' affair (inflation) it would succeed in increasing employment only 'insofar as it bamboozles wage earners into not claiming money wage increases equivalent to price increases'. All four agreed that an increase of investment in the world at large would stimulate employment by increasing the demand for Britain's exports, but Stamp wondered whether it would also have the effect of 'enhancing competition in established lines of our own — cotton and so on'.

Pigou, Henderson and Stamp all gave cautious support to the idea of a tariff. Henderson and Stamp thought that it would increase employment in those industries catering mainly for the home market; that insofar as it raised prices it would stimulate business confidence, but that it would also make exports less competitive. Pigou thought that its main effect would be psychological. It would increase employment, he said, 'insofar as it removed errors of pessimism or created errors of optimism in businessmen's minds'. ('Must they always be errors?' Keynes asked.) Here again Pigou, Henderson and Stamp were not abandoning their belief in free trade as the best means in normal circumstances of regulating world trading relations. They were making the assumption that conditions were not normal and asking themselves what device would be most beneficial to employment in the short term. They realised what many of the political supporters of free trade failed to, namely, that normal arguments for free imports and exports were not applicable to the current position.

To Robbins, on the other hand, free trade was more than just a theory for the optimum regulation of trading relations: it was a way of life. As such it should not be sacrificed in a moment of temporary stress. To Robbins, protection suggested economic nationalism rampant; it would play into the hands of every narrow and ungenerous sentiment in public life. The others might argue that tariffs were a temporary expedient to be removed when the crisis was over, but history showed that it was much easier to put them up than take them down, for what lingered on after the economic need for them had disappeared was the ideology which they had created. It was incredible, he concluded, that the finest minds in England were joining company with Beaverbrook and Rothermere in an '*Eldorado banal de tous les vieux garçons*'.

All four favoured a reduction in real wages on the grounds that it would reduce costs and improve business confidence. They realised, however, that a direct assault on wages was out of the question, and so they recommended various roundabout ways of achieving the same result — inflation, tariffs and so on. Indeed their advocacy of 'devices' was at least partly determined by their belief that these would ultimately bring the fundamental remedy — wage reductions — into play.

We have seen that Pigou, Henderson, Robbins and Stamp assumed rigidities in the wage structure to be the cause of unemployment. Keynes, on the other hand, attributed the crisis to a rigidity in interest rates. He argued that the levels of savings and investment were determined by two autonomous sets of decisons taken by savers and investors and that the only way of bringing them into harmony was through the 'natural' or 'equilibrium' rate of interest. Now if for some reason the actual (bank) rate of interest was higher than the rate required to bring savings and investment into conjunction, it followed that savings would exceed investment: prices would fall and businessmen would make losses. The key to recovery was the restoration of prices which alone would stimulate a satisfactory level of investment activity. This would be brought about by lowering the actual rate of interest so that it corresponded to the 'equilibrium' rate.

Maccapablanca's Rush Hour

Sir Oswald Mosley

'To O. M. who may one day do the things of which we dream.' (*John Strachey*)

But suppose the rate of interest would not come down? Keynes had by now come to believe that the operation of the gold standard had, so far as Britain was concerned, made impossible the restoration of the 'equilibrium' rate of interest. Also he was beginning to doubt, empirically, whether a low interest rate would bring about recovery after prolonged business pessimism, for he sensed that the interest rate — that rate at which it became profitable for businessmen to borrow in order to start fresh enterprises — had a component of risk in it which might loom much larger in their calculations than the actual discount rate. For these reasons he came to believe that more direct steps to stimulate investment would be necessary. In considering the effect of such investment he was helped by a powerful new analytic tool. One of the secretaries to the committee was R. F. Kahn, who had worked out a mathematical method of determining successive increments to employment produced by an initial outlay. This was the famous 'employment multiplier', which was first published in the autumn of 1931, but complete in all its essentials by the summer of 1930. It was shown to all five economists, but only Keynes grasped its importance. Lawrence Klein argues that the first time Keynes's work showed the influence of Kahn's multiplier was in 1933,[1] but this is in fact not so. He made full use of the concept in attacking the orthodox theory of public works in a paper presented to his fellow economists on the committee in September 1930.

The orthodox view, Keynes argued, was that a given expenditure was unproductive of any future employment unless it increased the capital wealth of the country, unless, in other words, it yielded an economic return. Kahn's argument was that secondary employment ensuing from the initial outlay did not depend on how the primary employment had been brought about. He calculated that in 1930 there would be an unemployment multiplier of two. The Government assumed that it cost £250 to employ one man for a year. On this basis £100m would provide work for 400,000. On Kahn's estimate, 800,000 would be employed. If in addition the £100m of 'excess savings' which now went abroad could be invested at home by developing domestic industries to replace imports under cover of protection, employment would be provided for an additional 800,000 men. By this combination, Keynes

[1] L. R. Klein, *The Keynesian Revolution*, 1952, p. 40.

thought, 'we might expect to have substantially cured the unemployment problem'.

Thus his programme of recovery consisted of an investment loan of £200m to be raised from 'idle' and foreign balances, under the cover of a tariff which would improve the balance of payments and at the same time enlarge investment opportunities at home by reducing imports. How feasible was it? In the first place, Keynes was probably over-optimistic about the effects of the 'multiplier', for he ignored the 'lags' and 'leakages' which subsequent experience revealed. Politically he ignored the effects on business confidence of a big public works programme, especially if carried out by a Labour Government. Despite the plentiful evidence of excess capacity, many businessmen still believed that any government spending was bound to divert resources from private spending. Orthodox theory admitted the existence of a whole range of projects which might not be remunerative in the fullest sense, but was hardly likely to approve of just handing out £200m irrespective of 'economic return'. A Keynesian programme of this type would certainly have increased employment, but not nearly as much as its author anticipated.

Although Pigou and Keynes argued furiously about their respective papers, they were still both classicists and their analysis was broadly classical also. Pigou concentrated his attention on rigidities in the wage structure; Keynes concentrated his on rigidities in the interest rates. Pigou's analysis led him to deflation; Keynes's to what was then called inflation. Their differences at this stage lay more in their assessment of business psychology than in economic theory. Keynes believed that an expansionist monetary policy was the easiest way to revive business confidence; Pigou inclined towards complete flexibility in wages. But both were agreed that the classical remedies of wage reductions and low interest rates would ultimately restore the system to full employment equilibrium. Keynes at this point did not yet see that investment opportunities might be limited by the lack of effective demand, a discovery which was to be his big subsequent contribution to economic theory.

However differently they might have tried to solve the unemployment problem if they 'had only themselves to please', Pigou and Keynes were brought together by the 'abnormality' of the times. They both recognised that their own particular solutions might not be feasible. They both, therefore, sought the most direct means of producing employment. Their philosophy was very much as Pigou described it in the following analogy:

> A man ordered to walk a tight-rope carrying a bag in one hand would be better off if he were allowed to carry a second bag in the other hand, though of course if he started bagless to add a bag would handicap him.

In other words, although complete market flexibility was the ideal, as it no longer existed many of the objections to government interference were thereby removed.

The economists' report, which was ready by 24 October, is not as interesting as the discussion which led to it. This was inevitable. It had to satisfy the economists themselves, which involved considerable ingenuity and proved in the end only partly successful (Robbins produced a minority report and Pigou made a number of reservations). It also had to be feasible, in other words useful to the Government; and this utility depended not on the correctness of any particular proposal but upon how much support could be mustered in favour of it. Hence the report was broadly orthodox, with space given to a number of the 'devices' which Pigou and others were prepared to recommend in an emergency situation.

The first section surveyed the causes of Britain's difficulties and the impact of the world slump. Long-term difficulties were attributed to demand changes away from the traditional export industries and internal rigidities which had prevented the required adaptations from being made. Chief among these was unemployment insurance. The main effect of the collapse in world prices had been to increase the burden of debt — government debt and business debt — which was fixed in monetary terms. The level of money wages had become inappropriate in the new conditions.

Internationally, falling prices had been aggravated firstly by the unwillingness of entrepreneurs to undertake new investment in falling price conditions, and secondly by the decline in standing, in the opinion of lenders, of many borrowers, in particular China, South America and Central Europe. To try to revive international lending 'a large joint pool of approved loans' might be formed by leading countries. 'Some far reaching effort at international co-operation', the report said, 'may be imperatively demanded.'

For Britain a number of proposals were put forward. The first, significantly, was the reform of unemployment insurance, 'which was urgently required in the public interest', because insurance and the 'dole' impeded mobility of labour, encouraged short-time working, held wage rates artificially high and constituted a definite tax on employers. The language here was the most forthright in the whole document. The economists clearly believed that unemployment pay, however humanitarian, was holding up the required shifts of labour and was moreover using up funds to keep men idle which might be better employed setting them to work.

A confusing section on wages followed. The report toyed with two expedients, either lowering wages or raising them! Both, it was argued, would increase employment. Lowering wages in the highly sheltered trades (those catering mainly for the home market) would attract more labour to them and also cheapen exports. Raising wages would increase home demand and thus employment and the cost could be met by saving on unemployment benefit. Its disadvantages were that it would create balance of payments difficulties, would have a bad effect on businessmen, might lead to demands for still higher wages and might raise prices. For these reasons a general rise in wages was rejected, but there was cautious support for subsidising additional employees in the sheltered industries at a rate less than that of unemployment insurance, Hubert Henderson dissenting. Wage reductions were recommended as a last resort and, if made, only in conjunction with reductions in salaries, dividends and rents.

Turning to home development, the committee urged that an attempt should be made to bring down the long-term rate of interest, recommended a tax on foreign lending, and proposed a big public works programme. The 'treasury view' was repudiated quite decisively:

> We do not accept the view that the undertaking of such work must necessarily cause any important diversion from employment in ordinary industry.

No use was made of Kahn's multiplier. The old phrase about works being 'useful and productive' made a familiar appearance, and the committee concluded that 'care would have to be taken not to alarm public opinion by a hastily improvised programme of dubious projects'.

Keynes, Henderson and Stamp went on to advocate a general tariff of 10 per cent. Pigou was less forthright, but conceded the case for 'some protective import duty'. Robbins's minority report showed his disinclination to tinker with 'devices'; it consisted in the main of a more strident restatement of classical remedies, and the complete rejection of a tariff.

Despite some confusion in analysis and remedy, the economists' report was a radical document with a comprehensive programme of action consisting of three main ingredients: first, a recasting of unemployment insurance on terms less favourable to the unemployed and less onerous to the Government, to go hand in hand with a policy of home investment on a large scale and a general tariff to yield both revenue and protection. If these measures in combination failed to increase employment, then there would have to be wage reductions in the sheltered industries.[1]

iii. CIVIL SERVICE VIEWS

To show that no solution was to be barred MacDonald, before his departure for Lossiemouth, sent Sir John Anderson, the head of the secretariat, a copy of the Mosley memorandum, with the following note:

Examine the proposals made here and see what is in them:

1. We should have in handy form the result of examination in figures of raising the school leaving age.
2. The proposal for roads in the short term section:
   (*a*) what can be done.
   (*b*) cost.
   (*c*) value in terms of employment.
   (*d*) length of time taken to complete.
3. Pensions proposals:
   (*a*) clear statement of what they are in figures.
   (*b*) persons they affect.
   (*c*) offsets because they would relieve other funds.
   (*d*) cost of such pensions.
4. Any other points that strike you.

Set this out in as tabular a form as possible so as not to cover up in long blocks of type the essential points.

J.R.M. 12/7/30[2]

---

[1] The material for this account of the committee of economists is to be found in the Keynes Papers, E.A.C. 4. It is not yet sufficiently well arranged to be systematically classified.

[2] MacDonald Papers, Mosley Memorandum File.

Sir John Anderson's civil service career had been extremely distinguished. A Scotsman, he was one of a remarkable group[1] who, without any advantage in background or early education, had entered the civil service at the beginning of the century and had risen rapidly to high position. He had passed out top in the civil service examination list in 1905, excelling in all subjects except economics, in which he gained 126 marks out of 500. A man of fine intellect, he was nevertheless heavy and portentous in manner, earning the nickname of 'Pompous John' from some of his colleagues.[2]

There is no record of Anderson's reply to MacDonald's request; but on 31 July he wrote to the Prime Minister to give an account of the investigations carried out by his secretariat in its seven weeks' existence, 'the results of which have been in the main negative'. Anderson made three main points:

(1) Unemployment statistics gave an exaggerated view of the magnitude of the problem, for 'a large number of people really abused the Unemployment Insurance Scheme'. This aspect should be thoroughly investigated 'if only on the ground that anything which tends to exaggerate the blackness of the outlook must operate to our prejudice both at home and abroad by spreading depression and tending to abate confidence in our ability to pull through'.

(2) The hard core of permanent unemployment was in the depressed areas. There was clearly a need for constructive work, 'but there is no escaping the conclusion that a fundamental attack on this part of the problem is out of the question so long as it is overlaid by the unemployment due to general world conditions . . . *the application of radical measures pre-supposes a healthy condition of general trade*'.

(3) Investigations had shown that 'we are now reaching the limit of works which will conform to any reasonable standard of economic utility or development. . . . The abandonment of any criteria of economic development with the consequential expenditure of public money at this juncture would be disastrous in the shock that it would give to the confidence which it is essential

---

[1] Such as Sir James Grigg and Sir Horace Wilson.

[2] John Wheeler-Bennett, *John Anderson, Viscount Waverley*, 1962. Wheeler-Bennett is wrong in thinking that Anderson was 'seconded to lead a team of civil servants collected from other departments and placed at Mr. Thomas's disposal'. He did not become actively involved in unemployment problems till June 1930; that is why 'no mention or acknowledgement is made [in J. H. Thomas's memoirs] of . . . Sir John Anderson' — an omission which Sir John Wheeler-Bennett naturally finds odd.

to maintain if the country is to get the benefit of the world recovery when it comes'. The Government, warned Anderson, 'must sweep away ruthlessly any lingering illusions that a substantial reduction of unemployment figures is to be sought in the artifical provison of employment'. [italics mine.]

How then could such a reduction be brought about? The answer was gloomy in the extreme. The Government's position was analogous to that of

> the captain and officers of a great ship which has run aground on a falling tide; no human endeavour will get the ship afloat until in the course of nature the tide again begins to flow.

MacDonald, over-impressed perhaps by this reference to the mysterious forces of nature to which he himself felt very close as he walked across the windy moors of Lossiemouth, wrote back: 'Your letter expresses exactly my own frame of mind'.[1]

The contrast in tone between Anderson's letter and the report of the committee of economists is striking. The country's most eminent economists were being forced by the pressure of facts to re-examine the whole basis of their beliefs in an effort to find remedies to meet a desperate situation, while a civil servant, who knew little about economics and who had studied the unemployment problem for seven weeks, announced that everything must wait upon the forces of nature! It is perhaps not unfair to speculate that, far from having thoroughly investigated all possibilities, Anderson had met a number of captains of industry and the City, over luncheon or dinner, at Brooks's or the Athenaeum, who had warned him that any 'radical measures' would undoubtedly so damage confidence as to produce economic collapse. In particular it is difficult to see at this stage any warrant for his assertion that 'a large number of people' were abusing the unemployment insurance fund, especially as Miss Bondfield was conscientiously producing figures from her department to show that there was little or no abuse.

Continuing his enquiries, MacDonald asked the Treasury for its view on the practicability of raising a large loan for home investment. He received a lengthy and grave reply which effectively closed the door in that direction. The central proposition of the treasury argument was that

[1] MacDonald Papers, Hartshorn Enclosures.

a state loan would in principle be legitimate if, and only if, the works were productive works yielding a money return to meet the interest and sinking fund charges of the loan.

This stern proposition appeared to rule out government-financed works such as road building, for although Morrison claimed that such work was beneficial in the broadest sense, he never suggested that a money value could be assigned to it which would meet the Treasury's conditions. If a loan were raised to finance projects which were in the least dubious or unsound, disaster, the Treasury predicted, would indubitably follow. Rates of interest would go up, there would in all probability be a flight from the pound, the war debt could not be converted into cheaper forms, the capital market would be depleted, the lop-sided character of industrial activity would be accentuated, for such works would concentrate on particular areas instead of 'diffusing prosperity over the country as a whole', and businessmen would be finally discouraged.[1]

Perhaps the Ministry of Transport had schemes for a large addition to the road programme? To Lossiemouth in the middle of August came a memorandum from Sir Henry Maybury definitively excluding that possibility. No large expansion would take place in the trunk road programme, said Maybury, nor could the rate of progress be greatly speeded up, as

schemes which could most readily and promptly be undertaken were naturally the first to be handled under earlier programmes; the more difficult and costly ones being postponed.

Rejecting any large national schemes, Maybury warned the Government to consider what effect these would have on the local authorities already preparing or carrying out large road programmes:

Would [they] be content to proceed with their works and continue to find their share of the cost if the government itself put other works in hand by direct administration on 100 per cent basis? Might not the dislocation and hesitation thus occasioned lead to a slackening of suspension of work which would counteract the amount of employment which would result from the new machinery?

If the Government did decide in favour of national schemes, they should not assume that an immediate start would be possible. The local

[1] MacDonald Papers, File 16, Unemployment. The Treasury memorandum is reproduced in Appendix V.

authorities would have to be appeased; surveys and engineering preparations would take much time; there would have to be negotiations with landowners, tenants and allotment holders; alternative routes suggested by the town planning authorities and the Council for the Preservation of Rural England would have to be considered; amenities could not be disregarded; displaced tenants would have to be rehoused. All this meant that the time needed to start government schemes would not be 'materially reduced' by direct control. Nevertheless, Maybury thought, there were some schemes that the State could undertake, such as the elimination of certain selected level crossings, which might eventually provide employment for 16,000 men a year.[1]

The final unemployment missive to arrive in Lossiemouth that summer was a memorandum written by Vernon Hartshorn, Thomas's successor as Lord Privy Seal. Hartshorn had been Postmaster-General in 1924, but had not immediately been given office in 1929 because he was, like Attlee, a member of the Simon Commission on India. When the Commission finished its work early in 1930,[2] he became available again, and MacDonald had taken the opportunity provided by the reshuffle in June to bring him into the Cabinet: Attlee likewise entered the Government as Mosley's successor.

Hartshorn accepted the view that the giant staple industries would never recover their pre-war position. The labour displaced could go either into new expanding export industries such as motor-cars, chemicals, electrical engineering and so on; or it could go into the development of home manufactures at the expense of imports. There was no immediate prospect of an increase in export trade: therefore it was necessary to consider the second alternative.

After fourteen months in office, schemes of work to the value of £43m were actually in operation, providing work for 67,000 men. Was that a satisfactory record? At first Hartshorn had thought not, and found the Ministry of Transport unduly pessimistic; Maybury's report in particular had been 'surprising'. But

> after fully examining the position, I am satisfied that not much more is possible than is actually being done.

[1] MacDonald Papers, Hartshorn Enclosures.

[2] The first volume of the Simon Report was published on 10 June 1930.

The limitations of a public works policy should be frankly faced. Instead, the Government should concentrate on a long-term policy of expanding agriculture, by increasing the production of pig, poultry and dairy products at the expense of imports, and should also encourage the growth of the newer industries. Was there enough finance, Hartshorn asked?

Under the heading of 'general factors', he wondered whether transport costs were not too high, whether it might be possible to improve sales and marketing organisation, whether 'some modification of fiscal policy' would be necessary (this veiled reference to tariffs was not pursued further). In conclusion he wrote that the Government must announce 'a bold and determined' industrial policy on a 'large number of points'.

MacDonald congratulated his deputy on 'one of the best statements of unemployment that has come under my hand', and added 'you set out the questions which we must consider and answer if the next session is to bring us any credit'.[1] However, the only real questions that emerged from the report were those Hartshorn asked himself: Where was the finance coming from? Would the Government consider tariffs? Hartshorn had joined MacDonald's band of earnest enquirers.

iv. THE TWO-PARTY CONFERENCE

Following MacDonald's first invitation to Lloyd George, on 19 May 1930, to join in a three-party conference on unemployment, Lord Lothian, the Liberal peer, suggested to Lloyd George that the Liberal special committee on unemployment be reconstituted to bring their programme up to date. Lothian added: 'it is obvious . . . I think, that the public works programme by itself is now insufficient to deal with a tidal wave'. Lord Lothian was expecting a 'political crash' in the autumn and thought that 'the country will follow any Party or group which really has an effective plan for dealing with the situation'. Lothian's mistake was the same as Mosley's. The main ingredients of the revised policy should be a vigorous programme of national development; economy in the public finances; revision of the income tax to lighten the heavy burden

[1] MacDonald Papers, Hartshorn Enclosures.

on industry and agriculture; anti-dumping legislation; an enquiry by the Government into the state of modernisation of certain backward industries, with credit facilities for rationalisation; a big agricultural policy; and finally an international conference on unemployment. The main new ingredient in Lothian's mixture, a highly significant one, was the emphasis on economy and reduction in taxation. The Liberals, like everyone else, were being infected with the current campaign for economy.

Lloyd George accepted Lothian's suggestion and he, Lothian and Seebohm Rowntree met, with their advisers, at Churt in the middle of June, to draw up a rough agenda for the enquiry. One of the decisions reached at that meeting was to ask Sir Arthur Salter, a Liberal of long standing and Britain's representative on the economic commission of the League of Nations, to produce a memorandum on Britain's position. This reached Lothian at the end of June.[1] Salter ascribed Britain's difficulties 'to a more static and less elastic economic system than we find . . . in any other country'. The main factors were

(1) The conservatism of industrialists and their pessimistic outlook. Their heavy commitment in old plant and their poor financial position — living off overdrafts — meant that the banks were masters, yet the banks felt no responsibility for management or re-equipment. For these reasons new capital was difficult to raise.
(2) The banks, while they had legal control (through overdrafts) over many industries, had neither the knowledge, tradition or sense of responsibility for re-organisation. They were 'a dead hand on development'. Centralisation had reduced elasticity of local financing, but had not secured the advantages of a collective policy as the big five did not co-operate.
(3) The dead weight of fixed charges and obligations was heavier than in any other country and increased automatically with every fall in commodity prices.
(4) The semi-monopoly structure of British industry prevented the quick transmission of wholesale price reductions into lower retail prices. This was particularly serious 'in relation to the cost of living in view of its bearing on the wages question'.
(5) The administration of income tax penalised frequent changes of plant.
(6) Industry was suffering from excessive real wages — 'prices have gone down, I believe, some 12 per cent in six years, while wages remain fixed in terms of sterling. The economic situation had not been such as to bear an increase of some 11 per cent in real wages in six years'.

[1] Lothian Papers, Box 214.

(7) The demarcation and traineeship systems were also important factors in 'discouraging adaptability and changes of occupation to a disastrous extent'.

These factors [Sir Arthur Salter argued] create an inelasticity of system to an unparalleled degree at a time when elasticity is most required. With reductions in effective competition, the fringe of custom is sacrificed as an alternative to reduction of price. Adaptability of function is sacrificed to a desire to remain at the same place and the same work. The advantages of new plant are impeded by taxation and financial difficulties.

Salter's memorandum was different in emphasis from *We Can Conquer Unemployment*. Essentially it was a plea for a more vigorous capitalism with an up-to-date continental, rather than a nineteenth-century British, model. Its robust attack on British economic institutions gave it an air of radicalism and placed it firmly in a long and continuing tradition of criticism that has looked to continental practice to rescue Britain from her economic dilemmas. It had little bearing on the immediate unemployment situation, but it offered a long-term framework for reconstruction which the Liberals were to appropriate in the advice they gave to the Government.

Rapid disillusionment was in store for the Liberal committee in their conversations with the Government in the two-party conference. Throughout the summer Lloyd George, Lothian and Rowntree held meetings with the government representatives. The Liberals would press on the Government the proposals of the 1929 pamphlet; the Government would agree with them in principle, but argue that it was financially and administratively impossible to undertake them in the time the Liberals wanted. A typical confrontation took place on 18 August. On the agenda was Sir Henry Maybury's memorandum,[1] which argued, broadly, that no major extensions were possible to the existing volume of road building. The Liberals were led by Lloyd George, Lothian and Rowntree, accompanied by one or two technical advisers; the Government were represented by Hartshorn and Morrison, accompanied by Hurcomb and Maybury from the Ministry of Transport. Lloyd George, opening the discussion, described Maybury's memorandum as 'impotent'. If it represented the final views of the Government there was no further basis for discussion. Maybury said Lloyd George had completely misunderstood his memorandum. The two men then became involved in a long and heated discussion on how long it

[1] See above, p. 218.

would take to survey a road. Lloyd George claimed that he had been informed by his professional advisers that a man could survey a mile of road per day. Maybury challenged this statement, whereupon one of the professional advisers present, a Mr. Humphreys,[1] said that he had told the Liberal leader that a competent man could take levels at the rate of a mile a day in easy country. On this informative note the meeting broke up.

Relating this confrontation to MacDonald, Hartshorn wrote:

> Lloyd George's tone throughout our talk this morning was distinctly truculent and I formed the impression that he was determined to misunderstand and to find a ground for breaking off negotiations, so as to be free to demonstrate in the House of Commons.

MacDonald agreed; nothing good could be expected of Lloyd George,

> but I do not understand why Rowntree and Lothian seem to support him in his attitude. I shall try to come across one or the other privately when I get to Town.[2]

Neither of them apparently considered the possibility that the Liberals really did want to expand and accelerate the road programme.

On 25 August the Ministry of Transport produced a detailed reply to the Liberal proposals. Generally speaking, it observed, the Lloyd George programme 'resembles in character programmes being carried out by the Ministry of Transport'. The differences of opinion had arisen over 'the justification for and practicability of the scale of expenditure proposed to the period of time within which it can be compressed'. Humphreys himself had admitted in discussion that the Liberal estimate was based 'on the hypothesis of a virtual dictatorship under which no regard would be paid to the protests of individuals, public bodies or even statutory undertakings'. Even if this were not considered an overriding objection, there were further, more practical, considerations:

> For instance, would it be possible to maintain nationally essential road communications if some thousands of weak bridges were rebuilt simultaneously and work started concurrently on all trunk roads and all rural roads; could the nationally indispensable services be maintained on railways and canals if all

[1] Mr. Humphreys was the director of a firm of consulting engineers, Howard Humphreys Ltd., who had advised Lloyd George on the technical aspects of the Liberal road programme.

[2] MacDonald Papers, Hartshorn Enclosures.

weak bridges were simultaneously undergoing reconstruction? Might not such far reaching operations give rise to a disastrous disorganisation of transport throughout the country and might not the general severing of communications render it practically impossible to transport the materials necessary for road and bridge reconstruction?

As an example of the legal difficulties to be overcome, short of dictatorship, the memorandum cited the case of the East Lancashire Road (estimated cost £3m) which had been approved in principle in 1924–5 and had then been delayed by five years by a whole series of court injunctions obtained by important interests. Even though emergency powers were used, their exercise was obstructed: when the Minister was on the point of making his order, the validity of his action was challenged in the High Court by the Manchester Ship Canal.[1]

This pattern of attack and counter-attack was repeated over the whole range of the Liberal emergency proposals. In the circumstances, they stood up remarkably well. However, they did not survive intact. When the Liberal pamphlet, *How to Tackle Unemployment*, the published version of the final Liberal proposals to the Government, was issued in October 1930, it was found that the public works programme had not only diminished in importance as a solution to the unemployment problem, but had undergone a marked change in emphasis.

In part this was due, inevitably, to the increase in unemployment. The Liberals still hoped to employ over 600,000 men on emergency works, but by October 1930 unemployment stood at well over 2,000,000. As no one at that time was prepared to pay men wages simply to dig holes and fill them up again, and as the Liberals had been duly impressed by the administrative difficulties of launching public works schemes, it is hardly surprising that the main emphasis should have shifted to long-term industrial reconstruction. Under this head, the Liberal pamphlet emphasised and elaborated the insights of Salter's memorandum:

The need for reduction in our manufacturing costs has, therefore, been greater than in that of almost any other country. At the same time, the securing of this reduction has been and is a more difficult thing for the British manufacturer than for any other, because in some respects Great Britain has a more static, less elastic economic system. This is probably by far the most serious and substantial cause of our troubles.[2]

---

[1] MacDonald Papers, Hartshorn Enclosures.

[2] *How to Tackle Unemployment*, October 1930, p. 12.

The pamphlet suggested that there were three alternative remedies: a direct reduction in our standard of life; the protection of our present relative inefficiency; an increase in our efficiency.[1] The first was rejected as 'a policy of defeat'. Protection was also rejected, predictably, on the usual free trade grounds. This left the third alternative, 'namely, a sharp reduction in our costs, to be secured by a great increase in our national productive and marketing efficiency'. It was estimated that the reduction would have to be in the order of 10 per cent.[2] The State should give a lead by a rigid programme of economy. 'If industry is to reduce its costs by 10 per cent or more, then the Government should, for its part, undertake itself to reduce costs in the same proportion.' To achieve this the Liberals recommended that the Government should appoint a small committee of businessmen, on the lines of the Geddes Committee,

> to make recommendations to the Chancellor of the Exchequer for effecting forthwith all possible reductions in the national expenditure on supply services, having regard especially to the present and prospective position of the revenue and to the effect of the present burden of taxation in restricting industry and employment.[3]

The other proposals for government action again bore the strong imprint of Salter's memorandum. Taxation should be changed to encourage installation of new plant;[4] pressure should be brought on the banks to become partners in enterprise;[5] trade facilities should be restored and export credits extended, especially with a view to increasing trade with Russia;[6] the Government should create and subsidise a research institute 'to bridge the gulf between science and industry'; finally, temporary help should be given to the rationalisation of private industry.[7]

As a contribution to the solution of the 'permanent' as opposed to the 'cyclical' unemployment problem, the Liberal pamphlet proposed a big new policy of agricultural development, designed over a period of years to settle 100,000 families on farms of between three acres and a hundred and thereby enable British agriculture 'to capture and hold a large part of the £400m market for foodstuffs within our shores now supplied from other countries'. This policy, it was estimated, would

1 *How to Tackle Unemployment*, p. 16. 2 Ibid. p. 20. 3 Ibid. p. 23.
4 Ibid. p. 25. 5 Ibid. p. 27. 6 Ibid. pp. 28–9.
7 Ibid. pp. 30–1.

result in an addition of '500,000 people directly employed in agriculture and its ancillary services'.[1] Moreover, if such a policy were to be started immediately, about 150,000 men would be employed in the first year 'in preparatory work' — reconditioning land, building new houses, re-equipping farms, improving soil, constructing dairies and so on.[2]

It is this employment that forms the new addition to the emergency programme and offsets the more pessimistic reappraisals of the possibility of road building, telephone construction and so on. However, the Liberals still hope to have an additional 250,000 a year working on the roads, arguing that the only difference between their proposals and the Government's 'is one of time'.[3] The housing policy was also somewhat expanded, and the Liberals hoped that suburban development could provide employment for 150,000 men a year.[4] Thus, by including the 150,000 men who would be employed for preparatory agricultural work and the 100,000 already being employed by government-assisted schemes, the Liberals reckoned that 650,000 men could be set to work within a year.[5] Once more the work was to be financed out of a national development loan.[6]

Although this Liberal document bore evidence of hasty compilation, its programme was up to a point logical and comprehensible. Both sides of industry — employers and unions — were urged to react more flexibly to shifts in demand, to the need for technological development and rationalisation; the banks were urged to become partners of industrial enterprise — 'industrial banks' as in the United States and Germany; the Government for its part was to provide specific forms of assistance — tax concessions on new plant, trade facilities and export credits, a research institute[7] and so on. Further, there was to be a deliberate policy of agricultural development, partly because a small-holding peasantry was considered healthy in itself, partly to lessen Britain's dependence on exports. In the greater emphasis given to these proposals we can detect Lloyd George's long-standing interest in agriculture,

[1] *How to Tackle Unemployment*, p. 58. [2] Ibid. p. 59. [3] Ibid. p. 63.
[4] Ibid. p. 72. [5] Ibid. p. 86. [6] Ibid. pp. 88–9.

[7] The Liberal interest in research institutes arose from a memorandum received describing the work of the Mellon Institute of Industrial Research in Pittsburgh, and Dr. A. D. Little's Institute in Boston, both of which were 'deliberately directing attention to the creation of new industries'. Lothian Papers, Box 214.

John Maynard Keynes

Miss Margaret Bondfield

'I lived only for the Trade Union Movement.'

backed on this occasion by Lord Lothian, one of the largest Scottish landowners. While these long-term adaptations were taking place, the Government should mount an autonomous investment programme to absorb a proportion of the unemployed and thus engineer an increase in effective demand which would have a cumulative effect. It is unfortunate that the one item of this Liberal programme that has generally been noted, in the light of its subsequent influence on events, is the plea for economy. This was by no means an integral part of the policy. Rather it was a bowing to the prevailing wind. Retrenchment in government expenditure was considered *psychologically* necessary to give confidence in government policy, and the Liberals adopted it to give businessmen confidence in their proposals. The important point was that it was intended as a small part of a *package deal*. Retrenchment in a number of services, including unemployment insurance, would be more than offset by a big expansion in investment and a generally constructive outlook. If a Government did nothing to break the psychological stranglehold of depression, then it was inevitable, in those circumstances, that it would eventually be forced back on retrenchment as the only possible constructive policy, in conditions of much greater financial difficulty than prevailed in October 1930.

V. FREE TRADE VERSUS PROTECTION

One of the foremost topics of debate in the middle of 1930 was the old question of free trade versus protection. The general argument in favour of free trade has been admirably stated by Gottfried von Haberler in his book *Theory of International Trade*:

> It can be proved that, at any rate under the usual assumptions of general economic theory (free competition, absence of friction and so on), the unrestricted international exchange of goods increases the real income of *all* the participating countries. The price mechanism, under competition, automatically ensures that each country specialises in the production of those goods which it is relatively best suited to produce and imports those goods, and only those goods, which it can obtain more cheaply, taking account of transport costs, in this indirect manner, than by producing them itself.[1]

---

[1] p. 221.

The most important point to note in this argument is the qualifying phrase 'under the usual assumptions of general economic theory (free competition, absence of friction and so on)'. As in so many other discussions, the 'usual assumptions' (which included the assumption of full employment) were not valid in the particular circumstances of 1930, even if the general argument was irreproachable. Thus in a depression a particular tariff might increase employment in a particular industry, even at the expense of 'real income'; a tariff might be a means of coping temporarily with particular problems consequent upon depression (such as balance of payments or budget deficits); it might be a means of protecting particular industries (such as agriculture) from the deflationary effects of competitive wage and price reductions, of cutting, in W. A. Lewis's words, 'the link between international trade and national production'.[1] Finally, it might be desirable to put up tariffs for tactical reasons so as to bring pressure on other countries to reduce theirs.

Traditionally, free trade was the ruling orthodoxy in Britain. It was well suited to nineteenth-century conditions, for it enabled manufacturers to enlarge their export markets when there was little competition and in return to obtain cheaply the necessary raw materials; by the same token cheap food meant low wages. However, the enormous optimism that had characterised the mid-nineteenth-century hey-day of free trade did not long survive the growth of foreign competition or the start of the boom–slump alternation of the modern trade cycle. Thus free trade was challenged in the 1880s and the early years of this century by Joseph Chamberlain; and protectionist feeling was bound to spread with the arrival of the greatest depression in modern times. As might be expected, Birmingham was foremost in the fight: in this case as in others, the genuine desire of manufacturers to protect their profits was linked to a paternalistic desire to protect their workers from the drastic readjustments in income and employment which the free trade solution would have entailed.[2] Throughout 1930 the ranks of the free traders were thinned by the desertion of economists, industrialists, bankers and trade unionists.[3] As Baldwin remarked: 'The age of free trade is passing . . .

[1] Lewis, *Economic Survey 1919–1939*, p. 165.

[2] See Asa Briggs, *History of Birmingham*, vol. ii, *1865–1938*, 1952, p. 281.

[3] We have already noted the betrayal of Keynes, Pigou and Henderson; industrial agitation for protection in the summer of 1930 crystallised in the

because no new free-traders are being born today.'[1] So strongly was protectionist feeling flowing that the Conservatives felt it was safe to advocate taxes on food — hitherto a sure election-loser. Even the Liberals, the traditional champions of the free trade cause, were beginning to have their doubts. E. D. Simon's outburst at the Liberal Party summer school drew a stern rebuke from the *Liberal Magazine*,[2] but a protectionist wing in the Party was rapidly developing under the leadership of Sir John Simon; Lloyd George was said to have an 'open mind' on the question. By the autumn of 1930 the only dogmatic free traders left were the Samuelite group of about twenty-five Liberal M.P.s; a few academic economists who could not bring themselves to sacrifice the elusive perfections of the free trade model; a large section of the City who regarded free trade as tied up with the gold standard, a thriving world trade and hence their own prosperity; and a few key men in the Labour administration, headed by Snowden.

The Conservatives had not advocated protection in their 1929 election campaign and up to the beginning of 1930 they were on the defensive on this issue, confining their efforts to urging the Government not to

formation by Sir William Morris (later Lord Nuffield) of a National Council of Industry and Commerce, on 25 September 1930, to urge protection and retrenchment on the Government, and protectionist pronouncements by the F.B.I. and the N.U.M. (see *The Times*, 5 November 1930); a Protectionist Bankers Manifesto was issued on 4 July 1930, signed among others by Reginald McKenna, former Liberal Chancellor of the Exchequer who had signed a Free Trade manifesto in 1926; for the trade union attitude see below, p. 230–1.

[1] *The Times*, 7 April 1930.

[2] 'In a regrettable outbreak', E. D. Simon, Liberal M.P. for the Withington Division of Manchester claimed that under free trade 'we were steadily losing our share of the world market to Germany' (*Liberal Magazine*, August 1930, p. 347). Simon's action precipitated what *The Nation* described as 'a considerable fluttering in the Liberal dovecot'. Walter Layton 'reacted with horror'; so did Ramsay Muir. Herbert Samuel considered his reference to a 10 per cent tariff 'unfortunate'; it 'could only have the effect of tending to confuse the public mind as to the general attitude of the Liberal Party on the fiscal question' (Letter, 13 August 1930). Keynes, on the other hand, did not doubt that it 'would help the situation' (Letter, 4 August 1930) and Hubert Henderson offered 'congratulations' on his 'fiscal indiscretion' but doubted whether such remarks would 'help Liberalism as an electoral force' (Letter, 5 August 1930). Quoted in Mary Stocks, *Ernest Simon of Manchester*, 1963, pp. 93–4.

dismantle the system of safeguarding which had been erected between 1924 and 1929. The Beaverbrook counter-attack proved a great embarrassment to the leadership, and Baldwin's concession of the referendum was, as J. A. Spender noted, 'an attempt to separate the parts of the tariff policy which [are thought to be] unpopular (food taxes) from those parts which [are thought to be] popular (taxes on manufactured goods)'.[1]

The world depression transformed the situation. The collapse of primary product prices, especially in arable products, threatened the British farmer with ruin, as other countries sought to unload on the unprotected British market. Wheat prices collapsed at the end of 1929 and there was much talk of Soviet and other 'dumping'. Much of this was exaggerated, but it did provide an embarrassed Conservative leadership with a safe opportunity to plunge into agricultural protection as part of the 'great' Imperial policy. By this time, the cry of 'dear food' no longer seemed objectionable as depression had become sufficiently widely diffused to rob it of emotional significance. By October 1930 the Conservatives had committed themselves to 'an emergency tariff' on manufactured goods to be followed by more 'scientific' protection to meet the special needs of particular industries. For agriculture, there was to be a wheat quota, a tax on imported barley and 'bounty fed' oats and 'protection' (unspecified) for smallholders and market gardeners against the 'dumping' of foreign fruits and vegetables. The emergency tariffs alone, Baldwin was confident, would 'at once stem the advance of unemployment and do much to restore hope and confidence to both employers and workers who to-day can only look upon the future with despair'.[2]

On the Labour side the pressure for the regulation of trade came from the trade unions. On 26 June 1930, the economic committee of the T.U.C. issued a report which pressed for 'as full a development as possible of the economic relations between the constituent parts of the British Commonwealth'. This report was 'leaked' to the Beaverbrook press before it was published and the *Daily Express* welcomed the 'T.U.C. crusaders': as a result the economic committee was told to take it back and add an explanatory memorandum dissociating it from

[1] *Daily News*, 6 March 1930.

[2] Baldwin to Chamberlain, 15 October 1930. *Gleanings and Memoranda*, p. 376.

Beaverbrook's proposals. On the other hand, the Council was divided on the question of a tariff. On 8 June a motion that the sentence

> In particular circumstances where it is desired to help a specific trade, a tariff may be justifiable. . . .

be deleted, was defeated by seventeen votes to five,[1] but right until the fall of the Labour Government the trade union movement remained 'undecided' about tariffs. Ernest Bevin tried to link the free trade/protection discussion to socialism. 'I have never accepted, as a socialist', he told the Nottingham conference of the T.U.C. in October 1930, 'that an inflexible free trade attitude is synonymous with socialism . . . I cannot reconcile the real operation of free trade with the organisation of industry under public ownership.'[2] Bevin clearly saw that the clamour of the basic industries for protection could be a lead-in for the reorganisation of such industries on socialist lines. By combining protection with compulsory reorganisation he sought to refute the free trade argument that a tariff would merely perpetuate inefficiency. Mosley appropriated this theme with relish in his speech to the Labour Party conference at Llandudno.[3] The policy had the great advantage of linking the Government's rationalisation policy with the general movement of opinion towards protection. Snowden, however, was likely to prove a formidable stumbling block, and his replacement as Chancellor would have been a necessary condition for its fulfilment.

vi. UNEMPLOYMENT INSURANCE

The background to the Government's 'thinking' on unemployment insurance was the growing campaign against 'abuses' and the ever more insistent demand for retrenchment. As we have seen, there was little opposition to the Unemployment Insurance (No. 2) Act, except from within the Labour Party. But with the growth of unemployment the climate of opinion underwent a most remarkable change. For one thing the unemployment fund came under immediate strain, and Miss Bondfield's repeated borrowings came to assume the character less of temporary

[1] General Council: Minutes of T.U.C. Economic Committee, 18 June 1930.
[2] T.U.C. *Annual Report*, p. 259. [3] Labour Party, *Annual Report*, p. 202.

loans than of debts which there was little prospect of repaying. In other words, they would eventually become a budgetary charge. This was in addition to the growing cost of 'transitional' benefit which by itself foreshadowed a large and mounting budget deficit. A feeling of drift, helplessness and even panic developed as the Government's work plan failed to stem the rise in unemployment while it refused to take remedial action to improve the finances of the fund. It was in this atmosphere that stories of abuses first began to appear in the national press. The general claim made was that the abolition of the 'not genuinely seeking work' clause had enabled 'cute' men and women to get benefits to which they were not entitled. Examples of this were ferreted out by enthusiastic journalists and spread thickly across the front pages, especially in the local press. But employers also bombarded the major Conservative national dailies with similar stories. The Government's ability to resist these charges had been weakened by the forecast of its own Actuary that such developments were to be expected. Throughout 1930 pressure was built up with the deliberate or unconscious motive of forcing the Labour Government to act against the unemployed.

There were, of course, several different lines of attack, with different motives behind them, some of which were quite serious and reputable. The economic point was made that by keeping men in the depressed areas and in depressed occupations, especially by its encouragement of short-time working, unemployment insurance prevented the necessary adaptations being made to shifts in demand. There was also Sir John Anderson's criticism that insofar as the live register was swollen by people who were not really unemployed or worked short-time and claimed unemployment benefit for part of the week, an exaggerated impression was given of the extent of unemployment. These serious charges should be considered separately from the more hysterical and sensational assaults on unemployment insurance, though both often made use of the same evidence, true or false.

The Government were handicapped in replying to opposition charges of 'legal' abuse of the provisions of the 1930 Act, by the forecast of the Government Actuary that married women and seasonal workers who were not really seeking employment would claim benefit. The figures relating to married women appeared to give substance to his contention. In October 1929 there were 86,000 married women claimants; in October 1930,

240,000.[1] Miss Bondfield tried to get round this by attributing the increased number of claims to the increasing unemployment in the cotton and pottery industries which employed large numbers of women, but it was later established that the increase in the number of married women claiming benefit in these trades far exceeded that in the number of single women.[2] The Opposition thus had a point, but the Interim Report of the Royal Commission on Unemployment Insurance which came out in June 1931 stated that the 'married women' problem had not been created by the 1930 Act, but by the 1927 Act passed by the Conservatives, which abandoned the 'one in six' rule.[3] In other words, the 'legal abuse' for which the Conservatives were now so vigorously blaming the Government was in large part their own fault.

Perhaps the most serious charge brought against the existing structure of unemployment insurance by its more sensible critics was that it encouraged short-time working. Unemployment insurance was being used as a subsidy for wages, a prop for inefficient industries which otherwise would be forced to rationalise. This was part of Salter's 'inelasticity' argument, and there was undoubtedly some truth in it. However, short-time working was far more a consequence than a cause of continued depression. Insofar as it occurred in industries affected by the world depression rather than in declining industries, it was designed to tide over purely temporary difficulties. In those, such as cotton and shipbuilding, which carried too many workers, it undoubtedly produced undue rigidity. But where in 1930 were these workers to go? Had the Government been prepared to start an active policy of industrial reconstruction, there would have been a strong case for penalising short-time arrangements. This was precisely the point of the Liberal proposals: reform of unemployment insurance was seen in the context of a constructive policy. In lieu of such a policy, short-time working, by spreading the load of work and by maintaining industrial peace, did more good than harm.[4]

[1] Parliamentary reply, 244 H.C. Deb. c. 175. [2] See below, p. 311.

[3] Cmd. 3872, p. 43. The 'one in six' rule stated that six contributions had to be paid for every one week's benefit.

[4] Employers were often able to use unemployment insurance to offset wage reductions, e.g. the following notice, circulated by the owners of a colliery in the summer of 1930: 'the pits will be so worked as to qualify the employees for three days unemployment benefit in alternate weeks. The unemployment benefit will more than cover the reduction in wages.'

Finally, there were the 'lunatic fringe' stories of abuse. Hundreds of instances of the abuse of unemployment insurance by individuals appeared in the press throughout the summer and autumn. Whenever they were repeated in the House of Commons Miss Bondfield or Jack Lawson, her parliamentary secretary, were able, on cursory enquiry, to show them to be baseless.[1]

The new spirit of antagonism to the unemployed brought into the open a submerged issue of the insurance scheme throughout the nineteen-twenties — the dole. We have seen that neither Conservatives nor Liberals were happy about having a 'dole' as part of an insurance scheme. The Labour Party, on the other hand, had always stood for the right to maintenance irrespective of contributions and had always opposed any distinction in conditions or rates of benefit between insurance and dole. Labour supporters had interpreted the 1930 Act, which had transferred responsibility for transitional benefit from the fund to the Exchequer as a first step towards a completely non-contributory system. The Conservatives, on the other hand, saw it as a first step towards a separation of the two schemes.

As the fund began to get more heavily into debt and as the burden on the Exchequer for transitional benefit began to increase, outlines of a plan of reform began to take shape on the opposition benches. The essence of the plan was to have a properly balancing 'insurance' fund on the one hand and an entirely separate system of relief, financed partly from the rates, for those who had fallen out of benefit on the other. In the insurance fund benefits would be strictly related to contributions; the relief fund would pay benefits on a 'less eligible' basis and with a means test. This structure became more explicit as the year wore on. At first Churchill had merely talked about 'a reformed Poor Law'.[2] Steel-Maitland, the former Minister of Labour, made the dubious assertion that 'everybody is agreed that the two things ought to be separated'; but his constructive proposals amounted to some kind of 'special authority',

[1] The *Nottingham Guardian* of 18 September 1930 quoted the case of a girl of sixteen who had received £150 unemployment pay in one year for a contribution of 24*s*. To have achieved this remarkable feat, Miss Bondfield claimed, 'she must have maintained, with dependants' allowances, not only herself but a husband or parent and at least twenty-three children'. 245 H.C. Deb. c. 1838–9.

[2] 237 H.C. Deb. c. 859.

acting with the 'local authority' in a 'national co-operation'.[1] The purpose of the operation was to save money. A properly balancing insurance fund would no longer run into debt while the cost to the Exchequer of 'transitional' benefit would be reduced by the combination of lower benefits, a means test, and a sharing of the finance with the local authorities — hence the significance of Churchill's reference to a 'reformed Poor Law'. In the absence of any constructive government alternative, proposals of this kind had become, by the end of 1930, the accepted orthodoxy. Even the *Manchester Guardian* affirmed in an editorial, on 22 December 1930, that

> The lines of reform accepted by most informed opinion were the strict division of the system into an insurance scheme with benefits limited by contributions, and a relief scheme for those no longer entitled to benefit, in whose case the question of payment according to need must enter.

The attack on unemployment insurance was part of the wider demand for retrenchment. We have noted the pressure brought to bear earlier in the year in anticipation of the Budget; during the summer and autumn businessmen waged the campaign for retrenchment with indefatigable vigour. Scarcely a day would pass without some industrialist or chamber of commerce being quoted as prophesying doom if the Government did not bring to a halt the ruinous expenditure on the social services.

An entertaining example of this concern was the setting up of the National Council of Industry and Commerce. On 18 September a letter went out, over the signatures of Sir William Morris and a number of prominent industrialists, summoning a meeting for the following week to discuss the formation of an organisation to promote 'practical common sense' in the discussion of economic questions.[2] The meeting duly took place on 25 September. *The Times* list of 'among those present' contained eighty-six names, mainly businessmen, but with a sprinkling of politicians, including Harold Macmillan. The occasion was enlivened by the following remarks from Sir William Morris who took the chair:

> No manufacturers could continue under the taxation imposed on British manufacturers. . . . The National Council wanted to see this altered, and also to see that our industries were protected. (Cheers) The crux of the whole matter was the need for a strong Government (cheers) (A voice — 'A strong man'), a Government of men who knew what they were talking about (cheers),

[1] 237 H.C. Deb. c. 1669–70. [2] *The Times*, 19 September 1930.

a Government of men who understood business (Cheers). The workmen of this country were neither Bolshevist nor Socialist (cheers) but what they were wanting was a real leader (cheers). . . .

One of the motives of this National Council was to get protection for British industry; but the meeting also resolved

that whatever Party may be in office for the time, our Government must keep its expenditure within the capacity of the country to pay and that a drastic reduction of taxation is urgently necessary if prosperity is to be restored to agriculture and industry.[1]

It was against this background that the Government's 'thinking' on unemployment insurance took place. Sir John Anderson had concluded, in his memorandum of July after a few weeks' study of the problem, that a large number of people 'really abused the unemployment insurance scheme'.[2] In a memorandum dated 13 June Hubert Henderson argued that the existence of the unemployment insurance scheme 'serves to swell the unemployment figures to an extent which is important but which it is impossible to estimate with any sort of precision'. However, he did reckon that most of the 'temporarily stopped' category of unemployed — about 500,000 — represented short-time arrangements. The significance of this — and here Henderson echoed Anderson — was the exaggerated impression given of the extent of unemployment and hence of Britain's economic difficulties, bad both for internal and external confidence. Henderson exonerated the Labour Government from blame, but he could not absolve it from its duty to take remedial action.[3]

In July the Government set up a committee of the Economic Advisory Council to investigate the problem. The chairman was G. D. H. Cole and the other members were Sir John Cadman, Sir Sydney Chapman,[4] and Hubert Henderson. The committee reported on 5 November. In view of the sympathies of the chairman its report is especially significant.

It started by tabulating the abuses which had grown up, which were not abuses in the legal sense, but loopholes in the Acts. The effects of these abuses were seen in 'the excessive and unjustifiable expenditure

[1] *The Times*, 2 September 1930. [2] See above, p. 216.

[3] MacDonald Papers, File 16, Unemployment Insurance.

[4] Cadman and Chapman were two of the 'practical' men on the Economic Advisory Council. Cadman had already helped Balfour draw up the 'business-man's answer' to Keynes and Cole earlier in the year. See above, p. 144.

from public funds' and 'the increase of economic friction and the encouragement of methods of industrial organisation which are harmful to trade and employment in general'. The main 'artificial rigidity' induced was 'the hindrance . . . to the rapid transfer from industry to industry or from place to place' which was especially necessary when 'the world is passing through a period of rapid technical change'.[1] There was, therefore, a strong case for the 'complete re-casting of the unemployment insurance scheme'. The broad principles of the plan were:

(1) Absolute separation of the finance of that part of the scheme which can properly be treated as insurance from that which cannot.
(2) Appointment of a Statutory Commission with wide latitude to make regulations for the working of the scheme.
(3) Extension of the scope of the scheme.
(4) Less rigidity in its working so as to allow special regulations to be framed for particular types of classes of workers.
(5) Application of radically different conditions for the receipt of benefit under the insurance and non-insurance scheme.
(6) Revision of the financial arrangements.[2]

Elaborating the fifth point the report proposed a means test for the non-insurance part of the scheme. 'After the expiry of insurance rights, benefit under Part II should be subject to an applicant's ability to establish his claim to the full amount of benefit on a basis of need.'

Here then was a complete endorsement of the Conservative case, produced by a committee of the Government's own Economic Advisory Council, headed by a leading socialist intellectual. Making it quite clear that the report's views were his own, Cole proceeded to publish an article in the *New Statesman* attacking the existing structure of unemployment insurance on exactly the same lines as in the report, so much so that Snowden on reading it accused him of abusing his access to privileged information.[3] It is also significant that whereas Cole and Cadman were on opposite sides over the question of a 'constructive' unemployment policy, they both agreed on the need to reform unemployment insurance.

Outside the Labour movement, there was near unanimity of comment,

[1] *Report of the Committee on Unemployment Benefit*, para. 24. (Henderson Papers, Box 1.)
[2] *Report of the Committee on Unemployment Benefit*, paras. 28–33.
[3] *New Statesman*, 15 November 1930, pp. 168–9.

both responsible and irresponsible, on the need to reform unemployment insurance. Such pressure might have been expected to have had an effect on persons less temperamentally infirm of purpose than MacDonald. On the Prime Minister the impact was formidable. The stories of abuses began to prey on his colourful imagination. He began to picture married women driving up in fur coats to draw benefit; and the retailing of such tales became a staple part of his conversation.[1] Whether he believed them or not, he was bound to recognise that, blazoned day after day across the front pages of a hostile press, they were extremely damaging to the Government. A more dynamic leader would have attempted to wrest the initiative from the Opposition. However, in the summer recess, political coups were difficult to conjure up. And whatever inclinations the Premier may have had towards a bolder unemployment policy were squashed by Snowden. Thus the Labour Government were faced with the prospect of having to reorganise unemployment insurance without being able to offer anything to their supporters in return. This in turn involved apparently insurmountable political difficulties.

Indeed in the summer of 1930 many of those supporters were still looking forward to a reorganisation of quite a different kind. Labour Members frequently asked Miss Bondfield when she intended to produce the second instalment of Labour's policy, and a lively discussion was carried on in trade union journals about the best way to organise a non-contributory scheme. Such plans were regarded by the Government as completely impracticable. Not only would Snowden not provide any more money for increased contributions: there was no chance whatsoever of carrying a reorganisation on non-contributory lines through the Commons. Indeed it is doubtful if Miss Bondfield herself ever really accepted the non-contributory principle.

During the summer of 1930 the 'Council of State' was never far from politicians' minds. MacDonald had revived the notion in his letters to Baldwin and Lloyd George; now Miss Bondfield contributed her quota. She concluded her speech in the Commons on 23 July as follows:

> We earnestly hope that the parties opposite will be willing to enter into consultation with us with a view to an agreed solution of these problems. We have our ideas; they have theirs. Let us pool them, and see if in this way we

[1] See M. A. Hamilton, *Up-Hill All The Way*, p. 54.

can obtain some measure of agreement on the next Unemployment Insurance Bill to be brought before Parliament.[1]

What were these 'problems' to which Miss Bondfield referred? In the course of her speech she had mentioned short-time working; a possible revision of conditions of the 1930 Act; the separation of insurance from transitional benefit; married women and seasonal workers; the overlapping with non-insured trades; the effects of rationalisation, and the future of the Poor Law. These topics were to form the rough agenda for such 'consultations' as might take place with a view to framing a comprehensive Insurance Bill. There was a ready response to Miss Bondfield's request. The Conservatives nominated Sir Henry Betterton, formerly parliamentary secretary to the Ministry of Labour, and Walter Elliot as their representatives; the Liberals selected Ernest Brown and Isaac Foot. Miss Bondfield and Vernon Hartshorn represented the Government. Thus was another inter-party or all-party conference launched.

The Ministry of Labour memorandum was far better than the opposition representatives dared hope and on the basis of it agreement seemed near. Lansbury has recorded that 'there is no doubt at all that agreement had been reached by the three Parties to push all transitional people on to the Poor Law'. But when Miss Bondfield brought her memorandum, 'which embodied much worse cuts than those which eventually found a place in the May Report', before the panel of Ministers, there was a violent reaction. The proposals were condemned as 'so disgusting . . . except by the Chancellor of the Exchequer and Miss Bondfield, that rather than allowing any danger of their publication, the P.M. insisted that each copy should be handed in — and I expect they were all destroyed'.[2] In these circumstances, the opposition representatives were informed that their services were no longer required, and the Government prepared alternative arrangements.[3]

[1] 241 H.C. Deb. c. 2190.

[2] Lansbury Papers, vol. 25n. 1–17, para. 3.

[3] There is little information available on the three-party conference. As it had the status of an advisory Cabinet committee, its proceedings were never revealed. Apart from Lansbury's account, we rely entirely on opposition statements made during the debate on the King's Speech, October 1930 (244 H.C. Deb. c. 50–51, 57, 83, 168–9).

vii. SUMMARY

It may be doubted whether the extensive enquiries which MacDonald initiated in the summer cleared up the confusion in his own mind. On many key issues he received directly contradictory advice. Against the attractions of a policy of capital development urged by the Liberals and the committee of economists would have to be set the loss of confidence which such a policy might produce among the business community; against the view that there still existed a large category of unfulfilled 'remunerative' public projects, the civil service contended that the 'limit' of useful works was being reached. The national development loan was vetoed by the Treasury; the proposal to centralise arterial road construction was opposed by the Ministry of Transport and vested local interests. As always there was a real intellectual tussle on the central issue of protection or free trade, the outcome of which would depend largely on estimates of the duration and intensity of the world depression. A strong case had been made that the existing system of unemployment benefit hindered the transfer of labour to new occupations and swelled artificially the numbers of the unemployed; on the other hand it was a guarantee of social peace and a security against wage reductions. Here again the question of whether drastic reform should take place hinged to a large extent on how long the depression would last. If there was little prospect of improvement then doubtless drastic modifications along the whole line of government unemployment policy would become urgently necessary. If, on the other hand, recovery was 'round the corner' as Hubert Henderson implied, then there was no impelling reason to alter the *status quo* if political survival could be assured.

Superimposed on these intellectual difficulties were the hazards of the political situation. Liberal support would be forthcoming for a policy of government investment, but this would run foul of the Treasury and the Conservatives. The Conservatives would support protection, but the Liberals and an important section of the Cabinet would be opposed. Both the Conservatives and Liberals, on the other hand, would support the overhaul of the unemployment benefit system, but this would create immense difficulties in the Labour Party. Indeed it was the potential Conservative–Liberal alliance on retrenchment in general and unemployment insurance in particular that posed the greatest threat to the Government's continued existence. In face of all these problematic choices, both intellectual and political, the obvious course for a Government as indecisive as MacDonald's was to gamble on a trade revival swift enough to rescue it from its long-term dilemmas, and in the interim to strive to prevent any Conservative–Liberal rapprochement over unemployment insurance. Fortunately the continuing divisions between the two Parties over the 'fiscal question' made this task comparatively easy, especially if the Government could contrive to make some concession to the Liberal view on capital development. The disadvantage of such a policy was that in the short term it would give the impression of drift and negation in face of the depression, while all the problems temporarily shelved would return with redoubled force if the depression failed to lift.

Meanwhile more traditional modes of thought and expression came to the fore as the Labour Party assembled for its annual conference at Llandudno. The Premier returned like a giant refreshed to face his critics, and his speech to the conference on the morning of 7 October was a triumph of political artistry and management. Tactically it was designed, as the *Morning Post* noted, 'to create an atmosphere in which it would be difficult to attack the Government on its failure to stem the increase in unemployment', and to do this MacDonald provided his audience with an excuse that was sure to appeal to them:

> So, my friends, we are not on trial; it is the system under which we live. It has broken down, not only in this little island; it has broken down in Europe, in Asia, in America; it has broken down everywhere *as it was bound to break down.* [italics mine.]

Thus the tables were neatly turned: it was the breakdown of capitalism, not the failure of the Government, that was responsible for the suffering and distress; and if the Government seemed impotent, was this not because it had no mandate for the only cure — socialism? Of course, the other Parties had their solutions — public works, protection — but these were no substitute for socialism, and no Labour Government could be expected to subscribe to them:

And I appeal to you, my friends, to-day, with all that is going on outside — I appeal to you to go back on to your Socialist faith. Do not mix that up with pettifogging patching — either of a Poor Law kind or of Relief Work kind.[1]

Throughout, MacDonald referred to public works as 'relief works' — to differentiate them from socialism, which was permanent reconstruction. If confusion lay at the heart of this analysis, it was the confusion of democratic socialism itself — the confusion that allowed a socialist party to take part in the ordinary political process, and yet sought to absolve it from responsibility for framing radical policies to meet concrete problems.

[1] Labour Party, *Annual Report*, 1930, p. 185. L. Macneill Weir, in *The Tragedy of Ramsay MacDonald*, 1939, wrote (p. 244), 'The tumultuous applause that followed the great peroration showed that MacDonald had retained his power as a spell-binder. . . . He had completely turned the tables on his opponents.'

II

THE FAILURE OF NERVE

i. THE KING'S SPEECH

AFTER a summer of enquiries, the Government faced Parliament again on 28 October 1930. In the intervening three months, unemployment had gone up by a further 200,000, from 2,000,000 to 2,200,000, a serious increase for the 'good employment' summer months. The King's Speech was eagerly awaited as the conclusion to three months of systematic examination of all the possibilities — by economists, civil servants, two-party and three-party conferences — under the personal direction of the Prime Minister. At the Imperial Conference which opened in London on 1 October Bennett, the Canadian Premier, had proposed a 10 per cent preferential empire tariff: here was a great opportunity for the Government to announce, in the King's Speech, that change of fiscal policy desired by so many. Underlying these hopes was a general feeling that if bold measures were delayed much longer, the psychological opportunity would pass beyond recall as increasing financial difficulties focused attention irretrievably on retrenchment.

Many hopes were cruelly disappointed as the undistinguished phrases of the King's Speech spelt out the message of 'business as usual'. The Government noted 'with grave concern and sympathy the continuance of heavy unemployment' but its only concrete promise was to introduce agricultural legislation. Unemployment insurance would be examined by a Royal Commission. A number of old favourites made their reappearance — taxation of land values, Bills to set up a Consumers' Council, to raise the school-leaving age and to amend the 1927 Trades Disputes Act. There would be a Bill to reorganise public transport in London; more significant, for its bearing on future Liberal–Labour relations, was a promise to introduce 'a measure of electoral reform'.[1]

[1] For the speech as a whole see 244 H.C. Deb. c. 5–7.

Much of this was useful and sensible. In a normal year this would undoubtedly have been considered a fair King's Speech. But where was Hartshorn's 'bold and determined' industrial policy 'on a large number of points'? All the contentious unemployment issues — tariffs, national development, unemployment insurance — were either omitted or shelved.[1] The agricultural policy could mean much or nothing, depending on the scale. As for the school-leaving and trade union proposals, they seemed curiously inappropriate at that moment, left-overs from past controversies. Even the proposal for electoral reform could only be made to seem relevant in the context of a Liberal–Labour alliance for a 'bold' unemployment policy: without such a constructive underpinning people were bound to see it as a shady manœuvre to keep the Government from an electorate it dare not face. As for MacDonald's comment that the agricultural and school-leaving age Bills were 'unemployment emergency measures' — that seemed quite fatuous;[2] his promise that, if given three more years of power, 'we will undertake to go a very much longer way in national reconstruction than is indicated in the Speech'[3] offered little comfort to those who clamoured for swift action.

Two comments that stand out from press and parliamentary reactions are that the Government had missed a magnificent opportunity for 'giving the nation a lead' and that it had shown no proper sense of priorities. The demand for 'strong meat' had been met with 'digestive bread and peptonised milk'.[4] 'Puny, pale and rickety' was how Lloyd George, in his most teasing vein, described the proposals.[5] 'What are the various offshoots of the Government programme doing in the King's Speech?' enquired the Liberal Major Nathan. 'There has been no leadership . . . no concentration of purpose or energy.'[6] The sense of opportunities lost was forcefully put by Boothby. The King's Speech was a 'terrible document . . . enough to strike terror into the heart of anyone who has the future of this country at heart'. Instead of subordinating everything to the fight against unemployment, as everything

[1] In fact, the Government had not made up its mind about tariffs or national development. Hartshorn, when asked to tell the P.L.P. Consultative Committee in November what he had been doing about unemployment, replied: 'How can I tell them anything? All my proposals were put in last August, and no decision has been taken on them yet.' Dalton, *Memoirs*, vol. i, 1953, p. 262.

[2] 244 H.C. Deb. c. 23. [3] Ibid. c. 28. [4] Ibid. c. 81. [5] Ibid. c. 53.

[6] Ibid. c. 248, 252.

had been subordinated to the task of winning the war, the Prime Minister had 'exhausted himself in frantic efforts to stop the construction of a couple of cruisers'; the Chancellor had 'intensified . . . deflation by every action he has taken'; Graham had spent his time 'trotting up and down to conferences at Geneva making futile appeals to foreign countries to stop doing this and that'.[1] Lloyd George put the blame squarely on MacDonald: 'I do not say he has not worked hard, but he has always worked hard at other things. He seems to be too busy to do his job.'[2]

The feeling that the Government had lost a great opportunity was given a note of extra urgency by a number of younger M.P.s who argued that its purely negative policy, by weakening the nation's confidence in the ability of politicians to solve the most pressing problems, was endangering democracy itself. The premise of this argument was that the nation 'demanded action' and that Parliament was, literally, on trial for its life. Captain Anthony Eden warned the House to

> make a close and careful study of the causes of the collapse of parliamentary government in Europe since the war. It has not always, or even usually, been because these countries are temperamentally unfitted to work the parliamentary machine. It has been for a far simpler reason, because Parliament has failed.[3]

A significant feature of the Speech was that it attracted hardly any Labour backbenchers to its support. Of the thirty-four Labour M.P.s who spoke in the debate on the address only two could be found to give generous praise to the Speech; one of them, a recent Minister, Ben Turner, who found it 'one of the most satisfactory Speeches that has been presented to the House of Commons during the present century', regretted a certain lack of 'fullness' in the section dealing with unemployment.[4] Most of the Labour speeches, mainly from I.L.P. M.P.s and supporters of the ex-Chancellor of the Duchy, Mosley, were furiously critical; the remainder reluctantly accepted it as the best that could be done in the circumstances, and salvaged their socialist consciences with the thought that no 'full-blooded' socialist measures were possible with a minority Government. From all the evidence, this was a general

[1] 244 H. C. Deb. c. 585–6. [2] Ibid. c. 55.

[3] Ibid. c. 614. For other comments of a similar kind see 66, 69, 118, 237, 408, 607.

[4] Ibid. c. 240–1.

backbench view and the Government naturally fostered it to excuse its own failings. Thus the simple syllogism that no cure was possible without socialism and no socialism was possible, was used to justify a policy of complete quietism. In these circumstances all that Labour backbenchers demanded of the Government was that they guarantee the unemployed decent rates of maintenance.

That this was a poor intellectual position from which to govern a capitalist country may readily be appreciated. If the Government had no faith in capitalism it should leave the handling of its problems to those who did believe in it, argued Lloyd George.[1] MacDonald, who was much practised in meeting objections of this kind from his own left-wingers, replied that this was an argument against political action altogether. How could one believe in political action if the opportunity of making it effective, namely taking office and 'moulding the transformation from one state of society to another', was refused?[2] This theory, which was really that of the inevitability of gradualness, was undoubtedly shared by MacDonald's followers, at least until the crisis of 1931, when he used it to justify the formation of the National Government. It was then that the Labour Party discovered that it did place certain definite limits upon 'taking office' in a capitalist society.

ii. REVIVAL THROUGH EXPORTS?

For a few weeks in November 1930, it seemed that the House of Commons might become a real 'Council of State'. Several M.P.s harked back to a golden age when Members, faced with a grave problem, would go into committee, sitting day and night till a solution emerged.[3] Now there was a similar wish to find accord, but deep divisions of principle, inherited with party allegiance, placed agreement perpetually beyond reach. Many of the younger M.P.s who wanted action regarded these

[1] 244 H.C. Deb. c. 711. [2] Ibid. c. 813–14.

[3] e.g. Winston Churchill, 246 H.C. Deb. c. 1139: 'Our ancestors would not have used so much parliamentary time on a single topic in this sporadic and ineffectual manner. . . . They would have pursued the topic with continuous persistence and with resolutions, descending from the general to the particular and throwing out at each stage those who disagreed with what was proposed so as to build up the main theme of House of Commons opinion.'

divisions as left-overs from by-gone controversies and demanded a pragmatic 'national' solution, premissed on the acceptance of the need for action. If only, they argued, discussions could be pursued free from party bias, a 'consensus' would soon emerge. The 'old gang' on the other hand seemed determined to 'play out to the end the old parliamentary game'.[1]

Foremost among the topics of debate in the autumn of 1930 was the question of free trade versus protection. At the start of the autumn session of Parliament, the Government soon made it clear that they had no intention of departing from their free trade principles. Baldwin moved the adoption of Bennett's Empire tariff proposals in an 'appalling speech'.[2] J. H. Thomas, the Dominions Secretary, now restored to his former perkiness, swept it aside in a 'brilliant' reply with the memorable remark: 'There never was such humbug.'[3] As we have seen, the Government had set their hearts on a tariff truce. Graham defended this policy in a lucid and persuasive speech. Britain's prosperity had depended on world trade. There was every prospect of a speedy world recovery: prices had reached rock bottom and the corner had been turned. Snowden in July had predicted recovery by the end of the year; Graham prudently postponed it till the following spring.[4] Any action by Britain to protect its own market, by diminishing the existing volume of trade, would jeopardise the excellent prospects of recovery.

In fact, during these months government-sponsored trade delegations roamed the world in search of export outlets. The Master Cutler of Sheffield left for South America on 1 August 'to undertake on behalf of Sheffield industries, an investigation of market conditions and trade possibilities in the principal markets of South America'.[5] An economic mission headed by Lord Kirkley left for South Africa. A delegation of coal owners headed by the Minister of Mines, Shinwell, were off to Scandinavia on 13 September, to be followed by the secretary of the Leicester Boot Manufacturers Association two months later. Sir Ernest Thompson headed a strong trade mission to China and Japan to in-

[1] Oliver Stanley, 244 H.C. Deb. c. 84.

[2] *Manchester Guardian*, 28 November 1930.

[3] 245 H.C. Deb. c. 1550.

[4] For Snowden's prophecy, see *Daily News*, 22 July 1930; for Graham's, 244 H.C. Deb. c. 516; for Graham's speech as a whole, cols. 514–30.

[5] *Board of Trade Journal*, 17 July 1930.

vestigate openings for the cotton trade and on 15 December the Government announced that Sir Arthur Balfour would leave shortly for Egypt. Even the Prince of Wales joined the export crusade, extolling the qualities of British manufacturers on a tour of South America.

In August the Government had appointed a committee of the E.A.C., consisting of Graham, Sir Charles Addis, Sir Arthur Balfour, Hugh Dalton, Keynes and Archibald Rose, to investigate the Chinese market. Rose, a textile maufacturer with great experience of China, argued at the second meeting of the committee held in November that trade via sea and river (the treaty port markets) had reached saturation point. The key to expansion was to improve the railways which were derelict owing to the ravages of war and banditry. In particular this would open up the province of Szechuan, at present accessible only by way of the Yangtze rapids. Rose read out a statement from the *China Express and Telegraph* of 27 November 1930 which in his opinion accurately indicated the possibilities:

It is not altogether fanciful to say that the most promising palliative for unemployment in this country would be a railway into Szechuan. The Tory party watch the figures going up with mocking glee, and the Socialists wring their hands and advertise their helplessness. Yet all the while Szechuan lies with her forty-five million potential consumers of British goods, virtually inaccessible.

The disturbed political position was a major obstacle. Sir Frederick Whyte in a letter to Rose from Shanghai dated 20 August was sceptical about possibilities, but noted optimistically that 'Chiang Kai-Shek himself, as usual is at his best when everyone else thinks the situation is at its worst. That quality is one of my strongest reasons for not losing confidence.' By 9 September Rose was able to inform Keynes that

a truce is in sight. . . . It will leave 3 or 4 strong factions unbroken and dissatisfied, the Young Marshal in Manchuria, Yen in the North, Feng in the Centre and Canton. The blight of the Kuomintang party machine hangs over them all, blocking decent decentralisation.

Even if the truce suggested that sufficient political authority could be established to open up the line from Harbin to Canton, the problem of finance still remained acute. Chinese credit was appalling: the drop in the value of silver had produced inflation; moreover the Chinese railway companies already owed the international consortium, which had been formed in 1908 to finance Chinese railway development, £17m. Repairs to the existing railways alone would cost another £10m. Who would be prepared to put up the money? Rose suggested an International Reconstruction Loan of £27m to be raised over three years to fund the debt and put the railways in working order. Keynes was impressed and suggested that Sir Arthur Salter might be the man to handle initial negotiations. Unfortunately preliminary reactions from China were unfavourable. Whyte cabled that the Chinese thought the plan smacked of foreign control.

The era of gunboat diplomacy was clearly over, symbolically affirmed by the handing over to the Chinese of the British naval base at Weihaiwei on 1 October. In these cirumstances an impasse had been reached. The E.A.C. committee reported on 18 December that whereas 'the revival and development of the trade of China would be a factor of first rate importance in reviving British trade', the only positive recommendation they felt able to make was that 'His Majesty's Government should consider whether it would be possible to appoint a special officer of experience in the engineering business world at His Majesty's Legation in Peking'. In addition, the British group in the international consortium should be 'informally encouraged' by H.M.G. to 'get into touch' with the Chinese Government 'with a view to initiating conversations in regard to railway rehabilitation and development'; so much for the six month exploration of the 'most promising palliative for unemployment in this country'.[1]

It is hardly surprising that others besides Sir Oswald Mosley came to the conclusion that the expectation of a trade revival was a chimera. But the dilemma remained that Britain's prosperity had always depended on foreign trade: if the outlook was so bleak what chance had she of recovering that prosperity? National self-sufficiency was out of the question. Import substitution might provide part of the answer, but only a small part. In seeking a way out, Conservatives were increasingly tempted by Beaverbrook's attractive vision of Empire Free Trade. In the Commons on 3 November Neville Chamberlain developed the idea of Imperial preference leading 'in a decade or two' to Imperial self-sufficiency. He envisaged a bloc of complementary trading countries, protected by external tariffs from the price fluctuations of world commerce,

[1] Keynes Papers, E.A.C. 5.

within which 'the expansion of productive capacity . . . shall steadily increase according to the natural growth of demand, instead of by spasmodic jerks . . . and sudden bursts of unemployment'.[1] Mosley, whose views had developed on the same lines, advocated an even more thoroughgoing Imperial *Zollverein*, with an empire bank to provide credit for what would increasingly become a domestic market.[2] The protectionists of this school were thus put in the paradoxical position of claiming that the ideals of free trade could only be realised in a 'common market' of nations, large enough to be self-sufficient, but linked closely enough politically or by sentiment to enable the development of common institutions and complementary policies.

The success of any such scheme depended on Britain being able to regroup her foreign trade on a sheltered free trade area where once again, with the elimination of competitors, comparative advantage would operate in favour of her traditional exports. In this sense the plan was an attempt to recapture, in a more limited area, the nineteenth-century trade pattern whereby Britain exchanged her manufactured goods for primary products. Mosley, indeed, made this the central premise of his scheme:

> It is a recognised fact that the Dominions for many years to come must be largely agricultural producers, and we must be largely industrial producers. In this natural exchange we have a natural balance of trade. . . .[3]

Was this not the classic nineteenth-century free trade case, shorn of its altruism and universality? Was not the whole concept of empire free trade a device to shelter obsolescence by removing successful competitors who would otherwise have forced adaptation or bankruptcy?

This interpretation becomes inescapable if one considers the figures for trade between Britain and the Empire countries, in which there was an unmistakable pattern. The Empire was becoming less dependent on Britain, while Britain was becoming more dependent on the Empire. In fact Britain's exports to the Dominions declined by only 9 per cent between 1913 and 1927, whereas those to all other countries declined by 30 per cent.[4] Yet this was in a period when world exports actually expanded by 18 per cent. With her increasing uncompetitiveness,

[1] 244 H.C. Deb. c. 513. [2] Ibid. c. 77–79. [3] Ibid. c. 78.
[4] André Siegfried, *England's Crisis*, 1931, pp. 183–5.

Britain was becoming more reluctant to 'go and fight it out' on the world markets, and increasingly reliant on the fidelity of her Empire customers.

What could this country expect to get from the Dominions and what would she be expected to give in return? The Dominions already gave preference to British exports, but this preference invariably took the form of a differential between two tariff levels — a reasonably effective tariff against British goods, a prohibitive tariff against foreign goods.[1] What Britain meant by Imperial preference was the lowering of the tariff against British exports. What Bennett proposed was merely a raising of the tariff against foreign exports: hence Thomas's 'humbug' remark. Britain, as the largest single market for Dominion exports, had much to offer in return. But the Dominions, being largely primary producers, were only interested in preference for such raw materials as wool, wheat and meat. In practice, discussion was almost entirely centred on wheat. As MacDonald remarked: 'The very first thing that every Premier says, and in some cases . . . the last thing, is "tax wheat". He added: 'We cannot do it'.[2] Even the Conservatives shrank from doing it, hence their elaborate 'quota' proposals.

Thus Empire free trade was equally a chimera: the Dominions did not want it,[3] and too much of Britain's trade — over 50 per cent — was still done with the rest of the world. Imperial preference was possible but would clearly require very hard bargaining and was only a very partial and long-term solution.

iii. CONSTRUCTIVE LEGISLATION — AGRICULTURE

If the Government showed no disposition to meet the protectionists on Imperial preference, they did make some effort to meet the Liberals on agriculture. Up to the summer of 1930 agriculture had been only very marginally an unemployment issue. The Labour and Conservative

[1] For example, Lancashire was faced with a 15 per cent tariff against its cotton exports to India, non-Empire countries with a 25 per cent tariff.

[2] 244 H.C. Deb. c. 28.

[3] e.g. the Canadian Prime Minister in proposing his 10 per cent preference said: 'This . . . should not be considered as a step towards Empire Free Trade. In our opinion, Empire Free Trade is neither desirable nor possible. . . .' (Quoted *Liberal Magazine*, 1930, p. 510.)

Parties looked to the revival of ordinary industry to cure unemployment; the Liberals' public works consisted mainly of road building. The reasons for the neglect of agriculture were familiar and long-standing. Major sections of it, such as wheat, had been declining, with brief interruptions, since the 1870s. Occurring in a completely domestic industry, this decline seemed irrelevant to the unemployment problem which arose from a loss of exports. Insofar as agricultural unemployment existed it was indirect; agricultural workers, undefended by unemployment insurance, sought jobs in the towns — thus producing urban, rather than rural, unemployment. There was little real interest in reviving agriculture. The triumph of the Manchester free traders in 1846 had marked the victory of the entrepreneur over the landlord. Cheap raw materials, cheap food and low wages overrode the claims of rural prosperity. While politicians might pay lip-service to the notion of 'healthy' agriculture and even encourage it in specific circumstances (e.g. war), the general feeling was that it was doomed to go on declining.

This view was not without its critics. People in the Labour and Liberal Parties had for years seen a return to the land as the answer to various ills of capitalism. A healthy society, they argued, required a much better 'balance' between industrial and agricultural sides than in England, where rural occupations had come by 1920 to employ only about 7 per cent of the labour force. Lansbury and Lloyd George were the foremost political advocates of this view. Land settlement was given some encouragement in the Small Holding Acts of 1892, 1906 and 1919. But more pressing justifications were required.

Although in the 1929 election only specific and rather unimportant developments in agriculture were offered as solutions to unemployment,[1]

[1] The Labour Party, for example, evinced some interest in afforestation and were confident that the speeding up of tree planting from 15,000 acres a year to 150,000 would provide 'permanent employment . . . to 120,000 forest workers at the end of eighty years' — about the only firm estimate in the Labour plans. (*A Labour Policy for Agriculture*, 1926, p. 35.) The Liberals also mentioned afforestation, but devoted more space to land drainage. An appreciative note on the efforts of the Quakers in providing allotments for 40,000 unemployed miners led to the suggestion that a larger provision of small holdings would 'afford a minor . . . contribution towards the solution of the unemployment problem'. (*We Can Conquer Unemployment*, 1929, pp. 40, 50.)

both the Labour and Liberal Parties had fairly detailed plans for restoring the profitability of agriculture. By the nineteen-twenties the drift from the land was proceeding at the rate of 10,000 workers a year. Both Parties saw that contraction through depression, by burdening the industry with debt, depleting its capital equipment and driving away the most enterprising farmers, would make it extremely difficult to call a halt to decline. An accumulated structure of obsolescence would continue to drag the industry down even when the market was potentially favourable. Thus both Parties favoured the swift incision of public ownership to cut a way through the antique complexities of land tenure and to promote investment and efficiency.[1] Both disclaimed the intention of establishing a state bureaucracy. The Liberal ideal was the owner occupier and small-holding state tenant who would retain or acquire most of the freehold rights.[2] Labour foresaw a more diversified system in which public farming on a co-operative basis would, over a period of time, ease out the individual farmer though there would always be a place for him.[3] In both proposals, nationalisation would be accompanied by state credit facilities and co-operative marketing to eliminate the profits of the middleman.[4] A significant addition to the Labour policy were the proposals to create Import Boards for wheat and meat, which were both largely imported, in order to secure a stable price for the domestic producer.[5]

The Liberal policy was motivated firstly by a belief in a 'healthy' agriculture[6] and secondly by a desire, economic and strategic, to lessen Britain's dependence on imports, especially when the Liberals foresaw a 'quasi-permanent falling off in demand for our exports'.[7] This motive was to provide a lead-in for serious interest in agriculture once the world depression had started. The Labour Party's main preoccupation was

[1] *A Labour Policy*, p. 5; *Land and The Nation*: Report of the Liberal Land Committee, 1923–5, p. 299.

[2] *Land and The Nation*, pp. 300–4.

[3] *A Labour Policy*, p. 6.

[4] Ibid. pp. 15–19; *Britain's Industrial Future*: Report of the Liberal Industrial Enquiry, 1927, pp. 329, 331–4.

[5] *A Labour Policy*, pp. 19–24.

[6] 'It . . . contributes to the health and well-being of the nation to a degree altogether out of proportion to the money profit which it returns.' (*Britain's Industrial Future*, p. 319.)

[7] Ibid. p. 320.

to raise the standard of living and status of the agricultural worker.[1]

The Conservatives had no such far-reaching plans. They emphatically rejected nationalisation.[2] They did not even whisper tariffs. As late as February 1930, despite the prompting of Leo Amery and others to reserve a 'free hand', Baldwin promised in a speech at the Caxton Hall not to tax food imports.[3]

Until the world depression started, the Government, which anxiously awaited a trade revival, saw no reason to give priority to its agricultural policy.[4] The Conservatives were also quiescent. However, the distress of the farmer gave them a live political issue, especially as they could say it was caused by Soviet 'dumping'.[5] By the autumn of 1930 they had come to favour a 'quota' or proportion of home-grown wheat in bread baked in this country; a 'tax' on bounty-fed oats and foreign barley; and protection for the market-gardener.[6] Thus it was the Conservatives who brought agriculture into the forefront of politics.

Quite independently, the rapid decline of world trade gave the question of import substitution a new urgency. Britain imported about £450m of the £700m worth of food she consumed. Much of this was in products where British agriculture, because of the closeness of the market, might be thought to enjoy comparative advantage. The Liberals were quick to see in a looming balance of payments crisis an economic rationale for

[1] *A Labour Policy*, Introduction, p. 8. The 1924 Labour Government passed the Agricultural Wages Act which laid down the principle of a 'minimum wage' for the agricultural industry.

[2] Baldwin's Election Address, *Gleanings and Memoranda*, January–June 1929, p. 610.

[3] L. Amery, *My Political Life*, vol. iii, pp. 22–3.

[4] Noel Buxton, the Minister, contented himself with buying the deer park of Luskentyre for the creation of small-holdings and sending a circular letter to London housewives urging them to buy British beef.

[5] Soviet dumping was one of the most persistent arguments used against the 'open door' in agriculture. Soviet wheat exports to Britain rose from nil in 1929 to 19m cwts in 1930. Even so this was a tiny proportion of total wheat imports. The Conservatives attributed this to political motives, but see M. Dobb, *Soviet Economic Development since 1917*, 1948, p. 238. The Russian Five-Year Plan relied on increasing agricultural exports in order to obtain the necessary foreign exchange to purchase constructional materials.

[6] Baldwin to Neville Chamberlain, 15 October 1930. *Gleanings and Memoranda*, June–December 1930, pp. 376–7.

their policy of home development to absorb the unemployed; only instead of roads, agriculture would be the new focus of activity. A vigorous 'free trade' plan for agriculture would both counter the evolving protectionism of Conservative policy and provide a firm basis for political co-operation with the Government.

The two-party conference on unemployment set up in June provided the opportunity to work out a joint policy. Previously, an agricultural sub-committee of the E.A.C. had endorsed the need for marketing reform.[1] The Liberal statement of policy issued in October, which embodied their contribution to the two-party discussions, placed agriculture in the forefront of the battle against unemployment. The basis of the new thinking was an acceptance of 'quasi-permanent' export decline, making necessary import substitution. As Britain would always require to import raw materials for her industry, agriculture appeared to offer the most fruitful field for development.

In what areas should this occur? The Liberals proposed to concentrate on products where British agriculture enjoyed a 'natural advantage': liquid milk, butter, cheese, eggs, poultry, vegetables, meat and non-tropical fruit. Their production could be increased by £200m. This kind of production required intensive farming: hence an integral part of the Liberal plan was a great expansion in small-holdings.[2] The family farm provided 'an extraordinarily good life for those who appreciate the countryside', while 'a countryside peopled with family farmers is a sound

[1] Protection was emphatically rejected:

> 'It should, in our opinion, be a cardinal principle of agricultural policy that it is the first business of the farmer to make his farm pay in the existing conditions of world markets. . . . We are convinced that permanent Government assistance in the form of guaranteed prices or acreage subsidies, which would make it easier to continue obsolete methods, should not be given.'

This report was signed by R. H. Tawney. It is touching to note his faith in the market mechanism, as well as his repudiation of the Labour policy of Import Boards ('guaranteed prices'). The report also rejected the policy of import substitution, which earned it some scathing criticism from Keynes. (Keynes Papers, E.A.C. 5.)

[2] The Liberals contended, with some expert backing, that the ideal unit in these cases was the small, specialist family farm rather than the large, diversified farm which relied on crop rotation, livestock to provide manure, etc. (*How to Tackle Unemployment*, p. 42.)

social foundation for a democratic State'.[1] On the other hand, distribution should be handled by co-operative organisations which would free the individual producer from his dependence on the middleman. The Liberal ideal was 'the specialist farmer, assisted by co-operation and proper marketing'.[2]

To implement such a policy, the state should nationalise three million acres of land.[3] It would then create 100,000 small-holdings (farms of up to fifty acres) 'within three or five years' as the first instalment of a national family farming system. The long-term effect of such a policy would be employment 'in agriculture and its ancillary services' of 500,000 men, or a total increase in the rural population of two million.[4] The start of the policy alone would provide work for 150,000 men on preparatory jobs.[5] The programme would be financed by a national development loan of £100m which would, however, only be required in instalments as the programme developed. The interest falling on the Budget would be merely £6m a year and the Liberals were confident that much of the money would be repaid by rents and the added prosperity of the agricultural community.[6]

This programme was brought before the Government in June and July and made more acceptable by the resignation of Noel Buxton, the Minister of Agriculture, through ill-health on 5 June 1930, and the promotion of his parliamentary secretary, Dr. Charles Addison, Lloyd George's erstwhile protégé, to his place. The doctor, if not brilliant, was amiable, persuasive and extremely energetic. He had been in effective charge of the Ministry for some months previously so there was no need to 'play himself in' before taking important policy decisions.

The King's Speech of 28 October announced

> Proposals . . . for the promotion of increased settlement and employment on the land, and of large-scale farming operations, and for the acquisition and improvement of agricultural land in need of re-conditioning; and for the organisation of producers for marketing purposes.[7]

This seemed very close to the Liberal plans: but whatever the intentions

[1] *How to Tackle Unemployment*, p. 44. The 'foundation of democracy' argument was somewhat weakened by appreciative references to Mussolini's land policy (p. 49).

[2] Ibid. p. 44. [3] Ibid. pp. 48–52.

[4] Ibid. p. 58. [5] Ibid. p. 59. [6] Ibid. pp. 59–60. [7] 244 H.C. Deb. c. 6.

of the legislation, the Treasury had to be won over, and at a time when there was increasing pressure for retrenchment. Had the Government changed their mind about a national development loan? Then there was the agricultural lobby, who had no great interest in rural resettlement: they wanted a guaranteed price. Rationalisation of marketing would obviously be long-term in its effects and in the meantime prices would go on falling; protection seemed the only immediately relevant measure.

The Land Utilisation Bill was given its second reading on 13 November. It did two things: it empowered the Minister of Agriculture, working through an Agricultural Land Corporation, to spend up to £6m buying land for large scale — 3,000 acre — experiments in farming, demonstration farms, and for the purpose of 'reclamation, draining and other work'. There was a complicated procedure for compulsory purchase which could be represented as 'creeping nationalisation'. The second part of the Bill dealt with small-holdings. Previously responsibility for providing them rested with the county councils. Now the Minister was given direct power to provide holdings and allotments for suitable unemployed persons and also for ordinary applicants where 'the council of any county have not provided sufficient small-holdings to satisfy . . . demand'. No financial limit was set to this section, but it was calculated that it would cost about £1m for each 1000 holdings, agreeing with the Liberal estimate of £100m for acquiring and equipping 100,000 small-holdings.

The Liberals thought nationalisation was the aim, and approved the proposals if not the tactics. Lord Lothian wrote to Lloyd George on 31 October:

> The proposal to make [land purchase] compulsory is really part of a general scheme of nationalisation, and there is no doubt that if the Government had been wise it would have introduced the Bill in this guise. Addison, however, feels that to introduce an entirely new and highly controversial principle of land acquisition as a side wind to a Bill dealing with reconditioning and small-holdings would be to imperil the Bill itself.[1]

Walter Guinness, the ex-Tory Minister, argued

> I must, in fairness, concede one very exceptional virtue to this proposal. It actually carries out a definite election pledge of the Socialist Party. In Labour's policy for the land the object of public ownership was put first. The Prime Minister has told us that people can be led to socialism by practical stages

[1] Lothian Papers, Box 214.

without mentioning nationalisation. However carefully the Bill shirks the name, it is very obvious that that is the real purpose of this scheme.... Already we see the germ from which may develop such a policy as exists in Russia.[1]

If Addison thought that by avoiding the word nationalisation he could disarm suspicion, he was sadly mistaken. Conservative speakers harped on this theme through the Bill's progress in the Commons. The Lords immediately deleted the clause setting up the Agricultural Land Corporation.[2] But the impact of the Bill as a measure for nationalisation and hence for immediate employment depended entirely on the expenditure anticipated in providing small-holdings for the unemployed; its power to provide them for other applicants was restricted by 'unsatisfied demand' which was extremely limited.[3] Addison's promises to the Liberals were fulsomely optimistic:

As regards finance [Lothian wrote] he says he can obtain from the Treasury all the money he can spend on small-holdings, if necessary up to £50m with Snowden's consent.[4]

Even if this was not quite the £100m proposed by the Liberals it was extremely promising. But swift disillusionment was in store.

On 27 February 1931, Addison said that he expected 10,000 holdings to be established 'during the next few years'.[5] Adamson, Scottish Secretary of State, reckoned the Bill would enable seven hundred

[1] 244 H.C. Deb. c. 1908.

[2] Other Conservative and farming objections to the Land Corporation were of the familiar 'direction from Whitehall' variety. Captain E. T. Morris, President of the N.F.U., said that the large scale farms were being set up to teach the farmer to do his job. 'They had been suffering from too many of these theorists for years past.' (*East Anglian Times*, 27 November 1930. Quoted *Gleanings and Memoranda*, Jan.–June, 1931, p. 52.)

[3] The figures for applications to County Councils given by the Ministry of Agriculture, July 1930, were: 1927: 3248; 1928: 2757; 1929: 2446. (241 H.C. Deb. c. 1095–6.) Undoubtedly these figures were influenced by the terms offered by the 1926 Act; but since about half of the applicants would be rejected as unsuitable, the Liberal plan of creating 100,000 holdings in three to five years seems excessively optimistic. Between 1870 and 1930 the numbers of small-holdings fell by over 50,000, twice the number of the statutory holdings created in the same period. (Lord Ernle, *English Farming Past and Present*, 1961, p. 429.)

[4] Lothian Papers, Box 214.

[5] *Daily Herald*, 28 February 1931.

families a year to be settled on the land in Scotland.[1] When Colonel Ashley, former Minister of Transport, moved that the amount spent on providing holdings in any one year be limited to £5m Attlee thought this 'not at all an ungenerous figure'.[2] But Snowden had no intention of approving even £5m a year. There was never any question of raising a development loan and the centre of political interest was rapidly shifting elsewhere. When the Bill finally became law in August 1931 it seemed an irrelevant epilogue; even the Lords' wrecking amendments, which threatened to raise the 'peers versus people' issue, were settled by the usual compromise. Crookshank commented not unfairly that the Bill wobbled 'between relief of unemployment and land settlement . . . it does not incline much in either direction'.[3]

Much more significant in the long run was the Agricultural Marketing Bill, introduced on 9 February 1931. Even when the land had been nationalised, 'the price received by the cultivator . . . will still be by far the most important factor in determining whether the industry is prosperous'.[4] Unfortunately the middleman absorbed 'far too large a percentage' of that price, a conclusion borne out by the report of the Linlithgow Committee in 1924.[5] Since 1929 a further collapse in the wholesale price of agricultural produce had occurred, and once more it was noted that retail prices were holding up better.[6] Both the Labour and Liberal Parties proposed to deal with the price question by setting up marketing boards to raise the price to the producer and lower that to the consumer, making possible agricultural expansion.

Addison's Bill proposed to allow producers of certain listed agricultural products — milk, potatoes, hops, wool, cereals, cheese and livestock (fruit was added later) — to regulate the marketing of their own products by boards elected by themselves. These boards would have the power to buy the particular product from the farmer, sell it, and fix its selling price. All producers of a given product would be compelled to take part in the scheme provided a majority of producers were in favour,

[1] 248 H.C. Deb. c. 341. [2] Ibid. c. 284–5. [3] Ibid. c. 344–5.
[4] *A Labour Policy*, p. 15. [5] *Final Report*, Cmd. 2008, para. 15–16.
[6] Taking 1924 as 100 wholesale agricultural prices declined from an average of 88 in the first six months of 1929 to 79 in the first six months of 1930; retail prices from 88 to 84 (*London and Cambridge Economic Service Monthly Bulletin*, 23 December 1930, p. 377).

but the Minister himself was not given power to establish a board, though he proposed to arm himself with 'Reorganisation Commissions' to make suggestions.[1] Finally, the usual Consumers' Councils were to be set up to safeguard the public interest.[2]

Like the Coal Mines Act, the Bill proposed to create producers' monopolies, with power to fix wholesale, but apparently little incentive to reduce retail, prices. There was, however, one important difference between the two cases. British farmers, unlike the coal owners, had no monopoly of the home market. Free trade was essential to the Labour–Liberal plan: the market mechanism would secure the required efficiency. This was precisely what the farmers did not want. They were not prepared to go on facing the 'fierce blasts of foreign competition'. But protection, their first priority, would destroy the whole point of the Labour–Liberal policy.[3]

The Conservatives were moving rapidly to a fully protectionist position on agriculture. Earlier they had exempted livestock from their protectionist schemes. Now, on 6 December 1930, Chamberlain noted in his diary:

> I have, of course, always wanted protection for agriculture, but it has appeared unlikely that we could get it until after the towns had been served. . . . Today public opinion is moving so rapidly under the pressure of increasing unemployment, that I believe we could go the whole hog with safety. And my studies at the Research Department have shown clearly enough that the future of British farming is not in wheat, but in livestock, dairying, pigs, and poultry. To build up those industries, so vital to the general prosperity of the country, a tariff seems indispensable, though it must of course be combined with other means.[4]

Thus the Conservative amendment to the second reading condemned a Bill 'which authorises the imposition of compulsory restrictions on the

[1] Characteristically the Liberals deplored this purely permissive legislation (*How to Tackle Unemployment*, p. 57). Lloyd George said he thought an 'element of compulsion' was necessary for the marketing schemes (244 H.C. Deb. c. 714).

[2] For the Bill as a whole see *Agricultural Marketing Bill* (No. 78), H.M.S.O., 18 December 1930.

[3] The Liberals had ruled out protection of any kind on the ground that it would perpetuate inefficiency. (*How to Tackle Unemployment*, pp. 45–6.)

[4] Feiling, *The Life of Neville Chamberlain*, p. 182.

sale of British produce without imposing any conditions on the sale of foreign produce'. As Viscount Wolmer said: 'You must take steps to prevent foreign produce from competing unfairly with home produce, and destroying any attempt at stabilising the price which the national organisation may achieve.'[1]

The farmers could not expect protection from Labour or the Liberals, but they could reasonably hope for all-party agreement on anti-dumping legislation. The Labour Party was committed to import boards, and there was a vociferous anti-dumping group of M.P.s headed by George Dallas, who sat for the wheat constituency of Wellingborough.[2] Among the Liberals Sir John Simon's supporters were increasingly adopting the whole Conservative policy,[3] and on the other wing Sir Archibald Sinclair, Lord Lothian and Lloyd George himself had all expressed willingness to act against dumping. Nothing could have done more to win the farmers over to the rest of the Government's agricultural policy.

However, when the question of import controls was raised in exploratory fashion earlier in 1930, the Labour Government had taken the view that it was impossible to restrict imports in view of international obligations.[4] On 1 August Snowden deferred all government action till the Imperial Conference, due to meet in October. Speaking at Leicester on 13 September Addison said: 'In my opinion, the Import Board is the only way to deal with the problem of imported wheat, and in the end I think we shall have to adopt it for a number of commodities.'[5] The Imperial Conference came and went with no further government announcement. In December, the Cabinet discussed

[1] 248 H.C. Deb. c. 78.

[2] 'When they found that they had to face bounty-fed cereals from Germany, bounty-fed flour from France, and convict-produced potatoes from Algeria, he said no industry could face competition of that character'. Report of a speech made by G. Dallas at Salisbury, 5 April 1930. (*The Times*, 7 April 1930.)

[3] Seven Liberal M.P.s supported a motion of Lt.-Col. Gault on 26 November 1930, deploring the Government's refusal to take action against cereal dumping. They were Sir R. Hutchison, Sir Murdoch MacDonald, G. Lambert, Rev. R. M. Kedward, P. J. Pybus, I. Macpherson, and Col. A. England. With the exception of Col. England they all sat for predominantly rural constituencies.

[4] Ten bilateral treaties and one international treaty prevented the immediate introduction of import controls. (242 H.C. Deb. c. 249.)

[5] *Daily Herald*, 15 September 1930.

import boards and quotas, and went on discussing them in desultory fashion for some months. But the free traders in the Cabinet were adamant.[1]

The refusal to give protection to agriculture cost the Government its last chance of getting the farmers on its side. The Land Utilisation Bill was dead before it ever reached the Statute Book: it is not even mentioned in the standard reference books.[2] The Agricultural Marketing Act had a better fate, especially after the cherished protection was conceded by the National Government. Yet by 1933 only the Hops Marketing Board had actually been set up; the Bill was no answer to the price question and had no effect on unemployment.

Perhaps the correct epitaph on the Liberal policy was pronounced by the Liberals themselves five years later. An exhaustive survey of small-holdings undertaken by Seebohm Rowntree and Viscount Astor concluded:

> the idea of securing a material increase in the agricultural population consistently with the maintenance of the national economic prosperity must be dismissed as chimerical.[3]

iv. MAINTENANCE — TOWARDS A ROYAL COMMISION

The promise in the King's Speech to set up a Royal Commission to look into unemployment insurance seems to have taken the Oppositions by surprise. Following the three-party conference, they had expected the announcement of legislation: the Royal Commission proposal meant a postponement of legislation to some future date in such a way as to make it impossible to force the Government into action in the interim. The trade unions, however, far from being pleased at this clever manœuvre on the Government's part, regarded the Royal Commission as a dastardly plot to strengthen support for reductions in unemployment pay.

[1] See below, p. 327.

[2] e.g. Ernle, *English Farming Past and Present*, 6th ed., 1961. The text is that of the fifth edition of 1936, which had been brought up to date. Even five years after the Act, it had been completely forgotten.

[3] King, *The Agricultural Dilemma*, 1935, p. 76.

That delay was the sole aim of the Government becomes clear from a remarkable interview between MacDonald, Hartshorn and Miss Bondfield and a deputation from the General Council of the T.U.C. held at 10 Downing Street on 2 January 1931. The Council representatives accused the Government of having conspired with the other two Parties to set up the Commission in order to 'fix' a result, unfavourable to the unemployed.

Citrine: The three-party conference agreed to set up a Royal Commission a month before the October announcement in the King's Speech.

P.M.: That is untrue.

MacDonald then outlined the position. The Government needed to secure supplementary borrowing powers for the insurance fund. It had decided that the necessary majority would not be forthcoming until it promised to do something about 'abuses'. Both the other Parties were opposed to a Commission and

The Commission was suggested by one of our own representatives as a way out to enable us to get our money and to tide things over for the next . . . six months.

Later he returned to this point in greater detail:

The Liberals and Tories did not force the Royal Commission on us in the sense that they asked us to appoint it. They were opposed to its appointment, because they asked for immediate action. They did force it upon us, however, in the sense that we could not have got the £10m . . . unless we had done something and the only thing we could do was to set up a Commission.

Miss Bondfield repudiated Citrine's contention that a commission had been agreed a month before the announcement. She referred to the Cabinet meeting of 23 October, five days before the opening of Parliament:

On Thursday night when the special Cabinet meeting was being held to settle the King's Speech, I had to report to the Cabinet about the three-party conference. . . . We had not finished our business and we were not able to produce a report. Mr. Greenwood, Mr. Hartshorn and I at that time had to go to the Cabinet and report that we foreshadowed there was no possibility of agreement and that we were convinced they would press for an immediate Bill. That was reported to the Cabinet practically at the same moment that a messenger was waiting to take the final draft of the King's Speech to the King.

I realised the difficulty of things being rushed at the last moment, but I do want to make this perfectly clear that at that stage the Cabinet were faced with what they had to put into the King's Speech, whether they were going to put in that a Bill would be introduced, or whether they were going to put in that a Commission would be appointed.

MacDonald supported this account, adding: 'We have always settled things at the last moment, ever since I have been in office.'

These excerpts make it quite clear that the Royal Commission was first and foremost a *delaying measure*. However, a difficulty arises from Miss Bondfield's report of the Cabinet meeting. The reactions of the opposition speakers in the Commons do not make sense unless the Government had led them to believe that the three-party conference would result in legislation. The opposition representatives, in other words, were expecting legislation. Such an expectation could only have been fostered by the government representatives, especially Miss Bondfield. This interpretation is strengthened by Lansbury's account to which we have already referred.[1]

It seems highly probable that while the King's messenger was waiting outside, Snowden and Miss Bondfield were pleading for early legislation; they failed to convince the Cabinet and the argument continued without agreement. In the end 'one of our representatives', presumably Hartshorn, had suggested a Royal Commission and this had been accepted, no doubt with bad grace on Snowden's part, as the only possible compromise.

As we have seen, the trade unions were deeply concerned at the news of a Royal Commision. They had not been consulted: they suspected that the purpose of the Commission was to produce a certain type of report. These suspicions were soon confirmed. Early in November, the government chief whip wrote to the Liberal chief whip giving him the date of the probable introduction of the new borrowing Bill and enquiring what the attitude of the Liberal Party was likely to be. Following this letter Miss Bondfield saw Sir Archibald Sinclair, Ernest Brown and Isaac Foot. The Liberals made it clear that it would be difficult to get the Party to support the Government unless the terms of reference and personnel of the Commission were announced before the new Bill was introduced; further, that the terms of reference should foreshadow the

[1] See above, p. 239.

kind of report that the Oppositions wanted — i.e. restoration of the insurance fund to a sound 'actuarial' basis by separating those in insurance from those on the 'dole'.[1] Little further progress was reported by mid-November. As the money resolution was scheduled for 1 December, the Government were left with about a fortnight to settle the terms of reference and the composition of the Commission.

Naturally the General Council were anxiously awaiting news. On Friday, 14 November Ince, Miss Bondfield's secretary, telephoned Transport House and asked to speak to Citrine on a 'very urgent and important matter'. Ince wanted to fix up a meeting on Monday afternoon between Snowden and Miss Bondfield and Citrine and Hayday (who had just become president of the T.U.C.) in order to discuss 'unemployment insurance'. Hayday had by this time left for the week-end for Nottingham, where he lived, and it proved impossible to get in touch with him.

On Monday, Ince telephoned at 10.45 a.m. to ask what arrangements had been agreed for the meeting. He was informed that no one had been able to get in touch with Hayday, but it was hoped to see him that afternoon. Meanwhile Hayday had arrived in London for the meeting of the T.U.C. economic committee. There he was eventually told of the various conversations and said that nothing could be done until a letter was received from the Ministry setting forth the points for discussion. During the meeting Ince telephoned once more but was told that Hayday was busy. Finally, after several more futile telephone calls, Miss Bondfield herself came on the line and told Citrine that the Cabinet were meeting in half an hour: was she to tell them that the General Council did not wish to discuss the terms of reference? Citrine repeated that if the Government had wished to discuss the Royal Commission with Hayday and himself a letter should have been sent, so as to give them a chance to hold a preliminary conference. He added that the Government's attitude in this matter was only one of several incidents which could not be separated.

Miss Bondfield related these incidents to the Cabinet who decided that no further effort should be made to contact the General Council before

[1] MacDonald Papers, Unemployment Insurance File 6. Sylvester (PS. to Lloyd George) to Thompson (Cabinet Office), 13 November 1930; Ince (M. of Labour) to Butler (P.M.'s office), 22 November 1930.

agreeing on terms of reference. The decision on this matter was reached on Wednesday, 19 November.

The abortive telephone negotiations produced lively discussion at the meeting on 2 January. The exchanges on that occasion convey vividly the relations between the Council and the Government:

Citrine: We were asked on Friday for Monday. . . . Then the Minister herself came on. (To Bondfield) And you asked me point blank whether we intended to come down and you said that the Cabinet were waiting for an answer, that you and the Chancellor had been deputed to see Hayday and myself about the matter and that the Cabinet were going to meet within half an hour. . . . I will tell you quite definitely that we were not prepared to come and see you within half an hour of the Cabinet meeting to discuss terms of reference without knowing what the subject was, without knowing what you wanted to discuss . . . without giving us any time to find out the opinion of our people, so that you in turn could communicate to the Cabinet a point of view that we ourselves did not know would be supported by our members. That is not the way to do business.

(MacDonald interjected that he was under the impression that adequate time had been afforded for consultation.)

Citrine (to P.M.): If you have been given the impression that time for consultation was afforded you were entirely misinformed, entirely misinformed.

(Switching his attack)

At the stage when we were first approached . . . you had already decided the terms of reference.

P.M.: No . . . you must accept my word. We had not decided on the terms of reference.

Citrine: I know they had been drafted in the Ministry of Labour and were in your hands. I know that much. I know what I am saying.

P.M.: The terms of reference were held up until you were consulted. They were not settled till 19 November. At the Cabinet meeting on the 17th, Miss Bondfield reported that Citrine had said that if consultation were desired the Cabinet should ask the General Council in writing.

Citrine: The reason why a letter was necessary was that unless such a letter setting forth the points of discussion should be sent to me in the first place no preliminary conference within the General Council and the constituent parts could take place.

Hayday: We were not told what the subject was.

Bondfield: Surely you knew it was on the subject of Unemployment Insurance?

P.M.: We were told that on the 14th a conversation took place over the telephone and that an appointment was made to see the Chancellor and the Minister on the 17th.

Citrine: That is absolutely incorrect.

Bondfield: I was given the impression that either Mr. Citrine or Mr. Hayday would try to come on Monday. The only difficulty was to get in touch with Mr. Hayday. We telephoned him three times at Nottingham.

Hartshorn: As a Trade Union official, what notice do you expect from the Government? You have been complaining that you were not kept in proper touch . . . but if you got notice on the 14th to come and discuss a matter upon which they did not reach a decision till the 19th, surely that is ample time?

Citrine: We think the opposite way, that the decision had already been reached on 28 October, when the King's Speech was read. The time for consultation was between 28 October and 14 November, but you wanted to consult us half an hour before your Cabinet meeting so that we were to be rushed into giving our point of view.

P.M.: The intention was not that you should come half an hour before the Cabinet meeting which was to have taken the decision, because the decision was not taken till Wednesday, 19th, the normal Cabinet day. Monday was a special meeting to discuss other matters and also to find out what had happened at the Conference which was supposedly scheduled for 5.30.

Hayday: That was not what we were told: Miss Bondfield misled us, then.

P.M.: After all, why did you not come and fight it out?[1]

The terms of reference were announced by Snowden in the House on 1 December. They were

> to inquire into the provisions and working of the unemployment insurance scheme and to make recommendations with regard to:
> (1) its future scope, the provisions which it should contain and the means by which it may be made solvent and self-supporting; and
> (2) the arrangements which should be made *outside the scheme* for the unemployed who are capable of and available for work. [italics mine.][2]

It can now be seen why the General Council were so suspicious of a government deal with the Opposition. The Royal Commission was given every encouragement to recommend on the lines of Conservative and Liberal proposals; it was not to be allowed even to discuss the non-contributory principle which formed the basis of Labour policy.

[1] General Council Papers, 157.83.D. [2] 245 H.C. Deb. c. 1785–6.

Having decided the terms of reference, it remained to recruit the personnel of the Commission, and once more the Government managed to offend the General Council. They were anxious to secure trade union representation, despite the grotesque misunderstandings that had arisen. But if they were to ask for General Council nominees they would have to invite employers' representatives as well. The Government, perhaps remembering the Sankey precedent, were hoping for a divided report which would provide an excuse for yet another delay.

Unfortunately arrangements were once more left in the hands of Miss Bondfield. On 20 November she telephoned Citrine inviting him to luncheon the following day. Citrine accepted, but said he would come as a private individual and not in his official capacity. He made the following note after the meeting:

> Miss Bondfield explained that it was the Government's purpose to appoint a Trade Union representative and the Government were anxious that I should accept nomination. I told her this was out of the question. Miss Bondfield then said that she had invited Sir Francis Floud, the new permanent secretary . . . to come along after lunch to meet me. I did not particularly like this course, but did not dissent. Sir Francis brought a letter for Miss Bondfield's signature which requested the General Council to nominate a representative and suggesting my name. I informed Miss Bondfield that I strongly objected to the letter being put before me in this way and to my being drawn into conversation in the presence of an official of the Ministry of Labour when Mr. Hayday and I had expressly refused to take part in official conversations.

Following this infortunate incident, the Prime Minister decided to dispense with the services of Miss Bondfield as an intermediary and got the Home Secretary, Clynes, to telephone Transport House on 26 November to ask the General Council informally whether it would agree to nominate members. Clynes was greatly respected, but he could not undo the damage. Hayday spoke to him: 'Johnny,' he said, 'to be perfectly frank we do not think it would.' So the letters inviting General Council and employers' representatives to serve on the Royal Commission were never sent and on 9 December 1930 the Prime Minister in announcing the appointment of Judge Holman Gregory as chairman told the Commons that there were to be no direct representatives of either employers or employed.[1]

[1] 246 H.C. Deb. c. 222–3.

Several significant points emerge from these negotiations, which were to play their full part in determining the course of the 1931 crisis.

Miss Bondfield clearly proved herself totally unable to win the confidence of the General Council. Suspicions of her dated from her signature of the Blanesburgh Report; they were reinforced by her attitude to 'not genuinely seeking work', and confirmed by her monumental tactlessness over the Royal Commission. There was deep suspicion too of Ministry of Labour officials. Otherwise it would be hard to account for Citrine's strong objection to the presence of Sir Francis Floud at his luncheon with Miss Bondfield. Miss Bondfield's ignorance of General Council procedure was amazing for one who had for six years been a member of it. In sending no written invitation or agenda, she committed a bad error of judgment which was largely responsible for the bitterness of the subsequent meeting. By misleading them about the purpose of the Monday Cabinet meeting, she also gave the General Council the impression that she was trying to blackmail them.

The lack of liaison with the Government was strongly felt and repeatedly stated. As Citrine put it:

> After the unfortunate lack of liaison in 1924 we hoped that this Government would at least have been working more cohesively with our movement than in fact has happened. For a period it did appear that cohesion was present . . . but of late that cohesion has almost disappeared and as far as I am personally concerned scarcely exists.

Hayday went so far as to say that 'the Labour Government have not been as fair as some of the other Governments'.

The General Council was by no means blameless. By allowing itself to be unduly offended by Miss Bondfield's heavy-handedness it lost a real opportunity to 'fight it out' on its members' behalf. Indeed, why did it have no point of view, on 14 November 1930, on the terms of reference? The Royal Commission was first broached on 28 October and according to Citrine the Council had expected it a month before. The terms of reference would clearly come up for discussion with the unions. Why then was it caught by surprise when Ince telephoned?

It seems certain that the Liberals were pressing for terms of reference excluding consideration of the Labour scheme. There is little doubt also that the Ministry of Labour was working for the same result. Citrine's suggestion that the terms had been drafted in the Ministry some time before is entirely plausible, though Cabinet acceptance was not a foregone conclusion. There would certainly have been more opposition within the Cabinet had the Council not behaved so stuffily.

V. A NATIONAL GOVERNMENT?

Jennie Lee has written in her memoirs that the negative attitude of the Labour Government in this period 'drove everyone under forty to the verge of madness'.[1] Beatrice Webb noted in her diary for 23 November that the parliamentary Labour Party was in a state of revolt; the relaxation of backbenchers was 'to talk, talk, talk, in little groups of the misdoings of the Cabinet'. There were rumours of a plot to replace MacDonald by Henderson, of a Cabinet move to get rid of Snowden.[2] The disaffection was not confined to the Labour Party. Younger Conservatives were sickened by Baldwin's lethargy and lack of drive, and in the winter of 1930 and spring of 1931 the clamour for his resignation reached its height. Liberals, too, sought to escape from the dilemma of keeping in office a Labour Government whose ineptitude was sure to drag down the Liberal Party to disastrous electoral defeat.

Beatrice Webb's comment on the Labour Party is exaggerated. The majority of Members, believing that the Government was doing its best in face of insuperable difficulties, and convinced that there was no possibility of socialism, remained resolutely loyal to the leadership. To

[1] Jennie Lee, *The Great Journey*, 1963, p. 115.

[2] There are several versions of the attempted putsch against MacDonald, but they all agree that Mosley, in the autumn of 1930, approached Arthur Henderson in the Foreign Secretary's private room behind the Speaker's chair and asked him to lead a movement against MacDonald, Henderson taking over the premiership. It is almost certain that Henderson refused, but MacDonald himself seemed to believe that he was intriguing against him. The *Manchester Guardian* of 10 November reported a story to the effect that Snowden was to be driven out of the Government because of his opposition to a National Development Loan, together with A. V. Alexander, First Lord of the Admiralty, and Wedgwood Benn, Secretary of State for India. Another version had it that Snowden's difficulties had arisen not over the National Development Loan, but over opposition to tariffs. Nevertheless the rumours were considered sufficiently serious to warrant an official denial. (*The Times*, 10 November 1930.)

all efforts to arouse them from their inertia they reacted 'like a load of damp cement'.[1] Nevertheless, three groups of dissidents did emerge, one mainly outside the parliamentary Party, two within it.

Early in November G. D. H. Cole, convinced that there was no inevitability of gradualness, started to get together a discussion group to work out a more secure intellectual foundation for socialism. He was anxious to recruit progressive trade unionists; the Countess of Warwick lent her country house, Easton Lodge, for week-end house parties; and early in December the first conference met, with Cole, W. A. Robson and Bevin, 'four or five young men from the L.S.E. and some of Cole's younger disciples from Oxford', including Hugh Gaitskell. A number of subsequent meetings led to the formation, in April of the following year, of the New Fabian Research Bureau and the Society for Socialist Inquiry and Propaganda.[2]

Within the parliamentary Party the two groups of dissidents were the I.L.P. and the Mosleyites who together numbered at their greatest extent about forty M.P.s. Earlier in the year the I.L.P. had taken steps to purge their parliamentary ranks of all who disagreed with the policy of the I.L.P. conference. This reduced their parliamentary strength to seventeen headed by Maxton who, however, surrendered the chairmanship of the party to Fenner Brockway. The secretary was W. J. Brown, who formed the link with the Mosleyite group. This was a less formal collection of about twenty-five left-wing M.P.s who, while rejecting the I.L.P. policy of *Socialism in Our Time* as unrealistic, nevertheless demanded a 'bold' unemployment policy, on the lines sketched by Mosley in his resignation and subsequent speeches in the House and at the Llandudno conference in October. Mosley's triumph on that occasion[3] undoubtedly strengthened his position in the parliamentary Party. The I.L.P., despite Mosley's half-hearted denials, correctly read his policy as an alternative to socialism; this and personal distrust kept the two groups apart and reduced their joint influence, despite the attempts of overlapping members to bring them together and despite occasional

[1] Jennie Lee, *The Great Journey*, p. 112.

[2] *Manchester Guardian*, 29 May 1931.

[3] Mosley's speech had been enthusiastically received and he had failed by only two hundred thousand votes (1,046,000–1,251,000) to defeat the executive. (*Annual Report*, 1930, pp. 200–4.)

joint meetings. John Strachey, of the Mosleyites, also attended Cole's conference at Easton Lodge, but Mosley's ideas found few adherents there, although Cole wrote to Beatrice Webb that 'the Mosleyites . . . might be quite useful — many of them — in a wider movement of a less melodramatic sort'.[1]

The first action of the new I.L.P. parliamentary group had been to move a critical amendment to the King's Speech. The N.E.C. had reacted by announcing that it would withhold endorsement from any candidate who claimed to follow the I.L.P. rather than party decisions. A test case soon arose at East Renfrew, a marginal Conservative seat in Scotland, where N.E.C. endorsement was refused after the I.L.P. candidate, Baillie Irwin, refused to give 'satisfactory answers' to questions put to him. Commented the *Manchester Guardian* of 22 November 1930, 'The Labour Party seems sometimes as ramshackle as the old Austrian Empire'. The Conservatives put up a well-known local amateur boxer, the Marquess of Douglas and Clydesdale, who greatly increased their majority. Throughout this period a long correspondence between Maxton and Henderson, trying to find some way of reconciling the decision of the I.L.P. conference in May with continued affiliation to the Labour Party, was exposing irreconcilable differences. A final letter from Maxton on 30 December said:

> We do not find it possible, however, to accept the Standing Orders and Disciplinary Rules of the Parliamentary Party without substantial qualification and reservation.[2]

There, for the moment, the matter rested.

The I.L.P. amendment had criticised the Government for its failure to implement 'socialist reorganisation' of industry and banking and secure a fairer income distribution. It had thirteen supporters (including the two tellers), four of whom — Batey, Horrabin, McShane and Brown — were also members of the Mosleyite group. F. W. Jowett, moving it, described the beneficent effects of income redistribution:

> An increase of wealth in a country is like manure. If it is all heaped up in the wrong place, it is a pernicious nuisance, but, if it is spread and distributed, it is a fruitful source of a new and better life.[3]

---

1 Passfield Letters, 1930. Item 70.

2 *Annual Conference Report*, 1931, p. 297.

3 244 H.C. Deb. c. 403.

The taxation of the rich, out of which this redistribution was to come, followed directly from the I.L.P.'s under-consumptionist analysis. As Brockway put it:

In our view the problem of unemployment cannot be separated from the general problem of poverty . . . the causes of unemployment and poverty are the same.[1]

It is not surprising that the I.L.P. thought Mosley's measures were mere tinkering. So did the orthodox leaders of the Labour Party. Ideologically they agreed with the I.L.P. Unfortunately, whereas the I.L.P. wanted to attack immediately, the Labour leaders considered the moment inopportune. The attack on poverty could, paradoxically, only be launched in times of prosperity. As Jennie Lee truly remarks, the Labour leaders 'had a policy for calm weather; no policy for crisis'.[2]

Yet she and her I.L.P. colleagues were caught in exactly the same dilemma. No bold policy was possible in 1930 that did not have the support of at least an important section of the capitalist community; yet the I.L.P. policy of massive taxation had no support at that moment outside the I.L.P. Precisely the same problem would have arisen had the Government had a majority. Admittedly in that case the Opposition would not have been able to defeat it. But what would have been the effect on the capitalist economy of trying to raise £200m by direct taxation and attempting to nationalise the banks? Were the I.L.P. prepared for a revolutionary situation? There is no evidence that they were.

Mosley and his supporters, on the other hand, grasped the crucial fact that the only hope of a bold policy lay in adopting the interventionist elements of the Liberal and Conservative programmes. It was the Mosley group, rather than the I.L.P., that attacked the argument that the Government could do nothing because it lacked a socialist majority. As Aneurin Bevan asked: why did it not carry out the Liberal plans?[3]

Most of the Mosleyite dissidents were young men. Of the seventeen M.P.s who signed the Mosley manifesto in December, eight were under forty and a further six under fifty — young in parliamentary terms. In addition all except Mosley himself and two elderly Members from mining seats had entered Parliament for the first time in 1929: hence their

[1] 244 H.C. Deb. c. 404. [2] Jennie Lee, *The Great Journey*, p. 109.
[3] 244 H.C. Deb. c. 759.

impatience with the parliamentary game. But there were more practical reasons for the type of action they wanted. Like the I.L.P. the Mosleyites were largely a regional grouping: eight of the seventeen came from the Birmingham area. This is not altogether surprising. As the full force of the depression hit the Black Country in 1930, many traditional Birmingham attitudes came to the fore. Feeling ran strongly for protection and against the Government's tariff truce; the chamber of commerce passed a resolution calling for a 'self-supporting' Empire; there was much talk in the local press of the need for a national Government or co-operation of all Parties to meet the emergency; a strong paternalist tradition expressed itself in the notion of capital and labour facing the crisis shoulder to shoulder.[1] These grass-roots pressures would find a natural home in the Conservative Party, but how were Birmingham's Labour M.P.s to react? The problem was not as difficult as it seemed. Just as Christian converts of early times had continued to worship in heathen temples, with a slight rearrangement in the order of the deities, so Birmingham socialism looked very much like Chamberlain toryism, with certain variations. Neither Mosley's temperament nor his philosophy offered any barrier to his adopting Chamberlain's policy; his supporters merely required the urgent prodding of local sentiment to follow suit. Thus the Mosley group can best be seen as a protectionist-imperialist cave within the Labour Party.

If the Labour Government's pitiful performance threatened to drive young Labour M.P.s to the verge of madness, Stanley Baldwin's lethargy was driving many Conservatives in the same direction. Throughout the summer and autumn of 1930 Chamberlain and Amery fought hard to secure Baldwin's assent for a 'great policy' on the Imperial question which would include a 'free hand' over food taxes. But the Conservative Party was tied by the promise of a referendum Baldwin had conceded to Beaverbrook in March, and for a time this hindered any fresh Conservative initiative.[2] Baldwin's own great counter-attack on the press lords in June succeeded in temporarily re-establishing his personal position, but as Chamberlain noted in his diary, how much better it would be if Baldwin attacked the Government instead of attacking Beaverbrook and Rothermere. By 26 July 1930 he had 'most reluctantly' come to the conclusion that 'if S.B. would go, the whole Party would

[1] See Asa Briggs, *History of Birmingham*, vol. ii. [2] See above, p. 166.

heave a sigh of relief'.[1] This was confirmed by a report from the chief agent in September that the demand for a change of leadership 'has grown from a faint whisper to a loud and continuous rumbling'.[2]

Chamberlain, in two important speeches in August and September, laid down 'my unauthorised programme' for a revitalised Conservative Party. This embraced drastic economy; reduction of direct taxation; thorough reform of unemployment insurance; an emergency tariff for manufacturers; a wheat quota; and finally, a 'free hand' for food taxes.[3] Bennett's offer of a 10 per cent Imperial preference in October seemed a great opportunity for freeing the Party from the incubus of the referendum and Chamberlain rushed off a letter to the press, over Baldwin's initials, accepting the principle of Bennett's offer and promising to submit it to the British people at the next election 'for their *final and definite* assent' (italics mine).[4] This disposed of the referendum: and a week later Chamberlain got Baldwin to put his initials to a further statement of party policy which embodied all the points of his 'unauthorised programme'.

Thus was Baldwin led, almost dragged, to accept the 'great policy'. But great policies require great spirits — and a number of younger Conservative M.P.s did not feel that the Party's 'old gang' fulfilled this requirement. A leading article in *The Times* of 17 October reckoned that the defeat of the Government at the previous election had been due largely to the belief that victory for Baldwin would have entailed the re-instatement of 'the same old gang' and added that Conservative prospects would be immensely improved by the knowledge that Baldwin 'was prepared to take office hereafter with a team that would be predominantly young and new'. Baldwin managed to resist a challenge to his leadership at a meeting of the whole Party at Caxton Hall on 30 October, when a motion of 'no confidence' was rejected by 462 votes to 116, but the forceful criticisms of the 'old gang' on that occasion moved a number of 'old gangsters' to consider vacating their positions of leadership.[5] On the same day as the Caxton Hall meeting the result of the

[1] Keith Feiling, *The Life of Neville Chamberlain*, p. 180. [2] Ibid. p. 181.

[3] See Iain Macleod, *Neville Chamberlain*, 1961, p. 137.

[4] *The Times*, 10 October 1930.

[5] Amery describes how, at a meeting convened for this purpose, Lord Hailsham read out a very stilted draft of a letter to Baldwin renouncing the

South Paddington by-election was announced, showing that the Beaverbrook–Rothermere candidate, Vice-Admiral Taylor, standing as an 'Empire Crusader', had won the seat from the official Conservative, Sir Herbert Lidiard. This immediately re-opened the leadership question, and in the weeks and months that followed, opposition to Baldwin steadily grew.

It is hardly surprising that disaffection spread among the younger Tory M.P.s. In the late nineteen-twenties a group of them had met from time to time to discuss a 'progressive' economic policy for the Tory Party and the result of their thinking was a book — *Industry and the State — A Conservative View*, which advocated, in somewhat ambiguous language, government intervention in the economy and, in particular, a policy of 'national reconstruction'. The authors, Boothby, Loder, Macmillan, Oliver Stanley, were sympathetic to the ideas of Mosley which, in many respects, closely resembled their own. The tardiness of Baldwin in formulating a modern policy, the insufficiency of that policy on the domestic side when it was formulated, and the lack of firm leadership when the country 'demanded action', drew these men, with a number of others, such as Walter Elliot and John Buchan, into closer contact with the Labour rebel.

Ties other than those of policy united them. With the exception of Boothby, who was too young, all of them, like him, had seen active service in the war, all had returned with a desire to 'build a land fit for heroes' and all had seen that vision destroyed by the harsh economic facts of the post-war world and the negligence of successive Governments. To those whose first consciousness of politics had been government intervention on an enormous scale in the war, the argument that the Government could do nothing to solve the economic problem appeared singularly unconvincing. Thus their war experience and subsequent disillusionment with the 'old gangs' gave to their anger a

claims of the 'old gang' to any prescriptive right to belong to a Conservative Cabinet, whereupon Amery, who thought the whole notion 'rather comic', drafted 'a simpler, if not altogether grammatic' alternative:

> 'We the undersigned old gangsters, keenly alive to each others' senility, wish to make it quite clear that we shall each be only too delighted to see any of the others bumped off, should you wish to do so.'

(L. S. Amery, *My Political Life*, vol. iii, pp. 36–7.)

quality at once akin to that of Mosley's and different from that of Mosley's Labour associates, whose political philosophy had precluded them from placing any hopes in the promises of the coalition. The Labour Mosleyites resented Mosley's flirtation with the Tory rebels, seeing in it a sign of his imminent return to the Conservative fold, and though in conversations at his home in Smith Square he tried to evoke a common front between his Labour and Conservative allies, it seemed doomed to failure. Nevertheless these discussions, which were also attended by the Liberals, Sir Archibald Sinclair and Henry Mond, reflected a genuine revulsion against party bickering.

It soon became apparent that no all-party group stood much hope of exerting influence unless it recruited leaders from among the 'old gangs'. The most sought after, on account of both his past record and his present dilemmas, was Lloyd George, though Churchill, perpetually straining on the party leash, was also mentioned. The Liberal leader had a bold policy and was known to have an 'open mind' on free trade. Moreover, the Party he led seemed to be on the point of disintegration. The Liberals found themselves being slowly dragged down by the unpopularity of the Labour Government, without being able to 'improve' its policy or performance. The official line — as reiterated by Lloyd George in an important speech at Tenby on 25 October, and in a long letter to the *Manchester Guardian* on 27 December — was still to keep the Government in office till the alternative vote had been passed or until a trade revival removed the appeal of protection. This implied at least two more years of office for the Labour administration. However, as hopes of improvement faded, the prospect of being tied to a moribund Government grew ever more unappetising. This dilemma would have taxed even a united Liberal Party: and it was far from being that. About a third of the Liberal M.P.s, including Simon, Runciman, Hutchison and Maclean, distrusted Lloyd George personally and abhorred his 'vigorous' unemployment policy;[1] another third, including Welsh

[1] Chamberlain noted in his diary of 21 November: 'Simon felt that the Government was a national danger and would accept office from the Conservatives. . . .' (Feiling, *The Life of Neville Chamberlain*, p. 184.) On 25 October Simon, writing to Lloyd George, had urged him to come out against the Labour Government. (*The Times*, 6 November 1930.) On 5 November he and four other Liberals, including Hutchison, the chief whip, voted for the Conservative amendment to the King's Speech.

Members, were definitely his adherents; the remainder, headed by Samuel, tried to keep the peace between them. But what if it were impossible to keep the Party together? From Lloyd George's point of view it was far better that the break-up should be part of a wider redeployment of political forces to produce either a new 'centre' combination under his leadership, or a more conventional coalition Government in which he could gradually sever himself from unwelcome associations. Thus in the autumn of 1930 he played a double game: officially he held to his policy of keeping the Government in office, privately he 'collogued' with Churchill, the press lords, Mosley, Garvin and others to discover what prospects there were for an alliance with the Tories[1] or a realignment of political forces.

It was left to J. L. Garvin, editor of the *Observer*, to give a lead to the campaign for a national Government or Party, whichever seemed the most likely. He brought to the economic crisis a long-standing predilection for 'national' politics and a hero-worship of Lloyd George. As early as March 1929 he had written to Keynes:

> I am sick and tired of party politics. I joined the Unionist party under Chamberlain's influence . . . and have spent my life fighting Conservatism. . . . From Liberalism I am divided . . . hopelessly for free trade reasons. . . . One must just 'pig it' until the House of Commons more nearly reflects the mind of the country. If only Ll.G. had preserved himself as a National man of emergency. . . .[2]

Thus Garvin in the autumn of 1930 encouraged the revolt of the young men. 'The rising generation in every party', he wrote, 'feels that if things are not put right in the next few years by a mighty and sustained effort of peace-energy on a war scale, it is going to be their funeral.'[3] Prospects for the break-up of old party alliances seemed good:

> No one remembers a time when discontents were so rife in all parties together and when movements were so kaleidoscopic. The whole country feels that fundamental changes are required. . . . Amongst the younger generation in all parties the strongest sentiment is in favour of 'clearing out all the Old Gangs.[4]

---

[1] Chamberlain, 21 November: 'Lloyd George's tactic was to frighten the Conservatives into a treaty by working with Labour'. (Feiling, *The Life of Neville Chamberlain*, p. 184.)

[2] Keynes Papers, Correspondence, 1929.

[3] *The Observer*, 19 October 1930. [4] Ibid. 2 November 1930.

The difficulty of translating this mood into action became clearer when Garvin speculated on possible leaders of a new combination: Beaverbrook, Rothermere, Mosley and Lloyd George. How many votes could they deliver between them?

By 9 November Garvin realised that the only possible national Government must incorporate the leaders of the old Parties. He even found nice things to say about MacDonald — 'a temperament broad and not pedantic' — and a fortnight later, 'as little of a partisan in intellect and heart as any man in Britain'. Eventually he selected Lord Reading as suitable 'national premier', but still he hungered after Lloyd George, who 'standing absolutely clear as an independent national statesman would be a mighty power yet'.

Lloyd George was by no means averse to such talk and from time to time spoke favourably of a 'pooling' of the 'best brains of all Parties' to 'extricate the nation from its emergency'.[1] Rumours were rife of meetings of ex-Ministers and 'other adepts at intrigue' to discuss a national Party.[2]

However, despite all the talk, rumour and intrigue, the only national combinations formed in the autumn of 1930 were those scribbled on the backs of menus at select dinner parties. No one emerged as Garvin's man of destiny. His assessment of MacDonald — 'as little of a partisan . . . as any man in Britain' was doubtless correct as far as it went and also applied to Baldwin. But the most characteristic expression of this impartiality was a chronic inability of both statesmen ever to make up their minds about anything. This left them at the mercy of external pressures, which in 1930 were not nearly strong enough to drive them into partnership. The young men's talk of 'crisis' and the 'nation demanding an end to party bickering' seemed to be mere spectres conjured up to frighten their elders.[3] Bernard Shaw remarked:

> The real world is a world of cinema poisoned ignorant romantic duffers who read the Daily Mail when they read at all, except the serial in the Daily Herald.[4]

---

[1] *Manchester Guardian*, 4 November, 6 December 1930.

[2] *Daily Herald*, 10 November 1930; *Morning Post*, 5 December 1930.

[3] It should always be remembered that the opinion-makers were centred on London and the south-east; whereas the heaviest unemployment and distress were in the north and Wales — remote from the comfortable parliamentary atmosphere at Westminster though not from Labour constituencies.

[4] Quoted in B. Webb Diaries, 30 November 1930.

Many expected Lloyd George to take the lead — but where was he to go? Moderate though his terms were for a bargain with the Conservatives,[1] they were too high for a Party which had every prospect of securing a substantial majority in any new House of Commons. The Shipley by-election of 6 November where a Labour majority of 4,961 had been converted into a Conservative majority of 1,665, confirmed the evidence of the municipal elections of the week before of a strong tide running for the Conservatives. The same assurance of victory soon caused those Tory M.P.s who had flirted with Mosley to confine their activities to their own Party which alone could offer them the expectation of ministerial office.

The only person who had taken the idea of a 'new combination' entirely seriously was Sir Oswald Mosley. Now, undismayed by the desertion of his Conservative allies and the dwindling interest in the whole idea, he pursued, with the inexorable process of a young man's logic, a course of action which was soon to place him in the political wilderness. The first step was the publication on 1 December 1930 of the Mosley manifesto, signed by seventeen Labour M.P.s and the miners' secretary, A. J. Cook. 'The years of talk', it concluded, 'are over and the hour of action has come.'[2]

[1] 'He did not want office for himself . . . but he would like to see something done for some other members of his Party.' Chamberlain's diary, 21 November 1930. Quoted in Feiling, *The Life of Neville Chamberlain*, p. 183.

[2] The signatories were: O. Baldwin, J. Batey, A. Bevan, W. J. Brown, A. J. Cook, W. G. Cove, R. Forgan, J. Lovat-Fraser, J. F. Horrabin, S. F. Markham, J. McGovern, J. J. McShane, Lady Cynthia Mosley, Sir Oswald Mosley, H. T. Muggeridge, M. Philips Price, C. J. Simmons, E. J. Strachey. The manifesto called for protection of the home market, long-term development through rationalisation, short-term public works based on slum clearance and a national loan, and Empire-orientated foreign trade; the whole to be supervised by a Cabinet of five 'overlords' subject only to 'the general control of Parliament'.

12

POINT OF NO RETURN

i. INTRODUCTION

ARNOLD TOYNBEE has described 1931 as the 'annus terribilis'. For the first time 'men and women all over the world were seriously contemplating and frankly discussing the possibility that the Western system of society might break down and cease to work'.[1] The fall in commodity prices accelerated, slowly dragging down the prices of manufactured goods in their wake; trade continued to decline; unemployment rose everywhere. In Germany, the figure stood at almost five million in January 1931; in the United States it was estimated at between six and seven million; even in France which had resisted the depression extremely well there were well over one million unemployed, and Italy approached that total. In these circumstances the financial and political structure began to crack. Four countries had been driven off the gold standard in 1929 and four more followed in 1930. Attempts to reduce budget deficits and cut wages were accompanied by revolutions, especially in the volatile South American countries; even in Australia serious rioting of the unemployed took place in Adelaide on 9 January. Elsewhere — in India, China and Spain — more conventional political disturbances reinforced the pattern of disintegration. Individual countries sought to protect themselves from the surrounding chaos by putting up tariffs: the United States led the way in 1930 with the gigantic Hawley–Smoot tariff and Canada, Cuba, Mexico, France, Italy, Spain, Australia and New Zealand rapidly followed suit.

Britain stood the strain relatively well. Its prospective budget deficit was considerably smaller than that of almost any other country;[2] and if

[1] *Survey of International Affairs*, 1931, p. 1.

[2] *World Economic Survey*, League of Nations, 1931–2, p. 269.

the unemployment figures were comparatively large, an important reason for this was the inclusion of short-time workers and the 'temporarily stopped' on the live register: on the same basis of compilation American unemployment figures would have been at least double what they were. The British unemployed worker was also protected by the most comprehensive scheme of national benefits in the world — in Germany, for example, the State had, in effect, transferred the burden of unemployment payments to the municipalities in a decree of June 1930; and American relief was still largely voluntary. If some countries sought relief from their difficulties by leaving the gold standard, many more attempted to reduce their standard of living in proportion to the fall in prices. Vigorous government did not generally mean expansionist policies, rather greater energy in enforcing deflation. And one of the most vigorous Governments of them all — that of Mussolini — was also one of the most deflationary.[1]

As we have seen, British statesmanship since 1918 had been based on the assumption that the damage done by the war was both partial and reparable. Hence its efforts had been devoted to securing political and economic disarmament as the precondition for a return to normality. These efforts continued into 1931. On 25 January the Council of the League of Nations decided to summon a World Disarmament Conference for 2 February 1932. Arthur Henderson, the British Foreign Secretary, was elected president in recognition of his services in that cause. Meanwhile Graham was still trying to persuade other countries to reduce their tariffs: in the third week of April there was a conference in London between British and French officials to try to work out a plan, but, predictably, no progress was made.

Indeed the world situation was singularly unripe for political or economic pacification. Bedevilling disarmament plans was the continuing antagonism between France and Germany. Brüning's Government, which had lost great prestige in the September 1930 elections, tried to restore its position by an adventurous foreign policy. First of all, in the autumn of 1930 it angled for a cancellation of reparations payments. This was bound to meet stern French opposition, but was by

[1] For details of the Italian cuts see the *Daily Telegraph* of 10 August 1931, which summarised, no doubt for the benefit of the Labour Government, the deflationary measures being taken abroad.

no means incompatible with the British view that the restoration of normality required, in the long term, the liquidation of war debts. Hence a conflict developed in British foreign policy between the desire to get French support for disarmament and the desire to solve the political and economic problems posed by the 'debt question'. There were in effect two British foreign policies during the months leading up to the fall of the Labour Government: that of the Foreign Office led by Henderson, and that of the Treasury and the banks led by Montagu Norman, with the acquiescence of Snowden and the reluctant support of MacDonald. Snowden's anti-French bias had been very evident at the Hague conference of 1929; Montagu Norman was so anti-French that he refrained for years from visiting French health resorts because he might have to meet French bankers.[1] His part in the reconstruction of defeated countries immediately after the war had given him an abiding dislike of reparations: he declared that no European recovery could come about by throwing 'Germany and Central Europe to the mercy of the French vindictive policy'.[2] As a central banker in the old tradition he felt that the French were not 'playing the game', a conviction that may have dated from the report he received in 1923 from Havenstein, President of the Reichsbank, that the French had seized German banknotes in deposit in the Ruhr and put them into circulation with the object of intensifying the already alarming inflation.[3] The French policy of hoarding gold was making it increasingly difficult for him to maintain the British sterling rate. MacDonald's dislike of reparations dated from the Treaty of Versailles which he considered to be an unjust peace, and the cancellation of war debts was a prominent feature of Labour's early post-war programmes.[4]

The French cordially reciprocated British feelings. They resented Norman's refusal to give France credits in 1926 at the height of the French financial crisis.[5] Moreover, there was a general feeling that Britain was played out, that Anglo-Saxon hegemony was giving way to French superiority in tardy justification of the physiocrats who had always claimed that commerce would be defeated by agriculture. This

[1] Paul Einzig, *Montagu Norman*, 1932, p. 126.
[2] Ibid. p. 115.
[3] Clay, *Lord Norman*, p. 207.
[4] See above, p. 38.
[5] Einzig, *Montagu Norman*, p. 71. He had stipulated a balanced Budget as a condition.

view was given expression in a widely-read book published in 1930 by André Siegfried entitled *England's Crisis* which showed a country enfeebled by obsolete attitudes and practices, unable to adjust to the demands of the contemporary world. This feeling of superiority was sustained by the unexpected fact of French financial strength. Paris, not London, was the master of Europe's destiny in 1931.

The ability of the French to stalemate the Germans on the reparations question led Brüning on to a new course. On 23 March 1931, after weeks of negotiations and rumours, the proposal for an Austro-German customs union was announced simultaneously in Berlin and Vienna. France, which feared Germany's renaissance and suspected the customs union to be the first step in the direction of an Anschluss, declared that she would never accept this plan. Henderson, conscious that the German initiative would harden the French against disarmament,[1] determined to get it buried as swiftly and as decently as possible. The general British reaction was that it was merely another nail in the coffin of the Labour Government's pacification policy.

London's financial dependence on Paris seriously handicapped the possibility of an independent British policy during this period. Between July and December 1930 there had been a persistent drain of gold and foreign exchange from London to Paris. In discussions with French officials, the debate followed a familiar pattern:

> The British spokesmen argued that France exercised an excessive pull over the world's gold, because she had undervalued her currency when she stabilised her exchange. The French replied that the influx of gold was due to the normal working of the gold standard; England should apply the orthodox remedy of a higher Bank Rate.[2]

The French argument that it was the British who were not 'playing the game' must have been particularly irksome. More galling was the reception of tentative proposals to raise a loan in Paris in January 1931. The French who regarded it as quite normal to bring politics into purely 'financial' matters insisted on British support against Germany's

[1] Doumergue, President of France, in a speech of 9 April had indicated that the cancellation of customs union would have to be a condition of France's participation in disarmament discussions. (Toynbee, *Survey of International Affairs 1931–2*, 1932, p. 37.)

[2] Clay, *Lord Norman*, p. 370.

position on reparations and disarmament. But the British were not prepared to mix finance and politics in quite such an open way. It was agreed by Norman and the Treasury that the 'political objections' to a loan in Paris were too great.[1] Moret, the Governor of the Bank of France, told a German informant that the British had been 'too proud' to accept a loan offered under 'certain conditions and limitations' by France.[2]

London's dependence on Paris checkmated another British initiative to promote recovery in the spring of 1931. In his memorandum of April 1930 Hubert Henderson had written that trade revival depended on 'the monetary policies pursued throughout the world'.[3] Hawtrey had made the same point when he argued before the Macmillan Committee that world credit should be so manipulated as to maintain a stable price level, a clear departure from orthodox central bank policy which regarded stability of exchanges as more important than stability of prices.[4] By 1931 the need to stop the catastrophic fall in prices had become even more urgent, especially for Britain which was so dependent on world markets. Indeed, this was a necessary part of any policy designed to promote 'international' recovery. The trouble was that the Bank of England was no longer powerful enough to initiate a reflationary move on its own; most of the world's gold was held in America and France: their co-operation would be essential.

Thus the 'Norman Plan' outlined by the British Governor at Geneva in April 1931 called for an 'international organisation for the conscious direction of money . . . towards those borrowers whose relief and

[1] Ibid. p. 370.

[2] Edward Bennett, *Germany and the Diplomacy of the Financial Crisis, 1931*, 1962, pp. 83–4. Berthelot, the French Secretary-General, made the following comment to the German ambassador on 23 February 1931:

> [He] explained that it was very difficult for the English, with their well-known pride in their hitherto leading position in the world of economics and finance, to enter into financial conversations with France. Even now, the English requests in these conversations are still unacceptable to France. But in view of England's general position, the necessity remains for her to reach certain agreements with France. Britain finds herself in a bad situation. The Empire is falling more and more apart, and in England itself the belief in her own ability to recover is disappearing. The British people also lack courage and the resolve to work (p. 84).

[3] See above, p. 143. [4] Macmillan Committee Evidence, 273 ff.

rehabilitation are an agreed object of policy'. Norman had mainly in mind Germany and eastern Europe, Australia, and South America, Britain's traditional markets. The plan envisaged that the most famous business organisations in the world should combine to subscribe £20m as ordinary capital of an international company to which the public would be invited to put up £100m against debentures. The great lending banks, acceptance houses and international companies should agree on conscious co-operation in their lending policy. The *Manchester Guardian* commented:

> The authors of the Bank of England Scheme believe that trade and industry could be stimulated throughout the world if some broad lines of investment policy, agreed upon in Britain, France, Germany, and the U.S.A. and other centres, could be jointly kept in mind, and the purpose of these discussions is to enlist, through the central banks, the help of private banks and producing companies of the world for such an attempt.[1]

This was an astonishingly imaginative scheme for the times; but the initiative came from the weakest of the major centres, though the one with most to gain from its success. Norman made a special trip to Washington in April, but he failed to enlist American support; and the French were equally hostile, seeing in the plan an attempt to unload British burdens on others, as indeed it was. London's financial weakness proved a fatal handicap.

Here we have another illustration of the breakdown of co-operation between the 'nucleus' of financial centres which had, till 1929, preserved the gold standard system. By 1930 two of the partners had virtually dropped out of the gold standard 'game', leaving to London sole responsibility for preserving what remained of the international financial structure. This fact should perhaps have been remembered by those who later accused British bankers of lending recklessly and desperately abroad. So they did, but what else could they have done? It was for a Government to impose a different order of priorities.

For Britain by 1931 the problem of breaking the vicious circle of deflation and depression had become acute. Unless world trade revived in the immediate future, she would face both a balance of payments and a budgetary crisis. The only real question was which of the two would produce the primary pressure on the exchange. The political difficulty

[1] 15 April 1931.

arose from the fact that no one, with the possible exception of the trade union leaders, was prepared to abandon the gold standard. This meant that as the pressure on sterling increased, the clamour for a positive policy to correct the financial position would increase with it; moreover, the longer the Government delayed, the more vociferous would become the clamour for retrenchment — cutting down the standard of life — as the shortest and most direct path to restoring financial equilibrium. Yet this course the Labour Party was almost certainly bound to resist. The alternative would have to be a policy designed to forestall the crisis, or, at the very least, to make sure that when it came, the Government had initiated alternative policies which it might offer as a *quid pro quo* for such retrenchment as was needed.

Certainly there was no shortage of alternatives. There was the Conservative policy of retrenchment plus protection. There was the Liberal policy of retrenchment plus borrowing.[1] There was the Mosleyite policy of protection plus borrowing. There was the I.L.P. policy of punitive taxation. On the international side the Conservatives, Mosleyites and trade unionists advocated, in some form or other, closer commercial ties with the Dominions and colonies; alternatively, there was the possibility of international action to correct the maldistribution of gold, and stabilise the world price level. All of these policies were designed to avert or forestall the financial crisis, whether by promoting national or international revival, or a combination of both; all of them contained elements of a 'package deal' which attempted to balance temporary sacrifices with positive measures designed to promote recovery. Alone of those in a position to contribute to the 'pool of ideas', the Labour Government offered nothing. The failure of Graham's tariff truce campaign left it totally bereft of any constructive ideas, either international or national. As Keynes wrote, it opposed any positive approach with an attitude of 'complete negation'.[2]

This attitude was embodied by Philip Snowden. He could block any

[1] The Liberal proposals were designed, in effect, to separate out the 'current' and 'capital' items in the Budget. This distinction, which was not very well understood at the time, has now become orthodox. Thus retrenchment on the 'current' account was perfectly compatible with borrowing for the 'capital' account.

[2] *New Statesman*, 7 March 1931.

policy of expansion: yet he could not enforce a policy of deflation. His manœuvrings on the latter point were both grotesque and tragic. His Jekyll and Hyde performances often occurred during the course of the same speech. Thus in the economy debate on 11 February, to which we shall refer again, he both emphasised the grave international dangers of an unbalanced Budget, and flippantly asserted that no real economies were possible. On 29 January 1931 the Treasury memorandum to the Royal Commission on Unemployment Insurance had declared that 'continued state borrowing on the present scale without adequate provision for repayment . . . would quickly call in question the stability of the British financial system'. It had declared that such borrowing was 'the ordinary and well-recognised sign of an unbalanced Budget'. Sir Richard Hopkins had warned of the 'adverse judgments' which foreigners would pass 'if, in fact, our finance became unsound'.[1] Yet a few months later Snowden was fiercely resenting any imputation that he was responsible for or associated with, these views.[2] More important, he

[1] *Minutes of Evidence*, pp. 381–91. See esp. para. 3294.

[2] 254 H.C. Deb. c. 86–7. When Sir Henry Betterton for the Conservatives said: 'I want to draw the attention of the Committee to the solemn warning which the Chancellor of the Exchequer gave last January through his officials', Snowden intervened with the words: 'Really, the hon. Gentleman has no right to associate me with that evidence. It was given by the experts of the Treasury and the Government Actuary. . . . They went there to express their views. As a matter of fact, they were directly invited. . . .' Yet as he admitted after a further exchange '[the] evidence was shown to me before it was presented to the Commission'. But 'it was not my evidence'. Of course, Snowden was right in claiming that he had no control over the Government Actuary. But his assertion that a public treasury statement merely expressed the private views of a treasury official was a novel interpretation of the relationship between a Minister and his civil servants. For example, the departmental memoranda issued by the Baldwin Government on Lloyd George's public works proposals in April 1929 were all signed by the Minister responsible, in order to protect their civil servants from the charge of meddling in politics. The issue of treasury intervention on major policy matters, apparently without the Chancellor's authorisation, had arisen shortly before. Citrine complained to MacDonald on 2 January 1931 that 'the Treasury, Mr. Snowden in fact, had written to the Banks suggesting that a movement should be undertaken by them for the purpose of reducing wages. . . .' He had written to Snowden who had assured him that the whole thing was absurd 'but not quite as absurd as one might have thought, because I happen to known that the document had been prepared in the Treasury itself, and I had seen the docu-

took no steps to act either on his own, or his department's, warnings. He conjured up fears, yet took no measures to dispel them.[1]

ii. POLICY DEBATE

In the first half of 1931 there were three academic contributions to the unemployment debate which aroused great interest. The first strengthened the hands of the deflationists; the other two attempted to rouse the Government from its torpor by suggesting active measures to break the stranglehold of depression and impending financial ruin.

On 11 and 12 June *The Times* published two long articles by Sir Josiah Stamp which summarised the views of the French economist Jacques Rueff, whose deflationary advice to Pierre Laval later brought the full rigour of the slump to France in 1934–5 and the Popular Front to power in 1936. Rueff attempted to restate the classical view that unemployment could be cured by sufficient wage flexibility with the aid of statistics drawn from the English experience of 1919–30. The statistical data was set out in the chart on p. 290.

Rueff's general argument was that in 1920 when prices started to fall rapidly, real wages went up. At the same time unemployment appeared. After a six months' lag, however, real wages started to go down, unemployment decreased and would probably have disappeared entirely had not real wages suddenly ceased to fall in 1922. 'The wage curve seems to have come down squarely on an obstacle which prevented any further decline.' Thereafter real wages rose again, and unemployment with

ment personally. . . .' To this MacDonald replied: 'That is not a document of Government policy . . . it is one of those abominable things where really we will have to see whether we can put our foot down.' (General Council Papers, 157.83D.) Here again is a document, prepared and circulated by the Treasury, not apparently 'authorised' by Snowden, which conflicted with government policy.

[1] Henry Clay, *Lord Norman*, p. 369, records that the 'first reports' to reach the Bank of England 'of distrust of sterling' started coming in after the middle of October 1930. On 15 October Snowden had delivered a widely reported speech to the Guildhall in which he had remarked: 'There is one item of national expenditure which is distressing me almost beyond measure, and that is the cost of unemployment.'

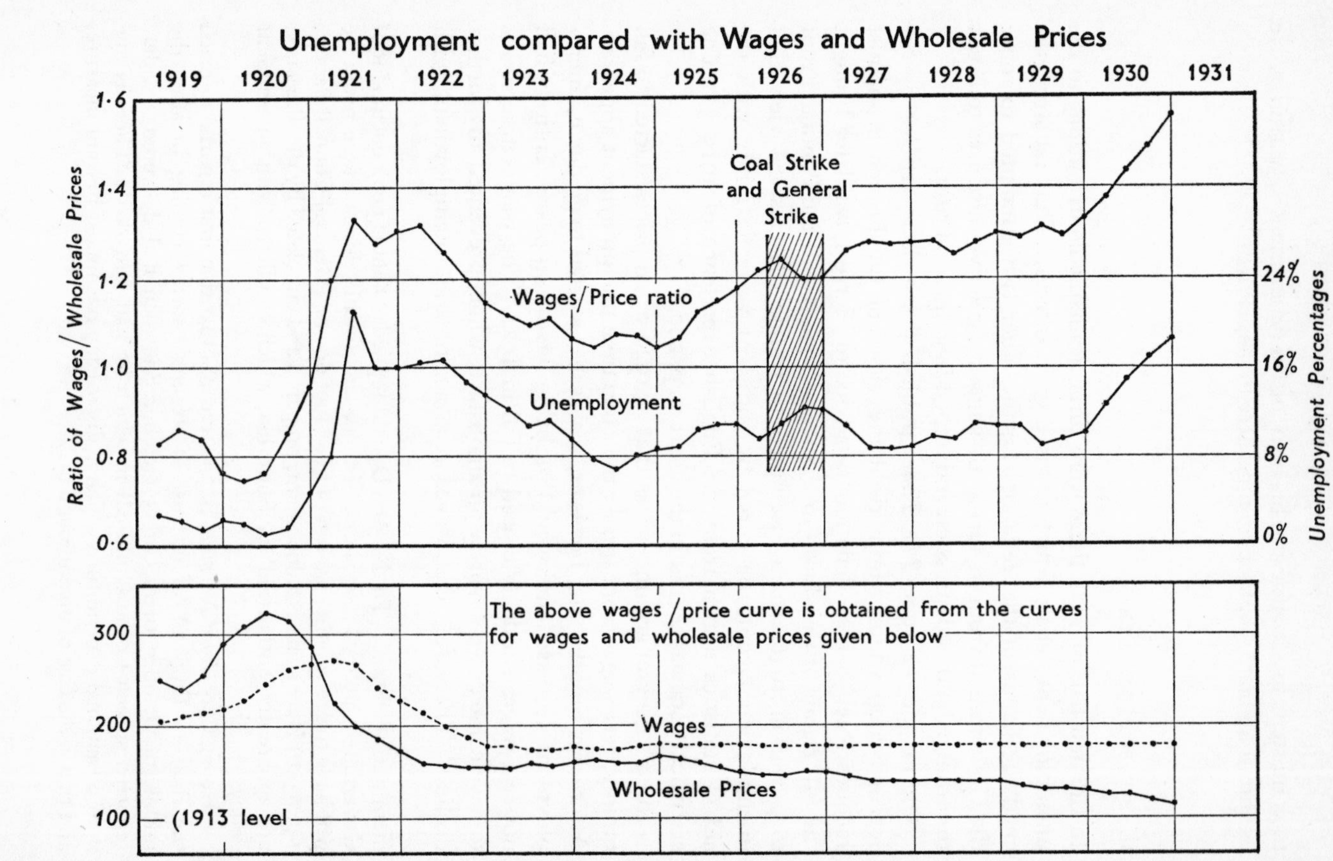

Unemployment compared with Wages and Wholesale Prices
1919
1920
1921
1922
1923
1924
1925
1926
1927
1928
1929
1930
1931
1·6
1·4
1·2
1·0
0·8
0·6
Ratio of Wages / Wholesale Prices
Coal Strike
and General
Strike
Wages/Price ratio
Unemployment
24%
16%
8%
0%
Unemployment Percentages
The above wages / price curve is obtained from the curves
for wages and wholesale prices given below
300
200
100
(1913 level
Wages
Wholesale Prices

them. The correlation between real wages and unemployment was found to be so perfect that Rueff formulated the law that 'any increase or decrease in the wages/price curve is accompanied by a similar movement in unemployment'.

Why did real wages stop falling in 1922? Rueff found the answer in the structure of unemployment insurance. 'In actual fact the wages level is a result of collective contracts, but these contracts would never have been observed by the workmen if they had not been sure of receiving an indemnity which differed little from their wages. It is the dole, therefore, that has made trade union discipline possible'. Rueff concluded: 'Therefore we may assume that the dole is the underlying cause of the unemployment which has been so cruelly inflicted on England since 1920'.

Generalising his argument, Rueff noted:

> Instead of allowing economic forces to operate freely, the tendency, since the War, has everywhere been in the opposite direction. The dole policy, the activities of the trade unions, and the employers' associations, and the various hindrances to migration have all interfered with the freedom of the labour markets. At the same time the activities of trusts, cartels, marketing schemes, and the various restriction and valorization schemes have all retarded or suppressed the indispensable movement of prices. In a word, the organism has been drugged and paralysed. Hence the present deplorable situation.

With this model, Rueff was able to dispose of all the 'fallacious' theories of the origins of the crisis. The British thought they had lost their markets through the War. But the loss of markets was commonplace before, and though adaptation caused suffering, unemployment was never permanent.

> When the profits and wages fell away in the declining industries [wrote Rueff] the workmen sought more remunerative employment in more prosperous industries. . . . It was indispensable, however, for wages and profits in the condemned industries to be reduced, for if wages had been pegged by a system of collective contracts there would have been no influence to restrict manpower where it was no longer needed. Similarly if an income almost equal to wages could have been obtained from unemployment insurance, the distribution of manpower would have remained unchanged.

Deflation as a cause of unemployment was also dismissed: everything would have been all right had wages come down.

Whether or not Rueff's argument was formally correct, there was little possibility of restoring complete flexibility of wages as a way out of depression: this was indeed the main reason why classical economics ceased to be serviceable during these years. Hardly anyone dared come out openly with the view that wages were too high,[1] though nearly all businessmen and economists held it privately. Rather, Rueff's argument added to the clamour for 'economies' in unemployment expenditure to relieve industry of its taxation burdens and to restore a budget balance. His statement of the classical case did, however, have wider implications. If the level of wages was a function of the level of unemployment benefit, then it followed that any reduction in unemployment benefit would break up the discipline that enabled the unions to resist wage reductions. From the union point of view any attack on the level of benefit was likely to herald a large-scale attack on wages, mounted with a greatly improved prospect of success. The writings of the French professor may thus have added an extra dimension to the struggle over the dole.

On 7 March 1931 Keynes, in an article for the *New Statesman* headed 'Proposals for a Revenue Tariff', publicly announced his conversion to protection. The core of Keynes's argument was that the country needed to expand demand, but that every known policy of expansion would threaten the sterling exchange rate and depress business confidence. Hence it had to be accompanied by measures taken to strengthen the exchange and to give businessmen confidence. The only measure that satisfied both conditions was a tariff. He proposed 'no discriminating, protective tariffs' but a flat rate or two flat rates, each applicable to wide categories of goods. The amount of revenue to be aimed at was £50–75m which might be achieved by having import duties of 15 per cent on all manufactured or semi-manufactured goods and 5 per cent on all foodstuffs. In addition to its other virtues such a measure would also

[1] An exception was the National Confederation of Employers' Organisations whose report, published on 12 February, stated Rueff's propositions in almost identical form. British industry was handicapped by philanthropic policies. The State was responsible for the rigid wage structure because the State and local authorities together formed the largest 'sheltered' industry in the country. If to the number of those employed by the central and local authorities were added those workpeople whose wages were fixed by trade boards or other statutory wage fixing machinery, plus those who received statutory unemployment benefit, then it could be seen that 'the State is in fact the largest controlling agent in the factors which set the general wage level of the country', whereas before the war it was the 'sensitive' exporting industries which set the trend. (*The Times*, 13 February 1931.)

relieve the strain on the Budget, thus forestalling the possibility of a financial crisis; and by substituting home production for foreign production, it would increase employment in this country. Keynes concluded:

> The Revenue Tariff is our iron ration which can only be used in an emergency. The emergency has arrived. Under cover of the breathing space and the margin of financial strength thus afforded us, we could frame a policy and a plan, both domestic and international, for marching to the assault against the spirit of contractionism and fear.

As was to be expected, the free traders sprang like lions to the defence of their cherished dogma. In a passionate and vituperative reply, Lionel Robbins said Keynes had over-estimated the yield of his tariff by £20m to £30m. As for the budget problem there were 'half a dozen ways of meeting it, each better both administratively and economically than this stale and dreary expedient of a tariff'. The only long-term solution to Britain's economic problems was to reduce wages; tariffs never came down: they simply grew.[1] Keynes with his greater realism replied the following week:

> Now Free Trade, combined with great mobility of wage-rates, is a tenable intellectual proposition.... The practical reason against it, which must suffice for the moment, whether we like it or not, is that it is *not* one of the alternatives between which we are in a position to choose. We are not offered it. It does not exist outside the field of pure hypothesis. The actual alternative is the policy of Negation.[2]

The argument raged to and fro for several weeks in the correspondence columns of the *New Statesman* and was taken up vigorously in the learned journals. The resolutely free trade *Economist* complained that a revenue tariff would raise the working-class cost of living — 'crocodile tears' Keynes said, as its own policy was to reduce wages by 10 to 15 per cent.[3] Indeed, most of the academic establishment showed themselves violently hostile to the results of Keynes's 'new process of cerebration', though J. R. Bellerby of Caius College, Cambridge, complained that none of Keynes's critics had touched on the real point in the controversy, which was whether or not the exchange should be defended in the first place. Increasingly the discussion became bogged down in arguments

[1] *New Statesman*, 14 March 1931. [2] Ibid. 21 March 1931.
[3] Ibid. 4 April 1931.

about the yield of the proposed tariffs, or in their effects on Britain's exports. Keynes struggled manfully with his critics. On 11 April he wrote that the assumption of the free traders that a reduction in imports would lead to an equivalent reduction in exports was true only in a world economic system in complete equilibrium and with perfect elasticity. In the existing circumstances 'it could only be by an improbable and extraordinary coincidence that the net effect on the value of our exports would be *equal* to the change in the value of our imports'. Yet he was rapidly tiring of the sterile controversy. His critics, he wrote, had ignored the problem that really interested him:

> the analysis of our present state, which occupied most of my original article and led up to the tariff proposal in the last paragraph. Is it the fault of the *odium theologicum* attaching to Free Trade? Is it that Economics is a queer subject or in a queer state? Whatever may be the reason, the new paths of thought have no appeal to the fundamentalists of Free Trade. They have been forcing me to chew over again a lot of stale mutton, dragging me along a route I have known all about as long as I have known anything, which cannot, as I have discovered by many attempts, lead one to a solution of our present difficulties — a peregrination of the catacombs with a guttering candle.

Politically, Keynes's new departure seemed to have little effect in the quarters where it mattered most. Conservatives, of course, welcomed his conversion, and added his arguments, somewhat inconsistently, to their own proposals for a tariff. The Liberals regretted his new stand and recalled his brilliant essays in defence of free trade written in 1923. Keynes sent a copy of his article to the Prime Minister who replied on 9 March:

> Thank you so much for your letter with the enclosed article. The position is getting a very critical one and the illness of the Chancellor[1] has enormously increased my difficulties. It will be a fortnight or three weeks before I can see him to exchange views on the budget.[2]

The Chancellor's response to these new ideas was all too predictable. Keynes had sent him a copy too, and Ethel Snowden replied on 7 March:

> I grieve to have to return your article unread by my husband, but he is really too ill to give his mind to anything. . . .

---

[1] For Snowden's illness, see below, p. 323.

[2] Keynes Papers, Articles, 1931.

I have read your article and will tell him the contents when he is able to listen. I dare say he will feel as sad as I do that you should think it necessary to take this line, for we are as strongly convinced that it is wrong (taking the long view) as you are that it is right.[1]

Garvin was more enthusiastic: the article had opened up familiar trains of thought:

If only you could make LL.G. adopt it — if Labour won't also — he would become the first man in the Country again and we would get somehow a National Government in the fullest practicable sense, or a National Majority which would do. . . .

To see a great people and a Great Empire sinking and fading without necessity makes me feel scornful as the devil towards all the three-party tripe-dressers; and towards mass ignorance helplessly enthroned and labelled 'Democracy'.[2]

Keynes had argued that an expansionist policy could not take place, given the existing rate of exchange, without import controls. The Macmillan Report, which finally appeared on 13 July, argued that the preservation of the existing rate of exchange was indispensable if Britain was to initiate that international expansionist policy which it saw as the main hope of overcoming the depression. Keynes was one of the signatories of that Report, but there was no contradiction between this and his earlier views, for in March he had argued for a tariff as a 'breathing space' to plan a policy 'both domestic and international'.

The argument against devaluation was stated with all that ponderousness reserved for authoritative pronouncements:

International trade, commerce and finance are based on confidence. One of the foundation stones on which that confidence reposes is the general belief that all countries will seek to maintain so far as lies in their power the value of their national currency as it has been fixed by law, and will only give legal recognition to its depreciation when that depreciation has already come about *de facto*.[3]

This was the general statement, but there was a more practical reason. Turning to the future, the Report argued that there was no more important requirement in the world than for a sound and scientific international monetary system, in order to restore confidence in trading relations, increase international liquidity and raise the world price level.

[1] Keynes Papers, Articles, 1931. [2] Ibid. 5 April 1931.
[3] *Macmillan Report*, para. 256.

The abandonment of the gold standard by Britain 'with the object of setting up a local standard with a sole regard to our domestic situation' would involve giving up the attempt to find a solution to the larger problem 'just at the moment, maybe, when, if we were able to look a little further forward, the beginnings of general progress would be becoming visible'.[1]

The prime objective of the international policy recommended by the Macmillan Report was that Britain should join with the United States and France in concerted action to expand credit.[2] This could not be left to the central banks since they were essentially private institutions dependent upon the willingness of private individuals to invest their money abroad. Just as there was hoarding at home, so there was international hoarding, reflected in the vast build up in the gold reserves of such creditor nations as the United States and France. And just as 'some of us believe' that in the domestic field it was necessary to 'invoke government enterprise to break the vicious circle' of deflation, so 'measures of an analogous kind' might be required in the international field. The first step would be an international conference devoted to 'The Restoration of International Trade', the result of which might be a series of international loans 'guaranteed by a joint fund' set up by the participating Governments.[3] However, the report stressed that 'in order that Great Britain may speak with authority in such discussions, it is essential that her financial strength should be beyond criticism'.[4]

Here was nothing less than a grand design for world reflation, revolutionary in its acceptance of the view that Governments could and should do something to interrupt the natural course of depression. Here at last was a policy designed to give some positive content to the Labour Government's vague internationalism. By coupling it with the Keynesian domestic policy of tariffs and public works, the Government would at last be able to present a positive unemployment policy on all fronts. Earlier, Snowden had rejected Norman's proposal that the British Government summon an international economic conference to concert a 'definite plan of action'.[5] Whether it would eventually have acted on the Macmillan Report we cannot tell.

[1] *Macmillan Report*, para. 253.
[2] Ibid. paras. 314, 315.
[3] Ibid. paras. 316–19.
[4] Ibid. para. 258.
[5] Clay, *Lord Norman*, pp. 369–70.

iii. GOVERNMENT POLICY

With the budget season coming up once again, the clamour for retrenchment grew predictably violent. The business lobby took the offensive with a stream of speeches, petitions and manifestos. Baldwin on 14 January, in an obscure phrase, spoke of 'the burden of taxation that was hanging like a nightmare on British industry'.[1] 'Our country . . . groaning under an unparalleled burden of taxation' intoned one of many similar letters to *The Times*.[2] Sir Arthur Balfour, Keynes's opponent on the E.A.C., thought that another threepence on the income tax would increase unemployment by 500,000.[3] The 'present mania for pensions' was 'un-English, immoral, degrading and disastrous' thought the publisher Sir Ernest Benn, while borrowing was 'a despicable dodge'.[4] The views of the National Confederation of Employers' Organisations have already been noted;[5] a Federation of British Industries memorandum of 11 March urged the supreme importance of a 'reduction in the burden of taxation and other charges'.[6] The chairmen of Barclays, Lloyds, Westminster, National Provincial and Martins Banks all, emphasised 'the crushing burden of taxation which harasses our industry, depletes our resources and saps our energies and enterprise'.[7] Nor were the right-wing Liberals any less insistent on the dangers of the existing position. Walter Runciman talked of the Government 'copiously bleeding the very life out of the country's resources',[8] while in a joint letter to *The Times* of 26 January from the Liberal Council he and Lord Grey asked their fellow countrymen to accept the following propositions: firstly that the weight of existing taxation was a prime cause of the stagnation of trade, second that the road of public waste was 'the road of want and privation' and third, that only by living within its means could Britain recover prosperity. A 'national non-party' economy campaign was inaugurated by Grey, Sir Robert Horne and Benn on 22 January,[9] and on 3 March Sir John Simon said that 'the limits of direct taxation have been reached'.[10]

[1] *The Times*, 15 January 1931.
[2] Ibid. 9 January 1931.
[3] Ibid. 15 January 1931.
[4] Ibid. 2 January 1931.
[5] See above, p. 292 n.
[6] *The Times*, 12 March 1931.
[7] Ibid. 20, 23, 28, 30, 31 January 1931.
[8] Ibid. 31 December 1930.
[9] Ibid. 28 January 1931.
[10] Ibid. 4 March 1931.

Snowden was doing all he could to allay business anxiety. He had rejected Miss Bondfield's proposal to increase the contributions from employers to the unemployment insurance fund on the ground that it would be psychologically disastrous; and in his speech at the Guildhall on 15 October 1930 he said:

> I stated in my Budget speech that I hoped that probably next year we should be able to avoid any increase in taxation. I think that the psychological effect of any increase in taxation will be very bad indeed. . . . I cannot say, but I shall do everything possible to avoid having to impose new taxation. Possibly I shall have to outrage my strict financial principles, and maybe do things that I could not justify in ordinary circumstances.

This last phrase was somewhat obscure, but it did not require much imagination to guess at its meaning: Snowden was saying that he might have to allow borrowing to continue for the unemployment fund rather than attempt to cover the deficit by fresh taxation. But this ran up against the campaign for economy and the dire warnings given by Sir Richard Hopkins of the Treasury. The Chancellor faced a formidable dilemma. Borrowing for the unemployment fund was unbalancing his Budget, and would frighten foreign holders of sterling. He might balance his Budget by increased taxation, but this would frighten and discourage businessmen; alternatively he might try to balance it by cutting down unemployment benefits, but this was politically impossible. Keynes's tariff would certainly help, but that offended the gospel of free trade to which he passionately adhered. As Snowden later recorded in his *Autobiography*:[1] 'I was appalled at the prospect of having to make another large addition to taxation, and yet I felt that the country could not afford a Budget which was not balanced. There were already signs that our national finances, and especially the continuously increasing load of debt upon the Unemployment Insurance Fund, were being watched and criticised abroad.'

The only alternative was some expedient which would at least postpone the moment of decision: by then trade might have started to improve. Fortunately, there was an appropriate delaying measure to hand. The Liberals in their proposals of the previous October had urged the Government to set up an 'economy committee' to recommend

[1] *Autobiography*, ii, pp. 890–1.

reductions in public expenditure, on the lines of the 'Geddes Committee' of 1922.

The opportunity of putting this plan into operation came in the first few days of February. The Conservatives put down a censure motion for 11 February accusing the Government of

> continuous additions to the public expenditure at a time when the avoidance of all new charges and strict economy in the existing services are necessary to restore confidence and to promote employment.

The motion was framed in such a way that the Liberals could support it, and there is some evidence that the Conservatives tried hard to get them into the lobby against the Government.[1] Unfortunately they had little to offer, whereas the Government could offer free trade, the alternative vote, and a bolder unemployment policy. In a speech on 30 January Graham stressed the opportunities for a 'progressive alliance' between the two Parties on the basis of maintaining free trade and 'the immediate programme to cope with unemployment', although decorum forbade him to mention electoral reform.[2]

The Conservatives were certainly right to think that the debates on 11 and 12 February were stage-managed. Instead of the Conservative motion, the Liberals put forward their proposal for an 'economy committee': this the Government promised to accept. For the following day the Liberals tabled the second half of their policy calling for capital expenditure. The Government maintained that there was no difference 'in principle' between the Liberal programme and their own. The main difficulty had arisen over the Liberal view that raising a loan should precede the programme, a course to which the Government had always objected. Now the Liberals agreed to drop this contentious point and accept the Labour alternative. Thus all the props had been carefully arranged when Sir Laming Worthington-Evans rose to move the

[1] See MacDonald's speech at Watford (*Manchester Guardian*, 31 January 1931): 'When the Opposition above the gangway pretends or professes to be horrified when we can get the Liberals into the lobby with us, they do not tell you that they have been moving heaven and earth . . . in order to effect a combination with the same Liberals to turn us out. This week they have been trying to do that. . . . They tried to bargain with the Liberals. They will go on trying to bargain. . . .'

[2] *Manchester Guardian*, 31 January 1931.

Conservative motion, in what turned out to be his last Commons speech before his sudden death three days later.

He cleverly exploited the twin themes of declining business confidence and London's international position, concluding:

John Bull has rivals everywhere. Many are envious of London as the financial centre of the world . . . if we are to maintain our pre-eminence, our public finance must be . . . unchallengeable.[1]

The first half of Snowden's reply was devoted to humouring his own backbenchers: if the Conservatives accused the Government of extravagance, what about their own record? — 'an ordinary debating reply' he noted in his autobiography.[2] He then turned to the Liberal proposal: certainly he would set up a committee, he had no objection to committees. The Government had already appointed seventy-two 'and one more will not hurt'.[3] In this part of his speech, the Chancellor appeared almost to be conspiring with his own Party: 'You need not worry,' he seemed to be saying, 'I have been forced to do this'. 'As a matter of fact,' he went on, 'I believe I could write its report tomorrow.'[4] So far there was nothing to cause the average Labour Member the least alarm. But abruptly the mood changed.

I say with all the seriousness I can command that the national position is so grave that drastic and disagreeable measures will have to be taken.

Any adverse expectations about the country's budgeting could well have 'disastrous consequences'. Expenditure which 'may be easy and tolerable' in good times 'becomes intolerable in a time of grave industrial depression'. Further taxation on industry 'would be the last straw'. Rigid economy was necessary even if it involved 'some temporary suspension, some temporary sacrifice . . . in order to make future progress possible'.[5]

What did it all mean? Labour M.P.s had little doubt:

The general conclusion is that Mr. Snowden had in mind, if not a reduction of unemployment benefit, at any rate such a revision of the administration of the unemployment scheme as would amount to a reduction of benefit, and also that he was giving a lead to employers in the country to call for wage reductions.[6]

---

1 248 H.C. Deb. c. 433–4.
2 *Autobiography*, ii, p. 893.
3 248 H.C. Deb. c. 446.
4 Ibid. c. 447.
5 Ibid. c. 447–9.
6 *Manchester Guardian*, 13 February 1931.

Was this then Snowden's way of preparing his Party for its moment of truth? That this was part of his motive there can be little doubt, and he himself later admitted it.[1] And others certainly thought so. W. J. Brown, in a furious attack, called the Chancellor's speech 'the most revolutionary single speech delivered in this Parliament . . . in . . . that it struck at the very root of the whole philosophy of constitutional and peaceful progression upon which the Labour movement has been built up'.[2] Yet if the Chancellor's sole purpose had been to educate his Party, why had he not disgorged these unpleasant truths in the comparative privacy of a party meeting? The reason is not perhaps difficult to find. If trade failed to improve, then, in Snowden's opinion, disagreeable economies would become necessary. No Labour Government could carry out such economies on its own. Quite apart from the sentiment of its supporters the electoral risks would be too great. And although the Conservatives and Liberals were prepared to urge economies in the abstract, they were careful not to mention any particulars. The fact was, as the *Manchester Guardian* noted, that no Party was prepared to put through unpopular economy measures.[3] Only a National Government would have sufficient authority to demand sacrifices from all classes. But no National Government was possible until everyone realised the gravity of the situation. Hitherto the Conservatives and Liberals had been scoring party points. It was time they realised that if the situation did become as bad as they said it was they would have to share responsibility for putting it right. As Snowden remarked in the course of his speech 'this is a question to be dealt with by no one party, but . . . in co-operation by all three parties in the House of Commons', and later 'no Government and no one Department can carry . . . out [economy] without the support of a united House of Commons'.[4] In short, his

[1] 'I had so phrased my statement as to prepare [Labour Members] for the unpleasant truth. . . .' (*Autobiography*, ii, p. 896.)

[2] 248 H.C. Deb. c. 494–5. [3] 12 February 1931.

[4] 248 H.C. Deb. c. 443, 447. See also his *Autobiography*, ii, p. 896: '. . . it is difficult to convey an impression of the effect of this statement. Members turned deadly serious, and listened with strained attention to this unexpected development of the debate. It was felt that a House which a few minutes before had been cheering the familiar reproaches of an ordinary Party occasion now realised that it was faced with a situation which would demand the co-operation of all Parties. The task was too big for one Party, and a united national effort would be needed to deal with the crisis.'

words were directed not only at his own backbenchers but at the Conservatives and Liberals as well. If cuts in unemployment pay became necessary all Parties would have to take responsibility for them.

The debate the following day seemed a complete anti-climax. Sir Herbert Samuel renounced the Liberal proposal for a big development loan: rather 'the various authorities, little by little, quietly and perhaps imperceptibly, might obtain the funds they need'.[1] The Prime Minister had no difficulty whatsoever in accepting this policy of imperceptible advance; even so it was too much for Sir Arthur Steel-Maitland who restated all the hoary civil service objections.[2] The debate was only enlivened by a hot speech from Sir Oswald Mosley who argued that the Government's plans of putting 'the nation in bed on a starvation diet are the suggestions of an old woman in a fright',[3] and a slashing attack on the City by Lloyd George which was the best face he could put on the destruction of his unemployment policy.[4] The Conservatives did not even bother to divide the House.

If the Government's reaction to the demand for retrenchment was to set up an 'economy committee'[5] how did it respond to the Liberal demand, however attenuated, for a bolder public works policy? In June 1930, it will be recalled, £111m worth of schemes had been approved, of which £44m were in actual operation, and the number of men being directly employed was 64,000. On the estimate that for every one man directly given work, another would obtain employment manufacturing the materials for the job, 128,000 men altogether had been given work

[1] 248 H.C. Deb. c. 644–5. [2] Ibid. c. 723–4. [3] Ibid. c. 691.
[4] Ibid. c. 731 ff.
[5] On 17 March the Prime Minister announced the appointment of Sir George May as chairman of the Economy Committee. He was just about to retire from the post of secretary to the Prudential Assurance Company. The other members were Sir Mark Webster Jenkinson, a director of Vickers Armstrong; Lord Plender, a 'distinguished chartered accountant', Alan Pugh, general secretary of the Iron and Steel Trades Confederation, Sir Thomas Royden, formerly Conservative M.P. for Bootle, and a director of shipping, railway and insurance companies, Charles Latham, a director of the Automobile Trades Association, and Ashley Cooper, a director of several companies. The terms of reference were 'to make recommendations to the Chancellor of the Exchequer for effecting forthwith all possible reductions in National Expenditure, having regard especially to the present and prospective position of the Revenue'.

after one year — just over a fifth of the number Lloyd George had envisaged in his scheme. On 16 April 1931 a Conservative censure motion gave the new Lord Privy Seal, Thomas Johnston, the opportunity to bring the figures up to date.[1] By the beginning of March, he declared, £173m worth of schemes had been approved, of which £101m were in operation, giving a total direct and indirect employment to 226,500 men. In other words, the programme after June 1930 had been on roughly the same scale as before. (For convenience, the various stages of the programme are given overleaf.)

Thomas Johnston in his speech of 16 April continued Thomas's habit of hopeful exploration. 'Only an improvement in world trade can benefit us in some directions. . . . It is common ground that the pacification and friendship of India and China would do more to provide economic and useful employment for Lancashire and other districts than anything else that we can well devise.'[2] He pointed to the success of a British exhibition held in Argentina — 'in one single order three hundred bathroom equipments were disposed of'.[3] On the domestic side, he asked the House to consider the possibility of converting coal into oil which offered 'great hope of prosperity in our coal-bearing areas'.[4] The development of the tourist industry was a promising prospect which could be assisted by building roads on the east coast of Scotland.[5] One tangible promise was to start a scheme for building rural houses. This arose out of negotiations between the Liberal, Sir Tudor Walters and Greenwood and Johnston in the two-party conference. Lloyd George as usual was excessively optimistic. The building of 100,000 rural cottages would provide employment for 150,000 men directly, another 100,000 indirectly — 250,000 in all. But the Government must undertake direct responsibility.[6] Little more was heard of this project. Captain Crookshank for the Conservatives denounced the Lord Privy Seal's speech as 'futile, fatuous and ridiculous': the Government were 'haphazard, self-complacent, children of the mist'.[7] And Chamberlain asked: 'What do they offer us. . . ? Seeds and fertilisers for allotments, bigger and better cemeteries, costly improvements of the best roads in the world,

[1] 251 H.C. Deb. c. 378–81. Johnston had succeeded Vernon Hartshorn who died suddenly on 13 March 1931.

[2] 251 H.C. Deb. c. 382–3.

[3] Ibid. c. 383.

[4] Ibid. c. 384.

[5] Ibid. c. 385, 386.

[6] Ibid. c. 419.

[7] Ibid. c. 391, 8.

	Total Value of Schemes Approved (£m)				Total Value of Schemes in Operation (£m)				Total number of men directly employed (000's)			
	June 1930	Oct. 1930	Jan. 1931	March 1931	June 1930	Oct. 1930	Jan. 1931	March 1931	June 1930	Oct. 1930	Jan. 1931	March 1931
Home Development Committee	27	28	34	34	8	26	32	34	—	7	10	10
U.G.C.	42	47	53	69	27	32	43	43	37	43	47	56
Road Programmes	43	49	54	56	9	12	16	20	27	29	30	33
Miscellaneous Colonial Development	—	12	14	14	—	—	—	4	—	7	13	14
TOTALS	111	136	153	173	44	70	91	101	64	86	100	113

These figures are taken from the various White Papers on Unemployment (Cmd. 3744, 3746, 4029) and civil service memoranda prepared for Ministers. Miscellaneous works include afforestation, land drainage, cleaning of ancient monuments, etc. The Colonial Development Act was thought to be providing 7,000 men with direct employment by March 1931. The low total of men being employed under the Home Development Committee was attributed to the fact that most of the employment being provided was indirect. The vast majority of grants from the Exchequer took the form of contributions to interest and sinking fund payments of loans raised by the authorities undertaking the works.

increased taxation, and a Royal Commission on Unemployment Insurance'.[1] Far from diminishing unemployment the Government's costly plans were actually increasing it. Sir Robert Horne, a Tory ex-Chancellor of the Exchequer, argued that the Government had damaged employment by (1) removing a number of safeguarding duties, (2) bringing in the 1930 Unemployment Insurance Act and (3) increasing taxation which 'depletes the reserves which people would otherwise put into their businesses'.[2] 'I say that that £173,000,000 [spent on unemployment] is the reason, to a very great extent, for the present figures of unemployment', concluded Captain Austin Hudson.[3]

Johnston's figure of 226,000 men directly and indirectly employed in fact represents the maximum extent of the Government's public works policy. Thereafter the number of men employed slowly declined as

> it was realised that, although substantial relief was being afforded . . . through the medium of grant-aided public works, not only were such schemes making little impression on the unemployment figures, *but the maximum results had been attained*.[4] [italics mine.]

In other words, it was no longer felt possible to justify *economically* a further expansion in the public works programme, for on no other criterion could it be claimed that 'maximum' results had been attained in providing work for 200,000 men out of an unemployed population of over two million. In March 1931 the U.G.C. was limited to considering schemes on which work could be actively started in October, and the economy measures of the National Government slowly brought the Labour Government's programme to a standstill.

This limit to public works policy was always inherent in the criteria used to justify it. For the scale of permissible expenditure was fixed, not by the volume of unemployment, but by the requirements of business accounting. All capital expenditure was required to pass the strict test of economic return, and while the Government were prepared initially to make political compromises on this point to expand employment, the pressure for retrenchment was bound to lead to stricter enquiries about the profitability of any scheme. The Liberals had argued that the provision of employment, irrespective of economic return, would increase demand and thus stimulate the economy, but this assertion was

[1] 251 H.C. Deb. c. 478. [2] Ibid. c. 430–2. [3] Ibid. c. 402.
[4] *Unemployment Grants Committee*, *Final Report*, Cmd. 3746, p. 10.

never accepted by the Treasury. Their second argument was that strict business accounting did not do justice to the economic return that would follow upon the building of roads, houses, and so on. Morrison argued the same way with Snowden but without much success. Indeed the method of financing local authority works put a premium on building cemeteries, sewers, recreation grounds, etc., which even the Liberals did not seek to include within their wider criteria of economic return. Thus the Government got the worst of both worlds. The type of works it was helping to finance, being in some measure 'relief works', alarmed important sections of the economic establishment. At the same time it was not doing enough to satisfy the interventionists. Above all it was providing a derisory amount of employment.

The effect of government activity on the level of demand cannot be calculated with any accuracy. Kahn estimated an employment multiplier of two in 1930. If we take the differential between the average weekly wage and the average unemployment benefit as being thirty shillings, the employment by the Government of 200,000 men may have added £16m to effective demand which, over successive increments of spending, probably kept a further 100,000 men in employment. But this estimate is extremely tentative.

The debate on unemployment was the last big House of Commons occasion before the presentation of the Budget on 27 April 1931. This has rightly been called a stop-gap Budget, for once more Snowden gambled on the future. He was faced with a deficit of £23,276,000 and a prospective deficit of £37,366,000. Both totals included a provision of about £60m for the sinking fund. Unlike the previous year he did not make any provision for the repayment of the realised deficit, saying 'it will be the duty of Parliament to deal with the matter when better times return', a step justified by citing Gladstone.[1] Turning to the prospective deficit, Snowden rejected both increased taxation and a revenue tariff as methods of dealing with it. Any increase in direct taxation would have a '[psychologically] depressing effect on industry'; moreover 'increased rates . . . would at this time produce a disappointingly low increase in yield'. As for the revenue tariff, it was simply a device for 'relieving the well-to-do at the expense of the poor'.[2]

Instead, Snowden reverted to Churchill's habit of raiding capital

[1] 251 H.C. Deb. c. 1397. [2] Ibid. c. 1402–3.

assets and rearranging the times of tax payments. From the dollar exchange account, set up during the war to purchase foreign currency in advance of requirements, he extracted £20m. By arranging for three-quarters of the income tax to be paid in January rather than June he gained £10m. The remaining £7m he obtained by increasing from fourpence to sixpence per gallon the tax on petrol. Except for this last item, these were 'once and for all' taxes, leaving an immediate prospective deficit for the next Budget of £30m. Snowden defended these unorthodox methods as 'temporary means' for dealing with a 'temporary emergency'. 'A revival of trade, when it comes, will be followed by an expansion of revenue and by a reduction on the expenditure side of the account in respect of unemployment.'[1]

There was indeed no attempt to cover the borrowing for unemployment, then proceeding at the rate of over £50m a year. On the 'treasury view' that such borrowing should be met out of current revenue, there was already a prospective deficit of £80m for the forthcoming year. Moreover, the Chancellor estimated his revenue at £766m — almost £6m more than the yield of the previous year, despite the general economic decline since then. The deficit was likely to be nearer £100m. However, 'if prosperity should return, it may well be that a margin will be found in the form of a yield from taxation in excess of the forecasts I have made'. And if it did not? Then 'reduction of expenditure will be the only alternative to increased taxation . . . it will be for the House to take carefully into account the proposals that may emerge from the work both of the Economy Committee and the Unemployment Commission.'[2]

For the Liberals Snowden provided a bonus. 'The main feature' of the Budget, he explained, was his proposal to set up immediately a valuation committee to plan a capital gains tax on land, to be levied at the rate of 1*d.* in the £.[3]

The dominant feeling among Conservatives and Liberals was, as Chamberlain put it, 'one of relief' that further taxation had been avoided,[4] though the Conservatives thought he had missed a 'great

[1] 251 H.C. Deb. c. 1404. [2] Ibid. c. 1408–9.

[3] Ibid. c. 1409–11.

[4] Ibid. c. 1469; though some Conservatives and Liberals attacked the plan to bring forward the date of tax collection as a roundabout way of achieving the same purpose (c. 1526, 1535).

opportunity' in not putting up a tariff.[1] On the other hand, many Conservative spokesmen felt the Budget was 'a complete gamble', 'fundamentally a dishonest Budget'.[2] The Chancellor had shown 'completely undue optimism with regard to revenue and certainly made an unpardonable omission with regard to expenditure'.[3]

In postponing any attempt to deal with borrowing Snowden had, of course, given many hostages to the future. If trade revived . . . but if it did not? E. F. Wise found alarming Snowden's 'apparent reliance on some miracle in the way of economy'.[4] For the moment, though, most Labour Members also felt a sense of relief that the political crisis which would have followed any attempt to cut unemployment benefits had at least been postponed.

Feeling perhaps that they had been robbed of the excitement of a real political crisis, the House of Commons decided to stage one all the same for the edification of the public. On 9 June Passfield wrote that Snowden was on the point of resignation and that the Government might well be defeated the following week. The point at issue was a clause in the Land Tax Bill. Apparently the Liberals had discovered that the proposed tax on capital gains would be additional to the ordinary Schedule A income tax on annual value. They proposed to let the owners off the income tax. A great debate developed: Snowden was obdurate — so were the Liberals. The Conservatives announced that they would support the Liberal amendment. As suddenly as it had arisen the crisis dissolved, a compromise being reached with both sides claiming the victory. Snowden's Bill was the last twitch of the great radical cause of land reform which in its heyday had come close to dominating English politics. His proposals, having emerged somewhat battered from their unexpected assault, were quietly shelved in 1932.

iv. THE ROYAL COMMISSION ON UNEMPLOYMENT INSURANCE

The Royal Commission on Unemployment Insurance had begun taking evidence on 19 December 1930. Its terms of reference had committed it to considering how to make the insurance fund self-supporting and

[1] 251 H.C. Deb. c. 1479. [2] Ibid. c. 1492, 1513.
[3] Ibid. c. 1492. [4] Ibid. c. 1518.

what provision to make for those who had fallen out of insurance. It was bound to consider 'legal abuses' which had figured so largely in the propaganda campaign against the administration of the existing scheme. It was, however, debarred from considering Labour's long-standing alternative — a completely non-contributory scheme, financed by the Exchequer with equal benefits to all adults, male and female, under the same conditions. It was only reluctantly that the General Council of the T.U.C. agreed to submit evidence.

Overshadowing the Commission's work was the financial strain caused by the borrowing of the fund and the mounting cost of transitional benefit, threatening to produce an unbalanced Budget: Sir Richard Hopkins's words echoed round the world. As the Commission was designed to buy off the Conservative and Liberal demands, its report was almost bound to fall in with opposition views. The *Manchester Guardian* had remarked in December that most informed opinion had come to accept a separation of insurance from the 'dole' and a tightening up of conditions: this, too, had been the view of the E.A.C. committee under Cole's chairmanship. Whether the Government had to act on the Commission's report would largely depend on the general economic situation at the time of its publication.

Sir Richard Hopkins gave figures to show the increasing cost of unemployment to the Treasury — the Treasury payments for transitional benefit and its contribution to the unemployment fund:

	£m
1928	11.75
1929	19.41
1930	36.97
1931	50–55 (estimate)[1]

Then he showed the increase in the rate of *borrowing* for the fund itself:

	Net borrowing during year	Debt at Commencement
	£m	£m
1928	11.43	24.53
1929	2.99	35.96

[1] *Minutes of Evidence*, Treasury Memorandum, pp. 381–91, para. 1.

	Net borrowing during year	Debt at Commencement
	£m	£m
1930	33–36 (estimate)	38.95
1931	40–50 (estimate)	72–75
1932		112–125[1]

He argued that 'orthodox canons' required that the fund build up a 'reserve' in good times, to meet its obligations during periods of stress, 'for state borrowing for an unproductive purpose — i.e. an object not producing a monetary yield which will provide the service of the loan — . . . is recognised to be unsound'. Thus it was necessary both to reduce borrowing and to provide for debt repayment, although Hopkins recognised that borrowing could not entirely be eliminated in the existing circumstances.[2] The idea of repudiating the debt was firmly rejected.[3]

The Government Actuary, Sir Alexander Watson, who gave evidence on the tenth day, filled out these suggestions with more concrete proposals. He stated that the fund could be restored to equilibrium only by a 50 per cent reduction of benefits, or alternatively a one-third reduction of benefits, plus an increase of sixpence in contributions. A more realistic proposal might be a reduction of 20 per cent in benefit, plus smaller increases in contributions. This would greatly reduce the borrowing. But as these measures were partly intended to enable debts to be repayed, Watson warned that benefits could not speedily be restored following a trade revival.[4]

Hopkins saw unemployment as burdening the Exchequer and threatening the Budget; Watkins saw only that the scheme had lost its 'insurance' character. These specialised reports were extremely relevant but they needed to be supplemented by non-actuarial considerations. After all, unemployment was first and foremost a human and social problem, which meant taking into account the human, social and political effects of different systems of benefit. The Ministry of Labour might have taken this broader view, but it was obsessed by 'legal abuses' which it tabulated at great length with statistics and illustration. The bias of ministry evidence was in favour of clearing up the 'anomalies' without any real attempt to estimate the social cost of doing so.

[1] Ibid. para. 3. [2] Ibid. para. 4. [3] Ibid. para. 6.
[4] Ibid. pp. 392 ff. paras. 15–17.

The Government Actuary had first raised the question of abuses by pointing out that 'the present scheme has been so comprehensively drawn as to give legal title to benefit in circumstances which the Trade Unions would not have recognised as unemployment'. Examples of this were benefit paid for short-time, for intermittent and seasonal work, and to married women.

The ministry evidence devoted much time to the question of the married woman. All she had to do was to show that she was 'available for work': it did not have to be full-time work and she did not have to show that she was making any efforts to obtain work. Admittedly she had to accept any 'suitable' job that was offered: however 'in the case of a married woman whose husband is at work or who has young children, it is difficult to offer employment which is suitable within the meaning of the Act, since employment which would necessitate her leaving home or removing to another district is unsuitable'.[1] As illustration, the Ministry cited the case of a woman

Aged 28; milk-round; left work on marriage in March 1929, and no work since; disallowed as 'not genuinely seeking work' in June and again in July 1929; now drawing benefit under transitional conditions, and registered as charwoman; there is a great surplus of charwomen on this register.

The Ministry produced figures which attempted to show that this was not an isolated case. The view that the increase in married women claimants was no greater proportionately than the increase in single women claimants was refuted by the following table:[2]

	Married Women			*Single Women*			
1930	North-West	Other Divs.	Total	North-West	Other Divs.	Total	Total
24 Feb.	57,399	71,619	129,018	61,375	105,143	166,518	295,536
13 October	109,956	128,871	238,827	96,629	141,797	238,426	477,253
Increase	52,557	57,252	109,809	35,254	36,654	71,908	181,717

There was a uniform increase throughout the whole country: hence the depression in textiles could not be cited as the dominant cause. The Ministry concluded that the big increase was due to the 1930 Act as before it had been possible to deal with doubtful cases under the 'not genuinely seeking work' provision.[3]

[1] Ibid. Ministry of Labour, *Note on Married Women*, pp. 69 ff. paras. 4–9.

[2] Ibid. *Note*, para. 11.

[3] Ibid. para. 15. But see above p. 233.

The memorandum received from the National Confederation of Employers' Organisations was more concerned with the 'burdens of industry' than with actuarial niceties.[1] Thus the employers argued that contributions should be lowered from eightpence a week (the existing level) to fivepence, with an emergency provision allowing an increase to sixpence. Likewise the fund's debt should be transferred to the Exchequer so that its service could become a national, rather than an industrial, charge. The Exchequer should retain responsibility for transitional benefit, but a means test should be employed and some of the burden should be shifted to the local authorities.[2] To offset the loss of income resulting from decreased contributions, benefits should be reduced by a third (para. 53), and there should be a strict limit on the number of weeks' benefit which could be claimed in any one year.[3] The Government Actuary, commenting on these proposals, observed that their 'nebulous character . . . makes it impossible to examine the financial effect of the scheme in any detail'. Nevertheless he concluded that with the reduced contributions the maximum number of weeks' benefit in any one year would have to be fixed at 'something between ten and twenty weeks' and that the additional cost to the Exchequer, through driving many of the unemployed on to transitional benefit, plus the transfer of the debt, would work out at over £20m. In other words, the employers' proposals were designed to save themselves money at the expense of the Exchequer. Their plan differed sharply from that of the Treasury, which was designed to relieve the Budget, and that of the Actuary, who was concerned above all else to maintain the 'insurance' character of the scheme. Here we have another hint of conflict between the 'business' and 'treasury' views.

If the employers wished to add over £20m to the Budget, the trade unions proposed to add almost £60m.[4] The General Council claimed

[1] The Confederation's proposal that a Board of Trustees should be empowered to adjust the rates of benefit from time to time was thought by the Actuary to contemplate 'the reverse . . . of a scheme founded on an actuarial basis'. (Royal Commission on Unemployment Insurance, *Final Report*, November 1932, Appendix No. 1, p. 503.)

[2] The advantage of this from industry's point of view was that the De-Rating Act of 1929 had relieved industrial undertakings of 75 per cent of their rates.

[3] *Minutes of Evidence*, pp. 1005–11.

[4] The General Council's written evidence is given in *Minutes of Evidence*,

that as the unemployed were not authors of their plight, but victims of the industrial system, the whole community should take responsibility for their maintenance. Both employers' and workers' contributions should be abolished and the entire charge placed on the Exchequer: in addition the existing debt should be cancelled. There could be no question of lowering benefits:

> . . . Nobody can conscientiously say that . . . thirty-two shillings is too much for a man, wife and three children. To any thinking person it is a constant source of wonder as to how the unemployed exist on such amounts. Many of those who urge a reduction of benefit would themselves spend such an amount on a single meal or for a seat at a theatre.[1]

Rather, the benefit should be increased to the levels recommended in the General Council's evidence to the Blanesburgh Committee — that is up to twenty and eighteen shillings for a man and a woman respectively[2] — and the waiting period should be reduced to three days. Such changes would 'probably' necessitate fresh taxation, and the General Council proposed a special 'unemployment levy' on all incomes, on a percentage basis, with unearned income being charged at a higher rate than earned.[3] The unions admitted some abuses which ought to be dealt with, but said they had been magnified out of all proportion: their elimination would have little effect on the finance of the scheme. Finally, as the unions were in much greater contact with the workers than the exchange officials, their own officers should 'be asked to take over for their members the administration of State unemployment Benefit from the Exchanges, including the placing of workers'.[4]

As the enquiry progressed, and Snowden's awful warning of 11 February came and went, opposition Members grew frantic about the delay in restoring the finances of the fund. When Miss Bondfield was obliged to ask the House to raise the fund's borrowing power once more, this time to £90m, Sir Arthur Steel-Maitland complained that the

pp. 967–975. The calculation of £57m as the additional cost to the Exchequer of its proposals was worked out by the Government Actuary (*Final Report*, p. 497). The Actuary calculated that the main increases would be £30m for the increased benefits and £13m for the reduction of the waiting period. In addition the unions' proposals to include agricultural and domestic workers within the scope of the scheme would cost another £8m.

[1] para. 60. [2] Ibid. [3] paras. 21–2. [4] para. 53.

Commission was only sitting two days a week, that Judge Holman Gregory was trying cases in the High Court, and that no attempts were being made to hurry things up.[1] The Government promised an interim report by May; two interim reports were finally published on 4 June, the minority one signed by the two Labour representatives, Councillor W. Asbury and Mrs. C. D. Rackham.

In its introduction, the majority report claimed that interim proposals had become necessary on 'matters which have been presented to us as urgent' especially the increasing indebtedness of the fund, the increasing cost to the Exchequer of transitional benefit and thirdly anomalies.[2]

On the first point, the majority report realistically concluded that the ideal of a 'solvent and self-supporting' fund was at that moment unrealisable. 'Nor do we think that its attainment is the sole or even the principal consideration to which we should have regard.'[3] Nevertheless the increase of borrowing should be stemmed, partly because borrowing had become financially unjustified, partly because it warped the essence of an 'insurance' scheme. In order, therefore, that borrowing should 'as nearly as possible' cease, the report advocated limiting benefit to twenty-six weeks in any one year,[4] raising the contributions of workers, employers and the State by between one and two pennies per week,[5] and reducing the rates of benefit by two shillings for each adult, male and female, and by greater or lesser amounts for the other groups.[6] The report attempted to justify these decreases by the argument that the cost of living had gone down.[7] For convenience, a summary of the various changes in the rates of benefit from 1929, actual and proposed, is given on page 315.

The report recognised that the limitation of ordinary benefit would throw many of the unemployed on to transitional benefit, and in order to reduce the cost of this it recommended a 'means test' for (i) single

[1] 248 H.C. Deb. c. 1273–4.

[2] *Interim Report of Royal Commission on Unemployment Insurance*, Cmd. 3872, para. 9.

[3] Ibid. para. 72. [4] Ibid. para. 81. [5] Ibid. para. 85. [6] Ibid. para. 87.

[7] The union reply was that if the real value of benefits had gone up, so had the real value of contributions; i.e. the value of the increased benefit was being financed by the increased value of contributions. (*Fair Play for the Unemployed*, p. 15.)

Age	1928 Men	1928 Women	1930 Men	1930 Women	Royal Commission Men	Royal Commission Women	Trade Unions Men	Trade Unions Women
	(shillings)		(shillings)		(shillings)		(shillings)	
Over 21	17	15	17	15	15	13	20	18
20–21	14	12	14	12	12	10	20	18
19–20	12	10	14	12	12	10	20	18
18–19	10	8	14	12	12	10	20	18
17–18	6	5	9	7/6	7	6	15	14
16–17	6	5	9	7/6	5	5	15	14
15	–	–	–	–	–	–	10	10
Adult Dependant.	7	7	9	9	8	8	10	10
Child	2	2	2	2	2	2	5	5

persons residing with relatives, (ii) married women living with their husbands, and (iii) persons receiving pensions of one kind or another; and in addition an extension of the term 'suitable employment' to cover 'work other than that to which they were accustomed but which they are reasonably capable of performing'.[1] Finally, a great tightening up was recommended in the conditions under which intermittent, casual, seasonal and short-time workers, and married women, might receive benefit.[2]

The effect of these proposals would be to reduce the annual borrowing of the fund from £40m to £8m and to reduce the exchequer charge for transitional benefits from £35m to £34m. On the other hand, the exchequer contribution to the fund would be raised from £15m to £18m so that the net saving would be about £30m. Thus instead of the Exchequer having to find £90m to balance the accounts for unemployment benefit, it would now require to find only £60m.[3]

Opinions about the report were sharply divided. The Conservatives and the Liberals welcomed it. 'A courageous document', noted the *Manchester Guardian* on 5 June. 'Postponement, questionable even six months ago, has now become possible', stated *The Times*. However, the Conservatives and Liberals were strangely vague about actual measures which they were prepared to take. As the *Manchester Guardian* went on to say:

[1] Ibid. paras. 96–102. [2] Ibid. paras. 103–26.

[3] The economies were made up as follows: (1) limit of benefit to twenty-six weeks: £9m. (2) Increase in contributions: £9m. (3) Reduction in ordinary rate of benefit: £9m. (4) Anomalies: £5m—making in all £32m. The additional cost to the Exchequer due to transfer from the fund (twenty-six weeks' rule)

But in insisting on immediate action being taken on the basis, if not on the actual letter, of the majority report we must clearly realise that we are handling the most ticklish politico-social issue that has arisen since the war. It is not a pleasant dilemma either for the Government or the Opposition. The Government has to put its regard for sound finance before all the professions of its supporters . . . the Oppositions, both Conservative and Liberal, have to count on the clamour that a large section of the Labour party is prepared to raise against anyone who reforms the 'dole'. . . .

In other words, no Party was prepared lightly to take the political risk of championing specific proposals to cut down benefit, however much it might fulminate on the need for economy. The German parallel was all too real. There the Government had introduced one emergency decree after another — the latest being on the very day that the Royal Commission reported — designed to restore the public finances, and the result had been increasing violence and the growth of extremist politics. On 22 June Lord Hailsham the Conservative leader in the Lords, was quoted in *The Times* as saying:

We have our own plans. I believe they are better than those of the Royal Commission. The last thing we should do is to reduce benefits and increase the contributions. . . .

which prompted the Liberal M.P. Ernest Brown to ask 'for a statement as to how the money is to be saved'.[1]

As a way out of this dilemma, commentators turned to the Australian parallel. By 1930 the decline in the price of wheat and wool and the curtailment of British lending had brought a balance of payments crisis, while the maintenance of a high level of social and unemployment expenditure had produced a budget deficit. Australia appealed to Britain for advice and the Treasury sent out Sir Otto Niemeyer, who 'did not hesitate to impress upon the Australian authorities the evils of . . . currency depreciation, and the necessity for drastic public economies'.

Sir Otto's advice produced a political crisis not only within the ruling Labour Party but between the Federal Government and the states, which was only ended in June 1931 by a 'National Treaty' based on

would be £9m making a total exchequer charge for transitional benefit of £44m. Against this would be offset £4m for reduction in benefits, and £6m for the new conditions, making a new exchequer charge of £34m (Ibid. pp. 47–8).

[1] 254 H.C. Deb. c. 98.

'equality of sacrifice', whereby a 20 per cent reduction in all 'adjustable' government expenditure was coupled with increased taxation and a 22 per cent conversion of the internal debt. Thus the sacrifices demanded from the wage earners and unemployed were to be matched by sacrifices on the part of the taxpayers and bondholders.[1] *The Times* of 10 June argued that the British unemployed could be asked to accept reductions in their standard of living only as part of a 'package deal' embracing the wealthier sections of the community. The General Council's proposal for a levy on all incomes, though designed to finance increased benefits, might conceivably have been adapted to the same purpose. Yet any proposals for a 'national treaty' in the English context would almost certainly require a National Government to give them effect.

The Labour Party's reaction confirmed the *Manchester Guardian*'s fears. The General Council's counterblast, *Fair Play for the Unemployed*, accused the Commission of having concentrated on the narrow issue of how to balance the fund, without considering wider questions. At a Cabinet sub-committee appointed to consider the report on 4 June Citrine warned Tom Shaw, Minister of War, that the General Council would oppose it. Shaw said it should go ahead but he 'hoped we would remember the difficulties of the men on the inside'.[2] In an official statement issued on 7 June the General Council announced preparations for massive demonstrations in the principal industrial centres against the report.[3] Strong support came in from the miners, engineers, shipbuilders and builders. 'A malicious attack on the already poverty-stricken conditions of the unemployed', noted the *Daily Herald* on 9 June. Parliamentary support for the industrial stand was equally prompt. 'If the Government touch the report, it is the end of the Government', wrote John Scurr, M.P. for Stepney, in the *Evening Standard* of 5 June. 'I am entirely opposed to the majority report', said Walter Ayles, M.P. for North Bristol.[4] Fenner Brockway, chairman of the I.L.P., dubbed the report an 'invitation to revolution'[5] and a meeting of the I.L.P. group called upon the 'working class to demand that the

[1] Brown, *The International Gold Standard Reinterpreted 1914–1934*, pp. 867 ff.

[2] General Council Papers, 157.83D.

[3] *The Times*, 8 June 1931.

[4] Quoted *Manchester Guardian*, 6 June 1931.

[5] *Daily Herald*, 8 June 1931.

Government shall increase benefits . . . extend unemployment insurance to agricultural workers, domestic servants, and . . . fishermen, and abolish the unfair conditions which at present disqualify applicants from receiving benefits'.[1] Finally, the trade union group of about a hundred M.P.s decided on 10 June that the recommendations of the Commission were 'wholly unacceptable'.[2]

By 12 June it was clear that the Government did not intend to carry out the main recommendations of the majority report. At a P.L.P. meeting the previous day MacDonald promised that they would not reduce benefits, or increase contributions, or shorten the period of benefit. On the other hand, he said, they proposed to deal with 'anomalies'.[3] 'These reforms will be good as far as they go', commented the *Manchester Guardian* of 12 June, but 'they are no relief to our national credit'. The financial situation would sooner or later compel 'major surgical operations'. In a wild article in the *Daily Mail*, Churchill wrote 'by every device, every dodge, every shift and almost every turpitude, they have managed to keep on paying for the longest time, in the loosest fashion, the largest doles to the largest number'. On 15 June a General Council deputation to 10, Downing Street, supported the Government's decision not to proceed with the major recommendations, but wanted more information about its attitude to anomalies. MacDonald said that the Government would shortly need more money to continue unemployment benefit and would therefore have to compromise on this point. Miss Bondfield indicated that the compromise might not be altogether unacceptable to her by proclaiming that 'many former shop assistants, now married, were coming back to work in shops for weekends only and they did not want to work for the rest of the week'. She did accept a General Council suggestion to set up an advisory committee of trade union officials and employers as part of the machinery of the new Bill, to look into disputed cases.[4]

On 18 June, following well-tried practice, the Government introduced simultaneously a Bill to deal with anomalies, and another to increase the borrowing power of the fund from £90m to £115m. The Anomalies Bill proposed to deal with four classes of workers: intermittent, short-time and seasonal workers, and married women. It empowered the

[1] *Daily Telegraph*, 5 June 1931. [2] *The Times*, 11 June 1931.
[3] *Daily Herald*, 12 June 1931. [4] General Council Papers, 157.83 D.

Minister, on consulting with an advisory committee, composed of trade unionists, employers and a treasury official, to make alterations in the conditions, the amount, and the period of benefit for these four groups. The advisory committee was really a concession to the trade union point of view, since it avoided the need to spell out for the unemployed the exact sacrifices they would be required to make; but at the same time it revived the principle of the Minister's discretionary power which the Labour movement had consistently challenged.

Even so, there was evidently considerable dissension within the Cabinet whether to go ahead with the Bill at all. We are told by Lansbury that when the interim report came out 'a section led by Snowden was in favour of putting . . . all [the proposals] immediately into operation . . . and it looked at one moment as if the Cabinet might break on this subject'.[1] Even after the decision had been made to produce a modified Bill there was strong pressure for postponement. On 1 July Miss Bondfield wrote to MacDonald:

> After the discussion at the Cabinet this morning I feel bound to put before you my serious apprehension at the possibility that the Anomalies Bill may be postponed until after the Summer Recess.
>
> Ever since the Royal Commission was appointed, we have constantly assured the House that we regarded the problem as urgent in order that we might legislate on the subject before the House rises.
>
> . . . If it is now decided to postpone any action until the autumn, my own position will be impossible and we shall be open to the accusation that we obtained the consent of the House to further borrowing on false pretences.

To this the Prime Minister replied, somewhat testily:

> I have your letter on the Anomalies Bill. The thing that surprised me at the Cabinet was that you yourself did not seem to press for the immediate enactment of the measure. Your hesitation took me very much by surprise. Unless I am strongly supported by Ministers whose business has been placed on the agenda, I cannot resist the pressure of others. . . . I propose at the moment to keep the Bill where it is.[2]

Miss Bondfield explained to the House on 22 June that the Government could not decide on the larger issues raised by the interim report till the final report came out.[3] Although the Conservatives and Liberals

[1] Lansbury Papers, 25 n. 1–17, para. 4.

[2] MacDonald Papers, File 6, Unemployment Insurance.

[3] 254 H.C. Deb. c. 72–3.

vigorously criticised the Minister's continued recourse to borrowing, they gave the Anomalies Bill itself a mild, even a friendly, passage. Walter Elliot said that 'nothing but a grave sense of the desperate position of . . . unemployment insurance could have moved the Minister to produce proposals such as this', and admitted that the 'saving of £5m is a large sum which cannot be attained without retrenching upon a wide field'.[1] Maclean for the Liberals agreed that it was a measure of 'great and far-reaching importance'.[2] The moderation of opposition spokesmen reflected their desire not to be too closely identified with further proposals for reducing benefit.

The one opposition criticism of substance was that the Bill was not 'sufficiently mandatory'. 'Is the right hon. Lady really in earnest. . . ?' asked Captain Waterhouse.[3]

The I.L.P. did not doubt the answer, and the Maxtonite and Mosley groups came together in the lobby to muster nineteen votes against the Bill's second reading. Thereafter they harried it unmercifully in an all-night session, when tempers ran high, and furious accusations were flung across the floor. Mosley's argument was that it was grossly unfair to make the poor suffer for the failings of the Government. Had his policy been adopted there would be no unemployed to strike off.[4] Buchanan emerged as the champion of the unemployed. His anger and eloquence spoke for the betrayed and dispossessed:

> The policy of the Labour party used to be 'work or maintenance', and now, they go and punish a man or woman for something over which he or she has no control. Who is there in this House who can say that the seasonal workers have any control over their lives? Who can say truthfully and honestly that the seasonal worker is idle because he or she desires to be idle?[5]

and on the married women question:

> What are we proposing to do now? A married woman must qualify after marriage. If she does not enter into marriage but cohabits with a man, she gets benefit. If you go straight-forwardly and marry, you are penalised, but if you live in sin you get benefit. That is the Bill.[6]

Buchanan's stand won much sympathy from the liberal Conservatives; Stanley pointed out that what divided him from Buchanan was not lack

[1] 254 H.C. Deb. c. 2115. [2] Ibid. c. 2125. [3] Ibid. c. 2125, 2157.
[4] Ibid. c. 2143 ff. [5] Ibid. c. 2132. [6] Ibid. c. 2130.

of sympathy, but a 'fundamental divergence' over 'financial possibilities and economic laws'.

He believes that State taxation does no more than inconvenience the rich who have to pay it while benefiting the poor who receive it. I believe that that taxation does more than inconvenience the rich. I believe that at the same time it damages the poor, and that the expenditure . . . is, in fact, putting a small benefit into their pockets every week and at the same time withdrawing from them for ever the chance of what they want more than doles — the chance of regular employment.[1]

But was Buchanan's the authentic voice of Labour? J. E. Mills, M.P. for Dartford, did not think so. He accused such I.L.P. champions as Maxton and Brockway of never having known a day's unemployment in their lives. The Bill was to stop 'wangling', which was deeply resented by a 'majority of our people' even more bitterly than by 'our political opponents'.[2] The Glasgow *Forward*, edited by T. Johnston, one of the most prominent of the Clydeside group in the early 1920s, wrote:

If the I.L.P. gets itself committed to any policy of defending abuses or sponging on the unemployment insurance benefit it will do an ill-service indeed to the unemployed.[3]

Other Labour and trade union comment followed MacDonald's argument that it was only by removing the 'spongers' that unemployment insurance could be made safe for the vast majority of the unemployed.

The all-night sitting of 15 July emphasised the depth of the cleavage between the I.L.P. and the bulk of the Labour Party. Thirty-three divisions were taken in all; in fact, the I.L.P. achieved little or nothing, except to convince themselves and others that their separation from the Labour Party could not be long postponed. As Buchanan said:

Loyalty I have to my party, and none more so, but, greater than that loyalty, the greatest loyalty to me, is my loyalty to the poor from whence I sprung, and nothing, not even secret meetings and a threat against my livelihood, will ever make me desert those folk who have given me bread.[4]

---

[1] 254 H.C. Deb. c. 2135.
[2] 255 H.C. Deb. c. 739.
[3] 4 July 1931.
[4] 254 H.C. Deb. c. 2134.

V. THE POSITION OF THE GOVERNMENT: JANUARY–JULY 1931

'Everyone expects the Cabinet will be out before the Budget. . . .', noted Beatrice Webb in her diary of 22 January 1931; and yet by 18 June she was writing, 'barring accidents . . . the Government will now go on indefinitely'.

No improvement in the Government's performance had produced this transformation. Admittedly there were successes, however transient, in the foreign field. MacDonald's farewell to the India round table conference which broke up in January was, noted Beatrice Webb, 'a gorgeous success — what an artist the man is, how admirably he thinks about external affairs — has enormously increased his prestige'.[1] The goodwill created by this imposing London gathering was reflected in the agreement reached by the Viceroy, Lord Irwin[2] with Gandhi, whereby the latter promised to discontinue the civil disobedience campaign.[3] On 1 March, following the visit of Henderson and Alexander to Paris, it was announced that the French and Italians had reached agreement on naval disarmament, thus rounding off the settlement reached by England, America and Japan at the London naval conference the previous year.[4] These achievements, Beatrice Webb remarked, 'have revived the *morale* of the P.L.P. — the temperamental Jimmy immediately exclaimed: "In for six years" '.[5]

On the domestic front the situation remained black. Quite apart from the running sore of unemployment, the Government was soon in difficulties with its legislative programme. Sir Charles Trevelyan mishandled the denominational question in the School Leaving Age Bill and an 'unsavoury union between Catholic socialism and Tory reaction' was consummated on 21 January when the 'Scurr amendment' postponing the operation of the measure till subsidies had been promised to the

[1] B. Webb Diaries, 22 January 1931. [2] Better known as Lord Halifax.

[3] *Daily Telegraph*, 6 March 1931.

[4] The agreement proved short-lived. 'Technical details' remained to be settled, and on 4 May Italy rejected the French proposals. 'Therewith, there disappeared, for an indefinite time to come, the hope of securing a comprehensive naval limitation agreement between all five of the principal naval Powers of the world' (*Survey of International Affairs*, 1931, p. 31).

[5] B. Webb *Diaries*, 8 March 1931.

Catholic schools was carried by 284 votes to 251.[1] On 18 February the Lords added to the Government's humiliation by rejecting the Bill by 168 votes to 22, and the best MacDonald could do was to announce that it would be passed under the Parliament Act. The Government had to withdraw the Trades Disputes Bill when a wrecking Liberal amendment on the definition of an illegal strike was carried in committee on 24 February,[2] and considered dropping, owing to its mutilation by the Peers, an Electoral Reform Bill which introduced the alternative vote and abolished plural voting and double-member and University seats. 'If government is to be carried on in accordance with the wishes of the people, the House of Lords — which watches over us like a pelican — will have to disappear', commented the new Solicitor-General, Sir Stafford Cripps.[3]

Death, disease and resignation added to the Government's discomfiture. Russell, the Under-Secretary of State for India, died on 11 March, two days before Hartshorn. Jowitt and F. O. Roberts, Minister of Pensions, were down with influenza; Parmoor was 'incapacitated'; MacDonald was thought to be unwell; Snowden was out of action for over a month after a prostate operation in mid-March. On 2 March Trevelyan gave up his thankless task at the Ministry of Education and launched a general attack on the Government in his resignation letter and at a meeting of the P.L.P. on 3 March. The *Daily Herald* described his letter as 'unjust, ungrateful and ungenerous'; at the parliamentary meeting his remarks were received in 'stony silence', while MacDonald was cheered for two minutes. Trevelyan was personally and politically unpopular, but he resigned at a bad period. Manifestos, *National Policies*, and statements rained down on a somewhat apathetic public as six Mosleyites made their characteristically flamboyant exit.[4] The I.L.P.

[1] MacDonald's statement that no question of resignation arose prompted Churchill to describe him as the 'boneless wonder': a comment on 'his wonderful skill in falling without hurting himself' (247 H.C. Deb. c. 1021–2).

[2] *The Times*, 14 April, carried a curious story that the Liberal amendment had in fact been drafted by a 'prominent member of the Government'. Sir William Jowitt dismissed such reports as 'a pack of lies' (Ibid. 14 April 1931).

[3] *Daily Herald*, 29 June 1931.

[4] The two Mosleys, Oliver Baldwin, Brown, Forgan and Strachey all resigned from the Labour Party at the end of February or early March: Brown and Baldwin did not join the New Party; W. E. D. Allen, Conservative

M.P.s found it more profitable for the moment to harass the Government from within the Party, though disaffiliation was repeatedly discussed. At the I.L.P. conference of 4–7 April Maxton laid down the dictum that the proper though 'irksome' course for the I.L.P. was to remain within the Labour Party, 'acting with it 90 per cent of the time, and 10 per cent of the time insisting on a clearer enunciation of Socialist principles and standing for them'.[1] Whether the I.L.P. position could be reconciled with the standing orders of the Labour Party was the subject of further correspondence between John Paton, the I.L.P. secretary, and Arthur Henderson, from May to July: agreement was as far away as ever when Parliament broke up.[2] The policy of 10 per cent disagreement led to the all-night session of 15 July on the Anomalies Bill; it also produced a string of incidents and minor acts of rebellion which alienated the I.L.P. from the bulk of the Party. On 13 March seven I.L.P. Members and two miners' M.P.s supported a Conservative motion to reduce the salary of Sir Ernest Gowers who had just been appointed chairman of the Coal Mines Reorganisation Commission set up by the 1930 Act: the Government majority fell to five. Early in July Kirkwood, Maxton, Brockway, Campbell Stephen, Buchanan and Kinley were all 'reported' to the National Executive for various breaches of discipline; McGovern was suspended from the House on 2 July and various I.L.P. members tried to prevent the Serjeant-at-Arms from removing him. The party leaders hit back vigorously. In his January message to the Labour movement, MacDonald wrote that 'some of our people . . . are more interested in proclaiming personal dissenting views for our enemies to use against us than in putting their necks into the collar and pulling all together for the success of the party and the well-being of the workers'.[3] Commenting on I.L.P. opposition to the Anomalies Bill Walter Citrine, secretary of the T.U.C., said on 9 July: 'I have regretted the scenes of the last few days in which a few men have arrogated to themselves the right to criticise in Parliament the considered and mature policy not only of the Trades Union Congress, but of the Labour Party of which they form a

M.P. for Belfast West, did, however, on 9 March; and on 15 March Harold Nicolson adhered as a 'humble recruit'.

[1] *The Times*, 6 April 1931.

[2] Labour Party, *Annual Report*, 1931, pp. 298–302.

[3] *Labour Magazine*, January 1931.

part'. The I.L.P., he went on, would get no support from the trade union movement.[1] Meanwhile the N.E.C. on 6 July declared that McGovern, who had been accused of improperly securing his selection as candidate for Shettleston after Wheatley's death, would no longer be acceptable as the Labour candidate in a future election.[2] Disaffection, however, was not confined to the I.L.P. Lack of Labour support contributed to the Government's defeat on a clause in the Electoral Reform Bill abolishing the university seats. At the N.E.C. meeting on 10 March 1931, the Prime Minister raised the question of thirty-three M.P.s who had been absent unpaired for a vote on the Unemployment Insurance (Money) Bill on 16 February: twenty-five M.P.s had been unable to give a satisfactory answer.[3] By April it was reported that since the Government had taken office, altogether 126 Labour M.P.s had voted against it on one occasion or more.[4] The party meeting of 23 April decided to accept a report of a joint committee of the P.L.P. and the N.E.C. advocating a joint standing committee to investigate all breaches of discipline with powers to report its conclusions to the constituency parties, unions or other nominating bodies, and also to recommend withdrawal of the party whip. The committee commented on 'the steady sense of loyalty in the constituencies which we would do well to emulate'.[5]

Death and resignation had led to a minor government reshuffle in March: Thomas Johnston was appointed to succeed Vernon Hartshorn; Lees-Smith became Minister of Education in place of Trevelyan; Attlee moved from the Duchy of Lancaster to become Postmaster-General; Morrison, as a reward for consistent competence and loyalty, was promoted to the Cabinet on 19 March.[6] But MacDonald planned further changes to strengthen the Government's position.

[1] *Daily Herald*, 10 July 1931. [2] *Daily Telegraph*, 7 July 1931.

[3] MacDonald Papers, Political 13 (Miscellaneous).

[4] *New Leader*, 1 May 1931. [5] MacDonald Papers, ibid.

[6] Apart from his responsibility for the road programme, Morrison spent most of the last few months of the Labour Government's life on his London Passenger Transport Bill, which had its second reading on 23 March. This provided for the transfer to public ownership of the various private transport undertakings in the London area. Passfield in a letter to his wife dated 22 April 1931 wrote: 'Herbert Morrison has carried through, with great ability and persistence, his great scheme for buying up, for transfer to a public authority, the whole of the London passenger traffic companies, on agreed

Early in the year the first rumours began of an impending major government reconstruction. The opportunities for such a change seemed steadily to improve. Early in January Sankey, the Lord Chancellor, was reported anxious to retire.[1] Snowden's persistent ill-health suggested relief from the burdens of the Exchequer by a peerage, which would also strengthen the Government in the Upper House where the Labour leadership under the octogenarian Lord Parmoor was deplorably weak: Earl Russell's death added to the work of the small contingent of venerable Labour peers, as he had been responsible for India, lunacy and motor-cars.[2] Passfield, too, was anxious to retire into private life. MacDonald wanted a change of management at the Exchequer, where Snowden's bleak negatives made any constructive domestic policy impossible. In the autumn of 1930 the Prime Minister had mentioned to the Chancellor a three-point programme for winning 'a clear majority at the next general election': no reduction in the social services; a forward programme on unemployment; and a 10 per cent revenue tariff.[3] To the last two points Snowden was vehemently opposed, while he had come to regard a reduction in the social services as a necessity. On the other hand Thomas, the Prime Minister's closest confidant in the top hierarchy of the Labour movement, was known to favour a tariff, so MacDonald toyed with the plan of promoting him to the Exchequer in Snowden's place. Unfortunately, the prospect of Thomas succeeding him was enough to make Snowden cling to office with redoubled vigour.[4]

Snowden's prostate operation on 16 March seemed to offer the ideal opportunity for putting the Premier's plan into operation. On 26 March Passfield was writing to his wife: 'P.M. to see Snowden and possibly Thomas on Sunday — maybe to talk about possible elevation to another

terms, which will avoid arbitration proceedings. This may so facilitate parliamentary proceedings that the Bill may go through this session — an immense coup'. (Passfield Papers, Section II.) This proved too optimistic: the Bill had to be carried over till the autumn.

[1] Passfield to Beatrice Webb, 14 January 1931.

[2] Ibid. 5 March 1931.

[3] Snowden, *Autobiography*, ii, p. 923.

[4] Ethel Snowden remarked to Beatrice Webb 'the City knows that Jimmy is a speculator on 'private information' and that is one of the reasons he wants the post'. Beatrice Webb continued that 'PS will not go to the Lords unless sure that J.H.T. is not made [Chancellor]' (B. Webb Diaries, 1 July 1931).

place'.[1] The meeting took place at Snowden's bedside on 30 March, when a buoyant convalescent informed the Prime Minister of his intention of introducing the Budget in person. What is more, he apparently refused to disclose his budget plans.[2] This was disagreeable news and by 24 April Passfield was writing: 'Let us hope that Snowden will insist on going to the House of Lords at Whitsuntide. . . .'[3] However, the Finance Bill dragged on into July, and the Chancellor's health seemed fully restored by the fight over his Land Taxes.[4]

MacDonald's tentative soundings on protection fared little better. On 11 May Alexander, the First Lord of the Admiralty and spokesman for the Co-operative Party, announced in Cabinet that he would resign rather than accept a wheat quota;[5] Snowden was as adamant as ever, and before these pressures MacDonald gave way. 'We finally disposed today of any proposal increasing the price of food, *under whatever alias*', wrote Passfield on 4 June, 'so there will be no "free trade" split in the Cabinet.'

Although the problem of Snowden remained for the moment insoluble, the need for a government reconstruction continued to be felt. On 18 April Arthur Henderson told the Webbs that MacDonald ought to make considerable changes in his Cabinet. The younger men must be brought on. 'But he saw little or nothing of the P.M. who did not associate with his colleagues.'[6] Henderson at this stage was apparently thinking of going to the Lords himself.[7] MacDonald, however, was keeping a number of possibilities open: 'Curious that J.R.M. made *no* peers in the Birthday Honours List', noted Passfield on 5 June. In point of fact, MacDonald's concern for strengthening the Government's position in the Lords dated back from the previous year when the Lords had wreaked havoc with the coal legislation. 'I want someone there who can put a reasonably sensible case to them', he told Citrine, and on 24 November 1930 he suggested that both Citrine and Bevin should go into

[1] Passfield Papers, Section II.

[2] Ibid. Passfield to Beatrice Webb, 31 March 1931.

[3] Ibid.

[4] 'MacDonald was not at all well at Cabinet today — said he had not slept. . . . Snowden, on the other hand, seemed quite well' (Passfield to Beatrice Webb, 8 July 1931).

[5] Passfield to Beatrice Webb, 11 May 1931.

[6] B. Webb Diaries, 18 April 1931.

[7] Snowden, *An Autobiography*, ii, p. 925.

the Lords. Both refused, though not without hesitation.[1] Now on 14 July he wrote to Passfield:

> As you know, I am in a most awful difficulty about the House of Lords. You may think that I have been doing nothing, but as a matter of fact I have been working at it for week-end after week-end, and am in a complete dead end. *We have not the material in our Party that we ought to have.* The solution will have to come, I am afraid, by moves which will surprise all of you. I am still working at it however. [italics mine.]

Both Beatrice and Sidney Webb concluded that this meant that MacDonald had decided to go to the Lords as Foreign Secretary, recommending Henderson as his successor. Henderson would omit Parmoor, Passfield, Amulree and possibly Miss Bondfield from a reconstructed Cabinet. The change of leadership would give hope of reconciling the insurgent elements within the Labour Party before the October Scarborough conference.[2]

Bassett, in his detailed survey of the 1931 crisis, accepts this as a reasonable interpretation of this letter, attacking the Webbs' later rethinking which saw it as a hint that MacDonald was planning a National Government.[3] Yet if the National Government interpretation shows signs of misleading hindsight, the Webbs' immediate reaction was equally strange. MacDonald's decision to relinquish the premiership to Henderson would certain have been a 'surprising' move: so surprising, in fact, that there is no hint of it except in Beatrice Webb's immediate comment. Certainly, MacDonald, who always liked to dwell on his difficulties, may have talked from time to time of retiring, but there is no evidence whatsoever that he was seriously contemplating this step. And it is indeed difficult to see how his going to the Lords would have solved the problem of the 'lack of material' in the Labour Party. There is an alternative possibility which had at least been privately discussed at length in the previous few months. Beatrice Webb says:

> Constant discussions have taken place between the 'big four' of the P.L.P. (P.M., Henderson, Thomas and Snowden) and Lloyd George and his inner cabinet — Lothian, Samuel, Sinclair; they meet every week or so, and it looks like the preparation for the appearance of Liberals sooner or later on the Labour Front Bench.[4]

[1] Citrine, *Men and Work*, pp. 310–12. [2] B. Webb Diaries, 14 July 1931.
[3] Bassett, *1931: Political Crisis*, pp. 409 ff.
[4] B. Webb Diaries, 31 May 1931.

These conversations were interrupted by the sham battle over the Land Taxes, but by the end of July Lloyd George was dictating the following memo of a conversation with the Prime Minister to his secretary, Frances Stevenson:

> Generally speaking, Labour would like an alliance. They would be prepared to drop some of their present Ministers . . . Ramsay would be Prime Minister, Lloyd George would be Leader (of the House) at the Foreign Office or the Treasury. . . .[1]

Here, then, was the most obvious and natural explanation of the 'moves which will surprise all of you'. Snowden was apparently willing enough to resign the chancellorship before the end of the Parliament, provided Thomas could be kept out of the succession.[2] His resignation would be the occasion for the entry of the Liberals into the Government, with Lloyd George taking his place at the Exchequer, and Henderson continuing as Foreign Secretary in the Lords.

A Labour–Liberal coalition was becoming increasingly attractive for both sides. More than ever it seemed necessary to hang together to avert the calamity of a protectionist victory; and this involved a guarantee of Labour office for two or three years to give world trade a chance to revive.[3] This in turn demanded a more formal relationship between the two Parties. From the Labour point of view, lack of parliamentary security was a constant and increasing threat, with the secession of the Mosleyites and the open rebellion of the I.L.P., who were now prepared to vote with the Conservatives. From the Liberal point of view 'responsibility without direct control', as Lloyd George put it,[4] threatened only disaster: the Liberals would gain no credit from the Government's success, but they would be borne down by its failure. Effective co-operation on an *ad hoc*, informal basis seemed unlikely after such major 'accidents' as occurred over Snowden's Land Tax Bill and the Trades Disputes Bill, both of which had started out as agreed measures.

[1] Quoted in Frank Owen, *Tempestuous Journey: Lloyd George, His Life and Times*, p. 717.

[2] Snowden, *Autobiography*, ii, pp. 926–7.

[3] There was the additional consideration that the Lords' mutilation of the Electoral Reform Bill meant that it would take two years to pass under the Parliament Act.

[4] *The Times*, 16 May 1931.

The immediate electoral prospects for both Parties were forbidding. In the thirteen by-elections of 1931 the swing to the Conservatives averaged about $7\frac{1}{2}$ per cent, rising to over 9 per cent for the last six of them. The Liberals did badly at almost every by-election they fought, showing a drop of over 6 per cent in their share of the three-party vote. Even allowing for a swing back to the Government of some 4 or 5 per cent, Labour stood to lose about fifty seats and the Liberals over thirty in an immediate general election, which everyone agreed meant a certain Conservative victory.

The growing conviction that the Conservatives would sweep the country reflected in part the political recovery of Baldwin and the ending of Conservative disunity. This had not seemed clear at the beginning of the year. On 23 February Chamberlain noted in his diary: 'the question of leadership is again growing acute . . . I am getting letters and communications from all over the country'; and on 26 February a memorandum from the Party's principal agent reported 'definite doubts whether the leader could carry the Party to victory'.[1] Churchill's withdrawal on 27 January from the Conservative Business Committee (the Shadow Cabinet) in opposition to Baldwin's India policy added to the embarrassment. In the by-election at St. George's, Westminster, for Worthington-Evans's seat, the official Conservative candidate, Moore-Brabazon, decided to stand down in favour of the Beaverbrook nominee, Sir Ernest Petter; it seemed that Baldwin would have to go, but at the last moment he found a staunch champion in Duff Cooper. Coming to St. George's to support his candidate, Baldwin denounced the newspaper magnates, in a historic phrase, for 'aiming at . . . power without responsibility — the prerogative of the harlot throughout the ages . . .',[2] and his authority was substantially confirmed when Duff Cooper won a majority of almost 6,000 in a straight fight against the Empire Crusader.

By the middle of 1931 the tactical advantage of a Labour–Liberal coalition had become obvious, at least to the leaders of the two Parties. But had it to their parliamentary supporters? On the Labour side hopes of a 'bold socialist policy' had by now vanished: the only hope of a 'bold' policy to restore Government credit seem to lie in coalescing with the

[1] K. Feiling, *The Life of Neville Chamberlain*, p. 185.
[2] *The Times*, 18 March 1931.

Liberals. And indeed, Lloyd George's pugnacious approach, in startling contrast to the apologetics of their own leaders, was now making him a more attractive figure to Labour M.P.s.[1] In a letter of 13 February, the left-wing Lansbury went so far as to beg Lloyd George to enter the Labour Party, suggesting that he would be made deputy Prime Minister and his followers given three or four Cabinet posts. Lloyd George replied that his coming over would 'antagonise millions of Liberals with hereditary party loyalties', but went on:

I can and will give effective assistance to the Government — if they mean business. At present I am genuinely perplexed and disappoined by the stickiness of some of your colleagues. They are always finding reasons for not doing things. They are too easily scared by obstacles and interests. Unless you inoculate them with some of your faith and courage, your Party and ours will be landed in overwhelming catastrophe.[2]

Lloyd George faced a dilemma. He led a coalition of which a large minority was definitely anti-Labour: any formal links with the Government would drive this group out of the Party. Even Liberal support might not improve the Government's performance sufficiently to give the Party a popular platform on which to fight the next election. The alternative vote might, in these circumstances, turn out to be a chimera. Conservatives played skilfully on these fears. In a letter to Lloyd George dated 3 December 1930, Lothian retailed a conversation he had had with Sir Samuel Hoare:

He said he thought that, according to the Conservative calculations . . . the alternative vote would be of very little value to the Liberals. . . . He thought that [the Conservative Party] would be quite willing to discuss an arrangement whereby all existing Liberals should be guaranteed their seats if the Government was turned out on a Liberal vote, and that so far as he could see it would be impossible for anybody to keep the existing Government in power indefinitely owing to its incompetence. I asked him whether the Conservatives would be willing to make an arrangement about policy, especially agriculture, and he said he thought they would be willing to discuss a policy about agri-

---

[1] E. F. Wise, an I.L.P. M.P., commented in a speech of 11 May on 'the regrettable tendency among some Labour members at this moment to fall for the leader of the Liberal Party' adding 'I am not at present one of that happy band' (*The Times*, 12 May 1931).

[2] See R. Postgate, *George Lansbury*, p. 265; Frank Owen, *Tempestuous Journey*, p. 715.

culture or anything else in a purely practical spirit. He said he thought it might be worth while for you sometime to have a talk to Neville Chamberlain who, you would find, would deal with the question purely as a matter of business.[1]

Lloyd George's hope of holding the Liberal Party together disappeared during the year as about seventeen Liberal M.P.s, led by Sir John Simon, were increasingly clearly headed for protection and the Conservative camp. On 24 March this number had voted at a meeting of the parliamentary Party against Lloyd George's promise to support any Government pledged to more vigorous public works, economy in the public finances, Indian pacification, free trade, electoral reform and agricultural development.[2] On 26 June, Sir John Simon, Ernest Brown and Sir Robert Hutchison formally left the Liberal Party, and there was a general exodus of the Liberal right, the departure of the Earl of Rosebery and other Liberal peers signifying the final dissolution of the Whig connection.[3] The movement of the Simonites into the Conservative camp made it all the more necessary for the thirty-odd Liberals who remained loyal to Lloyd George to reach a firm accommodation with the Labour Government to keep it in power. Lothian wrote to a Canadian friend at the end of April:

There is no doubt that there is a rapprochement going on between Labour and that two-thirds of the Liberals who follow Lloyd George. It is a rapprochement based partly on the realisation by the top story of Labour that their own socialist programme is impracticable as an immediate programme, and partly on the fact that an election with trade in its present condition would return the Conservatives to power for at least five years. . . . Pressure . . . on two partners in a common misery to stand together is pretty strong. I have little doubt that the people at the top would like to make a permanent arrangement to create a semi-Socialist Progressive party, but the rank and file of neither party would agree to it at present.[4]

---

[1] Lothian Papers, Box 193.

[2] *The Times*, 25, 26, 27 March 1931.

[3] Sir John Simon's resignation was the subject of a malicious attack by Lloyd George: 'I do not object in the least to the right hon. and learned Gentleman changing his opinions . . . but I do object to this intolerable self-righteousness. . . . Greater men . . . have done it in the past, but . . . they, at any rate, did not leave behind the slime of hypocrisy in passing from one side to another' (254 H.C. Deb. c. 1667).

[4] Lothian Papers, Box 193.

Looking into the future about the middle of July 1931 a Labour supporter might have been forgiven for feeling cautiously optimistic. The precondition for the Government's political survival seemed to be assured by the prospect of a firm alliance with the Lloyd George Liberals; the precondition for a more vigorous and imaginative unemployment policy by the impending retirement of Snowden and the accession of Lloyd George to the Government. Certainly future prospects seemed better than for some time, given a little time for favourable tendencies to establish themselves. But it was time that was running out.

13

THE FALL OF THE LABOUR GOVERNMENT

i. INTRODUCTION

No account of the financial crisis should presume too much on hindsight. Politicians have been blamed for clinging to an international monetary order that was doomed to pass away. Probably it was, for the nineteenth-century gold standard system basically lacked any efficient means of bringing the exports of the industrial countries into balance with the purchasing power of the underdeveloped nations; it was obvious by the late nineteen-twenties that private lending to debtors was inadequate to sustain full employment in the developed nations. The financial crisis broke before the world could devise new methods for dealing with this problem.

Yet though the system created by Britain was evidently disintegrating, it had brought too many real benefits in the past, and had too powerful a hold over men's minds and emotions to be surrendered without a struggle. English politicians, especially the older generation, sought the cause of its malfunctioning in the War, hence their efforts were devoted to restoring pre-war conditions. As late as 1931 economists and bankers were busily devising new means of shoring up the crumbling façade, even of making the gold standard system the instrument of world-wide recovery. There was optimism in the spring air. As the League of Nations *World Survey* somewhat sadly recalled:

> . . . there seemed to be a definite easing of economic and financial conditions. The early months of the year were calm, there was some return flow of capital to Germany and of gold to Great Britain, security prices rose somewhat in the spring, and money-market rates were extremely easy in the chief financial centres. . . .

There was ample evidence, therefore, of monetary ease in the chief creditor countries, and the accumulation of liquid capital funds. In past crises, such conditions . . . have always been the precursor of recovery from depression. . . .[1]

This was the atmosphere in which Snowden awaited a trade revival, in which Montagu Norman launched his big plan for an international consortium, in which the Macmillan Report found grounds for 'cautious optimism'. And when the financial blows of the late spring and summer started to rain down, they were brushed aside impatiently as irritating interruptions to recovery. More than ever it became necessary to make a stand against the irrational forces of financial panic that were threatening men's hopes, threatening the very foundation of future prosperity. This was the mood in which Britain made a last, supreme effort to preserve its past and protect its future.

ii. FINANCIAL CRISIS: INTERNATIONAL BACKGROUND

The plan for the Austro-German customs union had been held up by French opposition. Less than two months after its announcement Austria's largest bank, the Credit-Anstalt, in effect declared itself bankrupt. We will probably never know just how much the French had to do with this. Certainly there were good enough reasons for the insolvency of the bank. As the holding company for the mid-European Rothschild enterprises, its position was obviously threatened by the depression, especially severe in those parts. Nevertheless the timing of the announcement, on 11 May 1931, suggests French malevolence; Edward Bennett has concluded that 'the revelation of the losses at this particular moment' was highly suspicious.[2] For, as expected, the Austrian Government applied to Paris, its main capital market, for a loan to prop up its world-famous institution; and Paris made it clear that the price of any loan would be renunciation of the customs union.[3] Austria was on the verge of surrender, but in the last grandiose gesture of the gold standard era, Montagu Norman announced on 16 June an unconditional seven days' credit of £4½m. London thrilled to this affirmation of Britain's financial power; but Norman had destroyed the

[1] 1931/2, p. 70.

[2] Bennett, *Germany and the Diplomacy of the Financial Crisis, 1931*, p. 101.

[3] See *Manchester Guardian*, 19 June 1931.

carefully prepared French position,[1] which was a dangerous thing to do in view of London's reliance on Paris.

The Austrian collapse started the European financial crisis. Hodson has summarised the consequences as follows:

> . . . the banking system of a country has to remain liquid or perish. If one item among its assets, which had been regarded as liquid, becomes unrealizable for the time being, it must improve its proportion of liquidity by realising other assets. The failure of the Credit-Anstalt involved a complete loss of confidence in Austrian finance, and therefore a 'standstill' on all banking assets held in Austria. In order to cover their position, banks were forced to encash other foreign balances. . . . This beggar-my-neighbour struggle to maintain international banking liquidity, as one country after another 'froze' its foreign indebtedness, played an essential part in determining the course and the violence of the 1931 crisis.[2]

The first victim was Germany. For over a year the Brüning Government had faced the most appalling difficulties. Its deflationary policy, designed to defend the exchange and enable Germany to pay its debts and reparations,[3] produced massive unemployment and a violent assault on wages. This in turn created great political and social unrest expressed in big Nazi and Communist gains in the 1930 elections.[4] In order to counter domestic dissatisfaction the Government embarked on an 'adventurous' foreign policy aimed at cancelling reparations and securing an Anschluss with Austria. But this exposed Germany to French financial retaliation. France was a large creditor and already in October 1929 and September 1930 French-engineered capital flights[5] had

[1] Ibid. The loan not only enabled Austria 'to overcome her financial difficulties — temporarily at least — but also to maintain her freedom of action in the matter of the Austro-German customs union. . . .'

[2] Hodson, *Slump and Recovery 1929–1937*, p. 66.

[3] Germany had succeeded by deflation and import controls in reducing its imports by 26 per cent between 1928 and 1930 and maintaining its exports at 98 per cent of their 1928 value, thus increasing its balance of payments surplus. (*League of Nations Survey*, 1931/2, p. 64.)

[4] The percentage of votes cast for the Nazis rose from 2.6 in 1928 to 18.3 in 1930. Communist strength increased from 10.6 to 13.1 in the same period. The main sufferers were the Conservatives and the Socialists.

[5] The October 1929 withdrawal of French funds was occasioned by Dr. Schacht's refusal to accept the 'Young schedules'; the 1930 withdrawals followed the election. (W. A. Brown, *The International Gold Standard Reinterpreted 1914–1934*, pp. 936, 945.)

revealed the limits of political independence. Now, the freezing and depreciation of those securities held by German banks in Austria and Hungary made it difficult for Germany to meet its own short-term obligations; at the same time heavy losses of foreign exchange were being suffered because of French financial withdrawals and the huge budget deficit announced at the end of May, which threw foreigners into a panic. Large sales of American securities began in May and June and short-term funds were rapidly withdrawn. The Reichsbank lost RM 720m (about £35m) in the first fortnight of June and the raising of the Bank Rate to seven per cent only accelerated the flight.[1] It was clear that collapse was imminent unless Germany could get immediate credits or relief from its debts.

The cornerstone of gold standard morality was prompt payment of debts. It was therefore in the interest of all creditors to prevent debtors from defaulting. This partly explains Norman's loan to Austria. Credit-Anstalt owed British depositors £5m.[2] Germany was heavily in debt, especially to America but also to Britain, as Germany's reconstruction in the nineteen-twenties had been largely financed by foreign loans.[3] In June 1931, therefore, the German Government was able to confront its war-time enemies with a stark alternative: help us or we default.[4] Legally, Germany was entitled under the Young Plan to suspend reparations unilaterally; in practice this machinery was unworkable, for such a move would merely draw attention to Germany's plight and cause a run on the mark. Indeed, even Brüning's hint on 9 June that Germany might be forced to take this step was sufficient to treble the rate of withdrawals.[5]

On 18 June General Dawes noted after his talk with President Hoover:

[1] As Hodson remarks: 'In such times, possibilities of capital gain or loss, far exceed consideration of interest earned.'

[2] Ibid. p. 66.

[3] In 1929 no less than 45 per cent of all German bank deposits were foreign-owned. Since then there had been some liquidation, but the amount was still substantial. (Brown, *The International Gold Standard Reinterpreted 1914–1934*, p. 931.)

[4] The French believed the Germans were 'shamming' — that is deliberately exaggerating the extent of the crisis to force cancellation of reparations.

[5] In the first week of June the Reichsbank lost RM 180m; in the second week RM 540m.

If the Austrian bank failed, it was expected that Reichsbank would be compelled to take a moratorium. This would precipitate a world crisis, affecting our own country materially, as the New York banks alone were reported to have $500,000,000 of German acceptances.[1]

The anxiety of these New York bankers could well have been increased by the Reichsbank's promise when raising the Bank Rate on 14 June to impose exchange control if the situation worsened.[2] At any rate they now put strong pressure on Hoover to help 'in the European difficulty'. There followed an event which distorted reality by raising false hopes. On 20 June Hoover announced his plan for a one-year moratorium on all inter-government payments arising from the last war. This included reparations. After weeks of increasing crisis, news of the offer brought an immense upsurge of relief and confidence. Hoover's plan at last gave the promise of achieving psychological victory over the depression. As Owen Young, author of the Young Plan, commented: 'It only takes intelligence, courage and goodwill to make a prosperous world.'[3] Markets started booming everywhere: men talked of the end of American isolation, the final solution to the reparations problem, the start of a new era.

This mood lasted exactly a week. France had not been consulted and objected to Hoover 'laying down the law with an air of omnipotence'.[4] The French ignored the psychological implications of the proposal and saw it simply as a device to protect American investments in Germany. France, by this time, had withdrawn most of her money and so stood only to lose on the transaction, as she was owed a large sum in war debts. Further there was little hope of her obtaining any compensating political advantages, for Hoover had made it clear that his offer was unconditional. *Le Matin* said with characteristic bluntness: 'We would gain no political benefits by making sacrifices under Mr. Hoover's moral pressure.'[5] France's Foreign Minister, Briand, told the German Ambassador 'no French Cabinet could have survived if it had simply accepted the Hoover memorandum as proposed'.

The fortnight spent in haggling over terms in Paris plunged the world

[1] Bennett, *Germany and the Diplomacy of the Financial Crisis, 1931*, p. 137.

[2] Ibid. p. 143.

[3] *Manchester Guardian*, 23 June 1931.

[4] 'Pertinax' in *Echo de Paris*, 22 June 1931.

[5] 22 June 1931. The *League of Nations Survey*, 1931/2, p. 258, calculated that Germany stood to gain £77m, U.S.A. to lose £54m, France to lose £16m, and Great Britain to lose £10m, from the Hoover proposals.

At the Political Magicians' Dinner
The Man Above: 'They're all very funny tricks, but where's the magician who can produce some work?'
February 25th, 1931

The Long and Short of it

L. G.: 'Any nonsense from you, my lad, and over you go!'

January 10th, 1921

into the deepest gloom. Germany again started to lose money and the withdrawals reached crisis point with the failure on 3 July of the Nordwolle, one of the biggest industrial combines in Germany, which dragged down big banks, such as the Danat, associated with it. On 15 July, despite obtaining temporary credits, the Reichsbank was forced to declare exchange control, the precise eventuality which the Hoover proposals had been designed to forestall.

iii. THE FINANCIAL CRISIS: LONDON

On 15 July Montagu Norman received a cable from Harrison, Governor of the Federal Reserve Bank of New York:

> We are concerned and surprised at sudden drop in sterling exchange today. Can you throw any light on this?

Norman replied: 'I cannot explain the drop in sterling. It was sudden and unexpected.'[1] Up to 15 July the Bank of England had been gaining gold, mainly because Germany was losing it, and on that date its holdings were £165m — £15m above the 'Cunliffe' minimum. In the next two weeks it lost £33m of gold and another £33m of foreign exchange. The £33m of gold represents the net loss of gold for the whole period 15 July to 20 September when England was forced off the gold standard. After 1 August the brunt of the withdrawals was carried by the short-term credits which London was able to obtain from France and America. Over the whole period 15 July to 20 September England lost altogether £33m of gold and about £180m of foreign exchange.[2] It can thus be seen that the flight from the pound reached its maximum in the last fortnight in July. Thereafter the scale of withdrawals diminished and there were periods when the Bank of England actually gained gold.

Yet although more gold and foreign exchange was withdrawn between 15 July and 31 July than in any two-week period subsequently, this withdrawal cannot be said to have arisen from any crisis of confidence in the pound. That came only later. It is plain that it cannot be attributed

[1] Clay, *Lord Norman*, p. 384.

[2] The Treasury statement of 20 September 1931 said that 'more than £200 millions' were withdrawn from London (see Hodson, *Slump and Recovery*, p. 79). Bank Rate went up to $3\frac{1}{2}$ per cent on July 23, and to $4\frac{1}{2}$ per cent on July 30, where it remained till Britain was forced off the Gold Standard.

to the May Report which emphasised Britain's budgetary difficulties, for that was published only on 31 July. An alternative view seeks part of the explanation in the Macmillan Report which appeared on 13 July. On the whole this report dealt with long-term questions, but it did contain some figures purporting to show a net London short-term deficit in March 1931 of £254m. 'Extraordinary weight', according to Brown, was attached to these findings, since they seemed to indicate that London might find it difficult to meet foreign claims if her own short-term assets were immobilised by foreign moratoria as happened after 15 July.[1] Other commentators have made similar statements.

Yet there is no mention of the Macmillan Report, much less of this table of figures, in the French and American press in the week following publication; the Report itself was virtually ignored by the English press. As the *Economist* noted, people were much too engrossed with what was happening in Germany.[2]

The most likely explanation of the flight from the pound, and the one most frequently advanced at the time, is that foreigners were themselves embarrassed by the Central European moratoria, and sought to improve their liquidity by drawing money out of London. The *Manchester Guardian* explained on 28 July:

> The withdrawals of French money in the last fortnight must, in the main, be explained as measures for safeguarding their own liquidity at a time when, even in France, creditors and depositors were being disturbed by news of financial disasters abroad. . . .

Hodson has given the further reason that the French taxation system tended to deprive the Paris market of funds about this time of year 'which were made up by repatriation of foreign balances'.[3] Amsterdam and Zürich, however, probably withdrew for purely technical reasons.[4] The reason that the largest withdrawal of funds was from London was simply that London had more funds to withdraw than had anywhere else. As the world's greatest trading nation, Britain held more foreign

[1] Brown, *The International Gold Standard Reinterpreted*, p. 1020. The Macmillan Report (p. 112) estimated that in March 1931 London owed £407m and was owed £153m — a net liability of £254m. D. Williams, *Ec. H.R.* April 1963, pp. 527–8, argues that the £407m was probably too low.

[2] 18 July 1931.

[3] Hodson, *Slump and Recovery 1929–1937*, pp. 71–2.

[4] See Willard Hurst, *Journal of Political Economy*, 40 (1932), pp. 638–60.

exchange for ordinary commercial purposes than any other country; and London, as the world's greatest money market, was a repository for short-term foreign balances which she advanced abroad for short periods as part of her function of keeping money in circulation. With £90m of these advances locked up in Germany and a further £50m frozen in Central Europe, it was inevitable that 'panic' withdrawals should find London acceptance houses short of liquidity, with the result that demand could only be met by the export of gold. Quite simply, what was happening was that foreign investors were recouping their German losses by withdrawing from London, while London was unable to bring in its own money from Germany. The same pattern was repeated on a smaller scale in Zürich and Amsterdam.

The charge was made, especially by the Labour Party,[1] that London had lent too recklessly on the Continent. This was probably true; and in addition London lacked the financial strength to sustain the effort in face of a general financial collapse. But what else could she do? Britain was pursuing in 1931 her traditional policy of financing depression by providing adequate short-term credits until a new basis for long-term lending could be re-established.[2] Her motives were self-interested: she wished to safeguard her long-term investments and maintain trade. The vast increase in 'hot' or 'unfaithful' money made it a hazardous undertaking. It would have been better too had the financing been more equitably distributed between the major financial centres. Nevertheless such financing was necessary for the maintenance of the gold standard system, and once the French had started their political withdrawals from Central Europe in the spring of 1931, responsibility for averting complete financial collapse in Europe devolved more and more on London.[3] The one great effort made by Britain to escape from the impasse, the Norman plan, had come to nothing; the French had regarded it as a device for transferring burdens, as indeed it was. With the failure of international co-operation, London was forced to continue alone.

In July the Government made one last effort to save London from the full impact of the financial crisis. The Hoover timetable for recovery was

[1] See below, pp. 368–9.

[2] Brown, *The International Gold Standard Reinterpreted 1914–1934*, p. 1025.

[3] Britain's foreign lending had become much more European-oriented after 1918 when she had played a prominent part in the post-war 'stabilisation' of Central European currencies.

in ruins, for although the moratorium on war debts had eventually been agreed after a fortnight of tough negotiations in Paris, agreement came too late to prevent the German moratorium. MacDonald now issued invitations to the Americans, French and Germans to attend a conference in London on 20 July to try to solve the German problem. In reality, the hope was that such a conference might solve the British problem. The Government was trying to achieve two things: first, to get agreement for a big German loan which would release the frozen British funds, and secondly, to secure a final settlement of the reparations problem. The latter aim was pressed by Snowden in face of the opposition of Henderson who saw that it would ruin his beloved disarmament plan. However, the British and French positions were irreconcilable and unfortunately for Britain the French were masters of the financial situation, an unaccustomed role, but one no doubt which they enjoyed. Of the three centres from which Germany might conceivably obtain money, London was virtually out of action, New York was unwilling to act without the others and Paris demanded political guarantees, such as the abandonment of customs union, the 'pocket battleship' programme and any claims on Danzig. France, therefore, had only to insist on its political conditions, which were no more acceptable to the English and Americans than to the Germans themselves, to reduce the conference to a nullity.[1] Its sole result was to confirm the unilateral moratorium already in operation. This meant 'that there could be no external solution to Britain's financial problems'.[2]

As London continued to lose gold, borrowing became inevitable. Sir Robert Kindersley crossed to Paris on 26 July and arranged a credit of £25m with the Bank of France; a credit for the same amount was also opened with the Federal Reserve Bank in New York. Both were announced on 1 August. In order to avoid the deflationary effect of any further loss of gold, the Bank took the precaution of increasing the fiduciary issue — that portion of the note issue which did not require to be backed by gold — by £15m. There is no hint that the Bank found the slightest difficulty at this stage in raising the credits, nor that any con-

[1] As 'Pertinax' wrote in *Echo de Paris* on 22 July: 'The characteristic of the negotiations is the sustained and concerted effort of the English and Americans to prevent us from utilising the financial and economic upheaval in Germany for the ends of French policy.'

[2] Bennett, *Germany and the Diplomacy of the Financial Crisis, 1931*, p. 281.

ditions were attached. 'Nobody here supposes for a moment', wrote the *Manchester Guardian*'s Paris correspondent, 'that the Bank of England is unable to meet its international obligations. . . .'[1] The *Economist* recalled that in 1925 the Bank had obtained a credit of £40m to help re-establish the gold standard and thought it a happy augury that the credit had not been used.[2] Now that the pound was 'encompassed by the dollar and the franc' wrote M. Gerville-Reache in *L'Information*, its position as 'the leading international currency' was impregnably secured.[3]

iv. THE IMPACT OF THE MAY REPORT

Up to 1 August it would be true to say that insofar as it affected England the financial crisis was regarded as a *technical* matter, arising from the German moratorium and the unique position of the London money-market. In other words, it was not regarded as England's fault. Indeed Europeans tried to explain their withdrawals in terms of their own difficulties. The nature of the crisis changed radically with the publication of the May Report, and, even more important, with the conclusions drawn from it by influential sections of English opinion. It was now suggested that London might not be such a safe place to keep money as had been thought, because the Labour Government was bent on inflation leading to a devaluation of the currency. Once doubts of this kind had been suggested, it was also noted that Britain was running, in 1931, a balance of payments deficit which was interpreted as part of the same inflationary tendency. Hence a real crisis of confidence in sterling arose. In order to counteract these fears the Labour Government was urged to take immediate steps to balance the Budget and otherwise reduce incomes in such a way as to make it quite clear that the first objective of British policy remained that of maintaining the currency at par.

As we have seen, the May Committee was forced on the Government, which regarded it as a delaying measure. Snowden was, of course, desperately worried by the growing budget deficit, but there seemed no solution to it that did not involve the end of the Labour Government. His only hope was for the depression to lift and trade to revive, and this

[1] 30 July 1931. [2] 8 August 1931. [3] 1 August 1931.

was the premise of the 'stop-gap' Budget of April. The *Manchester Guardian* noted on 1 August: 'If all Mr. Snowden's risks had turned out well he could at a pinch have turned aside the recommendations of the Committee as unnecessarily drastic.' This confusion of hope with expectation was quite common in 1931 when the alternative of intensified depression was too awful to contemplate.

The publication of the May Report, with its revelation of a big budget deficit, at that moment was an unkind blow. Nevertheless much of its impact might have been averted by imaginative statesmanship. As an 'eminent authority' remarked to Arnold Toynbee: 'It was an act of incredible folly . . . to allow the May Report to be published without commentary or declaration of policy.'[1] But the same political difficulties which had impeded action on unemployment insurance in the past now impeded any rapid decision on the budget deficit. As before, the problem was to get the Labour movement to accept economies in the social services. As before, the Government sought refuge in delay. Following the publication of the Report on 31 July, MacDonald announced the formation of a Cabinet economy committee consisting of himself, Snowden, Henderson, Thomas and Graham to consider the Report 'during the recess'.[2] A day earlier Snowden had committed the Government to submitting to the House 'when it reassembles in October, the result of their consideration and deliberation' of the Report.[3] By that time he no doubt hoped that the financial crisis would have passed.

Both the majority report, signed by Sir George May and four of his colleagues, and the minority report, signed by the Labour representatives, Charles Latham and Arthur Pugh, agreed that the Chancellor faced a budget deficit for the year 1932–33 of £120m. It is interesting that the minority report did not query this total which was reached by the rather controversial method of including the 'normal' Sinking Fund provision of £55m and the whole borrowing (£50m) for unemployment insurance. Without these two items the deficit would have seemed distinctly less alarming at £15m. The majority report proposed to balance the Budget with economies of £97m, to come mainly out of unemployment benefit and other social services, the rest to be raised by taxation. The minority

[1] Toynbee, *Survey of International Affairs 1931–2*, p. 96 n.
[2] 255 H.C. Deb. c. 2623–4. [3] Ibid. c. 2512–13.

report accepted one or two of these economies, but sought the remedy mainly in additional taxation.

The economies of £97m were to be made up as follows:

	£m
Unemployment Insurance	
Reduction of standard rate of benefit by 20 per cent	15
Increase of weekly contributions by twopence	10
Extension of scheme to self-employed groups	5
Tightening up conditions for receipt of benefit	6
Limitation of benefit to twenty-six weeks in any year	8
Means test for transitional scheme	23
	67
Education	
Reduction of teachers' salaries by 20 per cent, etc.	14
Fighting Services	
Reduction in pay of all ranks by 10 per cent	2
Police	
Reduction in pay by 12½ per cent	1
Road Fund	
Postponement and slowing down of schemes	8
Miscellaneous	5
Total	97

The majority report said the deficit was caused by the cumulative extravagance of Governments forced to compete for electoral favours; the minority report explained it by deflation which had increased the burden of fixed debt. Thus it followed that the majority report sought to eliminate the gap by reducing expenditure in proportion to the fall in prices, while the minority report sought to tax the rentier. This difference represented an underlying conflict of social priorities. Sir George May and his business colleagues regarded social expenditure as essentially wasteful in that it diverted money from profitable business use. Hence they wanted to see a *permanent* reduction in the social services.[1] The Labour representatives, on the other hand, regarded an increasing state commitment to social security as good, not only because it obeyed the

[1] *May Report*, pp. 16, 173, 181, 192.

fundamental socialist maxim of redistributing income, but also because, in a depression, it maintained purchasing power. Thus both sides saw the argument over the Budget as the occasion for stating their competing social philosophies.

It may be thought that both reports, inasmuch as they agreed on the need to balance the Budget, were deflationary. However, insofar as the rentier's money was being hoarded or kept in idle balances, its appropriation to cover existing expenditure was clearly less deflationary than the proposal to reduce that expenditure. The majority report, moreover, proposed to carry deflation a good deal further: their goal was a permanent reduction in public expenditure. Thus they recommended that all exchequer grants for public works should be limited to 25 per cent and hinted that all incomes would eventually have to be reduced to bring down costs of production.[1]

The majority report, as Keynes noted, gave a cue to all the deflationists, whose theories had become somewhat suspect in the previous few years, to leap onto the deflationary bandwagon; and the more timid converts to inflation now vied with each other in abjuring their heresy.

That previously staunch supporter of the Liberal unemployment policy, the *Manchester Guardian*, now argued that the unbalanced Budget 'which saps the foundation of our credit' and the 'high costs of production . . . which sap the foundation of our export trade' were only different aspects of the problem of excessively high incomes and wages.[2] *The Times* stated that 'economy will be useless if it is ephemeral . . . cumulative and persistent economy is the only antidote to cumulative and persistent expenditure'.[3] The *Economist* was more explicit. The Government should not only balance the Budget, but readjust all salaries, wages and prices in order to make our exports more competitive.[4] Keynes was one of the few critics of the May approach, backed somewhat shyly by his old collaborator, Hubert Henderson. The report, argued Keynes, 'invites us to decide whether it is our intention to make Deflation effective by transmitting the reduction of international prices to British salaries and wages'. His own policy 'for so long as the slump lasts' was to suspend the Sinking Fund, continue borrowing for unemployment insurance and impose a revenue tariff.[5]

[1] *May Report*, p. 221. [2] 5 August 1931. [3] 7 August 1931.
[4] 22 August 1931. [5] *New Statesman*, 15 August 1931.

The connection between this debate and the question of the currency is obvious enough in general, but more difficult to pin down in detail. With Britain running a balance of payments deficit estimated at about £100m for 1931, it was clear that unless corrective measures were taken, Britain would soon be forced off the gold standard. Indeed, it is probable that in the months from July to September part of the loss of gold and foreign exchange went to meet the current payments deficit. The 'fundamental' correction required by the deflationists was to reduce British prices (via salaries and wages) to the world price level: Keynes's remedy was a tariff to reduce imports, pending international monetary action to *raise* the world price level. This was, in essence, the policy of the Macmillan Report. The Government, as usual, had not decided which of the two views to take, but there seems little doubt that given time it would have continued to press for world monetary expansion, with or without a British tariff, and would have rejected deflation.

Why the balance of payments deficit should have been considered by foreign opinion in 1931 to be less of a threat to sterling than the unbalanced Budget is a little difficult to understand; both were equally amenable to government policy, and the former, if unresolved, pointed much more directly to a currency depreciation than the latter. Probably the main answer is that the May Report specifically focused attention on the budgetary problem and therefore highlighted it as the main source of danger in the lurid imagination of foreign holders of sterling. But we must not neglect the special symbolic importance of the balanced Budget as a sign of 'sound' financial policy. There must always be some criteria by which to judge whether a policy is likely to be acceptable or not, and the balanced Budget was just such a 'rule of thumb', specially favoured by bankers and investors who lacked the detailed knowledge to attempt a more comprehensive assessment of possibilities.

The whole problem has been defined in terms of maintaining the value of the currency, since inflation and deflation have no meaning except in relation to a given value of money. Yet virtually no one in 1931 thought of defining it in any other way, for up to that time the maintenance of the fixed exchange parity was regarded as the cornerstone of policy to which everything else had to be adjusted. This philosophy, which was considered to be especially true for a country such as Britain, with its vast trading and financial commitments, had been given authoritative expression as late as July 1931 in the Macmillan Report.

If Britain devalued, it was argued, other countries would do the same: soon the whole world would be plunged into a welter of floating exchanges, tariff wars, and panic flights of money, all of them destructive of the trade, commerce and finance on which Britain's prosperity to a large extent depended. Similar preoccupations of self-interest underlay the argument that devaluation would constitute a 'default' on Britain's obligations, for Britain as the 'largest creditor nation' was particularly vulnerable to the nationalisation of her foreign property and assets if ever the gold standard morality collapsed. The frequent use of moral concepts in discussing the gold standard is particularly important, for moral behaviour has traditionally been held to require a non-human sanction and this is exactly what the gold standard was supposed to provide. Its greatest virtue was that it was automatic, fixed, beyond the control of politicians: a moral censor which expressed, in Sir Robert Kindersley's words, 'the results of the sins or virtues, as the case may be, of all inhabitants of a country', which created 'that anxiety which brings home to them that they are being extravagant. . . .'[1] Thus the maintenance of a parity fixed by tradition and custom solved any problem of economic or financial morality by 'automatically' setting in motion the correctives of deflation or inflation. It is significant that the Macmillan Report rejected any real possibility of 'controlled' devaluation, on the ground that once different groups of men in different countries started making autonomous decisions about the value at which their currencies should be fixed, there would be no hindrance to an accelerating spiral of depreciation as each nation sought to gain the advantage over the other. Thus the possibility of 'controlling' inflation once a country had abandoned the sheet anchor of the gold standard was discounted, for that 'anxiety' which would counter 'cumulative and persistent expenditure' with 'cumulative and persistent economy' would no longer operate.

That these arguments have not entirely lost their hold can be seen by the intense reluctance of major powers, even today, to contemplate devaluation, and their determination to exhaust almost every other resource before taking that step. Certainly hardly anyone in England in

[1] Macmillan Committee Evidence 1653.

1931 thought that the Government had any real choice in the matter.[1] It was one thing to be forced off the gold standard. But to leave voluntarily when resources still existed for defending it was regarded as unthinkable. There is no evidence that anyone in the Labour Government even raised the possibility of 'going off gold' in official discussion, although doubtless many members of the Cabinet wondered why it could not be done. Even Keynes was loyal to the 'established fact' of the gold standard almost till the end, although he probably thought the defence would require a tariff. Every official and unofficial memorandum the Government received from its advisers stressed the immense dangers — the dislocation of the world trading and financial system, uncontrollable inflation at home — which would result from any voluntary abandonment of the gold standard by Great Britain.[2]

If no solution to Britain's financial crisis could be sought in devaluation, it followed that the Government had to take measures to end the 'crisis of confidence' that had arisen. The May Report had focused attention on the budget deficit and this emerged as the main cause of the crisis of confidence. For an unbalanced Budget implied tolerance of inflation, or in other words a potential lack of loyalty to the fixed exchange parity. But we have also noted that the reason why the budget deficit figured so prominently in the crisis of confidence was the use made of the May Report by influential and respected opinion in this country. Broadly speaking, many prominent Conservatives and Liberals and the large majority of national newspapers used the May Report to bludgeon the Government into cutting down social services, especially unemployment insurance, which had been an opposition demand for over a year, and their exaggerated accounts of what would happen if the Government

[1] The main advocate of devaluation in the Labour Party was Ernest Bevin; and we shall consider the General Council's position below, pp. 367 ff. In his addendum to the Macmillan Report, signed with Sir Thomas Allen, he argued that if it proved impossible to initiate a credit expansion with Britain on the gold standard, then she should go off; and the Treasury and Bank should be considering 'an alternative basis in order to minimise disturbance if such a contingency should arise'. The point the defenders of the gold standard repeatedly made was that no alternative basis could be found, in the event of a voluntary depreciation, which would 'minimise' the disturbance.

[2] For Sir Henry Clay's memorandum to MacDonald on the effects of going off gold, see Appendix VI.

failed to act served to inflame the already exaggerated fears of the foreign holders of sterling.

In the days following the publication of the May Report, all the non-Labour national dailies made it clear that, in their opinion, the strain on sterling would only be eased when the Budget was balanced 'honestly', that is, not by the expedients that Snowden had produced in April, but on the lines suggested by the Report. 'The world is looking on and the world will judge' was the contribution of the *Daily Telegraph* on 10 August, typical of many. Banking comment stressed that the crisis was political, not financial, and could be solved only by the political authorities.[1] Sir Robert Horne, Lord Grey, Sir John Simon and Sir Donald Maclean were among those who made speeches stressing the immense danger which faced the country if the Government failed to take action.[2] Although this was ostensibly 'disinterested' comment, we do not have to look far for particular motives. The opposition press saw in the financial crisis a golden opportunity to bring to a successful conclusion their campaign against the existing unemployment insurance structure. They wanted to bring down the Government, even if they brought down the currency with it. The bankers too were quick to see the May Report as absolving them from any share of the blame for the financial crisis. Banking practice was perfectly sound: it was the Government's policy that was at fault. Finally, it is hard not to see in the speeches of Lord Grey and Sir John Simon the perpetuation of a private feud with Lloyd George and, in Simon's case, an attempt to rally dissident Liberals to his side.

The Labour Party was very slow to see the dynamite in the May Report. The Government had allowed it to be published without comment, and for twelve days gave no indication of its attitude to it. Meanwhile the Labour press saw the Report as a kind of bad joke, taking the line that no Labour Government would dare implement it; and if any of these commentators had their private doubts on this score

[1] See the comment of the 'distinguished banker' quoted in the *Manchester Guardian*, 7 August: 'If there is at present an emergency situation in Britain the relief must be found by political reforms. All the financial institutions of the country . . . are thoroughly sound. Any alarms there are should be met by a resolute effort to balance the Budget on the same lines as Australia, Brazil, etc., have been bidden to do by English preceptors these many years.'

[2] *The Times*, 8, 13 August; *Daily Telegraph*, 10 August.

their public comment was designed to make it impossible for the Labour Government to act.[1] Unfortunately this campaign developed at precisely the moment foreigners were anxiously looking for some sign that the Labour Government *would* balance the Budget. The Conservative and Liberal press were quick to argue that no remedy could be expected from a Labour Government,[2] which did not exactly allay foreign anxiety. The Labour press, striving to absolve the Government from any share of the blame for the financial crisis, made the tactical mistake of blaming it on the bankers and on 'panic' withdrawals by foreigners. As might have been expected the foreign press reacted by denying any such imputation and placing responsibility firmly with the Government. Thus *Le Temps* of 12 August said:

It is truly disquieting, in view of the gravity of the financial situation in England, to see responsible organs of opinion insisting on throwing onto other countries the responsibility for a crisis, the fundamental cause of which, as the May Report has established, is the bad administration of the finances. . . .

Thus foreigners got a retrospective justification for their July withdrawals and a justification for further withdrawals of funds if the 'bad administration' continued. As *Le Temps* stated on 4 August, the credits received by the Bank of England

[1] See *Daily Herald*, 1 August: 'Generally, the view was held that most of the Committee's recommendations were dead almost before they were born.' As late as 10 August, the *Daily Herald* was describing the May Report as a 'nine days wonder'. The *New Statesman* of 1 August thought that 'the one thing certain is that no Government, of any Party, will carry out' the May Report's proposals. E. F. Wise in the *New Leader* of 7 August thought it was 'almost unthinkable' that the Government 'can identify itself with a Report which reverses the . . . principles of the Labour movement'.

[2] e.g. *Manchester Guardian* of 1 August thought that the one thing certain was that the Labour movement would be utterly opposed to the May Report. The *Daily Telegraph* of the same day thought that there was nothing in the Government's attitude to the May Report to alleviate the fears of foreigners. *The Times* of 1 August thought that any Government that attempted real economy would be 'exposed to the attacks of a united Socialist Party'. In pursuance of these themes the opposition press carried rumours in the first ten days of August of government splits (*Daily Telegraph*, 7 August); on 2 August, MacDonald was denying that the Cabinet was split in its attitude to the report (*Daily Herald*, 3 August).

can in no way dispense the British Government and Parliament from putting an end to the disorder in their public finances, which will give rise, if it be allowed to continue, to a different kind of monetary peril, as serious as that resulting from the German crisis.

It is fruitless and probably impossible to disentangle the 'real' situation from what people believed to be the real situation: it was so because it was believed to be so. As Toynbee has observed:

. . . in the historical drama of 1931 . . . the psychological forces were the real actors on the stages, and . . . nations and states and Governments, bankers and politicians, commodities and currencies were their creatures, which moved under their impulsion like manipulated marionettes or like shadows thrown on a screen.[1]

And so what the *Daily Telegraph* said came to be true: the world looked on and prepared to judge.

V. THE ECONOMY COMMITTEE

August was holiday time and for a few days the financial crisis vanished from the headlines to make way for the gossip of the silly season. As Ramsay MacDonald, Prime Minister, left London for Lossiemouth, Jeannette MacDonald, Hollywood actress, arrived in the capital for the première of her new film, *The Midnight Lover*. Apart from a sudden drop in the sterling rate on 5 August, when apparently the Bank of England experimentally withdrew its support,[2] London ceased to lose gold and it was hoped that the credits would be sufficient to sustain the pound till the autumn.

The Cabinet economy committee, appointed to consider the May Report, was not due to meet till 25 August. Meanwhile its members would be supplied with detailed memoranda from all the leading departments to study at leisure, so that they could come to London with concrete suggestions.[3] On 5 August Snowden wrote to Samuel that the

[1] Toynbee, *Survey of International Affairs 1931–2*, p. 60.

[2] The Bank lost £4½m of gold in a single day, and immediately reversed its policy. (Clay, *Lord Norman*, p. 386.)

[3] In describing the meetings of the Cabinet economy committee and subsequently the full Cabinet I have relied heavily on the memoranda written by Graham and Greenwood immediately after the formation of the National

committee would not reach any conclusions till September.[1] MacDonald was quoted from Lossiemouth on 8 August saying he intended to return to London in about a fortnight's time, while as late as 10 August the *Daily Express* mentioned 24 August as the date on which the members of the committee were expected in London.

The Cabinet had dispersed without taking any decision, even on the principle of the May Report. No one except Keynes had suggested that the Budget should be left unbalanced. The criticism of the Labour press was entirely negative: it stated emphatically what the Labour movement could not accept, not what the Government ought to do. There was no General Council policy, though individual members might have their own ideas. Everyone waited to see what line the Government would take.

How did the Government see the political problem in the light of the May Report? As we have seen, there is good reason to suppose that MacDonald was planning to broaden his administration by including the Liberals. This was the long-term perspective. The immediate problem was how to carry economies in the social services which would not only be deeply unpopular in the Labour Party, but also widely resented in the country. In February Snowden had proposed all-party co-operation: now, just before Parliament broke up, he said that 'no Government . . . could take the full responsibility for . . . a reduction of expenditure of a drastic character'.[2] He later denied[3] that this was an invitation to the other Parties to join Labour in a coalition Government, but how could the Oppositions have been got to accept responsibility for Government policy unless they were part of the Government? In an interview with the *Daily Mail* on 10 August, MacDonald repeated that the whole House of Commons would have to take responsibility for carrying out economies. Both Chancellor and Prime Minister were clearly trying to get the Oppositions to share with the Government the electioneering risks of cutting the social services; perhaps they also felt that this was the only way of inducing the Labour Party to support

Government (Lansbury Papers), and I am indebted to the warden of Nuffield for permission to quote from Herbert Morrison's criticism of the first Greenwood draft.

[1] J. Bowle, *Viscount Samuel*, 1957, p. 267. [2] 255 H.C. Deb. c. 2512.

[3] *Autobiography*, ii, p. 932.

them. They could hardly have anticipated how popular this policy would turn out to be.

Nor indeed could the Oppositions, who were quite determined that the Government should take full responsibility. Neville Chamberlain wrote in his diary that 'to secure such a measure of relief, and *to do it through a Socialist government*, seems to me so important in the national interest that we must give it our support'[1] (italics mine). There was more to this remark than just electioneering: Chamberlain, like many others, thought that only if the Labour Party repudiated its past would foreigners really be convinced that the 'engines of extravagance' had been 'permanently reversed'. Nevertheless there were good enough electoral reasons for such a view; and the frequency with which opposition spokesmen stressed that the responsibility was Labour's and Labour's alone suggests that they were not blind to possible electoral advantage.[2] *Le Temps* of 12 August summed up as follows:

> It is common knowledge that Mr. MacDonald hopes to reorganise his Government on the basis of a coalition with the Conservatives and Liberals. It is hardly likely, though, that the Conservatives would allow such a political operation, which would have the effect of making the two opposition parties partners in the responsibilities which belong to the Labour government alone.

Seen in this perspective, national Government 'plotting' becomes less sinister, if somewhat unheroic. For if unpopular economies were necessary, as Snowden and probably MacDonald believed, it was at least prudent to attempt to share the risks. Equally it was in the interest of the opposition Parties to leave themselves a free hand.

The Government had made a grave psychological error in going on holiday without giving any indication of its attitude to the May Report or the question of balancing the Budget. Uncertainty is death to confidence, especially when it was reinforced by the suspicion that the Government would not be allowed by its own side to restore the public finances. There was a persistent exodus of short-term funds to the Continent. On 6 August Sir Ernest Harvey, the deputy governor,[3]

[1] Feiling, *The Life of Neville Chamberlain*, p. 191.

[2] e.g. Baldwin at Worcester, 1 August, had promised Conservative support in restoring the national finances but stressed that responsibility rested solely with the Government. (*The Times*, 3 August 1931.)

[3] Montagu Norman had collapsed from overwork on 29 July and was confined to his house till 16 August when he went on a cruise to restore his health.

The Sacrifice

Railway Director: '–Er–Gentlemen, as you already know, things–er–are not what they seem. We must–er–face the facts–ahem! and–er–do something big! As economy is imperative–er–and something is expected of us–er–I suggest that we sack the office boy!'

November 24th, 1930

The National Government

informed Snowden of the extent of the drain and added that foreigners expected an immediate readjustment in the budgetary position. The governor of the Bank of France said England was in the same position as France before Poincaré came in to balance the Budget in 1926. Walter Layton from Geneva reported the alarm of continental bankers: the stability of sterling was 'the one sheet anchor for Europe, and Britain the only country that could help Europe weather the storm; the British Government should borrow abroad and reassure its creditors by publishing at once a programme for dealing with the budgetary situation . . . '.[1] The same day, 6 August, leading British bankers addressed a memorandum to the Chancellor which stated that the crisis in the Budget and balance of payments had 'reached a point which, in our opinion, is threatening the depreciation of the currency with all its consequent evils'. The Government, they hinted, did not realise the extent to which foreign confidence had gone. Unless drastic economies were made at once, the credits would prove useless. 'What we have urged other nations to do', they concluded, 'we must now do ourselves, namely, restrict our expenditure, balance our budget, and improve our balance of trade.'[2] This was no longer the 'technical' crisis of July, but a real crisis of confidence. As Chamberlain was to write a little later: 'the cause of the trouble was not financial but political, and lay in the complete want of confidence in H.M.G. existing among foreigners . . . '.[3] At the same time the movement of funds had become too large to be handled by temporary inter-bank credits; the alternative was the negotiation of government credits, which 'raised explicitly the issue of Government financial policy, on which the lenders would expect to be assured . . . '.[4]

The bankers' warnings, together with a message from Snowden urging an immediate meeting of the Cabinet economy committee, reached MacDonald on Saturday, 8 August, and he left for London on Monday afternoon by overnight train, arriving at King's Cross on Tuesday morning. The *Daily Express* in a gossipy piece rumoured that Snowden was planning a conversion, but was otherwise firm on retrenchment, that Henderson, 'who voices the Trade Union point of view', was leading the opposition to any cuts in the social services and that the Prime

[1] Clay, *Lord Norman*, pp. 386–7. [2] Bowle, *Viscount Samuel*, pp. 268–9.
[3] Feiling, *The Life of Neville Chamberlain*, p. 191.
[4] Clay, *Lord Norman*, p. 387.

Minister seemed to be 'somewhat at sea about the whole affair'. With unusual prescience, the *Express* concluded that 'Sir George May . . . has fashioned a torpedo that may not only sink the Socialist Government, but may put party Government itself out of commission for a term'.[1]

Tuesday was spent in conference with Snowden, who had remained in London, and leading bankers,[2] who repeated that the crisis was political and could only be solved by political action. It was decided to hold the first meeting of the Cabinet economy committee at four o'clock the next day and MacDonald denied rumours of a Cabinet split. 'We are of one mind. We intend to balance the Budget.' This had a reassuring effect on the market.[3] Meanwhile, Baldwin, Chamberlain and Samuel,[4] apprised of the new turn in the situation by private informants in the Bank and City, were also on their way back to London. The *Daily Herald*, continuing its misreporting of the position, implied that MacDonald had returned to deal with the German crisis: the May Report it dismissed as a 'nine day wonder'. 'On every hand', it continued, 'there was an atmosphere of quiet assurance and a general feeling that Great Britain had weathered the storm.' The next day the editorial comment was: 'There can be little doubt that when the May Report is fully analysed and dissected it will be discovered that the picture is not nearly so black as painted'.

Although the sudden sagging of confidence had forced the Government to work out immediate measures, MacDonald did not abandon his hope for all-party co-operation. As the *Manchester Guardian* put it on 13 August, 'They (the Government) want in effect a preliminary three party agreement on an economy plan that can be presented in the House of Commons'. It went on to elucidate:

> The procedure to be followed appears to be this. The Cabinet Committee will formulate proposals of its own. The Liberals, through Sir Herbert Samuel, and the Conservatives, through Mr. Neville Chamberlain, will be invited to contribute suggestions. Over the week-end the Government will review the

[1] *Daily Express*, 11 August 1931.

[2] The Bank of England was represented in these discussions by Sir Ernest Harvey and Mr. Edward Peacock, one of the directors.

[3] *Daily Express*, 12 August 1931.

[4] Lloyd George underwent a prostate operation on 29 July which kept him out of active politics for the whole of the crisis.

pooled ideas, and, if the Opposition parties agree, a three-party conference will follow.

However, the *Manchester Guardian*'s comment that 'this is asking a great deal' was underlined by Lord Hailsham, Conservative leader in the Lords, who, on 12 August, told an *Evening News* reporter: 'I doubt whether it is our proper function to go any further than to offer the most sympathetic consideration to any scheme the Government may bring forward.' An editorial in the *Manchester Guardian* a day earlier stated that MacDonald would be far better employed in taking 'early steps to mobilise Labour opinion on his side'. It noted that the agendas of the Trades Union Congress and Labour Party conference 'show how far his own supporters are from the idea of co-operation between parties, or indeed from any policy of economy which touches insurance benefit or social services'.

When the Cabinet economy committee met on Wednesday, with Sir Warren Fisher from the Treasury in attendance, Snowden informed his colleagues, apparently to their surprise, that the May Report had *underestimated* the budget deficit by £50m. So much for the *Daily Herald* version. The Graham account states:

> No definite information was ever supplied as to the manner in which [the new estimate] was made up. Apparently, however, it took account of the loss due . . . under the Hoover moratorium plan, the serious decline in revenue compared with the estimates, due to a deepening industrial depression, and a larger call for transitional benefit and unemployment insurance. . . .[1]

The new figure of £170m included the full sinking fund provision. It meant that even if the full May Report economies of £97m were implemented, an additional £50m would have to be covered by taxation.

Before the economy committee was a paper from the Treasury with a list of economies amounting to approximately £90m. It was almost identical with the May list, except that the reduction in the standard rate of unemployment benefit was 10, not 20 per cent, and as an offset further economies were suggested in the defence estimates. After five hours of discussion that evening and the following morning the committee adjourned for the week-end, MacDonald returning to Lossiemouth. It met again on Monday and Tuesday of the following week. Meanwhile,

[1] Graham Memorandum, para. 4.

on Thursday morning and afternoon MacDonald and Snowden briefly explained the position to Samuel and the Conservative leaders, Baldwin and Chamberlain. In a press interview that night, Chamberlain said that the Government had put no concrete proposals before them, nor had they asked for any from them.[1]

'The one signal thing' which the Cabinet committee had achieved up to the week-end, in the *Manchester Guardian*'s opinion, was to

> have decided that the balancing of the Budget shall come through equality of sacrifice. . . . There must be no singling out of classes for penal sacrifices.

This decision, if applied with rigour, 'would take us right out of the restricted field of the May Report' and make possible a 'truly national effort' upon which the Government 'could bid for Liberal and Conservative support'.

In pursuing the theme of 'equality of sacrifice' Snowden and his Treasury officials were carefully examining the possibility of taxing all fixed-interest-bearing securities, government and industrial. The *Daily Herald* thought that this proposal was initially put up by the bankers who 'in signifying their approval of some form of abatement of interest on the War Loan. . . have borne in mind that on the same grounds a similar renunciation should be asked of the holders of other fixed-interest securities'. Conversion was 'ready at a moment's notice — envelopes have already been addressed to all holders of the 5 per cent War Loan'.[2] The proposal to tax the rentier was, of course, identical to that put forward in the minority report of the May Committee: the Government's guarantee to its own supporters that the sacrifice would be truly 'national' and not just fall on the poorest class. Bevin and Keynes had hinted at just such a 'national treaty' in their addendum to the Macmillan Report.[3] The prospect of winning support for such a policy was improved by the 'interesting discovery' that 'the Conservatives, though they preserve a free hand on any proposals the Government formulate, apparently accept the principle of equality of sacrifice and the corollary that the rentier cannot be exempt'. If this were so, then the Conservative leaders 'are taking risks with their

[1] *Manchester Guardian*, 14 August 1931; see also Bassett, *1931: Political Crisis*, pp. 66–7.

[2] *Daily Herald*, 13 August 1931.

[3] p. 200.

followers, not as great as the Government are prepared to take with theirs, but nevertheless risks not to be minimised'. The greater prospects of political reconciliation held out by the national treaty idea were expressed by the Liberal leader in the Lords, the Marquis of Reading:

> The economic position is sufficiently serious to require that party interests should be subordinated to the emergencies of the national situation. . . . A national Government would have many advantages, but there are difficulties, and if political exigencies make this impossible, then the only other course is by co-operation with the existing Government.[1]

But mere acceptance of equality of sacrifice furnished no guarantee of all-party agreement, only the prospect of hard bargaining, which, in fact, took place in the days preceding the break-up of the Government.[2] In getting the Labour movement on its side, the Government was greatly handicapped by the Treasury's eventual conclusion that a special tax on the rentier was administratively impracticable. This meant that Snowden, while being able to give full details of economies, was only able to promise taxation in general terms. As Citrine was to put it later:

> We were faced with the position either of accepting or rejecting the programme of cuts, and leaving to trust the operation of the principle of equality of sacrifice for other sections of the community.[3]

From the Graham memorandum it is possible to piece together what took place within the economy committee. MacDonald and Snowden told the others that very large economies were necessary; Henderson urged on the other hand that they should start with taxation 'in order finally to ascertain as low a total as was possible in attack upon the social services'. This course was rejected by the others. Henderson and possibly Graham then emphasised that they were not to be regarded as bound by anything that was agreed: 'they were merely engaged in a preliminary examination; after that examination there would be a report to the Cabinet, *not necessarily with specific recommendations*' (italics mine).

[1] *Manchester Guardian*, 15 August 1931.

[2] For example, the *Daily Telegraph*'s idea of 'equal sacrifice' was that the very poor should be obliged to pay taxes just as the rich did.

[3] Quoted in A. Bullock, *The Life and Times of Ernest Bevin* i, p. 483.

On the proposed 10 per cent reduction in unemployment benefit, Henderson and Graham said that the Labour Movement would never agree, so this proposal was deleted. 'The question of transitional benefit was never satisfactorily cleared up.' Both the May and Treasury Reports wanted to transfer transitional payments to the local authorities with a capitation fee from the Exchequer, the reduction to be effected by a stringent means test. 'There was agreement that some means test might be devised', but the matter was left in 'vague form'. The other proposals were considered, 'but no final decisions were reached or recommendations made'.[1]

On Monday and Tuesday MacDonald and Snowden reported their 'continuing conversations' with the bankers who had informed them that fresh credits were urgently needed, but would be conditional on balancing the Budget. The bankers considered a reduction in benefit to be indispensable. Henderson and Graham then asked to see the bankers, but Snowden objected on the grounds that 'these bankers were not accustomed to meeting politicians'. The possibilities of converting part of the war debt and of a revenue tariff were also discussed. Snowden promised to do what he could about the war debt, but the revenue tariff was defeated by four votes to one, with Thomas the sole supporter.[2] However, by four votes to one, this time with Snowden in the minority, the committee agreed that a revenue tariff was preferable to a cut in benefit. The memorandum is at pains to stress that no final decisions were taken, that the figures of economies 'changed from day to day and indeed from hour to hour, since there was never agreement as to what was definitely included or excluded', and that Henderson continued to stress that 'neither he nor anybody else was bound until the complete picture . . . was supplied'.

What was decided by the Cabinet economy committee? According to the Graham memorandum — nothing at all. MacDonald, Snowden and Thomas, on the other hand, felt that Henderson and Graham had backed down from proposals already agreed. Fortunately there is less difficulty in deciding this point than might be supposed, though of course it is difficult to estimate what 'mental reservations' were made during the discussions.

[1] Graham Memorandum, paras. 5–7.

[2] Ibid. para. 9.

We may start, first, with an inference that may be drawn from the time-table of the Cabinet committee's meetings. The full Cabinet was scheduled for eleven a.m. of Wednesday, 19 August. The sub-committee met at ten a.m. the previous day and, with a break for lunch, finished their work at six p.m. Commented the *Manchester Guardian*: 'It was hardly expected that the committee would rise so soon. Predictions had been made that they would sit until late tonight, and this early rising affords strong evidence that the committee have had no difficulty at all in reaching agreement.' Secondly, Bassett makes the obvious point that 'the committee certainly took one decision. They decided to submit a set of economy proposals to the Cabinet for the latter's consideration.'[1] But we may go further than that. Although the figures 'changed from hour to hour', there was obviously some point at which they stopped changing, since the sub-committee's proposal to the Cabinet contained detailed lists of economies (£78·5m) and precise figures for general taxation (£89m). Moreover the statement 'there was never agreement as to what was definitely included or excluded' is misleading to say the least. It was decided to exclude any proposal for a reduction in the standard rate or for a tariff — the controversial proposals. This was normal sub-committee procedure: to obtain as much agreement as possible and refer the remaining issues to the larger body.

The Graham memorandum stated that Henderson was 'waiting for the complete picture'. But what exactly were those parts of the picture which had not been completed? The memorandum states that the Chancellor never furnished precise details of how the revised estimate of the deficit was computed. Clearly this was not a point at issue since no Minister was in a position to challenge Treasury estimates of revenue, even though he might challenge particular accounting methods, such as including in the figures the borrowings for unemployment benefits or a sinking fund provision. Nor is there any evidence that Henderson or Graham ever raised this point. Perhaps, then, Henderson was waiting for fuller information about the new taxation? Yet, as the memorandum pointed out, the Chancellor 'quite properly' stated that the details of 'that side of the problem must be reserved for a Budget statement, strictly confidential in character until it was disclosed, with the application of the appropriate taxes, on the floor of the House of Commons'.

[1] Bassett, *1931: Political Crisis*, p. 70.

But Snowden certainly gave some information, as the memorandum records:

He mentioned in general terms that probably £62 millions would require to come from direct taxation, which was described as meaning an additional sixpence in the £ on income tax, the revision of surtax and death duties schemes, the withdrawal of certain tax concessions on the lower ranges of income and for the purpose of dealing with the *rentier* problem further differentiation against unearned income, which was explained as the only method by which, in the opinion of the Treasury, all sections of the *rentier* classes could be reached. . . . Only very general remarks were made regarding the new indirect taxation; but the Chancellor certainly stated that he could probably get a substantial yield by raising the duties of beer, tobacco, through a possible addition to the petrol tax, and probably by revision of the entertainments tax.[1]

Finally, Henderson and Graham may have felt justly aggrieved at not being allowed to meet the bankers — yet it is clear from the bankers' memorandum mentioned earlier that they would have received the same account as was retailed through MacDonald and Snowden. So as far as the economic and financial side was concerned, Henderson had as much of the full picture by 18 August as he was ever likely to have. What he was really waiting for was for Trade Union and Party reactions which would have become apparent when the Cabinet committee met the General Council and consultative committee on 20 August. This was the most important 'reservation' in the Foreign Secretary's mind.

vi. THE CABINET

From 19 August, the day of the full Cabinet meeting, the Greenwood memorandum takes over the story and opens extremely ambiguously:

The Cabinet was summoned for Wednesday, August 19th, when a foolscap sheet of figures dealing with possible methods of relieving the burden on the Unemployment Fund and of balancing the Budget was handed round. These particulars were put before the Cabinet as a basis for discussion. It was stated that the suggestions were purely tentative.

We are fortunate to have Herbert Morrison's marginal comments on the first draft of this memorandum, together with a letter to Arthur Green-

[1] Graham Memorandum, para. 10.

wood elucidating them. Commenting on the paragraph quoted above, Morrison writes:

> The document came, I think, from the sub-committee and I rather think the suggestions were a *little* more than tentative: e.g. the road and education economies were brought forward from the sub-committee rather emphatically.

Indeed the omission of any reference to the source of the 'foolscap sheet of figures' is an obvious falsification of the account, especially since it was headed: 'Committee on the Report of the Committee on National Expenditure'. Greenwood's account continues:

> As a result of the discussion which took place, though no general decision was arrived at, particular items relating to Unemployment Insurance were provisionally accepted and it was agreed that it was impracticable[1] to place even the partial maintenance of unemployed workers not in receipt of statutory benefit on the Poor Law, through the Public Assistance Authorities.

All the other economies were agreed fairly quickly, with the sub-committee insisting on the road and education economies 'rather emphatically'. The cut of 10 per cent in the standard rate had not been forwarded from the sub-committee and therefore did not come up, but when it was found that the economies which the Cabinet were prepared to agree were £20m short of the sub-committee's recommendation because of the deletion of the transitional savings, Henderson or Graham raised the possibility of a 10 per cent revenue tariff on manufactured goods as an alternative. Graham calculated that this would bring in about £25m. On a vote, fifteen members supported the idea and five — Snowden, Wedgwood Benn, Parmoor, Alexander and Passfield — opposed. As Snowden regarded this as an issue of principle, it was agreed to shelve the proposal and to set up a sub-committee of Greenwood, Graham, Johnston and Miss Bondfield to consider what to do about transitional benefit. Two further matters are mentioned in the Greenwood account. Thomas said that 'if the Government could not carry out a programme on lines similar to that put forward as a basis for discussion, we should be bound to support any Government which did'. This view, Greenwood remarks, 'did not receive general support'. Finally MacDonald 'adumbrated the possibility of a national Government'. We should very much like to know what form his adumbration

[1] Morrison's amendment for 'impracticable' is 'undesirable'.

took and how Ministers reacted to it, but there is nothing more. The Cabinet adjourned at 10.25 p.m., having sat nine hours.

From 10 August onwards the hidden hand of the trade unions becomes increasingly discernible. Why is it that the *Daily Herald*, which was in a better position to know the true facts than almost any other national newspaper, consistently got them wrong? We have seen that it misreported the real reason for MacDonald's return to London and consistently sought to minimise the crisis. On 19 August it reported that the Cabinet had before it proposals for (i) a 10 per cent revenue tariff, (ii) a temporary suspension of the sinking fund, (iii) a special tax on fixed-interest-bearing securities, (iv) an increased contribution to unemployment insurance 'with or without reductions of benefit' and (v) a conversion of the war loan. Four of these items were not in fact included in the proposals emanating from the sub-committee, and as to the other there was no proposal at this stage to reduce the standard rate of benefit. But the four unofficial proposals *were* identical to those put forward by the General Council a day later, and the *Manchester Guardian* of 20 August commented on the *Daily Herald* account:

> But there is still more reason to suspect that what we are hearing today about a revenue tariff is really propaganda from the industrial side of the movement. from men like Mr. Ernest Bevin . . . [who] are advancing the revenue tariff as an alternative and much more acceptable method of finding money.

The length of Wednesday's Cabinet sitting and hints of a split over the tariff suggested disagreements which *The Times* of 20 August found 'disturbing'. Meanwhile exhortations to the Government from the Tory press came fast and furious. On 13 August the *Daily Telegraph* had invoked Lecky's 'golden sentence':

> Nations seldom realise till too late, how prominent a place a sound system of finance holds among the vital elements of national stability and well-being; how few political changes are worth purchasing by its sacrifice; how widely and seriously human happiness is affected by the downfall or perturbation of national credit, or by excessive, injudicious and unjust taxation.

On 14 August it quoted Burke; by the seventeenth it had moved on to Gladstone. On 21 August it was ponderously hammering the same point home:

> What is at issue? It is not just the balancing of a Budget, highly important though that is. It is, to put it bluntly, the restoration of British credit in the

eyes of the world. This will not be done by any spectacular feat of clever balancing or by ingenious manipulations on either or both sides of the account. There is only one thing that will impress the people who know in this country and abroad, and that is a sight of an axe honestly laid at the upas-tree of colossal expenditure[1]. . . . New taxes are no substitute for a lessened burden. Even a revenue tariff . . . is no substitute. . . . Unemployment benefit is the crux . . . of the whole remedial plan, as it has been the culminating cause of the present emergency.

The Times was more prone to what Orwell has called the 'dying metaphor'. It wrote urgently on 12 August: 'Every hour which passes without some check upon the flood of national expenditure . . . adds fresh difficulties to the task confronting the Chancellor of the Exchequer. . . .' Turning from the general to the particular it gave the following sad example:

Only yesterday a trivial straw showed that the wind of extravagance was still blowing with gale force. It was announced that the Board of Education had approved the capital expenditure of £40 by the Holland Education Committee in order to make it more convenient for one solitary schoolboy to attend a council school.

By the seventeenth *The Times* was stating that 'unless immediate steps are taken to remedy the situation, the stability of the whole financial position of the country will be seriously imperilled' with 'depreciation of the currency and all the manifold evils which this would entail'. On 19 August it complained that 'the simple truth is that industry has already been sacrificed far too recklessly on the altar of the social services'. Next day it intoned:

There is no excuse for putting the cart of taxation before the horse of retrenchment. . . . Drastic economy alone will suffice, because drastic economy alone can give irresistible proof that the engines of extravagance have been reversed.

Unfortunately this was exactly the language Britain's foreign creditors and British holders of sterling wished to hear and they expected the Government to give immediate effect to the sentiments expressed by it. What was the alternative? Henderson 'waiting for the complete picture' provided none. The only concrete choice put before the Cabinet had been between cuts in unemployment pay and a revenue tariff and

[1] Upas tree: Javanese tree yielding milky sap used as arrow poison and held fatal to whatever came beneath its branches. (*Concise Oxford Dictionary*.)

Snowden had decisively rejected the latter, his argument being that it was more honest to have a straightforward cut in the standard of life than to proceed by the indirect route of raising the cost of living.[1] Snowden's position as Chancellor made him master of the Government's fate. MacDonald would have been happy to compromise on a tariff in order to hold the Cabinet together, even if this meant forfeiting Liberal support. He could not, however, afford the resignation of his Chancellor. Inexorably the Cabinet were being driven to curtailing unemployment benefit in some way or other as part of the 'national treaty'. However, alternative suggestions were not long in coming.

Thursday, 21 August marked the turning point in the political crisis. In the morning MacDonald and Snowden put the Cabinet's provisional economy plan to the Conservative and Liberal leaders and they rejected it as inadequate; in the afternoon they put the plan to members of the General Council who rejected it for the opposite reason.

The Cabinet had agreed that MacDonald and Snowden should meet the opposition leaders, and the 'three-party conference' which had been mooted so many times in the previous few days met at ten o'clock. Sir Herbert Samuel and Sir Donald Maclean represented the Liberals, Neville Chamberlain and Sir Samuel Hoare the Conservatives, Baldwin by this time being back in Aix. J. H. Thomas was also present. Accounts of what took place are confused. Samuel says that both Conservative and Liberal leaders, having heard the plans, 'agreed to recommend our Parties to support them'.[2] This is followed by Mowat.[3] On the other hand Chamberlain

> stressed two points; first, that in view of the increased estimate of deficit, to produce economies less than the aggregate recommended by May was wrong, and second, that if unemployment benefit were left untouched, the contemplated economies . . . would certainly be jeopardised. . . .[4]

It is not possible to get a consistent story from these accounts, but the likeliest supposition is that MacDonald and Snowden mentioned two sets of figures — the £78m recommended by the economy committee and the £56m provisionally agreed by the Cabinet — and that the

[1] See Bassett, *1931: Political Crisis*, p. 82.
[2] Viscount Samuel, *Memoirs*, p. 203.
[3] Mowat, *Britan Between the Wars*, p. 388.
[4] Feiling, *The Life of Neville Chamberlain*, p. 192.

opposition leaders accepted the first and rejected the second. Chamberlain's remark about unemployment benefit could scarcely have referred to the £78m, since of this £43m was to be saved out of unemployment benefit. Mowat's argument that MacDonald and Snowden compromised the Cabinet's position by mentioning the higher figure ignores the fact that they were trying for an agreed solution. This naturally required bargaining: hence some exposure of the Government's plans was inevitable.[1]

vii. THE GENERAL COUNCIL TAKES A HAND

The two men who more than anyone determined the outcome of the negotiations with the General Council were Arthur Henderson and Ernest Bevin. There is little doubt that MacDonald was relying on Henderson to swing the unions behind the Government. Either he did not take his 'mental reservations' seriously, or they were less obvious at the time than later. There was not the slightest rumour in the press of any dissension within the economy committee itself, or any hint that Henderson was anything but solidly behind the proposals of his colleagues: there was no repetition of the *Daily Express* story earlier in August that he was 'leading the opposition' to the cuts. Thus the outcome of the discussions with the General Council was at first viewed with some optimism. The *Manchester Guardian* of 18 August recognised that 'the reception of the Government's plans by the General Council of the Trades Union Congress and the Labour Executive on Thursday is going to matter more than anything else this week'. Conservative and Liberal support was assured and 'opinion, if not so unanimous, inclines strongly to the view that the T.U.C. and the Labour executive will accept [the proposals] too'.

[1] Bassett counters Mowat's criticism of MacDonald for mentioning £78m with the argument that the £56m represented an 'adjourned position'. 'It was surely legitimate, and even desirable, that the Government representatives should refrain from disclosing the precise state of the Cabinet's unfinished deliberations' (p. 86). He does not appear to realise that exactly the same argument applies to the £78m, which was equally part of the 'unfinished deliberations'. Both arguments, as is suggested above, are equally 'academic'; the Labour leaders were negotiating with the Oppositions for an agreed solution.

The crucial point, especially for the T.U.C., will be the cuts on unemployment. They will not be palatable, but neither would the overthrow of the Government be palatable, particularly as there is no guarantee that an election would follow. . . . Both Mr. MacDonald and Mr. Henderson will attend [the meeting] and *expound and defend* the Government's plans. [italics mine.]

By 19 August there was a less confident tone. The *Manchester Guardian*'s labour correspondent reported an 'extraordinarily strong' feeling in the General Council that 'whatever the consequences, a cutting down of benefit must be opposed. . . . Some members quite frankly fear that the Government will not be able to achieve its aim of balancing the Budget without splitting the Labour movement. . . .' In these circumstances 'the Cabinet committee are quite rightly going to [the meeting] prepared to exert, if need be, their full collective authority and influence'. But the *Guardian* was still confident that 'a falling pound and a Conservative Government are not ends that Labour . . . can possibly will'. By 20 August initial optimism had almost evaporated. The original calculation was that the Government plan would 'have a quick passage' through the T.U.C., the Labour Party and the Oppositions. 'But it hardly looks tonight as though it was going to be quite so simple a business as that.'

The most important public hints that the Government would not find it easy to persuade the General Council came from the *Daily Herald* whose editorial policy was controlled by the unions. From 19 August the *Herald* started to give prominence to what subsequently came to be recognised as the distinctive 'union view' on the economic crisis. We have seen how it interpreted the financial crisis, insofar as it accepted that there was a financial crisis, as a crisis of confidence in British banking, not in government policy. From this it followed that there was no need for the Government to give serious thought to the May proposals: and on 19 August it suggested, in fact, that the Cabinet were considering quite different possibilities. On 20 August under the misleading headline 'Cabinet Budget Plan Completed' it wrote, 'No reduction to be made in Unemployment Pay', and to underline the point said in an editorial:

In no circumstances will the Trade Union Movement agree to a reduction of unemployment benefit. . . .

We have seen too how the *Daily Herald* virtually placed the question of a revenue tariff on the Cabinet's agenda for Wednesday's meeting. All these attitudes betray unmistakably the guiding intelligence of Ernest Bevin.

Ernest Bevin had by this time emerged as the dominant personality in the trade union movement, with an intelligence and breadth of vision far beyond those of his colleagues, with the possible exception of the general secretary, Walter Citrine, with whom he worked closely. His economic education had been considerably extended by his membership of four bodies — the Mond–Turner group, the Macmillan Committee, the E.A.C., and the trade union economic committee, started in 1929 after suggestions that the General Council was ignorant of wider economic issues. The experience and knowledge he gained through these bodies gave him an essential background for creative economic policy making, and the necessary assurance to challenge Snowden's recipe for economic recovery.

His view of money as a means of exchange, a device to meet the needs of industry and trade, to enable men to manufacture, buy and sell goods, was unexceptionable, but he concluded from this that the international money market was a system of collective usury, 'a word he frequently used with the full Aristotelian flavour'.[1] From this it was not hard to conclude that the financial crisis

> has arisen as the result of the manipulation of finance by the City, borrowing money from abroad on . . . 'short-term' . . . and lending it on long-term. . . . As is usual, the financiers have rushed to the Government . . . attributing the blame for the trouble to the social policy of the country and to the fact that the budget is not balanced.[2]

This in itself should make the Government wary of accepting the bankers' advice, but quite apart from that Bevin had come to believe that the existing currency system based on gold was bound to break down; hence the bankers' policy 'which aimed at restoring the free working of the system' offered no remedy.

Bevin's own remedy, which he expounded in the summer of 1930 and in his addendum to the Macmillan Report, assumed that the old nineteenth-century laissez-faire system was gone for good. Instead the aim should be to create a regional grouping based on the Empire

[1] Bullock, *The Life and Times of Ernest Bevin*, p. 427.

[2] Report to the Executive of the T. & G.W.U. (ibid. p. 480).

in which there would be a rough balance between supplies of raw materials and foodstuffs on the one hand and manufactured goods on the other, a group of nations practising Free Trade between themselves, but putting up tariffs, if necessary, against outsiders, a group as self-contained as possible but with sufficient bargaining power to exchange products with other nations on fair terms.[1]

At home the plight of the great export industries offered a magnificent opportunity for extending Government control:

> He was prepared to agree to a protective tariff, but only on condition of the thorough reorganisation of the industries to be protected, not as a substitute for reorganisation, behind which inefficient industries could find protection from the need to put their house in order.[2]

Since such a programme could not be carried out with the existing gold standard, Bevin advocated devaluation and urged the Government, in his addendum to the Macmillan Report, to consider 'an alternative basis' for the economy.[3]

Such measures would, in Bevin's view, resolve the 'fundamental paradox' of a Labour Government trying to save a capitalist system from the difficulties which the Labour movement itself had created. Thus his opposition to the policy which the bankers were trying to foist on to the Government stemmed not only from the sectional interest of his own union members, but also from a long-term view of future development.

Bevin's vision of socialism was much more like Mosley's vision of capitalist *dirigisme* than like the traditional socialism of MacDonald and the Fabians. The basis of his view, as of Mosley's, was an immense distrust of 'international finance', which he was convinced was soaking industry for its own profit.[4] (This ignored the view that the London money market provided a necessary support for Britain's trade.) But what relevance had his measures to the immediate crisis? In a sense, of course, the crisis was a banker's crisis, inasmuch as it was a crisis of the international financial system which London upheld. But it was wrong to explain it in terms of the bankers' recklessness in borrowing short to lend long. Rather it was the inevitable result of

[1] Bullock, *The Life and Times of Ernest Bevin*, i, p. 441.

[2] Ibid. p. 445. [3] *Macmillan Report*, p. 240.

[4] Unfortunately, the two could never work together, Bevin regarding Mosley as an unreliable 'intellectual'.

London being forced between 1929 and 1931, almost alone, to finance the world depression. In order to realise the perspectives of the Norman Plan and the Macmillan Report, she was being called upon to make one supreme effort to save the currency. In this sense the alternative to Bevin's policy was not a restoration of the 'free working of the system' but of concerted international action to raise world prices. On the long-term policy, therefore, the issue was not quite as one-sided as Bevin presented it and the vast majority of expert opinion was against him. On the immediate issue, Bevin's policy of putting up a revenue tariff, suspending the sinking fund, taxing the fixed-interest rentier, and converting part of the War Loan was not designed to save the pound or balance the Budget but to inaugurate the new economic plan. As such it had no chance of passing the Commons and would have meant the resignation of the Government, before or after Britain had been forced off the gold standard. Nevertheless his policy did have this to recommend it: it would have enabled the Government to resign on a positive alternative to the banking and treasury view.

The question at three p.m. on the afternoon of Thursday, 20 August was: how far did the General Council endorse Bevin's view and how far were they open to persuasion? The answer to the latter part of the question depended very largely on Arthur Henderson. Earlier in the day — at about eleven thirty — he had, in the Premier's absence with the opposition leaders, explained the economy committee's plans to seven members of the Labour Party's consultative committee who gave it short shrift.[1] At three o'clock he and four other members of the Cabinet committee went to Transport House for the joint meeting with the General Council and the N.E.C. Snowden came with the greatest reluctance; he did not believe that the T.U.C. had any right to be consulted on Cabinet policy.[2]

MacDonald 'led off with what purported to be a review of the financial position . . . '.[3] He said the May Report had created panic about Britain's credit stability. The tremendous cost of dealing with unemployment 'was disturbing the minds of people outside the country'. If the salaries of public servants, teachers, policemen, etc., were to be reduced on cost of

[1] Bassett, *1931: Political Crisis*, p. 88. Chuter Ede reported that the programme would only receive the support of the lawyers in the party.

[2] Ibid. p. 73.

[3] Citrine, *Men and Work*, p. 281.

living grounds, the other Parties would regard that as an 'effective argument' for reducing unemployment benefit. That did not indicate the mind of the Cabinet, just what had been put before them by others. They were trying to meet the crisis by a combination of economy and taxation based on the principle of 'equal sacrifice'. He concluded:

> There is no change of policy. If anything has to be suspended it will be restored as soon as the Government is in a position to restore it. There is no abandoning of principles, only bowing to necessities. Everyone responsible for a department is a Trade Unionist, or a Socialist, or both, and the meeting can trust us.

Citrine said he was extremely dissatisfied with what the Prime Minister had told them. He had revealed no more than they could have found out from the press. Consultation was only possible 'if the Council was placed unreservedly in possession of information on which the Cabinet was to make its decision'. Until they were given this information they would express no opinion. But silence must not be taken as an indication of support.

Snowden then attempted to fill the mental vacuum left by MacDonald's statement with more precise figures. He said the deficit was very much more than £120m, and could not be met by taxation alone. They proposed to increase unemployment contributions by £15m and limit payments to twenty-six weeks, but there were no proposals for reducing benefit. He then described the rest of the economies. In reply to a question about whether the bankers' proposals were conditional, he said: 'The only part the bankers had played was to represent to them the seriousness of the international financial position.' Henderson remained silent throughout.

The General Council then retired to consider the position in the light of the two statements. 'Not one of the members . . . spoke in favour of the Cabinet's proposals.'[1] They rejected any 'worsening of the position of unemployed workers'; rejected salary cuts for teachers, policemen and military personnel, and the slashing of U.G.C. grants — 'the Council were of the opinion that such reductions, by lessening the only organised public works schemes which existed for the unemployed, would aggravate the position'. Instead they proposed to tax fixed-interest yields, convert part of the war debt and suspend the sinking fund. There was no decision about a revenue tariff and it was decided to refer the

[1] Citrine, *Men and Work*, p. 284.

matter to the T.U.C. Citrine says they also discussed 'a graduated levy upon all sections of the community in proportion to ability to pay,'[1] on the lines of the 'national treaty': presumably Snowden would have argued that this was being achieved by the Government's proposals. In any case it was inconsistent with the stipulation that there should be no 'worsening' in the position of the unemployed. Alan Pugh, who had signed the minority report of the May Committee, thought the salary cuts were justified.[2]

Greenwood carries on the story:

> The Cabinet met on Thursday evening at eight thirty and received reports of the day's meetings. They also received a report of the Sub-Committee on Unemployment Insurance which stated that even if further adjustments to save the financial situation were made, a considerable sum (£19½m) would still remain to be found.
>
> The Cabinet rose at nine thirty p.m. to enable the Prime Minister and others to meet representatives of the General Council of the T.U.C.

The deputation had in fact been kept waiting for an hour while the Cabinet sat. The General Council were represented by the chairman, Arthur Hayday, Citrine, Bevin, Pugh and Walkden, with Milne-Bailey and J. L. Smyth in attendance: on the other side were the Cabinet economy committee.

Citrine stated that 'after long and serious consideration' the General Council 'must record their opposition to the proposals relating to the worsening of unemployment benefit'. These proposals, it must be remembered, did not include any cut in the 'standard rate'. It was later stated that the Cabinet had never agreed to any 'cuts' in unemployment pay: in fact, as Morrison pointed out in his letter to Greenwood, both the special levy and the transitional arrangements provisionally approved by the Cabinet on Wednesday 'did involve at any rate the possibility of reduction . . . '. On the question of roads and the U.G.C. the Council felt it was *absolutely necessary* to expend large sums in carrying out these works and could not agree to any suggestions for drastic cuts. To accept

[1] *Men and Work*, p. 284.

[2] Meanwhile the national executive had met separately, but not with MacDonald who was a member. Henderson explained that no cuts were contemplated in unemployment benefits, and on this understanding the N.E.C. decided to leave the matter in the hands of the Cabinet. (For a more detailed account see Bassett, op. cit., pp. 94–6.)

wages cuts for teachers, policemen, etc., 'would be the signal for a wage cutting campaign in trades and industry generally'. Citrine then outlined the General Council's alternative programme of taxing fixed-interest securities, and suspending the sinking fund. They could not give their opinion on a revenue tariff as this was a matter for Congress. There was no mention of the graduated levy. Bevin added that the Council opposed the pay cuts in themselves, but resented even more the suggestion that the pay of these classes should come down without utilising the ordinary negotiating machinery. He emphasised that the Government's policy meant a continuation of the deflation to which the General Council were unalterably opposed. Snowden then asked whether the General Council were opposed to all the economies proposed that afternoon, to which the union leaders made the facetious reply that Cabinet Ministers' salaries had not been mentioned as yet.

Snowden, despite some provocation, replied that the General Council's position was 'quite comprehensible' and in normal times the Government would fully agree with their view. But he emphasised that if sterling went, the whole international financial structure would collapse and 'there would be no comparison between the present depression and the chaos and ruin that would face us in that event. There would be millions more unemployed and complete industrial collapse.' Bevin objected, but Snowden brushed this aside. The weight of debt, he went on, had been exaggerated. If the unions were so keen to tax the rentier why shouldn't the same cost of living argument be applied to teachers, etc? Bevin retorted that there was no analogy between the two: the value of the services rendered by teachers and policemen was very different from that of those performed by rentiers. Snowden then said that as far as the sinking fund was concerned 'certain obligations must be borne in mind'. About the revenue tariff 'he would not say anything at all'.

MacDonald then remarked, somewhat desperately, that nothing the General Council had said had been of the slightest help in the actual situation they had to face and Thomas asked Citrine what he would actually do in the 'desperate situation'? Citrine did not think the situation was that desperate. 'There were enormous resources in the country.' On this note the meeting broke up at ten thirty p.m. Henderson had not said a word, 'but no man present was more impressed by what he had heard'.[1] The complete picture was beginning to take shape.

The day had been one of almost complete disaster for the Government. They had failed the most crucial test of all, that of winning over the General Council. The two positions were apparently hopelessly at variance.

The Government had desperately mishandled their case. MacDonald's statement to the joint meeting had been so vague as to be almost useless. The empty melodious phrases were not enough: something tougher, more challenging, more concrete, was required. His listeners wanted to hear about the origins of the crisis, the true financial position, the political alternatives, the economic context, the electoral implications. It is doubtful whether MacDonald at his best could have convinced them; MacDonald at his worst stood no chance. In fairness to him, he was by that time physically and mentally exhausted. When the trade union obstacle came to be faced, he no longer had the reserves of leadership for a supreme effort. Snowden was, if anything, even worse, scarcely concealing the contempt he felt for these people who, as he saw it, were interfering with his plans, diverting him from the job in hand. He was negative and uncompromising, especially at the evening meeting. He, too, might have made concessions on the sinking fund and on the revenue tariff, as indeed he was obliged to do later on in the National Government; the trade union leaders might then have been willing to consider reductions in unemployment benefit as part of a 'graduated levy' which was, in fact, only a pretentious omnibus phrase covering economies and taxation. Instead his own intransigence brought out the intransigence of Citrine and Bevin. Finally, in the two crucial confrontations with the union leaders, Henderson said nothing. Was he waiting to see how MacDonald's appeal was received? Was he expecting Snowden to unbend? We shall never know: he sat silent and watched the Labour Party tear itself to pieces.

viii. THE LAST PHASE

The tragedy could not much longer be postponed. MacDonald had left the joint meeting in 'furious despair' and, after the trade union leaders

[1] Bullock, *The Life and Times of Ernest Bevin*, i, p. 484.

went that night, was close to collapse. A good night's rest, however, found him in a different mood. Sir Harold Nicolson suggests:

The refusal of the T.U.C. to move one inch to ease his difficulties, their overt attempt to dictate terms to an elected Government, outraged his political conscience, aroused his personal vindictiveness, and steeled his resolve.[1]

The Cabinet agreed that no Government worthy of the name could submit to dictation by an outside body: 'The General Council are pigs', Passfield told his wife,[2] and the *Manchester Guardian* of 22 August found it

a sad commentary on the machinery of democratic government that it should be possible for a body of thirty men, meeting with no preparation and discussing half-revealed proposals in a desultory fashion for several hours, to jeopardise the existence of a government.

However, the Cabinet was not prepared to go beyond the provisional figures agreed on Wednesday.

There was a discussion on rates of Unemployment Benefit but as a substantial minority was against an alteration, the question was dropped and other proposals considered relating to Unemployment Insurance. During later stages of the discussion reference was made to the raising of revenue, and to the sinking fund. The question of the Revenue Tariff was no longer pressed.

The £56m of economies thus became the Cabinet's agreed plan. Henderson was later to claim that it was accepted only if 'we carried our own people with us',[3] in other words that he was still waiting for the 'complete picture', but Morrison comments:

In making the statement . . . recording the position of the F[oreign] S[ecretary] it should be remembered that the modified programme conveyed to the Opposition Leaders was pretty definitely approved as one which we would be ready, given support, to go forward on.

Of course, the words 'given support' are ambiguous, but there can be little doubt that in the context, and given the Cabinet's reaction to the General Council's stand, they meant the support of the opposition Parties.

[1] Sir Harold Nicolson, *King George V: His Life and Reign*, p. 458.

[2] B. Webb Diaries, 22 August 1931.

[3] Bassett, *1931: Political Crisis*, p. 104.

That support was not forthcoming. At five o'clock that Friday, 21 August, MacDonald and Snowden saw the opposition leaders, Chamberlain, Hoare, Samuel and Maclean, who retired briefly to consider the Government's proposals but returned to make it clear that the economies were quite inadequate. The Conservatives at this point were insisting that economies must be the major balancing item, while the Labour plan left about 70 per cent of the deficit to be raised by taxation. As Hoare put it:

The general view of the Conservative delegates is economy first, the dominant part of the whole problem. . . . The crisis has arisen in our view from excessive expenditure, and therefore the first and foremost way of meeting it must be by a reduction of expenditure. New taxation, and additional forms of taxation, must take a secondary role.[1]

Maclean told the Prime Minister: 'You cannot divide the Conservatives and Liberals now.' This news again plunged MacDonald into deep gloom. Viscount Templewood (Sir Samuel Hoare) recalls that:

after the last meeting, he [MacDonald] asked Chamberlain and me to talk to him alone in his upstairs sitting-room. It was late in the evening, and the room was almost dark when, for many minutes, he soliloquised to us about his own troubles and the country's need for an all-party effort. His words, like the atmosphere, were obscure, but the conclusion that Chamberlain and I drew from them was the same. He had decided to resign, and to advise the King to send for the party leaders for consultation as to the next step.[2]

By the morning MacDonald's mood had changed once more.

The Cabinet were faced by the P.M. with the alternatives of a 10 % cut in unemployment benefit or the probability of a moratorium. A vote was taken as to whether the P.M. should approach the party leaders with proposals for a 10 % cut plus £7 millions other economies. It was agreed that the party leaders should be seen.

This account needs some elucidation. Herbert Morrison's commentary is as follows:

The word 'indication' should be substituted for 'vote'. . . . Indications were taken on 5 per cent as well as a 10 per cent reduction and this is not referred to in your document.

There is some confusion concerning the new total of economies implied by this acceptance. Snowden says that the additions came to £20m,

[1] *Manchester Guardian*, 21 August 1931.

[2] Templewood, *Nine Troubled Years*, pp. 17–18.

making a new total of £76m.[1] Nicolson, following Snowden, mentions £76m.[2] Samuel, however, on 14 September said that MacDonald and Snowden only mentioned a 10 per cent cut in unemployment benefit, then estimated at £12½m, which would have brought the total of economies to £68½m.[3] This was in fact almost identical to the total eventually imposed by the National Government. The opposition leaders considered the new figure of £68½m 'might be . . . adequate'.[4] Had the Cabinet agreed, the political crisis would have been over. But the Cabinet stipulated that 'it was to be an enquiry only. . . . The Cabinet as a whole remained uncommitted'.

It will be convenient at this point to summarise the various schemes of economies considered and to compare them with the National Government's Economy Bill (see opposite page).

The Prime Minister's reference to a 'moratorium' suggested that the financial situation had acquired a new urgency. On 13 August the Treasury had asked the Bank of England to sound New York as to the possibility of a credit direct to the British Government since, as Clay records, 'the movement of funds was now too large to be handled by temporary inter-Central Bank credits'.[5] Harrison, the governor of the New York Federal Reserve Bank, had replied that the British Government should raise £50m each in New York and Paris 'and that such a loan would be practicable in America, provided the programme of economy was adequate and received the approval of Parliament'.[6] There was nothing improper about this condition; the question of a government loan raised explicitly the issue of government policy. The Bank of England itself regarded its relationship with the Government as that 'between an ordinary bank and its client', and foreign bankers were likely to take this view even more emphatically. Perhaps this should not have been so; but this was the context in which the system of finance, built up by England itself, operated. A week later — on 21 August — the question of a loan became urgent, and Harrison advised the Treasury to get in touch with the Bank's New York agents, J. P. Morgan & Co. 'It had become', the Prime Minister was later to say, 'a question of

[1] *An Autobiography*, ii, p. 946.
[2] Nicolson, *King George V: His Life and Reign*, p. 459.
[3] 256 H.C. Deb. c. 550.
[4] Ibid. c. 550–1.
[5] See above, p. 355.
[6] Clay, *Lord Norman*, p. 390.

	May Report	Cabinet Committee	Cabinet Wed. 19 August	Cabinet 'negotiations' scheme Sat. 22 August	National Government
	£m	£m	£m	£m	£m
Deficit	120	170	170	170	170
Taxation	24	89	89	89	82
Sinking Fund	—	—	—	—	20
Economies					
(1) Unemployment Insurance					
Reduction standard rate	15	—	—	12	13
Increased weekly contributions	10	10	10	10	10
Extension of scheme	5	—	—	—	—
Anomalies	6	3	3	3	3
Limitation to 26 weeks[1]	8	8	—	—	—
Special levy of 2d.	—	2·5	4	4	—
Transitional saving	23	20	5	5	10
Total	67	43·5	22	34	36
(2) Education	14	11·5	11·5	11·5	10
(3) Fighting Services	2	9	9	9	8
(4) Roads	8	8	8	8	8
(5) Health	1	2	2	2	2
(6) Police	1	0·5	0·5	0·5	0·5
(7) Others	4	4	4	4	5·5
Total	30	34·5	34·5	34·5	34
Overall Total	97	78·5	57	68·5	70

[1] This was part of the National Government's scheme, but was included under transitional savings.

hours.'[1] The revelation of trade union intervention had completely offset the reassuring news of the Government's intention to balance the Budget, and the rate of withdrawals had suddenly increased. Hence the Prime Minister's urgent demand for a decision on the Saturday morning of 22 August. With the Cabinet's agreement to £68m of economies as a 'bargaining counter', Harrison was again approached with the new figure and replied 'that if the programme was approved *by all three Parties* it would be possible to raise a loan', but again referred the Government to

[1] Lothian wrote to Garvin, 21 August 1931, that the pound would be liable to go on Monday unless drastic action was taken over the week-end (Lothian Papers, Box 193).

Morgans. The latter had cabled the previous day that an all-party proposal should suffice to secure a credit.[1] Thus when the Oppositions agreed on Saturday morning that £68m might be adequate, MacDonald's task was to get the Cabinet to finalise the figure agreed with the Opposition. Then a three-party statement could be issued, preparatory to raising the credits in New York and Paris.

The Greenwood memorandum continues:

> When the Cabinet met in the afternoon, the P.M. reported that the oppositions would probably agree to this [the new figure]. It was then suggested that these proposals should be placed before the Bankers. Though there was a division of opinion on this it was decided to take this step. The Cabinet was not, however, to be committed to the 10 % cut plus £7m. The Bankers were to be told this and asked whether, if it were acceptable to the Government, it would satisfy New York.[2]

Once again, telegrams were dispatched across the Atlantic and the Cabinet agreed to meet the following evening (Sunday) to consider the replies.

By this time the resignation of the Labour Cabinet had become probable. As MacDonald was to tell the King on Sunday morning, on the latter's return to London from Sandringham, a powerful section of the Labour Cabinet, headed by Henderson and Graham, would probably not consent to the economies now being considered in New York. 'If they were to resign from the Government it would not be possible for him to carry on the administration. . . . The resignation of the Labour Government as a whole would then become inevitable.'[3] At the Saturday Cabinet meeting he had discussed once again the possibility of forming a National Government, but 'there was a general feeling' against it. By this time much of the Opposition's objection to a National Government had disappeared. Insofar as it had been as a device to enable a united Labour Government to share responsibility for unpopular measures, the Conservatives and Liberals had scorned it. But the new situation opened exciting tactical opportunities. For with the trade unions and important sections of the Labour Party ranged on

[1] Clay, *Lord Norman*, p. 390.

[2] Apparently there was still confusion about the exact figure which the Cabinet had authorised MacDonald and Snowden to place before the Opposition.

[3] Nicolson, *King George V: His Life and Reign*, pp. 460–1.

one side and the Prime Minister, the Chancellor of the Exchequer and other Ministers on the other, acceptance of National Government offered a good chance of splitting the Labour Party. Without it, MacDonald would have no option but to lead his Party in opposition, however unenthusiastically; and a Conservative-Liberal Government was likely to be an extremely sickly creature.

On Sunday morning the King saw MacDonald, and with his approval asked the opposition leaders to see him 'to hear from them . . . what the position of their respective Parties is'. Samuel was the first to arrive and impressed on the King the advantages of an all-party or National Government. Samuel recorded his actual advice as follows:

> We thought that, in view of the unpalatable character to the masses of the people of many of the economies which were indispensable, it would be to the general interest if a Labour government were in office during their enactment . . . if that solution proved to be impracticable, then a National Government of members of the three parties would be the best alternative.[1]

This, as we have seen, was exactly opposite to the view that MacDonald had originally taken. The unpalatable character of the economies made it preferable that they should be enacted by a National Government: only if that proved impracticable should a Labour Government try to carry them out. The wheel had turned full circle. Baldwin who arrived in the afternoon said that he would be willing to serve under MacDonald in a National Government.

> On Sunday evening the Cabinet met and opened with a speech from the P.M. placing before the members the alternatives of the provisional scheme including the 10 % cut or a moratorium.
>
> The discussion was interrupted to await the reply of New York on the proposals. It was gathered from a very guarded written statement which was read to the Cabinet that New York agreed to them.[2]

---

[1] John Bowle, *Viscount Samuel*, p. 271.

[2] The 'very guarded' reply was from J. P. Morgan. Morgan said that a public loan would be impossible till Parliament had actually enacted the proposed economies: but a short-term credit of 100 to 150 million dollars would be 'less difficult'. 'Are we right in assuming that the programme under consideration will have the sincere support of the Bank of England and the City generally and thus go a long way towards restoring internal confidence in Great Britain? Of course our ability to do anything depends on the response of public opinion particularly in Great Britain to the Government's announcement of the programme.' (Quoted Clay, *Lord Norman*, pp. 391–2.)

A minority of the Cabinet opposed the 10 % cut. The majority held that the Government could only adopt this proposal if there was complete or almost complete unanimity in the Cabinet. Everybody agreed that the position was such that it was impossible to continue.

It was agreed that the P.M. should report to the King that, with the proposed scheme, the Cabinet could not carry on and that the King be recommended to meet the three party leaders on the following day. . . .

From revelations made at the time, it appeared that the Cabinet split twelve-nine in favour of the economies,[1] the dissentients being Henderson, Clynes, Graham, Greenwood, Alexander, Lansbury, Johnston, Adamson and Addison. The Prime Minister had on his side Snowden, Thomas, Sankey, Passfield, Miss Bondfield, Morrison, Parmoor, Wedgwood Benn, Shaw, Amulree and Lees-Smith. MacDonald, looking 'scared and unbalanced',[2] went to the palace to advise the King to summon the three leaders the following morning, as the Cabinet had authorised, and a few minutes after his return the Cabinet dispersed. A few minutes later Sir Herbert Samuel appeared, to be followed by Baldwin, Neville Chamberlain, Sir Josiah Stamp and two governors of the Bank. The opposition leaders tried hard to get MacDonald to lead a National Government, but apparently he had still not decided when they left shortly after midnight.

The long agony ended on the Monday morning of 24 August. A statement from the palace issued at 11.55 stated simply:

His Majesty the King invited the Prime Minister, Mr. Stanley Baldwin and Sir Herbert Samuel to Buckingham Palace this morning, and the formation of a National Government is under consideration. A fuller announcement will be made later.

MacDonald returned and announced this decision to the waiting Cabinet

very well, with great feeling, saying he knew the cost, but could not refuse the King's request; that he would doubtless be denounced and ostracised, but could do no other. We uttered polite things, but accepted silently the accomplished fact.[3]

---

[1] The twelve included MacDonald.

[2] Nicolson, *King George V: His Life and Reign*, p. 464.

[3] Passfield Papers, Passfield to Beatrice Webb, 24 August 1931.

Lord Sankey proposed a vote of thanks to MacDonald which was passed unanimously and without further leave-taking his colleagues left the room.[1]

[1] MacDonald asked Snowden, Thomas and Sankey to serve with him in the National Government; they agreed. Later Lord Amulree, the Secretary of State for Air, also joined.

14

CONCLUSION

THE National Government failed to achieve the specific object for which it had been formed. Credits of £80m had been obtained on 28 August; on 8 September Snowden introduced emergency measures of extra taxation and economies designed to balance the Budget by 1933. But a mutiny of naval ratings at Invergordon on 16 September destroyed the confidence temporarily created; the flight from the pound could not be stemmed and on 21 September Britain was forced off the gold standard.[1]

In the following eight months eighteen countries abandoned the gold standard; forty countries raised tariffs or put on import controls; ten countries declared moratoria. Unemployment rose throughout the world. By the beginning of 1933 it was estimated at over thirty million, an increase of five to ten million over the preceding year.[2] Production and world trade continued to shrink; foreign lending dried up almost completely.[3] The fourth quarter of 1931 showed the biggest single

[1] MacDonald put the best face he could on this outcome by arguing that the formation of the National Government made it safer for Britain to go off the gold standard: 'The Budget is balanced, and we are in a position to control the situation' (256 H.C. Deb. c. 1273).

[2] League of Nations, *World Economic Survey*, 1932–3, p. 109.

[3] Taking 1925–1929 as 100, the volume of production fell to 96 in 1930, 84 in 1931, and 69 in 1932. (Ibid. 1932–3, p. 71.) The quantum, value and price of world trade (1929 = 100) were

	1930	1931	1932
Quantum	93	84	73
Value	81	58	39
Price	87	69	53

(Ibid. p. 213). U.S. lending ($m) fell from 905 in 1930 to 229 in 1931 to 29 in 1932; U.K. lending from 209 in 1931 to 102 in 1932 (League of Nations, *World Economic Survey*, p. 294).

downturn in economic activity recorded since the start of the depression.[1] This aggravation of depression constitutes in retrospect the chief argument for making the attempt to defend the gold standard in the summer of 1931.

Britain obtained immediate relief on its balance of payments, but the scale of retaliation made this short-lived. After a temporary reduction the unemployment figures continued to rise, reaching three million at the end of 1932. Even so, the formation of the National Government did help to restore confidence. Its immediate measures to balance the Budget and prevent dumping and the more extensive protective duties it imposed the following year gave businessmen hope and paved the way for eventual industrial recovery. But the problem of the 'special areas' with their million and a half unemployed was not solved till the re-armament boom of 1938.

MacDonald's parting from the Labour Party did not remain amicable or (as some hoped) temporary for long. On 28 September he was expelled from the Party by a 'rubber stamp'.[2] On 6 October Parliament was dissolved and on 27 October the National Government, appealing for a 'doctor's mandate' and aided by a vitriolic broadcast from Snowden denouncing Labour's programme as 'Bolshevism run mad', swept to the greatest electoral victory in English history, winning 556 seats to Labour's 52.

The National Government presided lethargically over Britain for the remainder of the decade. MacDonald, a sick man, retained the premiership till June 1935 when he made way for Stanley Baldwin. Snowden, created a viscount in October 1931, stayed in the Government as Lord Privy Seal till September 1932, when he resigned with the Samuelite Liberals (the Simonites stayed on to become Tories) in a final vindication of his free trade beliefs. He survived to publish his ferocious memoirs which mercilessly lambasted the failings of his former associates. Thomas, irrepressible as ever, but increasingly the tool of unscrupulous City speculators, was driven from the Colonial Office and public life by a budget-leak scandal in May 1936. Deprived of its best leaders in the

[1] Ibid. 1931–2, facing p. 64.

[2] See Citrine, *Men and Work*, pp. 288–9. He received a letter of expulsion headed 'Dear Sir' and signed with a rubber stamp and initials of the national organiser.

1931 débâcle, the Labour Party was led till 1935 by the aged Lansbury, while Arthur Henderson wore himself out in a vain effort to achieve world disarmament at Geneva. Most of the other Labour leaders slowly drifted back into Parliament and, under Clement Attlee, the Party recovered strength and cohesion. Many of the familiar names of this book were destined to play a prominent part in the rather happier circumstances of 1945–51.

The 'bold' men of the 1929 Parliament, disillusioned with the 'parliamentary game', vanished into limbo, on the fringes of the massive and passive 'National' majority. Lloyd George, after initial hesitation, rejected the National Government and all its works. Recovered from his illness, he returned to Parliament to lead a family group of four Liberals, cut off from both the Samuelites and Simonites. In 1935 he tried briefly end unsuccessfully to recapture the spirit of 1929, thereafter contenting himself with the cultivation of his orchard at Churt and the revision of his voluminous memoirs, all the while looking enviously to Germany where Hitler showed that public works could cure unemployment. Mosley, whose New Party was obliterated in 1931, went to Rome and, impressed by Mussolini, returned to lead the British Union of Fascists in a spectacular but ineffective assault on democracy. The I.L.P. disaffiliated from the Labour Party in 1932 and, deprived of its political base, became yet another little group on the fringes. Thus were the 'bold' men driven to political suicide, while Britain, complacent and insular, came to the verge of disaster.

For the inability of the Labour and National Governments to deal effectively with the economic problem (unemployment remained above one and a half million until the rearmament boom of 1938) had one important wider consequence: it helped to create and confirm a mood of national self-doubt, of pessimism regarding the future, in which appeasement could flourish. The refusal to stand up to the dictators was part of the refusal to stand up to unemployment; and the mood of resignation, of fatalism almost, which supported it was the same in one case as the other. People had been told for so long that there was nothing that could be done about unemployment, that they came to believe that there was nothing that could be done to stop a confident and self-assertive Germany. It was Hitler's excesses, not any recovery of national self-assurance, that brought Britain reluctantly to war in 1939.

It required Dunkirk to give the British faith in themselves once again.

The failure of the 1929 Labour Government thus determined the politics of the following decade. Could that failure have been prevented? Usually criticism of MacDonald and his colleagues starts with their handling of the financial crisis of 1931 rather than with their omissions over the previous two years. But whereas between 1929 and 1931 there were plenty of effective choices open to the Government, in 1931 itself there was virtual unanimity on the need to defend the gold standard. Even Keynes, who had his doubts, thought that the attempt to defend gold was 'inevitable'.[1]

MacDonald broke with his colleagues not over policy but over primary loyalty. As Prime Minister he considered his first duty was to the 'national interest' as it was almost universally conceived; the Labour Party saw its first duty to its own people. This conflict was not surprising, for whereas a Prime Minister is inevitably a national leader, his Party does not inevitably become a national Party. The Prime Minister could point to distinguished precedent for the action he took;[2] equally the Labour Party could cite precedents for its dissent. MacDonald appreciated this distinction of function. He did not try to win over his Party, doubtless hoping that they would show him similar understanding, and initially the parting did take place without recrimination.[3] The real criticism of MacDonald is not that he formed the National Government, but that under his leadership the Labour Government had drifted into a position which left it so little choice.

The absence of developed Keynesian theory was not a decisive barrier to the adoption of what might loosely be termed Keynesian policies, as is proved by the experience of the United States, Germany, France and Sweden which in the nineteen-thirties all attempted, with varying

[1] *New Statesman*, 29 August 1931.

[2] Peel in 1846, Gladstone in 1886 and Lloyd George in 1916 put their personal judgments above the need for party unity.

[3] See the *Daily Herald*'s editorial of 25 August 1931, quoted in Bassett, *1931*, p. 174. In a book on Labour's Scottish M.P.s written in September 1931, an anonymous author (actually the Labour Chief Whip, Tom Kennedy) says 'Mr. MacDonald has elected to move to the Right. No one blames him for doing so, or impugns his motives. No one has any right to rail at the trade unions or accuse them of sinister intentions for refusing to follow him.' (*The Scottish Socialists: A Gallery of Contemporary Portraits*, p. 89.)

success, to promote economic recovery through deficit budgeting. In Sweden this was done especially effectively by a democratic Labour Government operating a normal parliamentary system.[1] Even the 'climate of opinion' or 'conventional wisdom' which is often quite different from the state of academic knowledge was not nearly as monolithic in England as is sometimes supposed. A resolute Government would have done much more to exploit the differences between industry and the City. It was not primarily the industrialists who rejected a national development loan,[2] but the City and the Treasury. Naturally much would have depended upon the presentation of the policy and the ends to which such a loan would have been put. But again the Swedish experiment showed that a well-prepared and well-considered programme of public investment could gain business support;[3] and in Britain the Government's bargaining position was immensely strengthened in 1930 by industry's demand for a tariff. But the Government rejected Conservative protection, the Liberal national development loan, the Keynesian and Mosleyite amalgams of both, preferring instead the advice of the least progressive sections of the 'economic establishment'.

How far was this 'policy of negation' dictated by the absence of a majority? Admittedly the Government had no mandate for a 'socialist' solution. But did Labour leaders want one? They talked vaguely of reorganising industries by nationalisation, but when the Government introduced its Bill dealing with the coal mines it was the Liberals who insisted, against Government opposition, on *compulsory* reorganisation. It was they also who asked why the Government were not nationalising mining royalties — a step which a Conservative Government took a few years later. Again, Labour leaders rejected the underconsumptionist remedy of income redistribution as inappropriate to the existing economic situation — an argument which would have applied equally whether or not Labour had had a majority.[4] Finally, the 'socialist' proposals for import quotas were killed not by the parliamentary position but by the free traders in the Cabinet.

[1] See Arndt, *The Economic Lessons of the Nineteen-Thirties*, esp. pp. 207–20.

[2] Indeed employers argued repeatedly before the Macmillan Committee for government-subsidised investment. (Macmillan Committee Evidence, 2502, 2612, 3959, 3987; *Memorandum of the Association of British Chambers of Commerce*, p. 225, para. 15.)

[3] Arndt, *The Economic Lessons of the 1930s*, p. 219.

[4] See above, p. 160.

In any case, what was the 'socialist' solution? Nationalising a few obsolete industries would not obviously have made the slightest difference to the unemployment figures. Raising £200m by taxation in order to redistribute income and increase mass purchasing power, as the I.L.P. demanded, made little sense in a capitalist economy suffering from depression. Any attempt to do so would have produced a crisis of confidence, leading in all probability to the kind of resistance which every constitutional Party tries to avoid and which would have required leaders of much sterner stuff than MacDonald, Henderson, or even Maxton, to overcome. In any event, although such measures might have paved the way for the establishment of the socialist state, their immediate effect, owing to the political disturbance they would have occasioned, would have been to aggravate the economic crisis. Mosley was one of the few to see that in a capitalist economy the only way for a socialist Party to get action was by adopting the interventionist policies of capitalism's own spokesmen. Whether such an intervention marked an advance towards, or a retreat from, socialism he was prepared to leave for later 'theological' debate.

For a non-socialist solution (the only democratically feasible one) there was no lack of potential parliamentary support. Lloyd George's initial declaration of support for a 'prompt, bold and energetic' policy certainly seemed unequivocal, and throughout its life the Government received remarkably consistent Liberal support in the lobby.[1] Indeed the Liberals were constantly spurring the Government on to bolder action; and even if Labour leaders mistrusted Lloyd George, nothing would have been lost by putting Liberal promises to the test.

Although the parliamentary position did to some extent limit the Government's choice, the policy of negation weakened it even more. Effective measures to tackle unemployment on Liberal lines would have enabled it to bring pressure on its allies for a temporary revenue tariff or anti-dumping measures which Lloyd George was known to favour. Until the end of 1929 it held the parliamentary whip hand through its increasing support in the country. Even in 1930 a vigorous and imaginative policy would have given the electors a vivid contrast with Conservative and Liberal disunity. These sources of strength were thrown away. The Labour Government of 1964, in not entirely

[1] See above, pp. 163–4.

dissimilar circumstances, handled its parliamentary position much more skilfully.

It is true that the system of Government in 1929 was not geared to a vigorous unemployment policy. Arndt shows that in Sweden state intervention was an 'accepted tradition'. In Britain the central Government controlled and administered virtually nothing. Apart from a few public utilities, all economic activity was divided between private enterprise and the municipalities. The Treasury which came of age in the hey-day of laissez-faire was in no sense a Ministry of Economic Affairs; it simply controlled Government expenditure in the interests of balancing the Budget. Its conceptions did not embrace the new government departments created just before and during the war, which it starved of money.

Effective unemployment policy demanded first of all an appropriate executive instrument with adequate research and planning facilities. The Treasury was no instrument for initiating policy, though through its control of money it was admirably placed to block it. Hence a Ministry of Economic Affairs plus an expansionist Chancellor were indispensable: Bevin or Mosley in harness with Lloyd George at the Exchequer would have been the best combination. MacDonald recognised the need for extra-Treasury direction of economic policy when he appointed Thomas to head a rudimentary Economic Affairs Ministry and set up the Economic Advisory Council; but he never solved the problem of Snowden. The central Government would further have had to take direct responsibility for part of the public works programme. Local authority autonomy meant that delay was built into the Government's public works policy. The disproportion between the money allocated — £180m — and the number of men actually employed — 200,000 — inhibited the effectiveness of the policy and thus undermined public confidence in it.

There was considerable support for such steps. The Liberals and Mosleyites advocated government responsibility for road-building and housing and Lloyd George promised full support 'to overcome refractory and selfish interests'. The Labour Government and civil servants were horrified. The Lloyd George plan would require dictatorship. Arthur Greenwood replied to Sir Tudor Walters, Liberal advocate of state housing: 'I would rather trust the local authorities to solve the housing programme than any Hitler'.[1] Yet in 1937 the National Government took direct charge of the trunk road programme without protest and with some limited gain in speed of execution.[2] Nor would there have been insuperable difficulties in adapting the central government machine to the demand of vigorous policy. The instruments were all there: MacDonald had created some himself. They simply needed the right men to take charge of them. We have seen how close the Premier had come to admitting Lloyd George to the Cabinet in the summer of 1931. With Snowden out of the way, there is little doubt that the Liberal leader would soon, in Postgate's phrase, have 'blown away the vacillations of the wuffling MacDonald'.[3]

On the other hand, such changes would have run up against the non-interventionist bias of the civil service. Sir John Anderson thought that nothing could be done until in the course of nature unemployment disappeared; Sir Henry Maybury, following a long tradition of 'expert' advice which impeded the development of essential services, opposed any extension of the road programme; the Post Office argued that no one would use the telephones that Lloyd George wanted to instal; Sir Horace Wilson advised against compulsory rationalisation; the Treasury predicted disaster if any attempt were made to raise a development loan. The pioneering civil service tradition of Chadwick, Kay-Shuttleworth, Simon and Morant was quite extinct; a different attitude reigned, sceptical and ultimately pessimistic.

It may be objected that public opinion was not ready for what would have amounted to a revolution in English peace-time government. Lloyd George's purpose was to concentrate priority and speed up decisions. Advocates of a Government of 'national concentration' had the war very much in mind; its opponents argued that the two situations were not comparable: the unemployed were mostly far away from London, there was not the same feeling of urgency.[4] Could the conquest of unemploy-

[1] 246 H.C. Deb. c. 1095.

[2] The Ministry of Transport had argued that central control would not significantly speed up work on the roads. Under government direction it took five years from the inception of a road scheme to its completion. This was slower than Lloyd George had hoped for but faster than under the previous system: Snowden had complained to Morrison in 1929 that work was still in progress on the 1920 plan.

[3] Postgate, *Lansbury*, p. 266.

[4] See 244 H.C. Deb. c. 588–9.

ment have commanded the same order of priority as winning the war? Undoubtedly most people preferred 'business as usual'. Mobilising public opinion would have been a formidable challenge to a democratic leadership. What is indisputable is that there was no one in the Labour Government capable of 'giving the nation a lead'.

The more we examine the alternatives the more we are forced to conclude that the Labour Government's defeatism was largely self-imposed. Right from the start Lloyd George had considered it probable that 'the Socialists [would] make a mess of the job . . . because they have no men capable of handling a big task'.[1] 'It will not be easy to keep such Ministers in office', he was writing a year and a half later.[2] Certainly it would have required a Government considerably above average to cope effectively with unemployment. Ramsay MacDonald's Government was rather below average.

The Prime Minister himself was not an inspiring leader. His remoteness made him incapable of co-ordinating the work of his colleagues. There was no inner Cabinet to discuss and plan policy: the Big Five met only to consider day-to-day tactical problems arising from the parliamentary position. This meant that legislative programmes were settled at the last moment and depended largely on the persistence and advocacy of individual Ministers — 'a crowd of bookmakers jostling through a turnstile' as Mosley put it. There was no *camaraderie*, no sense of common purpose.[3] MacDonald was also incompetent as an executive. He lacked Asquith's effortless economy of labour to enable him to get through his business expeditiously and efficiently. He worked prodigiously hard, yet never, except on a few foreign policy topics, gave the impression of being *au fait* with what was happening. Certainly in his first year as Prime Minister he had little idea what the Government was doing about unemployment.[4] Even after his 'education' at the hands of the E.A.C. in

[1] Owen Frank, *Tempestuous Journey*, p. 170.

[2] *Manchester Guardian*, 27 December 1930.

[3] MacDonald was no better with the Party. When backbenchers came to see him with complaints or to discuss policy, he read his correspondence while they talked. As Snell, chairman of the consultative committee, remarked: 'The lack of spontaneous geniality on the part of Mr. MacDonald . . . undoubtedly led the rank and file of the Labour Members to believe he regarded them with disdain'. (Lord Snell, *Men, Movements and Myself*, p. 252.)

[4] As late as August 1930, two months after he assumed 'personal responsi-

the summer of 1930 had given him one or two ideas, he saw them purely in electoral terms, introducing the revenue tariff to Snowden with the words: 'I have been thinking how we can win a clear majority at the next General Election.'[1]

If fear of disaster at the polls at least stimulated MacDonald to unaccustomed speculation, Snowden's mind remained completely inflexible. He was admittedly an extreme case of ministerial identification with his department's opinions. 'How do you like your new Chief?' a Treasury official was asked soon after Snowden had succeeded Churchill as Chancellor. 'We are delighted at the change' was the reply. 'We feel we have moved from the pantry into the drawing room.'[2] The recalcitrance of his Party might stay the full-blooded execution of his deflationary views, but nothing could shift him from unbending opposition to any new idea. Powerless to enforce his own policy, he vetoed all others. Worse still, he countenanced public Treasury criticism of the policy for which he himself was responsible.[3] With him at the Exchequer, no Government stood much chance in the circumstances of 1929.

In general the Labour Ministers were propagandists with little knowledge of government.[4] Their inexperience, lack of assurance and the sheer volume of work helped to make them slaves to departmental views. Henderson, a successful Foreign Secretary, almost never intervened in home affairs except on matters of party discipline, and was almost entirely ignorant of economic and financial questions.[5] Passfield was so immersed in his department that his wife wrote: 'It is quite

bility' for unemployment, he was writing to Hartshorn: 'There is one little thing I have never seen, but which, from the point of view of Parliamentary debating, is very much required. Could you not give us a table showing the value of schemes sanctioned . . . the value of those actually in hand, the number of men actually employed and the number who would be employed at the peak period of the schemes? . . . Those of us who cannot devote enough time to master the whole of the details are often stumped.'

[1] Snowden, *An Autobiography*, ii, p. 923.

[2] Quoted Dalton, *Memoirs*, vol. i, p. 260 n.

[3] See above, p. 288 n.

[4] When MacDonald became Premier and Snowden Chancellor in 1924 it was the first time they had ever held government office.

[5] He apparently thought that the source of borrowings for unemployment was the Post Office Savings Bank. (Dalton, *Memoirs*, vol. i, p. 268.)

impracticable for him to think of unemployment.'[1] The trade union Ministers, coping with civil servants for the first time, were no better. Thomas and Miss Bondfield were completely in the hands of their official advisers. Hartshorn, who had come in eager to do something, was writing to MacDonald two months after his appointment as Lord Privy Seal: 'After fully examining the position, I am satisfied that not much more is possible than is actually being done.' The Ministers who fared best were usually those who had had a thorough training in local government, like Herbert Morrison, but even he could make little headway against Sir Henry Maybury, whose proposals Lloyd George described as 'impotent'.

By 10 November 1930 the *Manchester Guardian* thought the Government was exhibiting 'in marked degree those signs of senility which may be looked for in the ordinary way after three or four years'. Inexperience may well excuse administrative failure, but it does not entirely explain the want of courage, the intellectual paralysis that gripped the Labour Government. For that we must turn to the nature of the Labour Party.

For the failure of the Government was not just a failure of individuals but the failure of a Party and a doctrine. Arndt, writing of the Swedish experiment, remarks: 'The whole policy of the Labour Government was carefully worked out and, as far as that was possible for an opposition Party, planned in advance.'[2] Swedish socialism had clearly come to terms not only with economic reality but also with the parliamentary system, which may explain why it has held power continuously since 1932. The British Labour Party was far from such maturity. It owed its position not to its own merits but to the fact that the electorate abhorred the vacuum created by the splits in the Liberal Party.

Basically it believed that socialism was the cure for poverty, of which unemployment was simply the most vivid manifestation. It thought in terms of a total solution: but socialism would clearly take a very long time, for it would not be established until the majority of people were ready for it. In the meantime the Labour Party simply did not know what to do. It frowned on such attempts to force the pace as the I.L.P.'s *Socialism In Our Time*. Its own policies tended to be restatements of the 'socialist' attitude to problems, backed up with specific trade union or

[1] Passfield Papers, Beatrice Webb to Bernard Shaw, 2 December 1930.

[2] Arndt, *The Economic Lessons of the Nineteen-Thirties*, p. 217.

'palliative' proposals. The 'palliative' function of Labour Governments was much invoked. The unemployed were the victims of the system: therefore they were entitled to decent maintenance. On this the Labour Party was firmly united. But what if a Labour Government was running the system? Did it not have a responsibility to provide work? Even in office the Party kept up the myth of disassociation. 'We are not on trial; it is the system . . .', MacDonald told the Llandudno conference in 1930. Here trade union pressure was, perhaps inevitably, unconstructive. Their acceptance of unemployment as the price to be paid for maintaining wages made them less interested in increasing employment than in increasing unemployment benefits, thus complementing the 'palliative' notions of the parliamentary Socialists.[1] In short, there was no practical socialist economic policy, no theory of how to use Parliament for furthering socialist aims. Socialism explained the past and promised the future: it had nothing constructive to offer the present.

This failure to bring together socialism on the one hand with economic reality and parliamentary democracy on the other meant that Labour leaders who tried to work the 'system' were liable to have split personalities. In Snowden's mind socialism and public finance existed in two entirely separate, watertight compartments. Passfield perceptively describes the paralysis of will produced by this schizophrenia in Graham's case:

> He [Graham] always seems to be resisting and protesting — subconsciously . . . — against any kind of Progressive action. He doesn't really like any Radical or Collectivist proposals which he thinks are insufficiently considered from the standpoint of 'ideal' social philosophy. Also sceptical about any democratic reform which will always be tinged by corruption and tyrannical interference with individual liberty. . . . He has ceased to be competent for action.[2]

Without any adequate theory of the transition, the Labour Party was bound to be defeatist in the circumstances of 1929. Socialism was impossible and capitalism was doomed: there was nothing to do but govern without conviction a system it did not believe in but saw no real prospect of changing. It struggled to defend the working class as long as it knew how, and when it could defend them no longer it resigned.

[1] MacDonald's constant reference to 'relief works' (see 239 H.C. Deb. c. 1332, 1375–6; *Labour Party Conference Report*, 1930, p. 185) is symptomatic of the failure to grasp the dynamic function of government expenditure in promoting recovery.

[2] Passfield Papers, Passfield to Beatrice Webb, 15 September 1930.

APPENDIXES

I. LABOUR GOVERNMENT, 1929–31

	MINISTERS IN CABINET			JUNIOR MINISTERS ATTACHED	
P.M.	J. R. MacDonald	5 Jun 29–24 Aug 31			
Ld Pres.	Ld Parmoor	7 Jun 29			
Ld Chanc.	Ld Sankey	7 Jun 29			
Privy S.	J. Thomas	7 Jun 29			
	V. Hartshorn	5 Jun 30			
	T. Johnston	24 Mar 31			
Exch.	P. Snowden	7 Jun 29	*Treasury:*		
			F.S.	F. Pethick-Lawrence	11 Jun 29
For. O.	A. Henderson	7 Jun 29	*U-S.*	H. Dalton	11 Jun 29
Home O.	J. Clynes	7 Jun 29	*U-S.*	A. Short	11 Jun 29
Admir.	A. Alexander	7 Jun 29	*P. & F.S.:*		
				C. Ammon	11 Jun 29
			Civil Ld:		
				G. Hall	11 Jun 29
Ag. & Fish.	N. Buxton	7 Jun 29	*P.S.*	C. Addison	11 Jun 29
	C. Addison	5 Jun 30		Earl De La Warr	5 Jun 30
Air	Ld Thomson	7 Jun 29	*U-S.*	F. Montague	11 Jun 29
	Ld Amulree	14 Oct 30			
Col. O.	Ld Passfield	7 Jun 29	*U-S.*	W. Lunn	11 Jun 29
				D. Shiels	1 Dec 29
Dom. O.	Ld Passfield	7 Jun 29	*U-S.*	A. Ponsonby	11 Jun 29
	J. Thomas	5 Jun 30		W. Lunn	1 Dec 29
Bd Educ.	Sir C. Trevelyan	7 Jun 29	*P.S.*	M. Jones	11 Jun 29
	H. Lees-Smith	2 Mar 31			
Health	A. Greenwood	7 Jun 29	*P.S.*	Miss S. Lawrence	11 Jun 29
India O.	W. Benn	7 Jun 29	*U-S.*	D. Shiels	11 Jun 29
				Earl Russell	1 Dec 29
				Ld Snell	13 Mar 31
Lab.	Miss M. Bondfield	7 Jun 29	*P.S.*	J. Lawson	11 Jun 29
Scot. O.	W. Adamson	7 Jun 29	*U-S.*	T. Johnston	7 Jun 29
				J. Westwood	25 Mar 31
B.o.T.	W. Graham	7 Jun 29	*P.S.*	W. Smith	11 Jun 29
			P.S.	Overseas Trade Dept.:	
				G. Gillett	7 Jul 29
			P.S.	Mines Dept.:	
				B. Turner	11 Jun 29
				E. Shinwell	5 Jun 30
Transp.	(office not in cabinet)		*P.S.*	Earl Russell	11 Jun 29
	H. Morrison	19 Mar 31		A. Ponsonby (Ld)	1 Dec 29
				J. Parkinson	1 Mar 31

MINISTERS IN CABINET			JUNIOR MINISTERS ATTACHED		
War O.	T. Shaw	7 Jun 29	*U-S.*	Earl De La Warr	11 Jun 29
				Ld Marley	5 Jun 30
			F.S.	E. Shinwell	11 June 29
				W. Sanders	5 Jun 30
1st C. Works	G. Lansbury	7 Jun 29			

MINISTERS NOT IN CABINET			JUNIOR MINISTERS ATTACHED		
D. Lanc.	Sir O. Mosley	7 Jun 29			
	C. Attlee	23 May 30			
	Ld Ponsonby	13 Mar 31			
Paym.-Gen.	Ld Arnold	7 Jun 29			
Pensions	F. Roberts	7 Jun 29	*P.S.*	(*post vacant*)	
Postm.-Gen.	H. Lees-Smith	7 Jun 29	*Ass.*	S. Viant	7 Jul 29
	C. Attlee	2 Mar 31			
Transp.	H. Morrison	7 Jun 29	(*for Junior Ministers see above*)		
	(office in cabinet 19 Mar 31)				
Law Officers:			*P.S. to Treasury:*		
Att.-Gen.	Sir W. Jowitt	7 Jun 29		T. Kennedy	14 Jun 29
			Junior Lds of Treasury		
Sol.-Gen.	Sir J. Melville	7 Jun 29		J. Parkinson	11 Jun 29 –13 Mar 31
	Sir S. Cripps	22 Oct 30		C. Edwards	11 Jun 29 –24 Aug 31
				A. Barnes	11 Jun 29 –23 Oct 30
Ld. Advoc.	C. Aitchison	17 Jun 29		W. Whitely	27 Jun 29 –24 Aug 31
Sol.-Gen. Scotland	J. Watson	17 Jun 29		W. Paling	27 Jun 29 –24 Aug 31
				E. Thurtle	23 Oct 30 –24 Aug 31
				H. Charleton	13 Mar 31 –24 Aug 31

II. SELECTED STATISTICS

	1924	1925	1926	1927	1928	1929	1930	1931
1. Balance of Payments (£m)								
Merchandise Trade	−287	−393	−463	−386	−353	−381	−387	−282[1]
Invisible Exports	410	438	484	504	495	504	431	215
Current Surplus	123	45	21	118	147	123	44	−67
2. New Capital Issues (£m)								
For U.K.	89	132	141	176	219	151	127	33
For Abroad	134	88	112	139	143	94	109	46
3. Short-Term Foreign Account (£m)								
Short-Term Borrowing	—	—	—	419	503	451	435	407[2]
Short-Term Lending	—	—	—	140	201	176	161	153
Net Liability	—	—	—	279	302	275	274	254
4. Share Index (1924 = 100)								
Industrials	100	109	114	124	142	135	111	85
Fixed Interest	100	102	104	103	101	104	101	100
5. Production (1913 = 100)	95	93	—	105	105	111	102	92
6. Productivity (1924 = 100)	100	—	—	107	107	111	111[3]	—
7. Prices (1924 = 100)								
Wholesale	100	96	89	85	84	82	72	62[1]
Retail (Cost of Living)	100	100	98	96	95	94	90	84
8. Wages (1924 = 100)								
Money Wages	100	101	100	101	100	99	99	97[1]
Real Wages	100	101	102	105	105	106	108	113

9. Unemployment Benefits (1924 – 100)								
Money Benefits	100	120	120	120	113	113	113	113[4]
Real Benefits	100	120	122	125	119	120	125	131
10. Employment (000's)	9514	9599	9050	10,002	10,003	10,207	9785	9374[1]
Unemployment	1104	1338	1506	1179	1259	1251	1991	2700
Unemployment%	9·7	11·2	14·4	9·2	11·6	9·7	16·2	22·0

[1] First nine months, 1931. [2] March 1931. [3] First six months, 1930. [4] First six months, 1931.

Sources: London and Cambridge Economic Service, *Monthly Bulletin* (Special Quarterly Issue, 23 October 1931), pp. 321–5.
Ibid. 21 December 1931, p. 390.
Macmillan Report pp. 305, 309.
Interim Report, Royal Commission on Unemployment Insurance, p. 66.
Youngson, *The British Economy, 1920–1957*, p. 269.
Mowat, *Britain Between the Wars*, p. 261.

III. SCHEMES PREPARED BY THE ADVISORY MINISTERS, 1929–1930

Lansbury's main preoccupation was with schemes of land resettlement. He gave every support to Mosley's efforts to force a more radical unemployment policy on the Government; but his enthusiasms were reserved for placing men on the land — a policy that would both reduce unemployment and counteract the evils of modern urban civilisation. With this aim in mind he sent Thomas a memorandum on 22 July 1929. This contained some passages on the problems of the basic industries and a warning on the possibly ruinous effects of competitive transport improvements. But it was not long before Lansbury reached his favourite topic:

I therefore propose [he wrote] that we ask the minister of agriculture to consider *immediately* how best he can . . . formulate plans for utilising labour at present unemployed in mining and other areas for the purpose of re-establishing and developing every form of forestry and agriculture — in fact, to start the recolonisation of Britain.

Such a scheme would be 'for the good of Great Britain'. Young people would be only too glad to 'work in the open air'.

Miners now eating their hearts out in idleness and hopelessness could be put to work clearing and cultivating land, erecting buildings and cottages and thus creating settlements organised and set going on a co-operative basis.

There were 'many, many miles of Crown land', Lansbury suggested, which could be utilised for this purpose. 'Idle land and idle men stare us in the face and both are a sign and a symbol of decadence. . . . The only plan which offers a true remedy is to go back to the source of all wealth — the land.'[1]

These suggestions were duly rejected by the Board of Agriculture but Lansbury felt 'that it was impossible for me to accept the Board's memorandum as the last word'. In November he renewed his proposals

[1] Lansbury Papers, 19.d.88–93.

to Thomas's committee for national schemes. This time he proposed co-operative farming as in Denmark with

> each holding being worked as an independent unit, there being, as in Denmark, co-operation in collection, utilisation and marketing produce, by the creation of central creameries, bacon curing factories, poultry and egg grading establishments. . . . This proposal for an experiment on Danish lines has the merit of preserving individual initiative under state guidance and training and the very great advantage of a co-operative collecting and marketing.[1]

In the same memorandum he was also proposing to send unemployed miners to work on the land in France. These various suggestions were considered too broad for the consideration of the committee which was mainly interested in road schemes.

Discouraged but not defeated, Lansbury sent a copy of his first memorandum to the Prime Minister in April 1930: MacDonald sent a courteous reply but no more was heard of it.

This was not Lansbury's only attempt to settle men on the land. His early visit to Australia had created a lifelong interest in the possibilities of emigration to that continent. On becoming a Cabinet Minister, he was sent a scheme by Lord Passmore which proposed to settle 10,000 unemployed miners on the land in Western Australia to grow wheat. A company would be formed to finance the project: would Lansbury try to get the money out of the Government? Lansbury was enthusiastic and brought the matter before Thomas's committee in July 1929. It was handed over to Sir Horace Wilson for examination. He did not damn it out of hand, but argued that much more information was necessary concerning the suitability of the land, climatic conditions, etc.[2] Nothing more had been heard by the following spring; but following a further enquiry from Lansbury the following note was received from the Cabinet office:

> As a result of an investigation undertaken by the Overseas Settlement Department at the request of [Thomas's] committee last November, it has been ascertained that a considerable part of the area in Western Australia with which the scheme was concerned, has been found to be permeated with salt and therefore unfit for wheat growing.[3]

This appeared final: but Lansbury's interest revived when in August 1930 he received an enthusiastic letter from Sir James Mitchell, Premier of Western Australia, endorsing the whole project, but not

[1] Ibid. 20.d.277 ff.

[2] Ibid. 20.e.2–13; 3.73.

[3] 3 April 1930, ibid. 20.e.76.

offering to pay any contribution towards starting it. Lansbury sent a copy of Mitchell's letter to the Prime Minister who wrote to him on 19 September:

I meant, for the last three days, to speak to you about Western Australia emigration. I hope you have sent a copy of the note to the migration department of the board of trade, so that they might take the matter up and find out precisely what the prime minister of Western Australia has in mind. It would be a very good thing if something could be done. You probably will have noticed, however, that there is a great friction between him and his colleagues and that he is threatening to secede from the Commonwealth.[1]

MacDonald was wrong: the enquiry should have been addressed to the Dominions Office, not the Board of Trade. But it made no difference. A letter was received from Lunn, the Under-Secretary, on 22 October finally rejecting it.[2]

Johnston was never quite sure whether he was a full member of Thomas's unemployment committee; but he was Under-Secretary of State for Scotland and concerned with Scottish unemployment, which was higher than in England. With this in mind he submitted to the Prime Minister at the end of July 1929 a memorandum proposing the development of Scotland as a 'health centre and tourist resort', appealing to MacDonald 'as a Scotsman' to recommend his proposals to the Chancellor of the Exchequer.

Johnston's argument was that Scotland in every way matched Switzerland in scenic beauty with its 'great tracts of beautiful mountain and loch scenery'. It was both healthy and romantic — a combination likely to appeal to the Premier. Why then had it not become more popular as a tourist resort? The answer was that it was the preserve of the rich: 'It is no exaggeration to say that one-fourth part of the country is kept as a solitude for a six weeks or two months sport of a handful of plutocratic sportsmen and their retainers who go there to hunt wild deer.'

His actual scheme was very modest. He proposed the establishment of a Scottish development board which would be given £50,000 a year for three years to 'stimulate and create' tourist traffic; to advertise 'the health, scenic and romantic attractions of Scotland'. If tourists could be persuaded to come and spend money in Scotland the economy would be stimulated and employment increased.[3] MacDonald was sympathetic,

[1] Ibid. 20.e.30 ff. [2] Ibid. 20.e.93.

[3] MacDonald Papers, File 2. Unemployment.

but urged Johnston to consult the Treasury. There the scheme was eventually buried.

His other plan, connected with the same project, was to build a road round Loch Lomond to make it possible for tourists to come there. The Duke of Montrose objected, offering an alternative route. Even then it was only with the greatest difficulty that the Perthshire County Council could be persuaded to submit a scheme; and it was years before the road — from Aberfoyle to the Trossachs — was completed.[1]

Mosley was active in many fields. Any scheme which he thought likely to stimulate employment received his close attention. Thus we find him writing on 4 September 1929 to Lord Thomson, the Air Minister, in the following terms:

> We are now engaged in working out a new unemployment push for the autumn, and I am writing to you privately in this connection.
>
> From time to time I have discussed with people interested in the air the possibility of roofing over Termini on the South Side of London, such as Victoria Station, in order to make a central aerodrome. I recently asked my Treasury Secretary to get in touch with your Department with a view to finding out whether official consideration has even been given to such a project. I understand that it has been discussed, but rather as a possibility for the future than as an immediate contingency. Would it be possible for you to ask your experts to work out this project as an immediate proposition? . . . The factor of noise, must, of course, be considered, but I understand that design is approaching the elimination of this factor and there is no reason why we should not proceed a little ahead of design in a long-term project of this nature. In any event, I do not see that in modern conditions a slight increase of noise presents any insuperable objection. If the proposition is a technical possibility and the Ministry desired to take advantage of the present opportunity, we could press forward the plan on unemployment grounds. I suppose there is little chance of an economic return, but the continuation of employment with the great fillip such a project would give for air development might well justify a considerable Government subvention.

It is clear from this letter that Mosley was still expecting the Government to embark on larger schemes of employment that autumn. As for the project itself, with its vision of silent aeroplanes landing on the termini of Victoria Station, he wrote in a letter to Thomas on 3 October 1929: 'We are, of course, examining all kinds of possibilities, some hopeful and some a little fantastic.'

[1] See Johnston, *Memories*, pp. 104–5.

IV. MOSLEY MEMORANDUM MATERIAL

23 January 1930, *Mosley to MacDonald.*

My Dear Prime Minister,

I venture to forward to you my paper on the unemployment and general economic problem, and the organisation necessary to meet it which I told you in a previous letter was in course of preparation.

I have already sent a copy to Thomas, whom I have assured that the criticism of the present situation is in no way intended as a reflection upon him and that, indeed, the present limitations of policy and machinery in my view make his task impossible. I have also shown the document to Lansbury and Johnston who, I understand, are writing to you to say that they agree with the substance of it.

I hope very much that you will be able to consider it before any announcement is made or White Paper issued relative to the proposed economic staff. . . .[1] The policy suggested in the paper is not advanced in any dogmatic spirit and certainly not as any cast-iron formula. I am more than open to any alternative suggestions which can be shown to be superior. I have reached, however, the very definite conclusion after mature consideration that it is impossible to continue as at present.

Yours sincerely,

O. E. MOSLEY

23 January 1930, *Lansbury to MacDonald.*

Our colleague, Sir Oswald Mosley, after many discussions with us on the subject of unemployment and the Government's failure to reduce the figures, decided to spend a portion of the Christmas vacation summarising our views and experiences and also putting on record in skeleton form the sort of organisation and some of the steps which in his judgment are necessary if we are to deal effectively with this, the most vital of all domestic questions now before the country.

I have read his detailed examination of the present situation, and his criticisms of our present schemes for dealing with the problem, and without pledging myself to everything contained in the memorandum I must record the fact that I am in substantial agreement with him and I do most earnestly

[1] Reference to the E.A.C., set up on 12 February 1930.

beg of the Prime Minister and Lord Privy Seal to give their best and early attention to the memorandum prepared by our colleague.

In asking that this should be done I want to assure the Lord Privy Seal that our disagreements with him have no shape or shadow of personal feeling. Each of us at public meetings and meetings with Deputations have done our utmost to strengthen his hands, to explain his policy and ensure its success. I however believe that the limits within which he is working have set him an impossible task and am firmly convinced that the road we are now travelling affords us no kind of immediate or even early amelioration of our country's economic plight. The Lord Privy Seal has worked day and night and done all that one man could do within the limits he and his advisers have decided to work, but I believe that these limitations of present policy forbid success.

In these circumstances I feel it our duty, holding the views we do, to ask that the memorandum of our colleague shall receive the consideration it deserves. I hope that time will be found for the Prime Minister and the Lord Privy Seal to discuss with Sir Oswald Mosley in as full a manner as possible the present position in regard to unemployment and the proposals in relation thereto put forward by the Chancellor of the Duchy.[1]

2 February 1930, *Morrison to Thomas*.

My dear Thomas,

I have read the memorandum of the Chancellor of the Duchy dated Jan. 16, 1930. I cannot make detailed observations as to facts because, as requested by you, I have not consulted or mentioned the matters to officers. Nor in these observations am I concerned with Cabinet policy, but only with matters which concern me as Minister of Transport.

Your exceptional position as a Minister inevitably concerned with the work of a number of other Ministers could well have led to friction, particularly with myself as the Minister most involved in unemployment works in an immediate sense; you have, however, been careful to consult as a general rule, and things have worked with more smoothness than might have been anticipated; our relationships are and have been good, and I have to thank you for much assistance and support.

I am bound to say, however, that I view with apprehension the proposals as to new machinery made by Mosley. It would appear to involve such an overlordship of the executive responsibilities of Ministers that life would not be worth living. Clearly both you and Snowden are concerned with the magnitude of our road programme, and that has been understood by all of us, but my experience on the Committee on National Schemes makes me shudder at Mosley's series of committees with their many meetings and likely eternal arguments. They would tie the Ministers up with talk — and their officers — with evil effects on the state of one's nerves: it is better for

[1] Lansbury Papers, 20.d.332.

Ministers to settle policy between themselves in the light of Cabinet decisions, and to go to the Cabinet when disagreement cannot be bridged. Committees can be appointed when necessary, but they ought not to become a habit, for definite administration action is better than talk. Anyway, the Cabinet has now established the Committee of Economic Development which should meet the demand for broad views; but I am clear that if Ministers, subject to the P.M. and the Cabinet, cannot call their departments their own, nobody will be responsible for anything.

Further, under Mosley's plan, action would be slower and friction increased. Through the document there is manifested some distrust of the civil servants, apparently on the ground that they served under the last Government. Apart from the fact that in the end the same civil servants would in all likelihood be the most influential advisers of the proposed committees; my own experience does not justify anything but respect for their loyalty, ability and sincerity. I have and am effecting some substantial changes of policy at the M. of T. and I have received every assistance once policy has been decided: otherwise there would be trouble. Provided Ministers know their minds, I do not know that there would be available much better technical advice, generally speaking, than we get in the state departments. I am now considering, in a preliminary way, fundamental electricity policy: I am quite sure that I shall be able to submit better and quicker proposals to the P.M. and the Cabinet by combining my own views on policy with the technical facts and advice submitted to me by my people than by a series of meetings with businessmen, financiers and general research officers.

Whatever one's views as to the constitution of the inter-departmental committee on unemployment may be, I ought to make this clear. In accordance with what I should expect, my Permanent Secretary consulted me on important matters before meetings and reported after. So he always knew my mind.

I am not aware that Permanent Secretaries are influenced by the 'head of the civil service' as to the departmental advice they give their Ministers.

The document is much concerned with the Ministry of Transport and seems to be in some ways an offshoot of the interesting but rather wearisome debates and cross-examinations on the Committee on National Schemes. Clearly Mosley suffers somewhat from L.G.'s complaint: the road complex. A road is a means of transport: road work can assist, but it cannot possibly be a principal cure of immediate unemployment. Road transport must be considered in relation to other forms of transport. There should be and there is no bias in the department. And what better experience is there on the matter than that of the M. of T.? I listen to the railway, the road and canal interests, and keep coastwise shipping in mind, but in the end I must settle for myself what is sound. It seems to me curious to take the view that railway enthusiasts are blocking road transport as a more efficient means of transport and then to manifest a particular affection for canals.

It is not true that 'we have contented ourselves with continuing the policy of the Tory Government on a five-year basis instead of a one-year basis'. It is true that I refuse to be reckless with expenditure and to become the victim of road obsession unless the Cabinet tells me to do so. Spending Ministers, it seems to me, have as much a duty to have proper regard to economy as Labour understands it as the Chancellor of the Exchequer himself. Anyway, I have developed road commitments to such an extent that Snowden — as is his right — has begun to ask me questions.

It is not true that the depressed mining areas get less favourable treatment than areas like Brighton on road works: the black areas can and do get transfer terms. Whilst transfer policy has its difficulties, it has — with determined administrations — worked better than I anticipated and I do not think we have a case to drop it. But to assume that it would be easier if we nationalised municipal works is to ignore the fights the local authorities would intensify against imported state labour and also question time in the House!

If we get beyond existing grants or take over selected roads we shall collapse nearly all we are doing and penalise those who answered our call. Even talking about it is dangerous. My views on these matters are recorded in the papers of the Committee on National Schemes and had better be circulated to the Cabinet if they want to consider Mosley's document further. I have known no responsible person to accept the view of 100% grants for locally administered works; when you get to that point you must take away municipal powers, and face the parliamentary row.

The suggestion that we should 'frame the maximum possible programme of road construction etc. without regard to . . . expense of reaction on the railways' has only to be stated to be rejected.

Personally I was very careful in my election speeches, so that nothing I have written above conflicts with my pledges. Generally speaking, I believe it is sound to tell the people 'the truth, the whole truth, and nothing but the truth'.

Yours sincerely,

THE RT. HON. J. H. THOMAS, M.P.,
Lord Privy Seal

20 May 1930, *Mosley to MacDonald.*

My dear Prime Minister,

On 23rd January last I submitted to you a memorandum on unemployment policy, which was an attempt to work out in detail the programme of our party at the last Election and to provide a more effective alternative to the policy which the Government has pursued. In my covering letter, I explained that the memorandum was 'not advanced in any dogmatic spirit' and I was 'more than open to any alternative which could be shown to be superior'. I made it clear, however, that I had reached 'the very definite conclusion that it is impossible to continue as at present'.

The Cabinet subsequently decided to appoint a Committee under the

Chairmanship of the Chancellor of the Exchequer to consider the unemployment situation and in this connection to have regard to the memorandum. That committee presented a report which not only rejects in its entirety the memorandum, but also adopts a position which would involve the rejection of any effective alternative to present policy.

Since the report of the Committee you have been good enough to discuss with the Ministers charged with unemployment both the memorandum and the report. Unfortunately, those discussions have only served to emphasise our differences, while during their currency the Chancellor of the Exchequer has affirmed the position adopted by his committee as the policy of the Government in a public speech delivered to the British Banking Association on 14th May last. This policy was reiterated by the Lord Privy Seal in yesterday's Debate.

In these circumstances, I regret that I hold it to be inconsistent with honour for me to remain a Member of the Government. On the back benches, I shall remain in vote and action a loyal member of the Labour Party. In speech and in the advocacy of policy I shall claim the right always accorded by our party to its members to ask the party to adopt a policy which I believe to be more consistent with our programme and pledges at the last Election.

It is to me a matter of great regret that as a Minister I have no means of appeal to the judgment of our party except by resignation from the Government.

Yours sincerely,

O. E. MOSLEY

V. NATIONAL DEVELOPMENT AND STATE BORROWING: A NOTE PREPARED BY THE TREASURY, JULY 1930

1. . . . A serious deficit is more than likely for the 1931 budget due to (*a*) increasing calls from the Unemployment Fund and (*b*) diminished receipts from reduced activity in the current year. . . .
2. Further, the Chancellor in order to reassure businessmen held out the hope that further taxation would, if possible be avoided in 1931. Unless means can be found in 1931 to provide otherwise for the cost of 'transitional benefit' a charge which is not properly an exchequer charge and is now being reviewed further derangement of the finances and further taxation are inevitable next year.
3. Expenditure provided for both in 1930 and in 1931 includes a sum of £5m for additional debt redemption designed to recoup in part the realised deficit of £14m in 1929 and thus to maintain the Sinking Fund at its proper level. Money which is raised by taxation to pay off long term debt is by the very process of paying off the debt poured into the capital market and thus becomes available for industry and the general capital requirements of the country. The normal effect is widely beneficial and the policy of fixing a substantial sinking fund and regularly maintaining it at the prescribed level is not exclusively dictated by questions of Government credit: it serves the general interest as well. Nevertheless in case it be argued that in the difficult circumstances of the moment this extra provision for debt ought to be given up and the money applied to new purposes, it should be observed that this course is precluded by the logic of existing facts. The sum of £5m provided for extra debt falls short of the amount of the probable Budget deficit this year. If it were decided (by modification of the Finance Bill) not to make this provision, the only effect would be — by a departure from principles of sound finance — to reduce the amount of the prospective disclosed debt. . . . No money would be made available for any other purpose.
4. Borrowing is continuously proceeding to meet the current deficit on the ordinary U.I.F. This deficit is obviously a current revenue charge and borrowing is an inadmissible expedient. It is concealed because the fund is not part of the general structure of the Budget and condoned by usage and the immensely difficult conditions of the time. But it detracts from

the efficacy of such sinking fund provision as the Budget with its threatened deficit can yet provide. And further this vulnerable feature in our finance renders excessively dangerous any unsound measures of borrowing that might be contemplated in other Budgetary spheres. The Budget would become exposed to a double attack for its inability or unwillingness to pay its way in two separate spheres.

5. The rule governing legitimate borrowing for State development works is well recognised. Where the State directly undertakes capital developments of a productive nature capable of yielding a money return which will meet the interest and sinking fund charges on the requisite capital loan, the State is justified in borrowing the capital and normally does so. Telephone capital is a good example. This capital is productive and repays itself within the lifetime of the plant and equipment which the capital creates. Similarly postal and telegraph capital which at one time under an old practice was met from revenue, is now raised by loan. It is the same with public corporations set up under the aegis of the State to carry out undertakings of a public character. The Electricity Commission . . . possesses and exercises the power to borrow the capital it requires for remunerative capital works, and for a large part of this capital the guarantee of the Exchequer is statutorily available. Similarly the British Broadcasting Corporation has borrowing powers for remunerative works and the like powers will quite certainly be conferred upon the public authority projected by the present Government for the public management of the traffic of London.

6. Quite different considerations arise in regard to works which, though of a capital or durable nature, do not provide any return out of which interest charges or sinking fund can be met. In the case of local authorities with their limited field of financial operations, with their changing population and their inelastic field of revenues, it is obvious that large current expenditure on such objects as sewerage works, road construction, public buildings would not only seriously derange their annual finances, but might place an unfair burden on present ratepayers in respect of services the benefit of which will be shared by future ratepayers. Parliament has therefore allowed a practice of borrowing for such works to develop. But the position of the State is far different. Not only is it normally able to finance extensive capital works without inconvenient variations of taxation but such works as are not of a revenue producing character give little prospect of actual benefit to future taxpayers. Furthermore over the wide field of State activity the need for new works of a capital character is practically continuous. The inherent unsoundness of State borrowing for such purposes has been progressively recognised. The classic examples are the borrowings by pre-war Conservative Governments for naval works and public buildings. Works of this character are necessary but they are not remunerative they confer no direct and obvious benefit and more and

more are continually required as society progresses. If therefore their cost is borrowed in any year, the burden of that year's liability is cast upon posterity notwithstanding that posterity must either shoulder or similarly pass on to a still later generation the cost of the similar equipment it requires. . . .

7. Similar considerations govern expenditure upon the construction of new roads. There is already more than a risk of roads being built for which their is little or no traffic justification or which may only further cripple the railways. But however much they may add to the equipment of the country . . . they produce to the authorities who construct them no money return out of which to meet the interest and sinking fund on any loan. . . . The nation as a whole is likely to require heavy annual expenditure of this character for an indefinite period. On this ground the practice hitherto invariably followed of meeting the contributions of the Road Fund towards capital works of construction or improvement . . . out of the annual revenue of the Fund is in keeping with the sound principles which now govern national finance. (Note: the present position of the Road Fund is difficult. The commitments involved in the present programme can probably be met from the fund this year, but not in future years: and next year several millions must be found by increased taxation or by loan. Borrowing could be justified on the basis that the present abnormal programme is an anticipation of work which would otherwise have been done, but will not now be done, a few years ahead: this would involve prescribing that any money now borrowed will be repaid out of the Resources of the Road Fund over a short period of (say five years) beginning in five years time, in priority to all other claims upon the fund, whether for new capital construction or for other purposes. It is only on such a basis that borrowing could be made reasonably to conform to the accepted principles of British finance).

8. The (present) schemes in progress and projected have the common feature, — and so it is suggested, the common merit, — that they are almost without exception financed by loans which are not State loans. The development schemes undertaken by railways and other public utility companies under Part I of the Home Development Act are financed by capital raised by, or reserves, possessed by these undertakings. The schemes undertaken by local authorities through the agency of the St. Davids Committee — schemes which it must be feared, tend as time goes on and programmes increase to have less and less economic ground and more and more to resemble relief works, — are financed by loans raised by and on the credit of the local authorities concerned or by capital supplied in the case of the smaller authorities by the Public Works Loans Board. The part of the State is to make an annual contribution towards the interest and sinking fund on the loans. These contributions are often a large proportion of the total annual cost, they enable the money to be

readily raised and enable the local authority or other undertaker to bear without difficulty the balance of the annual charges for the loan. The system avoids the heavy detriment to Government credit which direct State borrowing would inevitably entail. It avoids also the obloquy and criticism which direct Government intervention in development works is liable so quickly to arouse. These annual grants from the State, being annual contributions towards interest and sinking fund, represent a continous State liability which may be estimated . . . at some £5m per annum on a capital expenditure of £100m (in the early years of the schemes).

11. With the aid of the State grants the capital for the enterprises above alluded to is readily obtained by those who seek it, — far more readily than it would be by the State which is cumbered with the vast liabilities of the War. A case for a State loan for development work would arise only if the State proposed itself to undertake by its own agency from its own resources development works additional to those which it is now promoting and expects to promote through the agency of local authorities and others. The argument in the earlier part of this note shows that such a State loan would in principle be legitimate if, but only if, the works were productive works yielding a money return to meet the interest and sinking fund charges of the loan. Before such a loan could be raised the programme of new State works must be framed and the detailed arrangements made for their execution. The ground covered by the existing system, embracing all the activities of public utilities (local authorities and the State itself) is extremely wide. . . . It is difficult to see where to find productive works on which to expend the proceeds of a direct Government loan unless (*a*) local authorities were superseded in their proper sphere, a course with very far-reaching reactions upon the scheme of British Government or (*b*) industries naturally fitted for intensive capital development were nationalised and brought under immediate Government control, or (*c*) the Government undertakes capital works in connection with schemes so speculative or as unattractive that private or rate-supported enterprise will not undertake them even with the promise of the heavy subsidies already available.

12. If, in spite of the difficulties surrounding this matter, a great programme of works additional to that now instituted was found a practical proposition and it were decided that the Government should carry them out with its own funds . . . the probable effects of such a Loan upon national credit and general prosperity must be considered. If the investing public . . . accepted these far-reaching additional schemes as useful and desirable and likely to correct the country's difficulties, it might be that despite the enormous weight of Government securities which now burden the gilt-edged market the money could be raised without great disturbance and without any really heavy fall in Government stocks. If,

on the other hand, the schemes were distrusted as extravagant and wasteful, if it were believed that this vast extension of direct Government activity would involve interference with private rights and the exercise of oppressive bureaucratic powers, — (and it is difficult to see how any vast programme of work could be set up without such powers being necessarily taken) — it is very unlikely that the money could be obtained save with great difficulty at very high rates and with serious effect of increasing the average rate of interest attracted by long-term loans, a rate which for the general good of the community urgently needs to come down. . . . It is a matter for serious reflection whether, if a great Government loan had to be raised in such circumstances . . . many investors would not come to the view that this country was a bad country in which to invest; there might arise something in the nature of a flight from the pound with all its serious reactions upon the exchange, upon short-term money rates in this country and upon the prospects of a trade revival. Any increase in the general rate of long-term interest postpones the prospect of conversion of the War Debt into cheaper forms. Any increase in short money rates increases the Exchequer charge for Treasury Bills and diminishes the sum which is available for redemption of Government debt and the consequent replenishment of the capital market. . . .

13. The Government would only be justified in entering upon such an additional development programme if it could be conclusively proved that (*a*) the issue of a new Government Development Loan would attract into investment monies at present lying idle; (*b*) that the above-indicated repercussions would be avoided, and (*c*) that the disbursement of this capital would be sufficient to start a general revival of trade irrespective of the utility of the works undertaken.

14. There are already abundant openings for investment available in the gilt-edged market, and there is no reason to believe that the offer of a new Government Loan would attract any substantial amount of money which would otherwise not be invested or employed in financing some form of trade activity. On the other hand, the extension of Government development schemes would in all probability tend to accentuate the lop-sided character of our present industrial activity, instead of diffusing prosperity over the industries of the country as a whole. Meanwhile the wholesale expenditure of Government money regardless of economic return, so far from tending to cure the present depression, would be more likely to increase than to diminish the discouragement of the business community.

VI. EXTRACTS FROM *The Pound and the Gold Standard*: a Note prepared by Henry Clay (August ?, 1931) for the guidance of the National Government (Lothian Papers, Box 219).

The Gold Standard means *more to England* than to any other country because England depends more than any other country on trade. . . . If the Gold Standard goes, the trade of the world would be plunged into a welter of depreciating currencies and fluctuating exchanges, in which trades will not know from week to week how they stand or whom they can trust.

English currency means *more to the world* than any other currency. London is the chief centre of international banking, the agency through which a large part of Europe's transactions with the rest of the world are financed. If the pound goes the currencies of half the countries in Europe will also go. . . . Foreign countries that have trusted us will lose thereby — but no other country can immediately take our place and the whole of the world's financial relations will be thrown out of gear. Revolution will follow in Central Europe, leading possibly to the triumph of international Communism.

The industries of the world are depressed. Recovery can only come if confidence in the future is restored. Already traders everywhere are contracting operations because doubts have been cast on the stability of the pound. No blow to confidence could be more shattering than the departure of England from the Gold Standard. What trade revival requires is confidence; the restoration of sterling to its old unquestioned position will do more than anything else to restore confidence.

Suppose England went off gold. There would be an immediate flight from the pound, holders of sterling throughout the world seeking to convert their holdings into some other currency. The value of sterling in terms of other currencies would slump heavily — far below the value of sterling as measured by comparative purchasing power. What effects would this have? This country is dependent on large imports. More than half its food and a large part of its raw materials come from abroad. The cost in pounds of all these imports would go up. . . . Where at present, with the pound worth 4.86 dollars, a quarter of wheat costs us 20/-, with the pound worth only 3.64 dollars, a quarter of wheat would cost us 26/8. This would mean a penny on the loaf and three halfpence on the lb. of beef.

There could be no increase in wages or doles to meet the increased cost of food. If wages and doles were increased, the value of the pound would slump further, and neutralise any increase in money wages. That is the vicious circle of inflation, to which the departure from the Gold Standard lays us open.

Although the increase in cost of imports would be counter-balanced by a decrease in the cost of exports, we export mainly luxury goods, which can be dispensed with by the rest of the world in times of difficulties, while [our] imports are foodstuffs and essential raw materials which we have to buy whatever the price.

Above all, the abandonment of the gold standard would remove the chief obstacle to inflation. The Government could incur expenditure without thought of covering it by taxation and expand the floating debt to cover the deficit. This would cause a fall of sterling on the exchanges and a rise in prices at home. This is advocated as the simplest way of cutting real wages and other charges. But it might stimulate demands for wages increases which would lead to further inflation and further sterling depreciation. In other words, the process of inflation is a vicious circle. By raising the cost of living it stimulates demands for wage and salary advances; these increase the expenses of Government and promote further inflation; this raises prices still further and starts a new cycle of advances and borrowings. This was the experience of England during the war and of most Continental countries since the war. The only way to stop it is to balance the Budget, which might as well be faced while we are still on the Gold Standard as deferred until we have gone off it and involved the whole world in confusion.

SELECT BIBLIOGRAPHY

i. PRIMARY SOURCES

(a) *Manuscript*

Hubert Henderson Papers
Keynes Papers
Lansbury Papers
Lothian Papers
MacDonald Papers
Morrison Papers
Mosley Papers
Passfield Papers
Strauss Diary
T.U.C. General Council Papers

(b) *Printed*

(i) Hansard

(ii) Newspapers: *Manchester Guardian* continuously, others for selected periods.

(iii) Periodicals: *The Nation*, *New Statesman* (they amalgamated in January 1931), *Economist*, *Gleanings and Memoranda* (Conservative Central Office), and *Liberal Magazine*.

(iv) Government Publications include:

Minority Report, Royal Commission on the Poor Laws, 1909. Cd. 4499.

Blanesburgh Report, 1927.

Morris Report, 1929, Cmd. 3415.

First Report, Royal Commission on Unemployment Insurance, 1931, Cmd. 3872, and Minutes of Evidence, HMSO, 1931.

Macmillan Report on Finance and Industry, 1931, Cmd. 3897, and Minutes of Evidence, HMSO, 1931.

May Report, 1931, Cmd. 3920.

Various White Papers on Unemployment, 1929–31.

(v) Party Literature on Unemployment includes:

Labour Party:

The New Unemployed Bill of the Labour Party, I.L.P., 1907.

Unemployment, The Peace and the Indemnity, 1921.
Unemployment: A Labour Policy, 1921.
Work for the Workless, 1924.
Revolution by Reason, I.L.P., 1925.
The Living Wage, I.L.P., 1926.
On the Dole or Off, 1926.
Labour and the Nation, 1929.
How to Conquer Unemployment, 1929.

Liberal Party:

Britain's Industrial Future: Report of the Liberal Industrial Inquiry, Ernest Benn, 1928.
We Can Conquer Unemployment, Cassell, 1929.
How to Tackle Unemployment, London, 1930.

ii. SECONDARY SOURCES

(*a*) *Economic Background*

1. Arndt, H. W., *The Economic Lessons of the Nineteen-Thirties*, O.U.P., 1944.
2. Brown, W. A., *The International Gold Standard Reinterpreted 1914–1934*, vols. i and ii, National Bureau of Economic Research, N.Y., 1940.
3. Clay, H., *The Post-War Unemployment Problem*, Macmillan, 1929.
4. *Commercial Policy in the Inter-War Period*, League of Nations, 1942.
5. Haberler, R., *Prosperity and Depression*, Lake Success, 1946; *Theory of International Trade*, William Hodge, 1936.
6. Hancock, K. J., 'The Reduction of Unemployment as a Problem of Public Policy 1920–1929', *Ec.H.R.* December 1962.
'Unemployment and the Economists in the 1920s', *Economica*, xxvii, 1960.
7. Hicks, U. K., *The Finance of British Government 1920–1936*, O.U.P., 1938.
8. Hobson, J. A., *Economics of Unemployment*, Allen & Unwin, 1922.
9. Hodson, H. V., *Slump and Recovery 1929–1937*, O.U.P., 1938.
10. Keynes, J. M., *Essays in Persuasion*, Hart-Davis, 1951 (reissue).
11. Klein, L., *The Keynesian Revolution*, Macmillan, 1961.
12. Lewis, W. A., *Economic Survey 1919–1939*, Allen & Unwin, 1949.
13. London and Cambridge Economic Service, *Monthly Bulletins*, 1929–31.
14. Nurkse, R., *International Currency Experience*, League of Nations, 1944.
15. Sayers, R., 'Return to Gold' in *Studies in the Industrial Revolution*, ed. Pressnell, U.L.P., 1958.
16. Siegfried, André, *England's Crisis*, Cape, 1931.
17. Tawney, R. H., 'The Abolition of Economic Controls, 1918–1921', *Ec.H.R.* 1943.

18. Tillyard, Sir F., *Unemployment Insurance in Great Britain 1911–1948*, Thames Bank Publishing Co., 1949.
19. Williams, D., 'London and the 1931 Financial Crisis', *Ec.H.R.*, April 1963.
20. *World Economic Survey 1931–2*, League of Nations, 1932.
21. Youngson, A. J., *The British Economy 1920–1957*, Allen & Unwin, 1960.

(*b*) *Political Background*

1. Bassett, R., *1931: Political Crisis*, Macmillan, 1958.
2. Bennett, Edward W., *Germany and the Diplomacy of the Financial Crisis, 1931*, Harvard University Press, 1962.
3. Butler, D. E., *The Electoral System in Britain 1918–1951*, O.U.P., 1953.
4. Cole, G. D. H., *A History of the Labour Party from 1914*, Routledge & Kegan Paul, 1948.
5. Dowse, Robert E., 'The Left Wing Opposition During the First Two Labour Governments', *Parliamentary Affairs*, Spring 1961.
6. MacDonald, J. R., *Socialism and Society*, I.L.P., 1905; *Socialism Critical and Constructive*, Cassell, 1921.
7. Middlemas, R. K., *The Clydesiders*, Hutchinson, 1965.
8. Milliband, Ralph, *Parliamentary Socialism: A Study in the Politics of Labour*, Allen & Unwin, 1961.
9. Mowat, C. L., *Britain Between the Wars*, Methuen, 1955.
10. Ross, J. F. S., *Parliamentary Representation*, Eyre & Spottiswoode, 1948.
11. Scanlon, J., *The Decline and Fall of the Labour Party*, Peter Davies, 1932.
12. Taylor, A. J. P., *English History 1914–1945*, O.U.P., 1965.
13. Toynbee, A. J., *Survey of International Affairs 1931–2*, O.U.P., 1932.
14. Wertheimer, Egon, *Portrait of the Labour Party*, Putnam's, 1929.
15. Wilson, Trevor, *The Downfall of the Liberal Party 1914–1935*, Collins, 1966.

(*c*) *Memoirs and Biographies*

1. Amery, L. S., *My Political Life*, vol. iii: *The Unforgiving Years 1929–1940*, Hutchinson, 1955.
2. Anonymous, *The Scottish Socialists*, Faber & Faber, 1931.
3. Blaxland, Gregory, *J. H. Thomas: A Life for Unity*, Muller, 1964.
4. Bondfield, Margaret, *A Life's Work*, National Book Association, 1948.
5. Boothby, R., *I Fight to Live*, Gollancz, 1947.
6. Bowle, John, *Viscount Samuel*, Gollancz, 1957.
7. Brockway, Fenner, *Inside the Left*, London New Leader, 1942.
8. Bullock, Alan, *The Life and Times of Ernest Bevin*, vol. i., Heinemann, 1960.
9. Citrine, Lord, *Men and Work*, Hutchinson, 1964.
10. Clay, Henry, *Lord Norman*, Macmillan, 1957.

11. Cross, Colin, *The Fascists in Britain*, Barrie & Rockcliff, 1961.
12. Dalton, Hugh, *Memoirs*, vol. i: *Call Back Yesterday, 1887–1931*, Muller, 1953.
13. Einzig, P., *Montagu Norman*, Kegan Paul, 1932.
14. Elton, Lord, *The Life of James Ramsay MacDonald*, Collins, 1939.
15. Feiling, Keith, *The Life of Neville Chamberlain*, Macmillan, 1946.
16. Foot, Michael, *Aneurin Bevan: A Biography*, vol. i, MacGibbon & Kee, 1962.
17. Graham, Thomas, *Willie Graham*, Hutchinson, 1952.
18. Grigg, P. J., *Prejudice and Judgment*, London, 1948.
19. Hamilton, M. A., *J. Ramsay MacDonald*, Cape, 1929; *Arthur Henderson*, Heinemann, 1938.
20. Harrod, Sir Roy, *Life of John Maynard Keynes*, Macmillan, 1951.
21. Hobson, J. A., *Confessions of an Economic Heretic*, Allen & Unwin, 1938.
22. Johnston, Thomas, *Memories*, Collins, 1952.
23. Jones, Thomas, *Lloyd George*, O.U.P., 1951; *A Diary With Letters 1931–1950*, O.U.P., 1954.
24. Lee, Jennie, *The Great Journey*, MacGibbon & Kee, 1963.
25. McNair, J., *Maxton, The Beloved Rebel*, Allen & Unwin, 1955.
26. Morrison, Lord, *An Autobiography*, Odhams, 1960.
27. Nicolson, Sir Harold, *King George V: His Life and Reign*, Constable, 1952.
28. Owen, Frank, *Tempestuous Journey: Lloyd George, His Life and Times*, Hutchinson, 1954.
29. Postgate, R., *The Life of George Lansbury*, Longmans, 1951.
30. Samuel, Viscount, *Memoirs*, Cresset, 1945.
31. Snell, Lord, *Men, Movements and Myself*, Dent, 1938.
32. Snowden, Viscount, *An Autobiography*, vols. i and ii, Nicholson & Watson, 1934.
33. Stocks, Mary, *Ernest Simon of Manchester*, Manchester U.P., 1963.
34. Templewood, Viscount, *Nine Troubled Years*, Collins, 1954.
35. Thomas, J. H., *My Story*, Hutchinson, 1937.
36. Williams, Francis, *A Pattern of Rulers*, Longmans, 1965.
37. Young, G. M., *Stanley Baldwin*. Hart-Davis, 1952.

INDEX

Notes. 100 (n.) indicates both text *and* footnot e.
The entries and numerals in bold type refer to the main treatment of the subjects.

EVERYMAN'S LIBRARY

EVERYMAN,
I WILL GO WITH THEE,
AND BE THY GUIDE,
IN THY MOST NEED
TO GO BY THY SIDE